Architecture & Academe

College Buildings in New England before 1860

BRYANT F. TOLLES, JR.

UNIVERSITY PRESS OF NEW ENGLAND

HANOVER & LONDON

University Press of New England
One Court Street, Lebanon NH 03766
www.upne.com
© 2011 Bryant F. Tolles, Jr.
Manufactured in the United States of America

Designed by Katherine B. Kimball
Typeset in Minion by Passumpsic Publishing

Unless otherwise indicated, photographs and illustrations are by the
author.

For permission to reproduce any of the material in this book, contact
Permissions, University Press of New England, One Court Street,
Lebanon NH 03766; or visit www.upne.com

Library of Congress Cataloging-in-Publication Data
Tolles, Bryant Franklin, 1939–
   Architecture & academe : college buildings in New England before 1860
/ Bryant F. Tolles, Jr. — 1st ed.
      p. cm.
   Includes bibliographical references and index.
   ISBN 978-1-58465-891-7 (cloth : alk. paper)
   1. College buildings—New England—History. 2. Campus planning—
New England—History. I. Title. II. Title: Architecture and academe. III.
Title: College buildings in New England before 1860.
   NA6603.T65 2010
   727'.30974—dc22   2010032754

5 4 3 2 1

Frontispiece: Old Row, Amherst College, Amherst, Massachusetts.
Left, Williston Hall (1857–58); *left center,* North College (1822–23);
center, Johnson Chapel (1826–27); *right,* South College (1820–21).
Photograph © 1985 by Bryant F. Tolles, Jr.

To the memory of former professor John B. Armstrong, Department of History, Boston University, for his encouragement of my interest in the architecture and campus planning of New England colleges and universities before 1860 and for serving as committee chair for my Ph.D. dissertation devoted to the northern New England region.

Contents

Illustrations

Preface

It is extremely gratifying for me to collaborate again with the University Press of New England on the publication of another book treating a facet of the architecture and related history of the northeastern United States. The completion of *Architecture and Academe: College Buildings in New England Before 1860*, however, has been a long time in the making, as the project dates back forty years, to the research work I undertook while I was a graduate student in the American and New England Studies Program administered by the History Department at Boston University. The culmination of my work at B.U., and the primary inspiration and basis for this book, is my 1970 Ph.D. dissertation, "College Architecture in Northern New England Before 1860: A Social and Cultural History." Since completing the dissertation, I have conducted additional research throughout the New England region and elsewhere, expanding the geographical scope and subject definition of the projected book topic. This book is an enlarged and modified outgrowth of the dissertation and is also derived from several articles published over the years in scholarly as well as popular historical and architectural periodicals.

Although others have written books on specific educational institutions, and higher educational buildings and campus planning nationwide, there exists no prior study devoted solely to the pre–Civil War college and university architecture of the New England region. While it is largely structured by institutional and campus planning origins and development in the broader context of higher educational history, the book focuses primarily on the architecture and related history of individual buildings, their origins, their functions, and their interrelationships with other buildings in their respective campus environments. The predominant campus planning models discussed include the open quadrangle and row schemes, and other innovative though less common planning solutions. Sixteen four-year liberals arts and science higher educational institutions are treated in the text, arranged chronologically as well as topically—Harvard, Yale, Brown, Dartmouth, Williams, Bowdoin, Vermont, Middlebury, Norwich, Amherst, Holy Cross, Tufts, Trinity, Wesleyan, Colby, and Bates. Intentionally excluded are two-year seminaries or "junior colleges" and specialized medical, law, or theological schools and their buildings. Hence, pre-1860 women's seminaries, such as Mt. Holyoke and Wheaton, do not qualify for inclusion. Educational building types described, analyzed, and compared include multipurpose main buildings; academic structures containing classrooms and faculty offices; residence halls (dormitories); ecclesiastical structures (churches and chapels); commons (dining) or athletic buildings; and scientific facilities (chemical laboratories, observatories, etc.). Examples of domestic architecture (presidential, faculty, and staff housing; social clubs) in higher educational settings are considered outside the purview of this study, as they were not a unique college and university building type. The book also excludes buildings acquired from noneducational or primary and secondary educational institutions, and converted to meet new college/university functions.

Following the front matter, *Architecture and Academe* commences with a brief introductory treatment of the English and European background, and subsequent American adaptation and innovation. It concludes at the beginning of the Civil War period, after which campus planning assumed new, rapidly expanding forms, buildings were conceived in innovative, late Victorian eclectic styles or amalgams of these styles, and individual building uses became more specialized. The main body of the text is devoted to a discussion of the historic origins and evolution in New England of college and university building design and campus-planning principles. Although the primary emphasis of the book is architecture, related economic, social, cultural, and intellectual history is woven into the narrative. Particular attention is directed to the relationship between architecture and educational philosophy and practice, and the individual contributions of institutional founders, trustees, presidents, faculty members, students, alumni/ae, campus planners, architects, and builders are highlighted.

The captioned illustrations in the book include both historic and contemporary photographs of individual buildings or building groups, a few exterior detail or interior shots, and photographic reproductions of printed views and architectural plans, both exterior wall configurations and interior floor layouts. The illustrations, both black-and-white and color, emphasize extant structures. These striking images of early higher educational architecture in the New England region serve as essential documentation supplementing the textual narrative and providing an element of visual realism as well as pictorial artistry.

Fortunately, for purposes of narrative discussion, personal observation, and illustration, well over 50 percent of pre–Civil War New England's college and university structures—almost sixty in all—have survived into the twenty-first century. This is primarily the result of excellent initial design and construction, the use of durable and attractive building materials, periodic renovation and upgrading, watchful care and use supervision, and a strong ongoing commitment to historic preservation by the ma-

jority of institutional trustees and chief administrators. Of indispensable aid in the recent documentation and preservation effort are the publication products of numerous historians and other writers—institutional histories, campus architectural histories, town and campus guides, local histories, and periodical articles. It is hoped that this book, supported by the prior work of these authors, will further the knowledge and appreciation of pre-1860 New England college and university buildings and foster their ongoing study and preservation in future decades.

As I intend for this study, like my other books, to reach readers of both scholarly and popular publications, I have endeavored to compile the narrative in an authoritative, factually informative, and readable style. In doing so I have made every effort to satisfy the highest scholarly standards, using a variety of manuscript and printed sources, and including extensive endnotes, a detailed bibliography, and an index. The aesthetically appealing and invaluable collection of black-and-white and color illustrations accompanying the text are photographs by the author or are derived from original printed and photographic views contained in the collections of institutional libraries and archives, historical societies, public libraries, or other organizations mentioned in the book's acknowledgments section and illustration credit lines. The resulting publication, combining textual narrative and analysis with extensive illustration, focuses principally on architectural as opposed to general higher educational history. It is hoped, consequently, that readers of this book will gain new knowledge and perspectives of the architectural and campus planning history and legacy of New England's distinguished group of pre–Civil War colleges and universities.

Concord, New Hampshire   B.F.T., Jr.
September 2009

Acknowledgments

As mentioned in the preface, I conducted the research serving as the foundation for this book at various times over a forty-year period at institutional libraries and archives, public libraries, historical organizations, and other types of repositories in the northeastern United States. I wish, therefore, to express my sincere gratitude for the research assistance I have received from numerous individuals, many of whom either are no longer active professionally with the many repositories I will mention below or have relocated to other repositories. Some, sadly, are deceased.

First and foremost, I want to credit the following individuals for their inspiration, ideas and guidance that encouraged me to conceptualize and develop the book topic. These include John B. Armstrong, former professor of history, Boston University; Walter Muir Whitehill, former director and librarian, Boston Athenaeum; Abbott Lowell Cummings, former director of the Society for the Preservation of New England Antiquities (today, Historic New England); and John P. Coolidge, former professor of fine arts, and former director of the Fogg Art Museum, Harvard University.

For materials pertaining to pre–Civil War college/university architecture and campus planning in all six New England states, I accessed pertinent collections at the following institutions and organizations: the Hugh M. Morris Library, University of Delaware, Newark (Susan Brynteson, director; and staff); the Fine Arts Library, University of Pennsylvania, Philadelphia; the American Antiquarian Society, Worcester, Mass. (Marcus A. McCorison, former director; Georgia B. Barnhill, curator of graphic arts; and library staff); the Winterthur Museum Library, Winterthur, Del.; The Athenaeum of Philadelphia (Bruce Laverty, curator of architecture; and library staff); the Society for the Preservation of New England Antiquities (Historic New England) Library, Boston; the Francis Loeb Library, Harvard University Graduate School of Design, Cambridge, Mass.; the New England Historic Genealogical Society, Boston; the Boston Athenaeum Library; the Hagley Museum and Library, Wilmington, Del.; the Boston Public Library (Sinclair Hitchings, former curator of prints; and library staff); and the Stephen R. Mugar Library, Boston University, Boston, Mass.

For the Connecticut institutions treated in this study, I conducted general research at the Connecticut Historical Society and the Connecticut State Library, both in Hartford. I was provided assistance with Trinity (Washington) College history and source materials by Glenn Weaver, former professor of history, and Peter J. Knapp, a longtime member of the college library staff and today the special collections librarian and college archivist. For my research on Wesleyan University, I worked with Olin Memorial Library special collections and archives staff members Elizabeth A. Swaim, Suzy Taraba, and Valerie Gillespie. At the Yale University Library, in the manuscripts and archives division, I have received invaluable help in my Yale research undertakings since the mid-1990s from Richard V. Szary, Judith Ann Schiff, and Mary C. LaFogg. For additional Yale resource materials, I also visited the library of the New Haven Colony Historical Society.

In my efforts to locate pertinent sources and expand my knowledge of Brown University in Rhode Island, I conducted research in Providence at the Rhode Island Historical Society, the Rhode Island Preservation and Heritage Commission, and the John Carter Brown Library and John Hay

Library, both at the university. At the latter library, in special collections and the institutional archives, Samuel Streit, Martha Mitchell, Raymond Butti, and Gerald Gaidmore assisted me greatly over the years.

For general materials documenting the history and architecture of early Massachusetts higher educational institutions, I have engaged in research at the Massachusetts Historical Society and the Massachusetts State Library, both situated in Boston. At Amherst College, I made visits to the Robert Frost Library, where I was assisted in archives and special collections by Daria D'Arienzo, John Lancaster, and most recently Maria Sakrejda-Leavitt, Marian Walker, and Peter Nelson. My work at Harvard University has been principally based in the library system at the Harvard University Archives, where I have been the beneficiary of extensive aid by longtime archivist and curator Harley P. Holden, recently retired, as well as Robin McElheny, Robin M. Carlaw, and Michelle Gachette. At the College of the Holy Cross, I have had the pleasure of working with the following staff in the archives and special collections of the Dinand Library: Reverend Eugene J. Harrington, Paul S. Nelligan, Sarah Campbell, and Mark Savolis, former assistant archivist and now archivist. In addition, Richard Phelps of the public affairs office was very helpful in responding to my questions. At Tufts University, I received assistance from Russell E. Miller, former professor of history and university historian-archivist, and the following members of the Wessell (now Tisch) Library institutional archives (today, digital collections and archives) staff: Robert Johnson-Lally, Barbara Tringali, Susanne Belovari, Lauren Miller, and Anne Saurer, the current director and university archivist. For published and unpublished sources of information about Williams College, I have consulted with several members of the institutional archives and special collections division of the library, including Norma H. Fox, Nadia McIntosh, Sharon Band, Lynne K. Fonteneau, Sylvia Kennick-Brown, and Linda Hall. Robert L. Volz, the current head librarian, Chapin Library, and formerly at Bowdoin College (see below), has been a recent contact person for me at Williams.

On several occasions since the 1970s, I have conducted general Maine institutional research at the Maine Historical Society (E. Marie Estes) in Portland, the Maine Historic Preservation Commission (Earle G. Shettleworth, Jr., current director) in Augusta, and the Farnsworth Art Museum (Marilyn C. Solvay) in Rockland. At Bates College, I have benefited from the assistance of Iva W. Foster, Edward F. Blount, Mary Riley, and Elaine Ardia, members of the general Corum or Ladd library staffs, and specifically special collections (now the Edmund S. Muskie Archives and Special Collections). My research efforts at Bowdoin College were based largely at the Hawthorne-Longfellow Library in special collections and archives, where I worked or had contact with Robert L. Volz (now at Williams College; see above), Susan Ravdin, Gregory Colati, and Daniel Hope. Providing additional assistance at the Bowdoin College Museum of Art were John Ward and Patricia M. Anderson, whose book on the college's architecture has been an indispensable source. I also wish to credit two former Bowdoin faculty members, William N. Shipman and Brooks W. Stoddard, for the help that they offered me. For materials relating to the first campus of Colby (Waterville) College, I received assistance from the staffs of the Waterville Historical Society, the Waterville Public Library, and the Colby College Archives (Elizabeth Libbey, Nancy Reinhart, and Patricia Burdick) at the Miller Library.

In developing a source base for my treatment of Dartmouth College architecture, I was aided by staff members of the New Hampshire Historical Society library (Mrs. Russell B. Tobey and William N. Copeley) and the New Hampshire State Library (Stella J. Scheckter), both in Concord; the Carpenter Art Library at Dartmouth College; and the Dartmouth College Library (Baker Memorial Library, Archives Department; today, the Rauner Special Collections Library) (Walter W. Wright, Mildrid Tunis, Kenneth C. Cramer, Phillip Cronewett, Stanley W. Brown, Sarah Hartwell, and Jay Satterfield, the current director of special collections).

For the three pre-1860 Vermont higher educational institutions considered in this book, I did general research in the collections of the Vermont Historical Society, Burlington, where over the years I worked with Grace Quimby, Laura P. Abbott, former director Charles T. Morrissey, and Reiden Nuquist. To locate and utilize research materials pertaining to Middlebury College, I received assistance from faculty members W. Storrs Lee and Glenn M. Andres, and the following staff members of the Middlebury College Library, most associated with rare books and special collections: Richard Serena, Ralph W. Franklin, Lockwood Merriman, Robert Buckeye, Danielle Rougeau, and Andrew Wentink, the current curator of special collections and the college archivist. I also examined the collections of the Ilsley Public

Library and the Sheldon Art Museum, Archaeological and Historical Society (Mrs. Richard Mudge and Polly C. Darnell), both in the town of Middlebury. For Norwich University sources, initially at the Chaplin Memorial Library and then at the Kreitzberg Library, I had contact with Gary Lord, professor of history, and these library staff members, all of whom served in various capacities with archives and special collections: George M. Brich, Jacqueline S. Painter, Julie Bressor, Kelly Gonzales, and Gail Wiese. My archival research at the University of Vermont libraries was facilitated by T. D. Seymour Bassett, David Blow, J. Kevin Graffagnino, Connell Gallagher, John Buechler, Sylvia Knight, and, most recently, Jeffrey Marshall, currently the head of special collections and archives, and a former library staff member at the Vermont Historical Society.

In conclusion, I wish to express my sincere gratitude to the many family members and friends who provided me (and my wife, who often accompanied me) with accommodations and hospitality while I was on research visits throughout the New England region. These visits, in addition to illustration preparation, were generously supported by research funding provided by the Office of the Dean, College or Arts and Science, University of Delaware. Most significantly, I would like to offer my enthusiastic appreciation to my wife, Carolyn, for her constant encouragement and support, for her critical review of the textual narrative, for her assistance in preparing the illustrations, and for undertaking the illustrations permission process. I also wish to extend my thanks to those individuals whom I may have inadvertently failed to mention or whom I did not specifically identify by name. While this book project was a long-term process, it was a very pleasant and gratifying experience for me, in large part due to the many personal and professional connections I have made since its inception.

INTRODUCTION

INCREASINGLY, THE PUBLISHED LITERATURE treating American higher educational building design and campus planning is effectively serving two vital roles. On the one hand, it is expressing an appreciation of and concern for the physical legacies of our colleges and universities. On the other, in a broad historical sense, it is profitably discussing the interrelationships between architecture, society, culture, economics, and higher educational theory and practice. The need for and desirability of this approach is clear, and this study represents an effort to achieve this, focusing attention on the New England region prior to the Civil War.

As other authors have demonstrated, early American college/university architecture may be productively examined and analyzed by pursuing a national focus, but perhaps even more successfully by concentrating on separate regions. Highlighting a single, clearly delineated geographical area, distinguished from others by natural features, climate, economy, and population, facilitates analysis and comparison of buildings and campuses. Inevitably, the resulting general conclusions have implications for the national scene. Because of its uniqueness as a region, its pioneering heritage in higher education, and its distinctive architectural imprint, New England is particularly worthy of and appropriate for such a study. Its pre–Civil War collegiate structures, both alone and in groupings, offer artistic and utilitarian merit to the people of the twenty-first century, yet they also tell us about the life and thought of previous generations and suggest valuable guidelines for those that will follow. In the architecture of the sixteen institutions included in this book, one can observe a creative and imaginative individualism that has characterized and in all likelihood will continue to characterize the development of the American spirit.

The substance of the book is organized around three major themes. The first concerns the relationship of higher educational needs and objectives, as exemplified in basic learning philosophy, to functional and aesthetic architectural planning, both in individual building and in general campus conceptions. As architectural historians such as Albert Bush-Brown have asserted, the architecture that was, and still is, most effective educationally is that which is in cultural harmony with the goals and operational practices of the academic institutions where it is located. In developing this theme, it is possible to illustrate the relationship, where it existed, between architectural "form" or "style" as expressed visually on building exteriors, and function, as implemented in materials selection and utilization, structural design, technology, and interior layout. In nearly all higher educational architecture of the pre–Civil War era, a comfortable blending of form and function may be observed.

Another significant generality emanates from an examination of this first theme. As subsequent chapters will detail, educators, in developing the physical plants of higher educational institutions, were influenced by long-standing but still viable theory and practice. Like their English antecedents, particularly the universities at Oxford and Cambridge, the majority of pre–Civil War collegiate institutions were laid out so that all their functions, whether academic, social, residential, religious, or administrative, could be interrelated as closely as possible within individual structures or building groups. The seventeenth-century buildings at Harvard and William and Mary first adopted this format, to be followed during the next hundred years by those at Yale, Princeton, and King's (Columbia), arranged according to English-originated open quadrangle plans or Yale-initiated row plans. Proponents of such an approach have long commended its successes in providing diversified yet integrated educational experiences for students in all academic areas, and some nonacademic areas as well. By ensuring the physical proximity of living, learning, and religious activities, American educators kept the "Oxbridge" educational philosophy viable and supplied architecture, with some variations in planning, that had many similarities to that employed in the English residential college system.

At the heart of the English and the American colonial educational philosophy was the concept of moral guardianship, which obligated institutions to provide for the complete educational, spiritual, and social life of their students in a suitable architectural setting. Education at America's first colleges — Harvard (est. 1636), William and Mary (est. 1693), and Yale (est. 1701) — was predicated on using a theological and classical curriculum to train young men for service as leaders in religious and public life. As time passed, the curriculum emphasis gradually shifted to mathematics and the sciences, with the result that by the 1790s, educational offerings had been greatly broadened. Gradually diversified but still integrated educational opportunities were made available to students in all academic as well as nonacademic areas. Such was the heritage of Benjamin Franklin's multifaceted learning theory and of the Renaissance Italian humanism from which Franklin's idea for the development of the universally educated man derived. By consolidating educational functions, the early campuses and buildings at Harvard, William and Mary, and Yale reflected such a belief, as did the physical plants of their successor pre–Revolutionary War institutions in America. A pattern was thus set that persisted at American colleges and universities throughout the first half of the nineteenth century.

Practical as well as theoretical, this educational philosophy, and the architecture that was its outgrowth, also re-

flected the continuing importance attached to the family unit as an educating force, primary social unit, and principal agency of cultural transfer in colonial American life. It was thus considered important to foster close personal relationships and intellectual productivity in the higher educational environment through the use of flexible, multipurpose, single-unit building designs and coherent campus plans. In this way, as Bernard Bailyn explained in his book *Education in the Forming of American Society* (1960), learning could involve not only "the purposeful acquisition of merely technical skills, but new ways of thinking and behaving." Individualism, a trademark of character and social order, was thereby reflected in as well as fostered by an architecture of humanistic versatility.

Specialization in facility planning, the hallmark of the modern higher educational campus, did not prevail in the United States until the last half of the nineteenth century, when the university movement, with its emphasis on a varied curriculum, became increasingly dominant. Its origins lay even earlier, in the grand, French-inspired communal campus conceptions of Joseph-Jacques Ramee at Union College (1813) and Thomas Jefferson at the University of Virginia (1817), in which individual units were planned for separately defined academic functions. Because of the long popularity and application of specialized facility planning, many modern-day educators have insufficiently recognized the practices and accomplishments of their predecessors who adhered to more traditional learning theory. Other college and university leaders have successfully reapplied the positive features of the integrated facility approach to campus planning, despite pressures for expansion and ever-changing site demands. In recent years, this tendency has become a discernible trend. The early higher educational institutions of New England effectively illustrate this older but still-viable ideological conviction in the structures that housed their programs and activities.

The second major theme concerns the relationship between architectural form (or style) and function, and the specific conditioning regional factors associated with the six New England states. In the manner of general architecture in this area, most college buildings there were rationally conceived, inelaborate, solidly constructed, and highly functional. In an aesthetic as well as utilitarian sense, they reflected the conservative, practical, and substantial characteristics of the people who planned and erected them. Because of the related problems of geographical remoteness and the lack of sophisticated transportation and communications systems, designs of interior academic institutions sometimes lagged stylistically behind those of coastline population centers, which were in more direct contact with foreign influences. Builders thus brought their own originality to bear on architecture that otherwise was the outgrowth of past forms or standard design books. This circumstance led to the use of native wood, stone, and brick materials in structural fabrication because of their availability and inexpensiveness in a local setting. Highly variable and undependable climatic conditions encouraged skillful and meticulous building practices. Foundations were made of stylized stone blocks; walls of wooden siding or stone or brick masonry; roofs of thick wooden shingles, slate slabs, or, ultimately, metal sheathing; and interior support framing of sturdy, well-joined horizontal and vertical support timbers. Roofs and wall surfaces were kept as plain and uncomplicated as possible in order to minimize weathering and deterioration. Such considerations lent an indigenous quality to these works of architecture, which, though influenced by existing national style vocabularies, made them unique, if not peculiar unto themselves.

Other regional factors had an impact on physical plant development at New England institutions of higher learning. None of the six states could be described as affluent prior to 1860, though Boston and other smaller urban areas offered selective opportunities for institutional financial support. Although the vitalizing and enriching effects of the American Industrial Revolution had begun to have impact, each state was largely oriented toward agricultural or seacoast economic pursuits. For this reason, funds for projects such as educational buildings were not readily available. As a response to the thriftiness necessitated by these circumstances, colleges and universities attempted to secure the utmost quality and quantity of building from modest expenditure. Furthermore, in situations where they appeared, individual philanthropic donors had their own ideas as to what exterior form and interior layout a building should assume. The end result for institutions, in the vast majority of cases, was the need to maximize function and durability at the expense of artistic ornamentation. Circumstances did change, however, when eclectic revivalist architectural styles became popular starting in the 1830s and 1840s.

When one considers the formidable role that the above factors played, it seems surprising that architectural charm and effectiveness were successfully realized in so many individual buildings. Structurally attractive yet eminently practical, these edifices created a rational and humanized relationship with the environment of which they were in part the product. They clearly belonged to their respective backgrounds and landscapes, and they candidly reflected educational realities, a resourceful people, and an uncomplicated way of life. They were direct manifestations in architectural terms of the very social conditions animating this section of the colonies and the new and developing nation prior to 1860.

The third major theme of this study involves the relationship between architectural form (or style) and function, and cultural trends and tastes at particular points in time. Although educational concerns and specific regional factors exerted the most forceful impact on collegiate architecture, fashion fads and preferences were also instrumental in determining building shapes, and external and internal appearances. Until the third decade of the nineteenth century, higher educational structures in New England carried forward general building styles that were derived from England and had prevailed in the colonies and the new United States since before the American Revolution. Their broad, traditional descriptions may be embodied in the terms "colonial," "provincial Georgian," and ultimately "Federal."

Institutional buildings conceived in these vernaculars were customarily of moderate size and were largely blockular in form, with rectangular floor plans, which was characteristic of public, commercial, and the most impressive residential structures of the time. Some were constructed of wood, and others of brick or stone, or a combination of building materials. Those of brick, despite the pleasantly varied textures of their walls, sometimes justified Thomas Jefferson's comment, "But that they have roofs, they might be mistaken as brick kilns!" Roofs were either pitched, hipped, or gambrel in form, marked by chimneys, and were often topped by a cupola or belfry. Gabled projecting pavilions were occasionally employed to break the monotony of long, flat wall surfaces and to provide additional interior space. Classical elements, interpreted by and derived from the English Renaissance, were used discreetly and sparingly as embellished style accents—a variety of moldings, corner blocks, balustrades, pilasters, columned porches, lintels, architraves, and so on. As a result, architectural impact depended largely on fundamentals such as proportions, fenestration configuration, and the relation of pavilions to any existing wings.

The most significant and precedent-setting examples of the earliest styles, most of which were located in New England, were the College Building (1695–1700) at the College of William and Mary (Virginia), attributed to Sir Christopher Wren; Harvard Hall II (1674–82), Stoughton Hall I (1698), Massachusetts Hall (1718, etc.), Harvard Hall III (1764, etc.), Hollis Hall (1762), and Holworthy Hall (1811–12) at Harvard College; the First College House (1717–18), Connecticut (South Middle) Hall (1750–52), the Old College Chapel (The Athenaeum) (1761–63), Union Hall (South College) (1793–94), Berkeley Hall (North Middle College) (1801), and the Connecticut Lyceum (1803–4) at Yale College; Robert Smith's Nassau Hall (1755–57) at the College of New Jersey (Princeton); Robert Crommelin's "First Building" (1756–60) at King's (Columbia) College (New York); University Hall (1770–71) at the College of Rhode Island (Brown University); Dartmouth Hall (1784–91) at Dartmouth College; West College (1791–93) and Old East College (1797–98) at Williams College; the "College Edifice" (1801–7) at the University of Vermont; Benjamin Latrobe's Old West College (1803) at Dickinson College (Pennsylvania); Old Queen's (1809) at Queen's College (Rutgers University) (New Jersey); and buildings at the College of Philadelphia (University of Pennsylvania), the University of North Carolina, and South Carolina College (University of South Carolina). Up to the 1830s, other New England structures adopted the features displayed in this impressive collection. As will be discussed and illustrated throughout this book, most of the region's early college/university buildings were arranged in straight lines according to variations of the row plan, thereby contrasting with the traditional closed and open quadrangles of the English universities. In a unique and simple manner, they were expressive of the instinctive, innovative tendencies of the New England heritage that spawned them.

From the 1830s to the early 1860s, the earliest styles in higher educational design were succeeded by historic eclectic or revivalist expressions. During this period Americans, in their search for national and individual self-awareness, embraced and adopted the prime attributes of previous cultures and civilizations. This tendency was first manifested architecturally in Greek and Roman classicism. Some of the most outstanding results in higher educational architecture were Ramée's Union College plan (1813); Jefferson's University of Virginia plan (1817); Old Centre (1819) at Centre College (Kentucky); Bentley Hall (1820) at Allegheny College

(Pennsylvania); the Washington College Building (1824) at Washington College (Washington and Lee University) (Virginia); Gideon Shryock's Old Morrison (1830–34) at Transylvania College (Kentucky); Old College (1834) at the University of Delaware; Thomas Ustick Walter's Girard College complex (1833–48) (Philadelphia, Pennsylvania); and several outstanding Greek temple structures at Davidson College (North Carolina) and the Universities of Pennsylvania, Georgia, North Carolina, and South Carolina. In New England, the earliest expressions of the Neo-Classical, specifically of Greek inspiration, were designed by Isaac Damon for Amherst College in 1826–27 (Johnson Chapel), and by Solomon Willard for Washington (Trinity) College in 1824–25 (Jarvis and Seabury halls). Slightly later, outstanding examples of the Greek Revival style were Manning Hall (1834–35) at Brown University and Reed Hall (1839–40) at Dartmouth College. These examples featured characteristic temple shapes, columned porches, triangular pediments, architraves, friezes, and other typical details. In New England, however, with its adherence to more traditional styles, Greek and Roman classicism did not gain the wide support that it did in regions to the south and west, and we are able to witness few examples there of its representation in higher educational architecture. The mark of the Neo-Classical was evident largely in the details and overall proportions of an architecture whose essential form belonged to a preceding period.

For many of the same reasons, the Neo-Gothic or Gothic Revival gained even less favor at institutions of higher learning in pre–Civil War New England. Though it would later be adopted as an ideal architecture for college and university campuses, and its enthusiastic use extended well into the twentieth century, it was somehow considered alien to staid life in nineteenth-century New England, possibly because of its medieval and established church associations. Furthermore, buildings designed in this style were expensive to raise and were thought to prohibit adequate admission of light and ventilation for academic purposes. Nonetheless, its sense of high human aspiration and endeavor was recognized and endorsed by some educational leaders. Two of its principal examples in this country were Richard Bond's Gore Hall (library) (1838–41, etc.) at Harvard and Henry Austin's Old College Library (1842–47) at Yale. Both edifices were conceived, however, in the more generally accepted English Perpendicular Gothic, inspired by King's College Chapel at Cambridge University and other academic buildings in England. North of Massachusetts, this limited heritage made an even less tangible impression, and there were no higher educational structures there of pure Gothic inspiration. The closest approximation of the Gothic there was Richard Upjohn's Bowdoin College Chapel (1844–55), but this was designed essentially in the German Romanesque style and stood in reasonable harmony with its rural Maine surroundings.

The Italianate or Italian Revival style met a warmer reception than the Neo-Gothic or Gothic Revival on mid-nineteenth-century college and university campuses in the United States. This seems quite logical, however, when one considers the extent to which this manner of building design carried forward the spirit and actual use of certain provincial Georgian and Federal style elements. Nonetheless, the introduction of a new block massing and new roof, door, and window treatments suggested that the high cultural standards and accomplishments of Renaissance Italy could yet blend in with the American scene. Though this style had widespread use in the Midwest, where some private liberal arts institutions employed it for full campus plans, it was also prevalent in individual buildings in New England. Examples in the region were provocative and of

extremely high quality: Henry A. Sykes's Woods Cabinet/ Lawrence Observatory (The Octagon) (1847–48, etc.), Morgan Library (1852–53), and Appleton Cabinet (1855, etc.), and Charles E. Parkes's Williston Hall (1857–58; 1950–51) at Amherst College; Richard Bond's Lawrence Hall (Scientific School) (1847) and Richard Schultze's Appleton Chapel (1856, etc.) at Harvard University; Lawrence Hall (1846–47) at Williams College; Gridley J. F. Bryant's Ballou Hall (1852–54) and Thomas W. Silloway's East Hall (1860) at Tufts College; and Gridley J. F. Bryant's Hathorn Hall (1856–57) at Bates College. Outside of the Italianate style and the aforementioned revivalist styles, no others received major attention from New England college/university building designers and campus planners. Concerns for economy, ingrained regional tastes, and function continued to be the principal factors in determining the patterns of higher educational physical plant development. Educators of the day were still inclined to employ variations of the traditional, refined, and direct building type emanating from American colonial- and national-era colleges in contemporary buildings. This planning tendency, with its deep historical roots, has continued to be evident in American higher education from the post–Civil War years to the modern era.[1]

I

THE COLLEGES OF THE
COLONIAL PERIOD

HARVARD AND YALE

Planning and Design Precedents Are Established

AS NEW ENGLAND'S first higher educational institutions, Harvard and Yale established individual building design and campus planning precedents that influenced the physical development patterns of every pre–Civil War college and university in the region. Incorporating a variety of functions, buildings at both institutions expressed simplicity and utility in their rectangular block forms, with modest, traditional classical architectural style elements. While Harvard's leaders and planners chose to adopt the open and closed quadrangle plans of the older English universities, those at Yale initiated the row plan, which became the predominant campus scheme in New England before 1860. Throughout the entire region, colleges and universities participated in active cultural transfer, sharing evolving concepts of living and learning within continually changing physical environments.

Harvard: The Pioneering Leader

The original section of Harvard University's campus, adjacent to Harvard Square in the center of Cambridge, Massachusetts, has, in the words of architectural historian Bainbridge Bunting, "constituted the vital core of the community both culturally and topographically." Following its founding in 1636, however, Harvard had modest though brief architectural beginnings in a 1633 wooden residence purchased from William Peyntree in around 1637; this structure served general college purposes and housed Harvard's president until its demolition in 1644. Succeeding this spacious structure on the southern side of today's Harvard Yard were a new house (c. 1644) for the president and an adjacent residence acquired from Edward Goffe in 1651 and converted to a student dormitory named Goffe College. These two structures, vernacular in form though larger than other houses in the town, ceased to be used in the 1670s and were likely torn down, their sites later occupied in 1726 by the Wadsworth House, the fourth presidential residence, which has survived in modified form to the current era.

Concurrently, Harvard officials had erected the college's first academic building, commenced in 1638 and completed by 1644, and distinguished as the largest building of any type erected in the English colonies until that time. Lacking an official name during its lifetime (it has historically been referred to as The College, Harvard College, First Harvard College, and Old College), it has been called Harvard Hall I by recent college architectural historians to distinguish it from its

Fig. 1-1. The Old College (Harvard Hall I, 1638–44) from the Yard, Harvard College. North-elevation drawing by Harold R. Shurtleff, c. 1933, from Samuel Eliot Morison, *The Founding of Harvard College* (1935), opposite p. 271. Courtesy of Harvard University Archives, HUV 2038 pf.

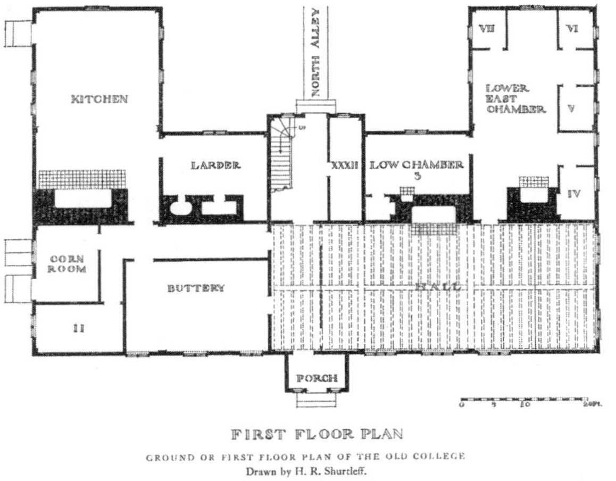

FIRST FLOOR PLAN
GROUND OR FIRST FLOOR PLAN OF THE OLD COLLEGE
Drawn by H. R. Shurtleff.

Fig. 1-2. The Old College (Harvard Hall I, 1638–44), ground- or first-floor plan, Harvard College. Conjectural restoration drawing by Harold R. Shurtleff, c. 1933. Courtesy of Harvard University Archives, HUA 935.57.

two successors, Harvard Hall II and Harvard Hall III. Situated in the middle of a narrow 1⅛-acre yard, the substantial E-shaped, largely symmetrical wooden edifice (fig. 1-1) was positioned to the north of Harvard's initial structures on Braintree Street (later Massachusetts Avenue). Funded by a colonial government grant and a generous bequest from John Harvard, Harvard Hall I ultimately cost £1,000 to complete. Reconstructed in plan and appearance in around 1933 by historians Harold Shurtleff and Samuel Eliot Morison, this building, like most New England houses of the time, was two stories tall (plus garret space) and was wood-framed, with clapboarded walls and a shingled roof. Windows were of the iron casement type. Penetrating the steep-pitched roofs with their several gables and dormers were long, paneled brick chimneys, and a cupola at the building's center point contained the college bell.

The long, flat brick side walls of Harvard Hall I faced south, while the projecting center section (containing the main entrance) and the wings faced north, creating a courtyard opening on Kirkland Street and subsequently leading to the use of the term "Yard" to define the oldest portion of Harvard's campus. Contained on the first story (fig. 1-2) of this multipurpose building were a large hall used for religious services, dining, lectures, recitations, and college functions; a kitchen with pantry; a buttery; a large bedroom chamber; six study spaces; and a stair tower. On the second floor, according to conjectural restoration, were the

college library; three large and two single bedroom chambers; fourteen small studies; and smaller closet alcoves. Pinched by the sloping roof planes, the third floor accommodated two suites, each with a chamber and four studies, and four additional studies in the top section of the stair tower. These various spaces are believed to have been modeled after those contained in the colleges of Oxford and Cambridge universities in England.

With the lack of professional architects in the American colonies at the time, Morison attributes the design of Harvard Hall I to John Wilson. Wilson was a member of the Harvard Board of Overseers, a Boston church minister, and a former resident of Eton in England, the location of the Old School quadrangle at Eton College, which was similar in arrangement to Harvard's first major building. John Friend of Ipswich, Massachusetts, is documented as the chief contractor. Harvard Hall I met the college's multifaceted needs for over three decades, but gradually deteriorated, and by 1671, the construction of a replacement, Harvard Hall II, had begun. This building was totally demolished in 1680. Scholars of Harvard architecture have speculated that its premature demise may have resulted from a combination of the harsh New England climate, poor structural design, inadequate construction supervision, and possibly termite infestation. It should be noted, however, that the brief lifespan of this innovative American educational edifice was similar to that of many seventeenth-century New England buildings.[1]

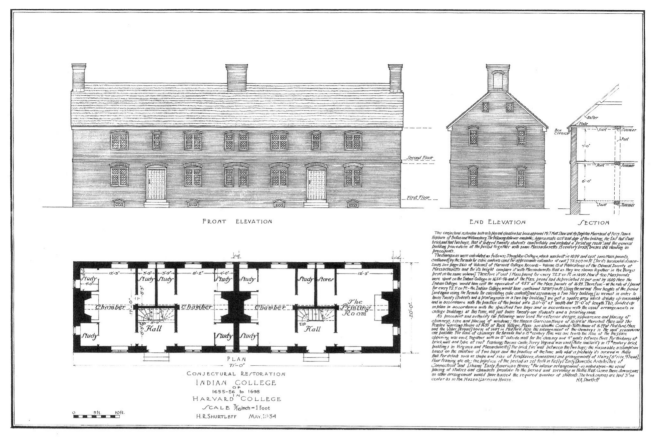

Fig. 1-3. Indian College (1654–56), Harvard College. Front and end elevations; section and first-floor plan. Conjectural restoration drawing by Harold R. Shurtleff, c. 1933. Courtesy of Harvard University Archives, UAI 15.25 pf.

The next major building project on Harvard's first campus was the brick Indian College (fig. 1-3), raised in 1654–56 on a site just to the west of Harvard Hall I, toward present-day Harvard Square. Financed by an English charitable foundation, the Society for the Propagation of the Gospel in New England, the new edifice was intended to house twenty Indian students, but after 1665, when no candidates enrolled, it served as a dormitory for other students and housed the college's printing press. After the press closed in 1692, it stood idle for a few years and was finally demolished in 1698, and its bricks were used in the construction of Stoughton Hall I. As Harold Shurtleff has reconstructed it, Indian College, a two-story, rectangular block, was capped by a pitched roof and likely possessed no roof gables, since there were no rooms in the attic. With the completion of this project, the college's first campus possessed four randomly arranged buildings (the major ones being Harvard Hall I and Indian College) and small related outbuildings,

precluding the possibility of visual order. By 1670, Harvard's lands had increased to approximately nine acres in the western third of today's Harvard Yard, and the next phase of physical growth was thereby facilitated.[2]

After it was determined that Harvard Hall I should be demolished, a successor structure was planned for the college property opposite the burial lot at the north end of Harvard Square. Conceived in 1671, financed by several Massachusetts towns, and put up between 1672 and 1677 by Cambridge master builder Samuel Andrew, Harvard Hall II (also called Old College and Harvard College) was the first component of the new, extroverted, west-facing, English-inspired open quadrangle, which would bring order and building interrelationships to the institution not present in the first campus. Due to the existence of a superb engraved view (fig. 1-4) of the open quadrangle executed by William Burgis in 1726, one may gain an accurate impression of the campus without having to rely on conjectural restorations

Fig. 1-4. "A Prospect of the Colledges in Cambridge in New England" (Harvard College). Engraving by William Burgis (1726), revised by William Price (1743). Left, Harvard Hall II (1672–82); center, (Old) Stoughton Hall I (1698); right, Massachusetts Hall (1719–21). From William L. Andrews, ed., *A Prospect of the Colledges in Cambridge* (1897), frontispiece. Courtesy of Harvard University Archives, HUV 2143 pf.

of the appearances of its three buildings, commencing with Harvard Hall II.

Considered by many to be one of the most significant structures built in New England before 1700, this long, 97-by-42-foot brick edifice was an intriguing though somewhat awkward blend of Medieval Jacobean and Renaissance design features. Two stories tall to the main cornice, it accommodated two more stories under a complex, seemingly disjointed gambrel roof, which possessed an amazing total of fourteen gables and ten dormers, reflecting late Gothic practice. In the early eighteenth century, school officials considered replacing the roof with a flatter version to alleviate the threat of deterioration, but this never came to pass. Windows were regularly spaced and of various rectangular sizes, some with Medieval-originated mullioned and diamond-pane casements. Reminiscent of Renaissance and more recent English practice was the use of certain classical details to highlight critical features—the molded brick pilasters framing the entrance doorways; the ornamented brick cornices of the first-floor windows supported by brackets; the double belt courses between the first and second stories; the thin chimney pilaster strips; and the water table, most likely of pressed brick fabrication. An octagonal lantern adorned the roof, along with a balustrade that was added in 1691. Whether these multiple elements were well integrated is certainly subject to some debate, but there should be little doubt that Harvard Hall II was a provocative architectural composition.

Fortunately, due to the existence of the Burgis engraving and other evidence, Harold Shurtleff was able to provide an accurate reconstruction of the interior layout of the building. Like Harvard Hall I, it served multiple purposes, accommodating academic, residential, and administrative functions. On the first level, the two main entrances opened into stair halls. Between these entries was a great hall, which served as a chapel, dining hall, lecture room, and special events center. The hall was flanked by a buttery, a kitchen, and two living chambers with studies. On the second floor above the hall was the main library, with four student and tutors chambers with studies on either side. The two upper levels under the gambrel roof provided additional space for student living chambers, each consisting of a common bedroom and two small closets, an older feature of the English universities. Certain of these spaces were later converted to classrooms and a scientific laboratory as other new residential buildings were erected and opened on the campus. This successful combination of living and learning functions, involving both faculty and students, remained viable and active until the unfortunate loss of the building to fire, and its subsequent demolition, in 1764.[3]

Following the completion of a third house for Harvard's presidents, facing Harvard Hall II, Stoughton Hall I (Old Stoughton) was erected as a dormitory in 1698 as the third or back side of the west-oriented open quadrangle (see fig. 1-4). Formalized planning was thereby introduced to the Harvard campus. Named for William Stoughton, lieutenant governor of Massachusetts, who donated £800 for the project, the new building measured 23 by 100 feet, stood four stories tall, was protected by a pitched roof with dormers, and was able to house up to forty students. The placement of the four chimneys and the symmetrical facade, illustrated in the Burgis engraving, indicates that the building consisted of two entries accessing two chambers with associated studies per floor in each entry. This plan, derived from that of Indian College, was subsequently used for other dormitories at Harvard, as well as Yale and other eastern colleges/universities. In the decorative elements of Stoughton Hall I, Harvard clearly abandoned Medieval design practices for Early Georgian, introducing orderly fenestration, a well-defined main cornice, corner quoins, stringcourses, an inscription panel with pediment, and doorways framed by pilasters and topped by segmental-arched pediments. Though these various features were well articulated, Stoughton I, the product of deficient construction practices, was never stable or weather resistant, and after further damage by troops quartered there during the Revolutionary War, the decision was made to demolish the building. This unfortunate task was performed in 1781.[4]

Harvard University's oldest surviving major building is Massachusetts Hall, commenced in 1719 and completed in 1721 to provide living quarters for the institution's expanding student population. Erected on the site of the former third president's house, it completed the balanced composition of the open quadrangle, with its well-defined courtyard (see fig. 1-4) in the tradition of Oxford and Cambridge universities. Funded by a £3,500 appropriation of the pro-

vincial legislature, it reproduced in three stories and garret the two-entry plan of Stoughton Hall I but was twice as deep, providing living space for sixty students and two tutors. One of the tutor rooms was later used as the "Apparatus Chamber" for scientific studies. More sweeping interior alterations were made in 1870, when the aging edifice was totally gutted and converted to academic uses, creating four large spaces, each two stories tall, for lecture rooms, laboratories, and reading and examination rooms (fig. 1-5). Following a fire in 1924, Massachusetts was rebuilt on the interior as a residential hall; however, in 1939 the first two floors were again remodeled, this time for administrative offices, now including that of the president. Little change has occurred since, except for the addition of unobtrusive metal window sashes in 1974. The original designer has yet to be documented, though President John Leverett has been cited as a possibility.

As an architectural composition, Massachusetts Hall (fig. 1-6), even more than Stoughton Hall I, embraced the Early Georgian vernacular and displayed little evidence of the Medieval design tradition. The relatively plain main facade and brick end walls lack the sophisticated decorative elements customarily associated with buildings of this style. Nonetheless, this pleasantly proportioned 50-by-100-foot structure possesses significant aesthetic attributes: the gambrel roof with dormers and balustrades hiding the upper roof planes; the paneled, paired chimneys at each gable end; the clock face in the upper west gable; the brick

Fig. 1-5. Massachusetts Hall (1719–21), interior of reading room, The Yard, Harvard University. Photograph, 1876. Courtesy of Harvard University Archives, HUV 30 (1-4).

Fig. 1-6. Massachusetts Hall (1718, etc.), The Yard, Harvard University. Photograph, 2009.

Fig. 1-7. Holden Chapel (1742), The Yard, Harvard University. Photograph, 2009.

belt courses and water tables defining the floor levels; the segmental-arched and flat window lintels; and the front doorway surrounds with pronounced, flat lintels. Until their unfortunate removal in 1790, these doorways were protected by hoods supported by scrolled brackets, perhaps the most interesting decorative as well as functional feature of the building. With its solid exterior appearance, which one may still view today, Massachusetts Hall, in its relative simplicity, reflects the conservative, practical values of its creators, along with their need for fiscal restraint.[5]

Harvard's next significant building chronologically is the diminutive Holden Chapel (fig. 1-7), constructed in 1742 and attributed to John Smibert of Boston. Positioned just to the west of the row formed by Hollis and Stoughton II halls, between two small quadrangles, it is the college's first exclusively religious structure, though it only served this purpose for just over two decades. Initially its main facade, framed by paired brick pilasters and topped by a Tuscan entablature and gable displaying florid wood carving, was in the west end wall facing the Cambridge Common. The current arched entrance, with its flanking pilasters and entablature, is believed to have been designed around 1850 by architect Gridley J. F. Bryant (see chapters 5 and 7); it replaced a tall square-headed door that was enclosed within a crenellated porch in 1800. The side walls of the nicely proportioned pitched-roof building contain three identical round-arched windows separated by pilasters, with brownstone caps and bases nearly identical to those on the west facade. Today the rear or east facade, originally devoid of architectural embellishment, possesses the main entrance with entablature and pediment, all added in 1850 when campus buildings were refocused inward toward the open Yard. In 1880, when the former west entrance was sealed, the west pediment's florid Baroque relief, which featured the Holden family arms, was reproduced in the east pediment. Financed by a £400 gift from Mrs. Samuel Holden, the widow of the former governor of the Bank of England, Holden Chapel, with its sophisticated High Georgian form and embellishment, set the precedent for Harvard architecture for the next half century. After it ceased to function as a religious sanctuary, it was divided into two stories and served numerous roles—the first quarters of the medical school; physics and chemistry laboratories; lecture rooms; an anatomical museum; and recitation rooms. Also in 1880, the intermediate floor was removed, returning the interior

to a single-story space, and it has since been used for choir and glee club rehearsals and instruction, and for classes devoted to music and elocution.[6]

Other than Massachusetts Hall, Holden Chapel, and Harvard Hall III, the other surviving eighteenth-century building at Harvard is Hollis Hall (fig. 1-8), situated just north of Harvard Hall III and adjacent to Holden Chapel. Facing growing enrollment and benefiting from economic prosperity in the late 1750s, college officials again appealed for a new dormitory. In 1762 the colonial legislature responded positively, appropriating £2,500 for the project. Completed over the next year under the direction of master builder and possible architect Thomas Dawes, the building was named Hollis Hall in recognition of a family that over many years had generously funded endowments for the library, professorships, and student scholarships. The conscious placement of Hollis between Harvard Hall II and Holden Chapel created a second but smaller open quadrangle facing westward toward the Common and suggesting the college's wish to relate closely to the Cambridge community.

Although the interior format of Hollis is similar to that of Massachusetts Hall—both have two entries and are two suites deep—its exterior appearance, apparent on both its

Fig. 1-8. Hollis Hall (1762–63), The Yard, Harvard University. Photograph, 2009.

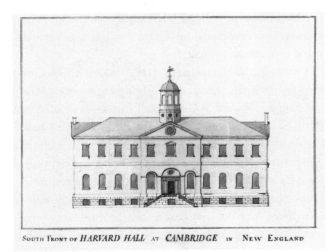

SOUTH FRONT OF *HARVARD HALL* AT *CAMBRIDGE* IN NEW ENGLAND

Fig. 1-9. Harvard Hall III (1764–66, etc.), The Yard, Harvard College. Front-elevation drawing (1764) by Pierie du Simitiere. Courtesy of the Library Company of Philadelphia.

east and west facades, is strikingly different and more characteristic of middle or late Georgian architecture. Establishing precedent for later pre–Civil War New England higher educational structures, the four-story Hollis is a balanced, 105-by-44-foot, three-section brick composition dominated by a center, slightly projecting pavilion supporting a closed classical pediment. The end result, of positive visual impression, and the existence of the pavilion did not negatively impact the rectangular interior floor-plan configuration. To create a west as well as east central axial focus for the three-section design, the builders placed on the first floor a false central entrance containing two narrow vertical windows as on the floors above, ultimately separated by a brick fire wall installed in 1875. As architectural historians of Harvard have recently observed, Hollis differs from Massachusetts in several other respects: its roof is hipped rather than gambrel; the windows of the top story are shorter than the ones below; and the main entrance surrounds have flat pilasters, Corinthian capitals, and a dentil course rather than the more traditional, plain architrave moldings. Just one of the original door frames, for the center false door of the west facade, has been preserved (its original segmental-arched pediment was removed). The frames of the flanking west doors, formerly the front entrances, were removed in 1898, long after the early college buildings were reoriented toward the present-day Yard. Initially back doors, the two entrances on the east facade—the only ones still functioning—are original but of modest articulation, as they were considered secondary when they were installed.[7]

On 24 January 1764, soon after Hollis Hall was completed and opened for use, nearby Harvard Hall II was destroyed by a catastrophic fire, the worst in the college's history. Lost along with the building were students' possessions, furnishings, scientific apparatus, and the entire five-thousand-volume college library collection. Funded by the colonial legislature, Harvard Hall III was promptly raised on the same site based on designs by the Royal Governor, Sir Thomas Bernard, with Thomas Dawes serving as chief contractor. The construction process was concluded in June 1766. Because it would have been prohibitively expensive to accommodate all the functions housed in the former building, college officials determined that the new Harvard Hall would meet only academic and related needs, making it the first college structure in America devoted solely to this purpose—that is, the first such structure without residential space. Consequently, the new edifice contained a chapel and commons (above a cellar kitchen) on the first floor; and the new library, the Philosophical Chamber (Cabinet) for scientific instruments and natural history objects, the Hebrew School, and the Mathematical School on the second floor. The exterior design of the 107-by-40-foot, symmetrical, rectangular block building (fig. 1-9) could be characterized as plain, conservative, and uninspiring. It did, however, possess certain High Georgian qualities, such as the front central pavilion topped by a closed pediment, end gables, refined stone cornices, and a simple octagonal cupola with dome crowning the hipped roof at its center. In general, architectural historians have given Harvard Hall III high ratings, regarding it as one of the more sophisticated American college buildings of its period.

Over the course of its history, Harvard Hall III has been

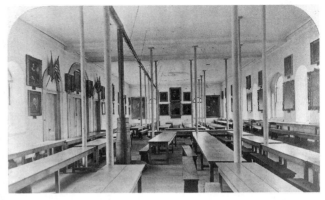

Fig. 1-10. Harvard Hall III (1764–66, etc.), common room, The Yard, Harvard University. Photograph, c. 1860. Courtesy of Harvard University Archives, HUV 31 (6-5a).

Fig. 1-11. Harvard Hall III (1764–66, etc.), after 1842 addition of two-story porch designed by Richard Bond, The Yard, Harvard University. Photograph, c. 1860. Courtesy of Harvard University Archives, HUV 31 (4-5b).

Fig. 1-12. Harvard Hall III (1764–66, etc.), with 1870 front-facade addition designed by Ware and Van Brunt, The Yard, Harvard University. Photograph, 1986.

rearranged on its interior and twice enlarged, transforming its exterior appearance. In 1815, when the commons, kitchen, and chapel were relocated to University Hall, the first floor was converted to classrooms, a mineralogical cabinet, and laboratories, and the second floor was devoted exclusively to the expanded library. Nearly three decades later, in 1842, the first floor became a single large room (fig. 1-10) for special functions and other purposes, and a two-story central pavilion (fig. 1-11), planned by Richard Bond, was added to the front facade, providing much-needed extra space, and duplicating the form and most details of the original central pavilion. In 1870, the building was again expanded, this time for the science department, and the corners of the then T-shaped first-floor plan were filled in with two one-story additions. Erected from designs prepared by architects Ware and Van Brunt of Boston, the new additions, along with the central pavilion, were embellished by flat Doric pilasters set between round-arched windows and a thick modillioned cornice, conscientiously preserving the Georgian flavor of the exterior. Although the interior underwent a total reconstruction in 1968–69, the exterior of Harvard Hall III looks much the same today (fig. 1-12) as it did in the late nineteenth century. In the estimate of many, it is Harvard's most significant extant pre–Civil War building, anchoring the two western-facing open quadrangles (fig. 1-13) until 1781 and the loss of Stoughton Hall I.[8]

Funded by a public lottery in 1795–96, a new dormitory, Stoughton Hall II (New Stoughton) (fig. 1-14), was built in 1804–5 over twenty years after the loss of the first

Fig. 1-13. "A Westerly View of The Colledges in Cambridge, New England," Harvard College. From left to right: Holden Chapel (1742); Hollis Hall (1762–63); Harvard Hall III (1764–66); Stoughton Hall I (1698); Massachusetts Hall (1719–21). Engraving, c. 1767, Josh Chadwick, del.; P. Revere, Sculp. Courtesy of Harvard University Archives, HUV 2167.2 pf.

Fig. 1-14. Hollis Hall (1762–63), left, and Stoughton Hall II (1804–5), right, The Yard, Harvard University. Photograph, 2009.

Stoughton Hall to fire and demolition. The final cost was $23,700, with over $18,000 raised by a lottery. The first Harvard building to be erected in the nineteenth century, it was planned by the highly esteemed Boston architect Charles Bulfinch (1763–1844), who was responsible for numerous major Boston building designs in the Federal vein, derived from English classicism. Situated just to the north of Hollis Hall, it also originally faced west toward the Cambridge Common. A near duplicate of Hollis in terms of building massing, materials, fenestration, and interior layout, Stoughton Hall II also featured a false door frame in the center of its west facade. Differences that are characteristic of the early phase of Federal architecture included white limestone window lintels; flush granite door lintels; the absence of belt courses and a water table in the walls; and the recessed granite frames of the two front (east) entrances. Dating from repairs made after an 1879 fire, the present cornice and hipped roof give an impression of heaviness that likely was not present in the original building statement. Subject to interior improvements made over the last century, Stoughton Hall II continues to provide living quarters for Harvard's students.[9]

Under the eighteen-year presidency (1810–28) of John T. Kirkland, the developing Harvard Yard was landscaped and provided with paths, and the commitment to a large rectangular quadrangle was furthered by the construction of two more important buildings, Holworthy and University halls. Designed by Loammi Baldwin in 1811 and completed in 1811–12, Holworthy Hall (fig. 1-15) was the first

structure to be positioned east of the open quadrangles. It was named for Sir Matthew Holworthy, an English merchant, in recognition of his earlier bequest to the college, although its $24,500 cost was funded by a state-sponsored public lottery. Set at right angles to the east facades of Hollis and Stoughton II, the new residence hall formed the north boundary of the original Yard, and continues to do so (fig. 1-16). Accessing three stairways and living units instead of two (as in the older dormitories), with a functional center doorway, the three front entrances display heavy, rusticated, granite block frames with splayed lintel blocks. Flat, angled cornices were placed over the windows of all four stories. The first Harvard dormitory to depart from the Medieval practice of closet-sized studies accessed from bedrooms, Holworthy possessed suites composed of a study with southern exposure and two bedrooms to the north, thereby providing good natural light and ventilation. For its first sixty years, this stunning, lengthy (138-foot) Federal-style edifice possessed a lower top story (see fig. 1-15) than it does today; the eave line was raised by two feet during the 1871 renovation of the dormitories in the Yard implemented by President Charles W. Eliot's administration.[10]

One of Harvard's most famous and architecturally meritorious structures is University Hall, erected in 1813–15 from designs drafted by Charles Bulfinch, and occupying a key position in the gradually evolving quadrangle of the old Yard. Although the idea was later abandoned, Bulfinch initially envisioned his new structure at the center of a large elliptical row of trees taking the shape of a large horse race-

Fig. 1-15. Holworthy Hall (1811–12), designed by Loammi Baldwin, The Yard, Harvard University. Photograph, c. 1861. Courtesy of Harvard University Archives, HUV 37 (1-1).

Fig. 1-16. Holworthy Hall (1811–12), The Yard, Harvard University. Photograph, 2009.

track (fig. 1-17). Nonetheless, in the end Bulfinch's idea of University Hall as the core Yard building confirmed the inward orientation of the Yard, with the new edifice located at the center of the long east side of the quadrangle, facing the east ends of Massachusetts Hall and Harvard Hall III (fig. 1-18).

Constructed of Chelmsford, Massachusetts, granite instead of brick, the new $65,000 structure, strategically positioned and elaborately embellished, was then, and in the view of many still is, the university's pivotal, monumental architectural landmark. Planned to incorporate public activities, including a chapel, dining halls, the president's office, and six classrooms, University Hall (fig. 1-19), like earlier buildings at Harvard, displays a three-unit composition—a two-story central section with large, round-arched fenestration in the upper level; a fully articulated entablature; and a roof balustrade, set between three-story wings with three window bays. Striking details include the paired white wooden pilasters with Ionic capitals framing the main arched doorways and upper windows in the eight-bay central section. The Federal-style character of the structure is further emphasized by the low-pitched roof, penetrated by tall brick chimneys and largely concealed behind the balustrade. Overall, the composition, with minor deficiencies, appears unified, defying the criticism of some who have questioned the configuration of the window apertures. The design also included a central rooftop cupola (never built) and, at trustee insistence, a central, one-story columned porch (see fig. 1-18) running across the west fa-

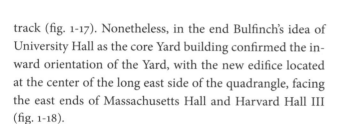

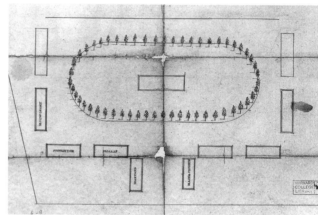

Fig. 1-17. "Racetrack" plan (1812–13), Harvard Yard, Harvard College, by Charles Bulfinch. Courtesy of Harvard University Archives, HUA: UAI 15.740 pf.

Fig. 1-18. "South View of the Several Halls of Harvard College." Engraving (first state, c. 1825), Fisher-Bowen view. Author's collection.

Fig. 1-19. University Hall (1813–15), designed by Charles Bulfinch, west facade, The Yard, Harvard University. Photograph, 2009.

Fig. 1-20. University Hall (1813–15), interior of faculty room, The Yard, Harvard University. Photograph, c. 1930. Courtesy of Harvard University Archives, HUV 39 (8-1).

cade, which was present until its removal in 1842. Showing foresight about the future growth of the campus, Bulfinch, supported by university officials, endowed the east elevation with an impressive granite wall surface and wooden pilasters on the western facade, allowing University Hall to function as an effective link between the old Yard and subsequent architectural development to the east.

While University Hall has been subjected to few exterior modifications, the interior has been recurrently remodeled since its construction. Although it has never required major alterations, the first floor, originally planned to accommodate four class dining halls, was converted to instructional usage, along with the basement kitchen, in around 1840. In 1868–69, after religious services were moved to the new Appleton Chapel, the second-floor chapel was divided horizontally as well as vertically into four classrooms, and the current dormer windows were installed to provide illumination and fresh air to the upper rooms. More recently, in 1896, these classrooms were removed and the old chapel restored as a meeting hall (fig. 1-20) for the Faculty of Arts and Sciences. Other, more recent changes include the

Fig. 1-21. Gore Hall (library) (1838–41, etc.), designed by Richard Bond, The Yard, Harvard University. Photograph, c. 1900. Courtesy of Harvard University Archives, HUV 48 (12-5).

addition of granite steps before the east front doorway in 1917; the placement of the legendary statue of John Harvard (1882) by Daniel Chester French in its current location in front of the hall in 1924; and the transfer of the president's office from the south end of the second floor to Massachusetts Hall in 1939.[11]

Departing from the developing quadrangle and any other formal campus scheme, Harvard's leaders located Gore Hall (fig. 1-21), the college library built in 1838–41, on part of the site of the present Widener Library facing Massachusetts Avenue. Named for Governor Christopher Gore, whose $100,000 bequest helped to fund construction expenses, the new building was the first Harvard structure devoted exclusively to library functions, including the storage of over 40,000 volumes. Designed by Boston architect Richard Bond, the perpendicular Gothic Revival–style edifice was built of Quincy, Massachusetts, granite and cost $273,000, twice the initial project estimate. With a length of 140 feet, Gore possessed a floor plan in the shape of a Latin cross, with insignificant transepts. Small octagonal towers were present on the front and rear facades of the main block and the transepts, in each case flanking large, traceried, broken-arched windows. Its picturesque design possibly inspired by King's College Chapel at Cambridge University, the library was widely admired in its day, though some of its details could be regarded as awkward and not well integrated, and the overall symmetrical composition had a somewhat stiff appearance.

Modern-day architectural historians have also expressed reservations about the ability of Gore Hall to func-

tion effectively. The spacious columned nave (fig. 1-22) of the Gothic structure served as the primary reading room, flanked by book alcoves set in narrow side aisles. Books were shelved in the narrow side aisles according to collection rather than subject categories, which was deemed inconvenient to readers. To his credit, the designer did attempt to minimize the threat of fire through the use of iron roof trusses and floor supports, combined with wooden trim. In its early years, however, Gore Hall was heated by steam, a system that attracted notice and produced humid vapors that clouded windowpanes and damaged the book collection, which by the late 1850s was considered the second largest in the country.

Typical of institutional library structures, Gore Hall underwent alterations and expansions as the collections and use demands grew. In around 1850, the 83-foot octagonal corner towers, which had posed structural problems, were reduced in height. In 1876, after failing to find a donor to fund a new library edifice, Harvard officials used general funds to construct a large stack wing (see fig. 1-21) on the east side of the building. The new wing contained experi-

Fig. 1-22. Gore Hall (library) (1838–41, etc.), interior, The Yard, Harvard University. Photograph, n.d. Courtesy of Harvard University Archives, HUV 48 (5-2).

Fig. 1-23. "Astronomical Observatory [1843], Cambridge, Mass.," Harvard University. Printed view (Mallory, del.; Worcester & Co.) from *Gleason's Pictorial* (1852). Courtesy of Harvard University Archives, HUV 2251.

Fig. 1-24. Lawrence Hall (Scientific School) (1847), designed by Richard Bond, Harvard University. Photograph, before 1871 remodeling. Courtesy of Harvard University Archives, HUV 170 (1-7).

mental metal shelving in which the weight of the books was conveyed downward to the foundations through steel book stacks instead of the framing system. This innovative stack design had been planned in 1874 by Boston architects Ware and Van Brunt, working with the head librarians. Electric lighting was installed in 1891, and another remodeling took place in 1895, on this occasion subdividing the old nave reading room into three tiers of stacks and a reading room in the top level. In 1906, a two-story administrative wing was added, but this expansion failed to adequately address the rapidly accelerating library needs of the university. Occupying the prime strategic location for the main Harvard library, Gore Hall was demolished in 1913, soon to be replaced by the resplendent Widener Library, still in use.[12]

Other Harvard buildings, too, were erected outside the Yard between 1820 and 1850 (see note 12). Two of these satisfying the subject definition of this book were the Harvard Observatory and Lawrence Hall, home of the Lawrence Scientific School. The older of the two structures, the Observatory (fig. 1-23), is located outside the North Yard to the north of Harvard Square. Erected in 1843 to replace a temporary observatory, it was planned by architect Isaiah Rogers (1800–1869) of Boston, known for his designs of hotels and commercial buildings in the city and elsewhere. In the tradition of the well-known Palladian scheme, it comprised a central section and identical pitched-roof, two-story side pavilions connected by one-story wooden wings. Atop the central section, housing the observatory equipment, was an octagonal dome positioned above a low attic. Extremely

formal and geometrical, the modest Italianate design featured broad, overhanging cornices, but no other recognizable detail. Initially, the east wing was a faculty residence, while the west wing, dating from 1851, contained a library and classrooms. Situated on a small rise overlooking the town, the Observatory was later enlarged, resulting in the loss of the wings in 1954 and 1960. Today only the original central section remains, nearly obscured by more recent scientific structures.[13]

The first home of the Scientific School endowed by Abbott Lawrence was Lawrence Hall (fig. 1-24), the design product of Richard Bond, the architect of Gore Hall. Erected in 1847 on the north side of Cambridge Street adjacent to the old Yard, Lawrence Hall, like the Observatory, was intended to be a five-section, symmetrical composition, but this was never fully realized, and a west wing to balance the professor's residence in the east wing on the other side of the central pavilion was never built. Architecturally cohesive and imaginatively embellished, Lawrence was Harvard's only example of the mature, brick-and-brownstone Italianate style, extremely tall and geometrical, with broad cornices supported by heavy brackets, hooded, round-arched windows, corner quoins, and other typical features. In 1871, under the direction of Ware and Van Brunt, the interior was totally reconfigured, and the exterior modified by the removal of the central doorway and the addition of a low third story, reproducing the detailing of the pediment of the pavilion. In 1970, after multiple academic uses over the years, the building was badly damaged by fire and de-

Fig. 1-25. Appleton Chapel (1856, etc.), designed by Paul Schulze, The Yard, Harvard University. Photograph, n.d., by the American Engraving Company, Boston. Courtesy of Harvard University Archives, HUV 53 (4-3).

molished to provide space for the new Undergraduate Science Center.[14]

Harvard's next two large-scale structures, designed by Boston and then Washington, D.C., architect Paul Schulze (1827–97), were dissimilar in terms of size, proportions, and building materials and were randomly placed outside the Bulfinch-envisioned closed quadrangle and the old Yard. Replacing the chapel in University Hall, the older of the two buildings, Appleton Chapel (fig. 1-25), was erected in 1856–57 and financed from a general $200,000 bequest by the trustees of the estate of Samuel Appleton, an affluent Boston industrialist. The rationale behind its location is still undetermined: the new chapel edifice was placed with its longitudinal axis at right angles to University and Gore halls, defining one side of an open space that would in time become the Tercentenary Quadrangle. While Appleton's major axis was focused on Holden Chapel, the off-center main tower negated any possible relationship with the older, much smaller structure. Curiously, though the tower and main facade faced westward toward the old Yard, the

intervening space was later occupied by a massive dormitory, Thayer Hall, isolating Appleton from the then organizing space.

In visual terms, Appleton Chapel was distinctly different from other Yard buildings, primarily because of its light-colored Nova Scotia limestone materials and its curious, moderately successful combination of Classical and Romanesque Revival architectural style elements. Particularly noteworthy were the heavy, square corner pilasters; the large, round-arched side windows set within round-arched panels; the off-center, triple-arched front entrance; and the ponderous, multistage, square corner tower with its numerous diverse apertures, thick, bracketed cornice, and spire topped by a metal finial and weather vane. In 1872, under the direction of the Boston architectural partnership of Peabody and Stearns, the acoustics of the interior sanctuary were improved, and the seating capacity was expanded to nine hundred by the addition of a gallery space. There were two additional remodelings in 1886 and 1919, and then the chapel was demolished in 1931 and replaced by today's brick Neo-Classical Georgian Memorial Church. While Appleton Chapel will be remembered for its incredible profusion of eclectic decorative details, it lacked the aesthetic cohesiveness and integrity that its creators had surely hoped to realize.[15]

Schulze's second Harvard commission, Boylston Hall (fig. 1-26), was arguably a more successful design than Appleton Chapel. Also occupying a site seemingly divorced from the old Yard, this symmetrical, rectangular (117-by-70-foot), two-story structure was constructed of rough masonry block granite from Rockport, Massachusetts, in

Fig. 1-26. Boylston Hall (1857), designed by Paul Schulze, The Yard, Harvard University. Photograph, before 1870. Courtesy of Harvard University Archives, HUV 47 (4-6a).

Fig. 1-27. University Museum, first section (1859), designed by Henry Greenough and George Snell, North Yard, Harvard University. Photograph, before 1871. Courtesy of Harvard University Archives, HUV 315 (1-2).

1857. Initially protected by a truncated hipped roof, Boylston received a new mansard-roofed third story in 1870–71 under the direction of architects Peabody and Stearns. Its most striking architectural features were the bracketed cornice band under the roof plane overhangs; the plain molding separating the stories; the round-arched windows with wooden mullions; and the main arched front doorway facing the center of the Yard. Erected using funds from a bequest by Ward Nicholas Boylston for a granite structure, Boylston is said to have resembled contemporary granite commercial buildings in Boston, particularly those of architect Gridley J. F. Bryant (see chapters 5 and 7), with their various, often contrasting surface textures. The total cost of this project was $50,000.

Boylston Hall could be considered a functionally innovative building, as it may well have been the first erected in the United States to house a chemistry laboratory and lecture rooms. It also accommodated an anatomical museum and a collection of mineralogical specimens and later in its history served many other purposes. The most recent renovation, praised by many associated with the university, was implemented in 1959 by The Architects Collaborative and contractors. Under their direction, the interior was entirely gutted, rebuilt, and reorganized, and the mansard dormer and arched windows in the walls were fitted with undivided, polished plates of glass. At the same time, an arched metal vestibule was installed, shielding the main entrance. The end result is a persuasive architectural statement, the granite walls effectively contrasting with the glass window surfaces.[16]

Harvard's last two pre–Civil War buildings, the Univer-

sity Museum and the Old Gym (later Rogers Hall), were built outside the Yard and were among the first manifestations of the university's growth beyond the confines of the original campus. Contributing to the architectural diversity and unsystematic planning of the North Yard was the immense University Museum, its various components erected between 1859 and 1913, implementing the dream of famous Swiss naturalist Louis Agassiz to assemble in a single complex collections relating to geology and all forms of life—plants, animals, and man. The first fireproof section (fig. 1-27) of the huge, factory-like complex, initially known as Agassiz Hall (Museum of Comparative Zoology), was designed by Boston architects Henry Greenough (1801–83) and George Snell (1820–93) and was funded from private and public sources. Forming the east section of today's north wing, the original rectangular brick building consisted of three horizontal divisions—a tall basement with windows surmounted by two zones, each divided into a principal story and a mezzanine above. As a result, each exhibition gallery possessed a main floor and a balcony surrounding a high central space, much like the interiors of other American scientific museums of the late nineteenth century.

Rather formal and restrained in appearance, this first unit of the University Museum possessed a six-bay front (east) facade, visually ordered by a projecting entrance pavilion with round-arched double doors. Surrounding the building were plain, molded cornices. Accenting the tall windows of the first and third stories were impressive Italianate brownstone lintels with supporting brackets. Early in its history, the original plan underwent modifications; the first, in the early 1870s, added a mansard roof to the unit when the second section was erected, thereby providing an additional floor for office space. Subsequently, other modifications were made to the original museum, but it has endured as a recognizable part of the full complex.[17]

Harvard's latest pre-1860 building, the Old Gym (fig. 1-28), formerly occupied the site of the current city fire station, at the triangle formed by Cambridge Street, Broadway, and Quincy Street. Built in 1859 for $9,500 and designed by Boston architect Edward Clark Cabot (1818–1901), this somewhat undistinguished octagonal 70-foot-wide brick edifice was used primarily for gymnastic exercise (fig. 1-29), though it also possessed two bowling alleys. Particularly noteworthy were the large round-arched windows in each of the eight wall surfaces, their form repeated in the

much smaller round-arched windows and door of the first level. On the completion of the Hemenway Gymnasium in 1878, the building, with the new name Rogers Hall, was used by the Engineering School and subsequently the Germanic Museum, until it was torn down in 1933. Despite this loss, Harvard University has retained ten of its pre–Civil War buildings, preserving an architectural legacy that has greatly influenced the physical origins and development of New England's colleges and universities.[18]

Fig. 1-28. Old Gymnasium (Rogers Hall) (1859), designed by E. C. Cabot, Harvard University. Photograph, n.d. Courtesy of Harvard University Archives, HUV 162 (3-3).

Fig. 1-29. Old Gymnasium (Rogers Hall) (1859), interior, Harvard University. Photograph, n.d. Courtesy of Harvard University Archives, HUV 162 (3-1).

Fig. 1-30. "The First Yale College House" (1717–18). Reproduced sketch from Edwin Oviatt, *The Beginnings of Yale* (1916), p. 354. Author's collection.

Yale: The Evolution of the Old Brick Row

In 1701, ten Congregational ministers founded "The Collegiate School" at Saybrook, Connecticut, but its stay there was brief, and in 1717 it was decided to move the fledgling institution to a more advantageous location. After much discussion, the New Haven trustees prevailed, and on 28 October of that year the Connecticut General Assembly issued a formal proclamation confirming the relocation of the new college to that city. Anticipating formal approval of the move, in early October the New Haven trustees had commenced the construction of a building for the college on a slight rise just west of the New Haven Green. The lot was at the corner of present-day Chapel and College streets, where Bingham Hall is situated today on Yale University's Old Campus. As the initial building was being completed in 1718, the institution was renamed Yale College in recognition of generous financial assistance received from Elihu Yale, a London capitalist of American birth.

Conspicuously positioned facing eastward toward the meetinghouse below, the Collegiate House (renamed the Yale College House in 1718) (fig. 1-30) was of vernacular appearance, resembling an inn or extended residence, and, except for its six tall brick chimneys, was constructed entirely of wood. Extremely long and narrow, the new three-and-one-half-story edifice measured approximately 170 by 21 feet, its square interior chambers with small studies extending the entire width and flanked by stair entryways. The largest ell rooms were the commons and chapel, and the library above it, on the south end, and a kitchen in a small ell addition. Reconstruction views show an ordered, repetitive facade with three pedimented doorways and a pitched roof broken by dormers and topped at its center point by a round, open cupola with concave dome roof, finial, and weathervane. It has been suggested that a possible model was Harvard's Stoughton Hall I, built in 1698 and inspired by earlier English university dormitories. Although the Collegiate House was much longer than Stoughton Hall I, this connection is more than likely, as Yale was founded by ministers who had attended Harvard, and Harvard was the only other college in New England at the time. Credited with the realization of the Collegiate House, estimated to have cost £1000, is Henry Caner (1680–1731), an accomplished master builder from Boston who also was responsible for other buildings in New Haven in later years. Gradually replaced by other structures, off line from the developing Old Brick Row, and of questionable construction, Yale's first headquarters was razed in stages between 1775 and 1782.[19]

Faced with a growing student population, in 1747 Reverend Thomas Clap, the college rector (a title soon changed to "president"), proposed a plan for erecting a new college dormitory. Seeking assistance with the design, he solicited advice from President Edward Holyoke of Harvard and received back descriptive information and plans for Massachusetts Hall, which Harvard had constructed in 1719–20. Connecticut Hall (later South Middle College) (fig. 1-31), named in recognition of financial assistance from the state General Assembly, was erected by Francis Letort and Thomas Bills in 1750–52 for the sum of £1,660. The builders

followed Holyoke's specifications and Clap's plans so closely that Connecticut Hall was a near duplicate of its Harvard predecessor. A three-story, rectangular, brick block capped by a gambrel roof (with garret) broken by dormers and chimneys, it was 100 feet long and 40 feet wide, and initially contained thirty-two "chambers" and sixty-four studies. For the most part, decorative elements were limited to belt courses and roof cornices. Similar to that of the Collegiate House, the floor plan, English in its origins, was developed around two lateral stair halls (entryways); the student chambers (eight on each floor) with studies were doubled across the width. Positioned just to the north of the Collegiate House, Connecticut Hall was set farther back from the street and the Green. Its siting anticipated the acquisition of additional land and future campus development.

Over time, like so many other early higher educational buildings, Connecticut Hall has undergone significant alterations on both its exterior and its interior. In 1796–97, college officials added a pitched roof over a new fourth

Fig. 1-31. "View of Yale-College, New Haven." Left, Union Hall (South College); center, Old College Chapel (The Athenaeum); right, Connecticut (South Middle) Hall. Engraving by John Scoles from *The Lady and Gentleman's Pocket Magazine* (August–November 1796). Courtesy of Manuscripts and Archives, Yale University Library.

Fig. 1-32. Connecticut (South Middle) Hall (1750–52), Yale College. Photograph, c. 1885, by Pach Bros., N.Y. Courtesy of Manuscripts and Archives, Yale University Library.

Fig. 1-33. Connecticut (South Middle) Hall (1750–52), Yale University. Photograph, 2009.

story (fig. 1-32), which remained in place until the original upper portion of the structure was restored to its initial form in 1905 under the direction of architect Grosvenor Atterbury of New York. As a result of two major interior rearrangements in the twentieth century, the primary one in 1952–54, the center of the building was rearranged for a meeting room, the former student rooms were converted to faculty offices and seminar rooms, and the small studies were eliminated. Satisfying academic rather than the original residential needs, Connecticut, in the words of architec-

tural historian Hugh Morrison, remains as "the only relic of the sound and simple architectural tradition of the eighteenth century" at Yale after the nineteenth-century destruction of the other remaining Old Brick Row buildings. In 1965, it was designated as a National Historic Landmark. Paired with its Georgian Colonial Revival near duplicate–McClellan Hall (1925), designed by Walter B. Chambers—it continues to have a commanding presence at the south end of the Old Campus (fig. 1-33), surrounded by various interpretations of collegiate Gothic Revival, mid-Victorian Gothic, and Richardsonian Romanesque architecture.[20]

Yale's next building, the Old College Chapel (see fig. 1-31), anticipated in its placement as well as its form and detailing the origins of a row scheme for the college. Built in 1761–63 just south of Connecticut Hall, its longitudinal axis was at right angles to that of Connecticut, its principal end-gable facade and attached steeple tower directed eastward toward the New Haven Green. Its construction implemented Thomas Clap's plan for a larger campus, which called for the creation of a balanced, three-building composition, the third structure to be placed on the south side of the chapel at some point in the future. Set behind the College House, the Old College Chapel (later known as The Athenaeum) was an unsophisticated, three-story, pitched-roof brick box, 50 feet long and 40 feet wide, containing a two-story first-floor gallery for religious and academic uses, and a second floor above for a library. The tall, 125-foot tower, topped by an open belfry and slender spire, was funded through the generosity of New Haven citizens and was to become the visual ordering point for the three-building row on its completion. Designed and built by Francis Letort and Thomas Bills, who had also been responsible for Connecticut Hall, the chapel was remodeled in 1824 for recitation and dormitory rooms. At the same time, it was provided with an octagonal upper stage, and the spire on the tower was replaced by a cylindrical dome and became the college's first astronomical observatory.[21]

Following Thomas Clap as Yale's next president was Ezra Stiles, who shared Clap's interest in the systematic growth of Yale's physical plant and grounds. In 1777, he provided the Yale Corporation with an informal plan for campus development, with the grounds configured as a rectangle, and five current (minus Collegiate House) and possible future buildings arranged in an open quadrangle facing the Green, very likely modeled after Harvard's first open quadrangle in the old Yard. Stiles had to delay expansion plans due to the negative impact of the Revolutionary War, a postwar recession, and public anticlericalism. Finally, after fifteen years had passed, Connecticut pledged $30,000 in tax arrears to Yale and expansion plans were revived, with the building of a second dormitory as top priority. The location of the dormitory, however, was subject to heated debate. Stiles urged that it be placed south of the College Chapel balancing Connecticut Hall, but corporation members voted to place it to the north of the row courtyard, at right angles to the line of existing buildings. Dissatisfied by this decision, the citizens of New Haven expressed their disapproval, favoring the more extroverted row plan, thereby improving the aesthetic character of the Green and better connecting the college campus with the city. For assistance in resolving this dilemma, Stiles turned to James Hillhouse, a Yale graduate, U.S. Representative, and force in New Haven's civic affairs. This action was to produce the first higher educational campus plan in America and combine the city Green and the college yard.

To assist in the preparation of the plan for Yale, Hillhouse turned to John Trumbull (1756–1843), a talented painter and amateur architect, a Connecticut native, and a Harvard graduate. Working collaboratively with Hillhouse, Trumbull produced in just one month, December 1792, a plan that argued against the corporation's preferred location for the "New College" and proposed an extended, symmetrical, five-building row scheme, depicted on paper with existing and proposed halls in elevation and floor diagrams, details, and explanatory notes (fig. 1-34). Based on this documentation, it is clear that Hillhouse and Trumbull were in favor of placing the next college building on the south

Fig. 1-34. John Trumbull plan (1792) for the Old Brick Row, Yale College. Courtesy of Manuscripts and Archives, Yale University Library.

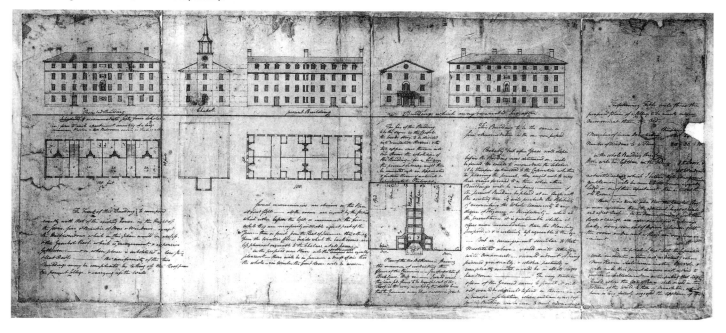

Fig. 1-35. Union Hall (South College) (1793–94), Old Brick Row, Yale College. Photograph, c. 1869, by William Norton, Montreal, Canada. Courtesy of Manuscripts and Archives, Yale University Library.

side of the College Chapel, thereby standing behind Ezra Stiles's original recommendation. In addition to this first plan sheet, the two men produced a second with front and rear campus yards, containing rows of trees and walkways, and in the rear a picturesque garden accessed by meandering paths. A close examination of these sheets makes it irrefutably clear that Hillhouse and Trumbull intended that the Yale campus form a nearly exact square—a self-contained block enclosed by streets on all four sides. Screened by the landscape design, the rear yard behind the proposed elongated row was conceived to accommodate smaller service buildings, their role to meet necessary though perhaps uninspiring functions of life on the campus. In the individual front-elevation building designs, Trumbull expressed the principles of the simplified American Federal vernacular, its origins rooted in the tasteful elegance of English Adamesque classicism.[22]

At its meeting on 1 January 1793, the corporation, on re-

viewing its original decision, approved the new third hall as Trumbull had drawn it, to be placed to the south of the College Chapel to create the three-unit row composition. Three months later, President Stiles led cornerstone laying ceremonies, and construction of the new brick, four-story structure (figs. 1-31 and 1-35), named Union Hall in recognition of Yale's reconciliation with the state, commenced. It was completed in July 1794 and later took the name South College. With dimensions of 100 by 40 feet (the same as Connecticut Hall), it was capped by a low hipped roof broken by brick chimneys and possessed little architectural detail except for thin belt courses and plain roof cornice molding. Departing from the floor plan of Connecticut Hall, Trumbull introduced a new arrangement for thirty-two suites, each combining a large common parlor and two bedrooms/studies, spanning the entire building width and providing improved interior light, heating, and ventilation. This revised suite configuration, expanding much-needed student accommodations, became a model for American collegiate dormitories throughout the nineteenth century and was employed as a planning module for Yale's twentieth-century campus. Unfortunately, the architect of this influential edifice has yet to be identified.[23]

Under the leadership of the next president, Timothy Dwight, selected in 1795, Yale continued the implementation of Hillhouse's and Trumbull's campus plan. In September 1796, the corporation authorized the Building Committee, chaired by Hillhouse, to purchase the property north of the campus, on which there were several unattractive and controversial buildings. Three years later, in 1799–1800, the college also purchased the remaining lots along College Street, then occupied by a poorhouse and jail, thus consolidating the entire street frontage facing the New Haven Green. In 1798, Dwight and the corporation committed to the construction of the second president's house, not accounted for in the campus plan, which in the next year was placed north and slightly east of the developing row, directed east toward the Green. Later used as an analytical laboratory, it was designed and built under the direction of Peter Banner of Boston, an English contractor and self-taught architect, and lasted until 1860, when it was destroyed.

Addressing the continuing problem of insufficient student housing and other demands, Yale Corporation leaders, supported by funding from the State Assembly, made the decision to erect two new buildings—a dormitory and an academic hall—at the north end of the row, perpetuating the Hillhouse and Trumbull concept of repetitive building types (see fig. 1-34). At its November 1800 meeting, corporation members officially approved the project but indicated that they intended to erect the dormitory first, leaving a gap in the row for the academic hall. Both buildings were designed and built by Peter Banner and were intended to blend with their row predecessors.

The construction of the additional dormitory, named Berkeley Hall (later North Middle College) for the Anglican bishop George Berkeley, a Yale benefactor, was completed in 1801–3. The timing made excellent strategic sense, as it allowed the college to expand enrollments and take in more student tuition income, part of which helped to finance the academic hall. In exterior appearance and interior layout, Berkeley was nearly identical to Union Hall, except that it lacked belt courses in the walls and contained additional study rooms to help with the ever-present quandary of student overenrollment. Highly functional and re-

sembling later New England industrial structures, the new dormitory was an immaculately pure if not inspiring representation of the Federal style.

Yale's first building devoted solely to secular functions, the new academic hall, later named the Connecticut Lyceum, was designed by Banner (fig. 1-36) to be used exclusively for classroom instruction and study, thereby relieving congestion in the dormitories, where classes were sometimes conducted in the entryways. Financed by a legislative grant and erected in 1803–4, this structure included study and recitation rooms on the first and second floors; a library, relocated from the chapel, on the third floor; and a chemistry laboratory and appendages in the cellar. In the rear of the building, Banner installed a cross-gable, result-

Fig. 1-36. Connecticut Lyceum (1803–4), Old Brick Row, Yale College. Front-elevation drawing (c. 1803) by Peter Banner. Courtesy of Manuscripts and Archives, Yale University Library.

Fig. 1-37. Connecticut Lyceum (1803–4), Old Brick Row, Yale College. Photograph, n.d. Courtesy of Manuscripts and Archives, Yale University Library.

ing in obstruction-free space for a large lecture room. In the placement of the square front tower with open belfry and dome cap, he departed from Trumbull's original design (see fig. 1-34) and created a churchlike front facade that underscored the importance of religion at Yale at the time. Other details, such as the round windows in the tower and open pediment, and the arched front doorway surround, added to the Federal-style articulation of the Lyceum (fig. 1-37). The completion of this well-proportioned edifice signaled the successful implementation of the 1792 Hillhouse-Trumbull plan for the five-building row, as is so attractively illustrated in Amos Doolittle's 1807 view (fig. 1-38), contained in the Manuscripts and Archives collections at the Yale University Library.[24]

The presidency of Jeremiah Day, successor to Timothy Dwight, saw the completion of the fully realized, seven-building Old Brick Row. In 1820–21, aware that only three-quarters of the student body could be housed on campus, Day moved ahead with the construction of a new dormitory. Appropriately entitled North College, this understated, four-story, rectangular, pitched-roof brick structure

Fig. 1-38. Amos Doolittle view (1807) of the Old Brick Row, Yale College. Left to right: Union Hall (South College); Old College Chapel (The Athenaeum); Connecticut (South Middle) Hall; Connecticut Lyceum; Berkeley Hall (North Middle College). Courtesy of Manuscripts and Archives, Yale University Library.

(fig. 1-39), closely resembled Berkeley Hall, leaving a space between itself and Berkeley for another chapel type to follow in the future. Paid for with college funds, the conservative structure was designed and built by Ira Atwater of Connecticut. Subjected to intensive use like the other row buildings, by the 1890s it had become adversely affected on the interior by "its sagging beams, its billowing floor [and] its crocked ceiling" (fig. 1-40). Its demolition ten years later proved not to be premature.[25]

In January 1824, ground was broken in the open space for the New or Second Chapel, which was completely built and readied for use in just eleven months. Reproducing the steepled, rectangular box form of its two ecclesiastical predecessors in the row, it was larger than the Lyceum and the College Chapel, with dimensions of 56 by 72 feet. Most notable about the design of the Second Chapel (fig. 1-41) was the Ionic-columned front, the two-story balustraded portico, and the central square tower, its embellished classical bell stage topped by a two-stage spire with finial. Considering the quality of the design, resembling that of the rebuilt Congregational churches on the nearby New Haven

Fig. 1-39. North College (1820–21), center, Old Brick Row, Yale College. Photograph, 1870s. Courtesy of Manuscripts and Archives, Yale University Library.

Fig. 1-40. Interior of Room 116, North College (1820–21), Old Brick Row, Yale College. Photograph, 1889. Courtesy of Manuscripts and Archives, Yale University Library.

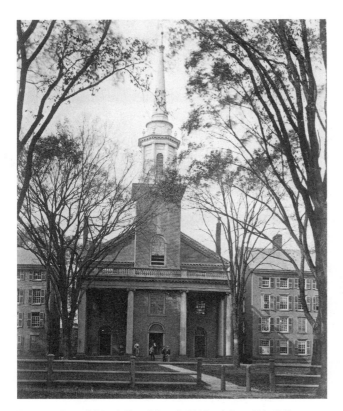

Fig. 1-41. Second (New) Chapel (1824), Old Brick Row, Yale College. Photograph, n.d. Courtesy of Manuscripts and Archives, Yale University Library.

Green, it is regrettable that the names of the builder as well as the architect remain unknown. As for its utility, the Second Chapel satisfied a variety of needs — the galleried, two-story main sanctuary for worship by a growing college congregation; student sleeping rooms on the third floor; and the college library in the attic space. It was used primarily as a chapel until 1876, then as a classroom facility until its demolition. Its presence in the Old Brick Row, as illustrated in the 1870s (fig. 1-42), signified the ongoing importance of theological concerns in the education of Yale undergraduates.[26]

The first building constructed behind (or to the west of) the Old Brick Row was the first Commons Hall or Old Laboratory (fig. 1-43), raised in 1782. Chronologically the fourth of Yale's buildings, it served as a student dining hall until 1820, when it took on a new function as Benjamin Silliman's chemical laboratory, formerly located in the basement of the Lyceum. It soon became recognized as one of the country's most important centers of chemical science. With dimensions of 90 by 30 feet, and built with college funds, it was located behind Connecticut Hall and the College Chapel next to the college pump, a significant watering and gathering spot on the campus. Of one-story brick construction, with a pitched roof topped by dormers, it was designed and built by Ira Atwater and enlarged in 1803.[27]

Fig. 1-42. Old Brick Row, Yale College. Photograph, 1870s. Courtesy of Manuscripts and Archives, Yale University Library.

Fig. 1-43. Old Laboratory (first Commons) (1782), Yale College. Photograph, c. 1880. Courtesy of Manuscripts and Archives, Yale University Library.

Fig. 1-44. The Cabinet (second Commons) or Philosophical Building (1819), Yale College. Photograph, c. 1870. Courtesy of Manuscripts and Archives, Yale University Library.

In response to student complaints about the lack of a suitable dining facility, President Dwight's administration replaced the old building with a new commons hall (fig. 1-44) in 1819. Placed to the west of the row, directly behind the Lyceum, it was the first building constructed for the college since 1802. Designed by noted Waterbury, Connecticut, church architect David Hoadley (1774–c. 1840), this interesting two-story, pitched-roof, 80-by-40-foot brick structure, later covered with stucco, displayed a late Federal/early Greek Revival east facade with repetitive, flat Ionic order pilasters on high bases supporting a plain entablature set under a molded, dentiled cornice. Positioned in the center and reached by a high stone stairway with metal rails was a double doorway surmounted by a semicircular fanlight. Over the years the building changed functions and was christened with new names — the Cabinet while meeting dining needs, as it also contained a mineralogical collection in large glass cabinets on the second floor; and, after 1842, the Philosophical Building while the departments of natural philosophy, physics, and astronomy were located there, along with a reading room that replaced the mineralogical collection in 1876, when it was relocated to the new Peabody Museum.[28]

Another addition to the random group of buildings de-

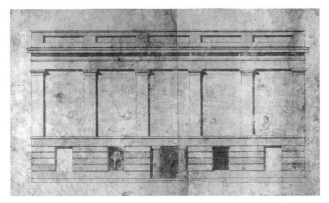

Fig. 1-45. Trumbull Gallery, Yale College. Elevation drawing (c. 1832) by John Trumbull. *Courtesy of Manuscripts and Archives, Yale University Library.*

veloping behind the Old Brick Row came in 1831–32, after painter/architect John Trumbull offered to bequeath his collection of historical paintings to Yale in exchange for an annuity and the construction of a picture gallery to display the collection. Designed by Trumbull himself (fig. 1-45), the Trumbull Gallery gained prompt distinction as the first art museum to be associated with a higher educational institution in the United States. Set directly behind the Second (New) Chapel and aligned perfectly with its center axis, it had a positive, formal relationship with the row in front. Like the adjacent commons (Cabinet), it possessed a symmetrical front (east) facade with flat, evenly spaced Doric pilasters placed above a first-story cellar and below a wide entablature (fig. 1-46). Particularly intriguing visually was the recessed, front central doorway, with its flanking, fluted Doric support columns. A theological lecture room filled the first floor, while the exhibition halls occupied the tall space above, illuminated by a square skylight set on a flat roof. The tomblike appearance of the Trumbull Gallery was highly appropriate, as the building also housed the crypts of Trumbull and his wife until they were later removed to nearby Street Hall. In around 1867, the paintings were relocated to a new fine arts building, and Trumbull Gallery, with new, tall side windows, became occupied

Fig. 1-46. Trumbull Gallery (1832), Yale College. Photograph, c. 1890, by Pach Bros., N.Y. *Courtesy of Manuscripts and Archives, Yale University Library.*

by the college treasury, central administrative offices, and the music department until it was razed in the early twentieth century.[29]

Yale's second surviving pre–Civil War building, after Connecticut Hall, is the former Yale College Library, planned and erected during the final years of President Day's lengthy tenure. In the late 1830s, when the administration commenced fund-raising for the envisioned structure, thought was given to the possibility of placing the new library in the existing Old Brick Row, to occupy the open space between North and Divinity colleges. Instead, the college's leaders choose to place the library behind the row, centered on the west boundary of the campus block on High Street, facing east. Clearly fire safety was a matter of great importance: the administration chose to isolate the new building, with its valuable book collections, from the residential halls and other campus facilities. Furthermore, the library's positioning suggested that the interior of the campus block, rather than the yard before the row on College Street, would be the focal point for the next major phase of campus development.

Breaking sharply and brilliantly from Yale's formal, classical design tradition, the College Library (fig. 1-47) was designed in the early but flamboyant perpendicular Gothic Revival style by New Haven architect Henry Austin (1804–91), the planner of other buildings in the city and nearby

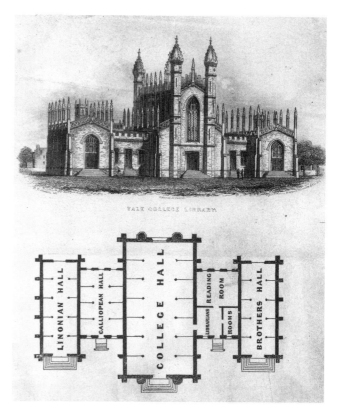

Fig. 1-47. "Yale College Library" (Dwight Memorial Chapel; Dwight Hall) (1842–47), Yale College, by Henry Austin, architect. Engraving, front (east) elevation and floor plan, Daggett Hinman & Co. after D. C. Hinman, del., *Yale Literary Magazine*, 1843. Courtesy of the Connecticut Historical Society, Hartford, Conn. Gift of Mrs. J. Coolidge Hills.

Fig. 1-48. Old College Library (Dwight Memorial Chapel; Dwight Hall) (1842–47), Yale University. Photograph, 1985.

Fig. 1-49. Nave interior, Old College Library (Dwight Memorial Chapel; Dwight Hall) (1842–47), Yale University. Photograph, 1880. Courtesy of Manuscripts and Archives, Yale University Library.

communities. Similar to Gore Hall (1838–41) of the same general style at Harvard, it also may have been inspired by King's College Chapel at Cambridge University. Foreshadowing Yale's extensive twentieth-century commitment to neo-Gothic design, the brownstone-fabricated library, symmetrical in floor plan, possessed tall, thin octagonal corner towers; wooden pinnacles (most never erected or later removed); staged, square corner pilasters; and lengthy segmental-arched windows that contributed to the forceful verticality of the overall architectural composition (fig. 1-48). Erected between 1842 and 1847, the skillfully articulated new library, Austin's first Gothic commission, reveals the architect's reliance on design books rather than personal familiarity with the style. Contained on the interior were a tall nave for the college book collections, artworks, and scientific specimens in the central section (fig. 1-49), with the books of student literary societies situated in the north and south wings. Over time, the various collections were moved to other specialized buildings on campus, and in 1931, under the direction of architect Charles Z. Klauder, the library was converted to its present function as the Dwight Memorial Chapel and Dwight Hall; it is now the center for Yale's social outreach undertakings and other religious and charitable organizations. Despite changing functions, the former College Library, with its picturesque profusion of Gothic revival elements, continues to contribute architectural beauty as well as a rich historical legacy to the current Old Campus.[30]

Alumni Hall, the only building raised on the college square during the 1850s, was erected in 1851–53 on a site at the corner of current Elm and High streets (now the location of Wright Hall), almost a hundred yards north of the College Library. Designed by the prolific architect Alexander Jackson Davis (1803–92) and built by Ithiel Town (1784–1844), Davis's partner, it was a perfectly symmetrical, stone, rectangular block expression of the castellated Gothic Revival style (fig. 1-50). Its most characteristic features included octagonal towers flanking a segmental-arched front doorway, and broken parapets on the front facade. Although the provocative structure is long gone, the towers and intervening wall at the center of the front elevation have survived, moved and incorporated as the entrance into Weir Hall (c. 1910–24) at nearby Jonathan Edwards College (fig. 1-51). Later known as Graduate Hall, this $24,500, multipurpose structure housed student society rooms in the upper story, and a large 96-by-48-foot single room (fig. 1-52) on the first

Fig. 1-50. Alumni Hall (1851), Yale College. Front-elevation sketch, n.d., by Alexander Jackson Davis. Courtesy of Manuscripts and Archives, Yale University Library.

Fig. 1-51. Alumni Hall (1851–53), relocated central facade, Weir Hall (c. 1910–24), Jonathan Edwards College, Yale University. Photograph, 1985.

Fig. 1-52. Interior of Examination Room, Alumni Hall (1851–53), Yale College. Photograph, c. 1878, by Kingsley Historical Illustrations. Courtesy of Manuscripts and Archives, Yale University Library.

Fig. 1-53. Old Gymnasium (1859), Library Street, Yale College. Photograph, c. 1880. Courtesy of Manuscripts and Archives, Yale University Library.

story for recitation, examination, admissions testing, and meetings, and occasionally for dining.[31]

Yale's last major pre–Civil War structure was the Old Gymnasium (fig. 1-53), erected in 1859 from plans by New Haven architect Sidney M. Stone on a plot of land (today on the south side of the Harkness Quadrangle) on Library Street, which was at right angles to High Street. A chaste, pitched-roof, 50-by-100-feet brick edifice of one tall story over a raised cellar, it was devoid of architectural ornamentation except for its roof gable and side band cornices, with their pronounced dentils, and the arched front entrance door, beautifully articulated with a Greek Doric surround consisting of flanking square pilasters and a low triangular pediment above a frieze of alternating triglyphs and metopes. In 1892, when a new University Gymnasium opened, the Old Gymnasium was fitted out as a dining hall to accommodate up to 450 students. After 1902, and the opening of a new Commons Hall, it became the Herrick Psychological Hall, fulfilling this role until its demolition fifteen years later in 1917.[32]

By 1870, it had become increasingly evident that Yale's leaders were contemplating a development plan for the campus block with future buildings lining the perimeter and forming a large closed quadrangle surrounding the Old Brick Row and the several buildings to the rear. The row, worn and deteriorating from long use, was regarded as obsolete and would continue to meet institutional needs for an indefinite future. In 1869, Yale commenced the inevitably controversial dismantling of the Old Brick Row and the enclosing of the current Old Campus. The first building to go was Divinity Hall during the same year. Though new

buildings rose, there was no further demolition until the presidency of Timothy Dwight, a strong champion, with some reservations, of the evolving closed quadrangle. After his election to office in 1886, the demolition was recommenced. Following a plan for the systematic development of the quadrangle, Dwight carried out a cycle of destruction and construction that entailed tearing down the following buildings: the first Commons Hall or Old Laboratory in 1888; the second Commons (The Cabinet) in 1890; the College Chapel (Athenaeum) and Union Hall (South College) in 1893; Berkeley Hall (North Middle College) in 1895; and the Second (New) Chapel in 1896. To his successor, Arthur Twining Hadley, Dwight left the task of destroying the remaining Old Brick Row structures—the Lyceum and North College—in 1901. The Trumbull Gallery was razed the same year, followed by Alumni Hall in 1911. Today, all that remain of Yale's pre-1860 structures are Connecticut Hall, the only Old Brick Row survivor, and the Yale College Library (Dwight Memorial Chapel; Dwight Hall). In eliminating most of its early buildings, largely for practical, operational reasons and the desire for "modernism," the university became more self-contained and inwardly focused, and less connected with the surrounding city. This continued to be reflected in Yale's twentieth-century architecture, centered on the development of the residential college system. In the razing of virtually all of the Old Brick Row and adjacent structures, Yale also lost most of its historic building legacy. Regrettably, its record of historic preservation is the least impressive of New England's early colleges and universities, greatly surpassed by that of Harvard and other regional institutions.[33]

2

BROWN AND DARTMOUTH

The Persistence of Colonial Traditions

THE VENERABLE PRE-CIVIL WAR campuses of Brown University and Dartmouth College, given their generally positive historic preservation records, continue to possess and display prominent higher educational building exemplars and defined building groups reflecting the influence of Harvard, Yale, Princeton, and their English university forerunners. In the individual structures, one may still observe the influence of late Georgian, Federal, and Greek Revival architectural styles, interpreted and forcefully expressed by several notable architects/master builders. Campus building arrangements were modeled either on the formalized, English-inspired open quadrangle plan or the Yale-originated row plan. Their buildings and surrounding landscapes continue to express the pioneering and enterprising spirit that characterized their respective origins and subsequent historical development.

University Hall and the Brown University Row

Brown University's first permanent building, University Hall (fig. 2-1), is one of the genuine icons of early American collegiate architecture and dates from the first years of the institution, when it was known as Rhode Island College.[1] Erected in 1770–71 on a gradual hillside site east of downtown Providence, Rhode Island, it was initially known as the College Edifice. A substantial multipurpose facility, it was the first of a group of four buildings that would eventually constitute the Brown row, inspired by Yale's New Haven row plan, on the Front Campus facing Prospect Street. In its early years it housed all of the college's functions, including offices, classrooms, a library, a refectory, and residential quarters. It has been conjectured that the institution's first president, James Manning, who had Princeton connections, influenced the design for the College Edifice, as it was unquestionably a simple provincial variant of Nassau Hall (1754–56) at Princeton (fig. 2-2). There is also a distinct possibility that Philadelphia's Robert S. Smith (c. 1722–77), credited with the design of Nassau Hall, may have visited Providence as the College Edifice was in the planning stage and may have contributed sketches for it. Traditionally, the design has been attributed to Joseph Brown (1773–85) of Providence, illustrious Brown family member and amateur architect and scientist, though this assumption has been generally rejected in modern times. Thus, the mystery as to who actually drafted the plans continues to this day, and it is generally assumed that the building's design was a collaborative committee effort involving trustees and college officials.[2]

Fig. 2-1. "A S.W. View of the College in Providence, together with the President's House & Gardens," Brown University. Engraving, 1800, by S. Hill after a sketch by David Leonard. Courtesy of Brown University Library.

Fig. 2-2. Nassau Hall (1754–56), detail from "A North-West Prospect of Nassau Hall, with a Front View of the President's House, in New Jersey." Frontispiece engraving from Blair, *An Account of the College of New Jersey* (1764). Courtesy of Princeton University Library.

The first documented reference to a building for the new college appears in Hezekiah Smith's diary, in which he comments on the 5 September 1765 meeting of the corporation:

I was with the Corporation in Newport which sat upon the College business, and was elected one of the Fellows of the College. Although but part of the Corporation, we subscribed nineteen hundred and ninety-two dollars for the BUILDING, and for endowing the College.

At the corporation meetings that soon followed, committees were appointed to find a location for the College Edifice, draft instructions, prepare a building model, purchase materials, and solicit subscriptions. On 8 September 1769, a committee composed of Stephen Hopkins, Joseph Brown,

and John Davis issued a report recommending the initial plan:

1st. That a suitable place be procured for erecting the College edifice on the easiest terms. . . .

2nd. That the building do not exceed sixty-six feet long, and thirty-six feet wide, and three stories high;—that it be a plain building with walls of best bricks and lime, the doors and window frames of red cedar;—that there be a cupola for a bell;—that the first building be so situated as to be one wing of the whole College edifice, when completed.

Over the next several months, additional appointed committees issued other reports proposing somewhat different planning guidelines. Finally, on 9 February 1770, the day after the question of location had been determined, the corporation adopted a final plan:

Voted, That the College edifice be built according to the following plan, viz.: That the house be one hundred and fifty feet long and forty-six feet wide, with a projection of ten feet on each side (ten by thirty,) and that it be four stories high.

Under the direction of a special Building Committee, the land acquisition was finalized, materials were acquired, and construction coordinated by Nicholas Brown and Company proceeded apace. The laying of the cornerstone occurred on 14 May 1770. By the end of 1771, the fifty-six-room College Edifice had been largely completed on the exterior, two floors were finished and in use, and the remaining two floors awaited completion in 1785 and 1788, after the Revolutionary War. The total cost, which included the adjacent president's house, was approximately $9,000.[3]

Renamed in January 1823 after the college had become Brown University (1804), University Hall (figs. 2-3 and 2-4) is of modest cruciform design. Of rather plain, utilitarian character, more so than Nassau Hall at Princeton, it recalls the highly functional, unembellished designs of early Rhode Island industrial structures, particularly textile mills. As Henry-Russell Hitchcock stated in his classic work *Rhode Island Architecture* (1939), "Academic design could hardly be further reduced to its essentials of solid mass, sound proportions and regular rhythm." Few details are present. The four stories are separated by thin, horizontal, molded stringcourses and are broken by evenly spaced, segmental-arched, double-sash windows. At the center of both the west and east main facades are central projections, also with stringcourses at the floor levels, and topped by plain pediments penetrated by oblong-shaped lights. Protecting the structure is a low hipped roof above a molded wooden cornice, broken by eight tall brick chimneys and displaying a wooden balustrade; on the roof deck sits a gracefully proportioned octagonal open bell cupola. In the book *Buildings of Rhode Island*, William H. Jordy attributes the structure's monumentality to the "extent of its wall surfaces" and the "repetitive accumulation of its openings, domestic in scale and functional in treatment." Because of this and other enhancing design qualities, University Hall possesses a charm and dignity that befits one of America's oldest higher educational institutions. Its designation in 1963 as a National Historic Landmark is well justified.[4]

During its long history, University Hall, always subject to intensive use, has several times undergone both exterior and interior renovation and restoration. During the Revolutionary War, the building was used as a hospital for French soldiers and a barracks for American troops, resulting in significant damage and necessitating major repairs in 1782–83, paid for by the U.S. government in 1800. After the construction of nearby Manning Hall in 1834–35, University Hall, no longer in vogue and in a state of decay, had its outer walls covered with a coat of cement to create a match with Manning. At the same time, the fragile wooden roof balustrade was removed. In 1850 and in the immediate years following, important changes were made to the interior when the former chapel and dining hall (Commons Room) were converted to recitation rooms and the original corridors were divided in the middle by partitions, making movement within the structure more difficult. In 1883, after a delay of several years, the interior of the building was subjected to a sweeping, somewhat controversial renovation according to plans by the partnership of Gould & Angell, modified by J. H. Brown of Worcester. This renovation was made possible by $47,000 in funds generated by subscription and left over from the erection of Slater Hall next door to the south. As a consequence, areas of the old chapel and commons were converted to two-story rooms with galleries (fig. 2-5), interior rooms were enlarged by the conversion of hallway space, new stairways were installed, gas light and steam heat were introduced, the balustrade was rebuilt, small-paned windows were replaced by ones with large panes, the long-absent bell was returned to the cupola, and the exterior cement was painted olive green.[5]

Additional major projects carried out in the twentieth century have returned University Hall to its original ex-

Fig. 2-3. University Hall (1770–71), main west facade, Brown University. Photograph, 1934, by Arthur Haskell. Courtesy of Historic New England.

Fig. 2-4. University Hall (1770–71), rear east facade, Brown University. Photograph, 1986.

Fig. 2-5. University Hall (1770–71), central classroom interior, Brown University. Photograph, c. 1916. Courtesy of Brown University Library.

Fig. 2-6. "Brown University, Providence, R.I." Left, Hope College; center, University Hall. Lithograph, c. 1828, after drawing by James Kidder, published by Senelr Lith. Co's Rooms, Boston. Courtesy of Brown University Library.

Fig. 2-7. Hope College (1821–22), west facade, Brown University. Photograph, 1987.

terior appearance and have improved the interior to meet ever-changing demands. In 1905, through the generosity of Marsden J. Perry, the building was again renovated, resulting in the removal of the exterior paint and cement and restoration of the brickwork, the replacement of the large-pane windows with historically correct twelve-over-twelve double-sash types, the further enlargement of the chimneys, and the restoration of the belfry to its original form as illustrated in old engravings. A further reworking of the building occurred in 1939–40 under the direction of Perry, Shaw, and Hepburn when the old, crumbling foundation was replaced; more new, historically accurate chimneys and windows were installed; the cupola was restored; and the repeatedly altered interior was rebuilt to its present state. Though it had a long history of residential and other uses, since the 1939–40 renovation the building has almost exclusively accommodated administrative offices (those of the president, vice president, deans, the registrar, admissions, and the Graduate School), reception rooms, conference studios, and a large room for faculty and corporation meetings. A rededication ceremony occurred on 4 May 1940.[6] Some additional, more modest improvements have been made since, ensuring that University Hall will long endure as the pivotal edifice of Brown University's highly revered row, and the symbol and leadership center of its prominent role in American higher education.

Also situated on the Front Campus facing west, toward Prospect Street, is the second of Brown University's buildings, Hope College, raised in 1821–22. It is positioned at the north end of the line of buildings flanking its predecessor, University Hall, its near architectural twin, though it is somewhat more formalized and refined in subtle detail, with small-scale elements (fig. 2-6). Of late Federal styling, Hope was the first of Brown's structures to serve wholly as a dormitory. Financed by the second Nicholas Brown, for whom the university was named in 1804, the new edifice, at his suggestion, was named for his only surviving sister, Hope Brown Ives, the wife of his business partner and trustee Thomas Poynton Ives. The total cost of the project was $5,200 for the land and $21,000 for materials and labor. Constructed of brick and set on granite foundations, Hope College, as conceived by a special committee of the university corporation, was 120 feet long and 40 feet wide, four stories in height without a cellar (until 1894), and contained forty-eight rooms for nearly one hundred students, and officers and two student literary societies, the Philermenian and the United Brothers, that were forerunners to Brown's fraternities. On the opening of the new building, in a letter to the members of the corporation, benefactor Nicholas Brown stated, "I avail myself of this occasion to express hope, that Heaven will bless and make it useful in the promotion of Virtue, Science and Literature, to this University for education." In every way, Hope College had an auspicious beginning.[7]

In architectural terms, Hope College (fig. 2-7) generally followed the precedent of University Hall and earlier residential structures at Harvard, Yale, and other institutions in the Northeast. While not pace-setting in design, it leaves a neat, ordered, and aesthetically positive impression. Capping the building is a low hipped roof above narrow dentil molding punctured by eight tall brick chimneys and surmounted by a narrow, rectangular wooden balustrade. In the center of the west and east facades are slight projections topped by closed pediments with dentil molding and enclosing semicircular lights. Departing from certain colonial-era technique practices, as evident in the original College Edifice, Hope College possesses elliptically shaped toplights with granite lintels and keystones over the entrance doorways on each facade, and rectangular granite lintels above each double-sash window aperture. Unfortunately, to date the designer/builder of this distinguished structure has not been identified, but this does not detract from its significance in the annals of early New England college and university architecture. Its very presence introduced the campus row plan to Brown University, perpetuating the row concept and individual building design initiated at Yale a century before.[8]

It is interesting to observe that Hope College had a number of deficiencies in the mid- and late nineteenth century that were not uncommon to dormitories and other building types at Brown or at other colleges and universities. As a consequence, student living circumstances there were hardly luxurious! Because Hope had no cellar until late in the century, sanitary conditions were poor, drainage was limited, and there was no safe place to deposit ashes from the coal stoves in the closets of each room. A central heating system was not installed until the 1890s. In addition, water had to be brought into the interior from an old well at the rear of the building, as there was no modern plumbing or bathtubs there or elsewhere on campus until the late 1850s. For several decades students lacked any kind of interior night lighting other than candles. This deficiency was partially alleviated when gas was introduced in the 1890s. There was just one meter in the building, and the students immediately formed the Hope College Gas Light Association to collect bill payments. At one point, when a bill was unpaid, the Providence Gas Company removed the meter, and lighting was temporarily suspended![9]

Subject to great wear and tear, dormitory structures at Brown, as well as its sister institutions, have required extensive periodic renovations to meet residential and general educational needs. In 1876, President Ezekiel Robinson publicly described what he perceived as the deplorable conditions of both University Hall and Hope College. Finally, in the summer of 1891, Hope, "which was much out of repair—the north wall cracked, timbers rotting, and the whole interior worn and dingy," was totally renovated on the interior (fig. 2-8) at a cost of $35,000 under the direction of Marshall Woods, chairman of the real estate committee of the Board of Trustees.[10] A reconstruction project was proposed in 1941–42 but was deferred due to World

Fig. 2-8. Hope College (1821–22), student room interior, Brown University. Photograph, 1897. Courtesy of Brown University Library.

Fig. 2-9. Hope College (1821–22) during restoration (1957–59), Brown University. Photograph, c. 1958. Courtesy of Brown University Library.

War II. As a result, no additional major improvements were made until 1957–59, when the Boston architectural firm of Perry, Shaw, Hepburn and Dean directed a massive $500,000 reconstruction of the building (fig. 2-9). It was rededicated with much ceremony in September 1959, and today is a coeducational dormitory with sixteen single and thirty-one double rooms, and lounges.[11] Few other pre–Civil War New England college buildings have served the same purpose for so long.

Flanked by University Hall to the south and Hope College to the north, Manning Hall was erected in 1834–35 as the pivotal centerpiece of Brown University's original three-building row (fig. 2-10). With its longitudinal axis at right angles to the line of the row, the new, simplified rubblestone and stucco-covered version of a classical prostyle Doric temple may be considered an excellent example of Greek Revival architecture, in fact one of the best Ameri-

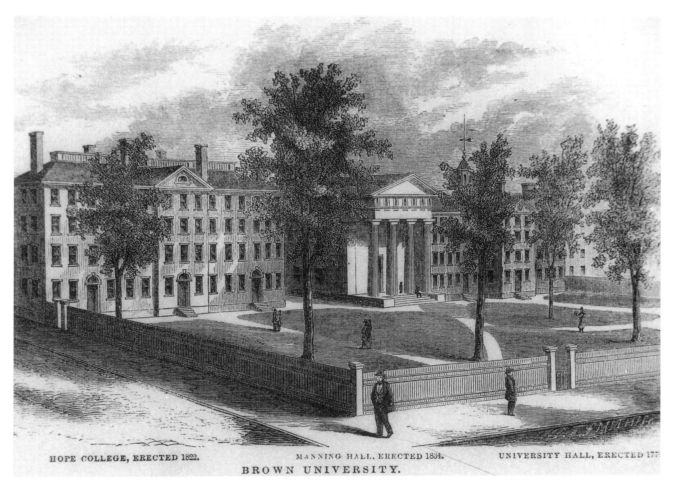

HOPE COLLEGE, ERECTED 1822.   MANNING HALL, ERECTED 1834.   UNIVERSITY HALL, ERECTED 177

BROWN UNIVERSITY.

Fig. 2-10. "Brown University." Left, Hope College; center, Manning Hall; right, University Hall. Signed lower left by "McLear," and lower right by "D. T. Smith & Co." Engraving from Guild, *Life, Times and Correspondence of James Manning and the Early History of Brown University* (1864), opposite p. 107. Courtesy of Brown University Library.

can higher educational structures executed in this style (fig. 2-11). It is believed to be a replica of the Temple of Artemis Propylaea at Eleusis in Greece, but with dimensions (including the portico) of 90 by 42 feet, and a height of 40 feet, it is twice the size of the prototype. The plan is believed to have been taken from the 1837 publication *The Unedited Antiquities of Attica, comprising the Architectural Remains of Eleusis, Rhamnus, and Thericus.* This quite stunning, monumental structure, like Hope College before it, was totally funded by Nicholas Brown, and at his request was named in memory of the university's first president, James Manning. The approximate cost is estimated to have been $18,000.[12]

At the dedication of Manning Hall on 4 February 1835, Brown's president Francis Wayland delivered an address, "The Dependence of Science on Revealed Religion," in

Fig. 2-11. Manning Hall (1834–35), main west facade, Brown University. Photograph, 1987.

Fig. 2-12. Manning Hall (1834–35), interior of the second-floor chapel, Brown University. Photograph, c. 1875. Courtesy of Brown University Library.

Fig. 2-13. Manning Hall (1834–35), rear east facade, Brown University. Photograph, 1987.

which he included a brief but useful descriptive passage about the building:

The Library occupies the whole of the first floor and is a beautiful room. In the center, it is ornamented with a double row of fluted columns. The Library is sixty-four feet by thirty-eight, and is thirteen feet high. The Chapel [fig. 2-12] is on the second floor. It exhibits the most graceful proportions. Its length and breadth are the same as those of the Library. Its length, however, is not less than twenty-five feet. The front of the edifice is ornamental with four fluted columns, resting on a platform thirteen feet from the walls. It is of the Doric order, and is said to be one of the finest specimens to be found in our country.[13]

The Doric order is magnificently expressed not only in the front-facade portico, its round brick columns surmounted by an entablature and pediment above, but also in the flat Doric pilasters, entablature, and pediment of the rear facade (fig. 2-13). Both the two entrance doorways and windows are rectangular and lack embellishment.

In his dedication comments, President Wayland identified Russell Warren (1792–1860) as the architect of Manning Hall, Daniel Hale as the master mason, and the partnership of Tallman (William) and Bucklin (James C.) (1801–90) of Providence as the master builders. More recent sources, however, also grant Bucklin the attribution as architect. This seems the most logical possibility, though Warren had joined the partnership in 1827 and likely played a role in conceptualizing the designs. Over the years Bucklin and Warren collaborated on several projects, including the extant Westminster Street facade of the Providence Arcade in 1828. A leading exponent of the Greek Revival, Bucklin has been credited with the design or codesign of numerous outstanding buildings in Providence in the mid-nineteenth century. The Tallman and Bucklin firm was one of the largest and most esteemed contracting firms in New England at the time, a fact the trustees and officers recognized. Bucklin's work in planning Manning Hall for Brown University was clearly regarded as successful, for he was hired again just a short time later to prepare the designs for the new President's House and Rhode Island Hall.[14]

As required and anticipated, numerous improvements have been made to Manning Hall since its construction and opening. In the summer of 1857, the chapel interior was redecorated with funds provided by Robert H. Ives and the late Moses Brown Ives, and a marble tablet honoring Nicholas and John Carter Brown was installed in the east wall. The original coat of plaster stucco on the exterior was replaced in 1861. Gas was introduced in 1873, followed ultimately by steam heat in 1886. In 1878 the library was relocated to a new, specialized library edifice (today named Robinson Hall), and the president's lecture room (after 1889), the Museum of Classical Archaeology (after 1889), and other rooms occupied the vacated space (fig. 2-14). In 1894 the chapel was deemed inadequate, services were moved to nearby Sayles Hall, and the resulting space taken over by the Department of Architecture and then the Department of Art into the twentieth century. The former chapel was used for these and other purposes until March 1959, when the chapel, with seating for two hundred people, was rededicated to its original function after a $49,000 restoration and redecoration directed by architect Thomas Mott Shaw of Perry, Shaw, Hepburn and Dean. The lower floor continues to serve classroom purposes. Highly regarded by university officials for its Greek Revival excellence, historical character, and serviceability, Manning Hall will in all likelihood continue to receive consistent preservation attention in the future.[15]

At the extreme south side of the Front Campus row, bordered by George Street, and beyond Slater Hall (1879), a Victorian eclectic dormitory, is Rhode Island Hall (fig. 2-15), an unadorned vernacular stone and stucco-sheathed Greek Revival edifice. It was erected in 1839–40 for the Department of Natural History and other sciences. The last of Brown University's pre–Civil War buildings, it was designed by James C. Bucklin, the architect of Manning Hall, and built by the partnership of Tallman and Bucklin. In the design, Bucklin departed from the conventional Greek Revival plan, placing the main entrance in the west-facing side wall, incorporated in a vestibule projecting 12 feet from the center of the 70-by-42-foot structure. The traditional temple form was further compromised in 1875, when a pitched-roof ell (fig. 2-16) with four flat Doric pilasters supporting a plain entablature and pediment mimicking those of the main block was appended to the center of the east rear wall. Particularly eye-catching is the central rear doorway, with its flat stone upper lintel and side post molding strips.[16]

In the early 1880s, *King's Pocket-Book of Providence, R.I.* described the interior contents of Rhode Island Hall:

On the lower floor are lecture-rooms [chemistry and natural philosophy], and in the upper story is a natural-history museum, containing about 30,000 specimens in zoology [fig. 2-17], 10,000

Fig. 2-14. Manning Hall (1834–35), Brown University. Lecture classroom in former library space on first floor. Photograph, 1887 class album. Courtesy of Brown University Library.

Fig. 2-15. Rhode Island Hall (1839–40), Brown University. Photograph, c. 1890. Courtesy of Brown University Library.

Fig. 2-16. Rhode Island Hall (1839–40), east-facade ell, Brown University. Photograph, 1987.

Fig. 2-17. Rhode Island Hall (1839–40), interior of Jencks Natural History Museum, Brown University. Photograph, c. 1885. Courtesy of Brown University Library.

in mineralogy, 5,000 in geology and paleontology, together with a collection of coins and medals, and a number of Indian and other barbaric implements and curiosities. Recently an ell was added to the building, the lower floor of which is used for a physical laboratory, and the upper story for a portrait gallery. The basement is used for a zoological laboratory.[17]

While its functions continued to change over the next century, the building, constantly subject to interior rearrangement, still houses faculty offices and classrooms.

The Rhode Island Hall contracting project, like those of its predecessors, took several years to complete. At the annual meeting of the corporation on 8 September 1836, it was voted that "a committee be appointed to devise means for erecting a building for lecture rooms, and rooms for the reception of geology specimens." Progress was slow, but by 1838, $2,500 had been raised from several supporters. Then

in March 1839, Nicholas Brown presented land for a new president's house on Waterman Street and a science building on George Street. In addition, he pledged $7,000 for the president's house and $3,000 for the science building, with the stipulation that other donors must match these amounts through subscription by the first of May. The campaign was a success, with most of the funds contributed by Rhode Island residents, and for this reason the new structure was called Rhode Island Hall and dedicated on 4 September 1840.

Except for the 1874 addition and a small addition in 1904 (since removed) to the south side primarily for the natural history collections, the building has not been expanded or its decorative elements modified on the exterior. Interior renovations have occurred in 1915, in 1982, and at other times, but these have not been detrimental.[18] In 2008–9 the university undertook a comprehensive interior and exte-

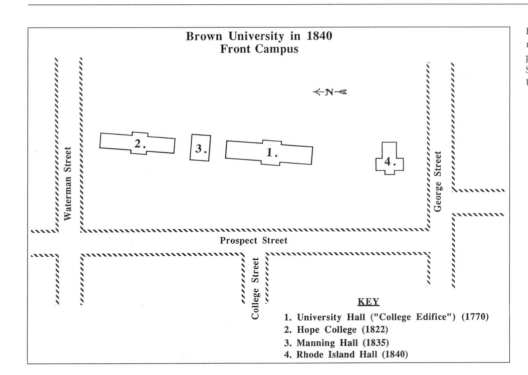

Fig. 2-18. "Brown University in
1840—Front Campus." Diagram
prepared in 1986 by Jon E.
Scharf, graduate student assistant,
University of Delaware.

Brown University in 1840
Front Campus

←N←

KEY
1. University Hall ("College Edifice") (1770)
2. Hope College (1822)
3. Manning Hall (1835)
4. Rhode Island Hall (1840)

rior rehabilitation of the building, with respect for its architectural integrity and seemingly with positive results. Brown University's historic row (fig. 2-18) of architecturally significant structures, anchored at the midpoint by University Hall, continues to make a pronounced physical statement about American higher educational life and learning in the nineteenth century.

Dartmouth College: Evolving Campus Forms

From its 1769 founding to the Civil War years, Dartmouth College grew from a small, near-wilderness institution devoted primarily to the education of male Native Americans to a substantial men's liberal arts and science college. To satisfy current philosophical demands and accommodate changing educational functions during this period, its campus underwent an architecturally and historically significant transformation. Early in its history, following the first New England precedent at Harvard (see fig. 1-4), the college adopted and modified the English-inspired open quadrangle plan for its initial two building groupings situated on the spacious Hanover, New Hampshire, town common (green) and on the adjacent hillside to the east. Three decades into the nineteenth century, under the direction of a single architectural designer, Ammi Burnham Young

(1798–1874), a Yale-inspired row scheme (see fig. 1-31) was developed on this same hillside site, resulting in the Old Row, with majestic Dartmouth Hall at the center much like University Hall in the row at Brown. By the middle of the century, the campus evolved further, and the row was incorporated into a third extended version of the open quadrangle idea (fig. 2-19). This changing pattern of planning preferences at Dartmouth was unique among higher educational institutions in New England before 1860.[19]

The initial educational structure at Dartmouth was Old College (1769–71), which with Commons (College) Hall (1770–74) formed two sides of what college historian Frederick Chase referred to an "an incipient quadrangle" on the southeast corner of the town common. Thanks to various items held at the Dartmouth College Library, including early written descriptions and alumnus William W. Dewey's valuable 1847 sketches and notes concerning this and other Dartmouth buildings, Old College and Commons Hall have been thoroughly documented. Derived from the Dewey manuscripts is an undated blueprint reconstruction drawing (fig. 2-20) of this first complex (c. 1774) showing the two brick buildings proximate to each other and college president Eleazar Wheelock's first "log hut" and mansion house just to the east.[20]

With its longer dimensions on a north-south line, Old

Fig. 2-19. Old Row and Reed Hall, Dartmouth College. Left, Wentworth Hall (1828–29); left center, Dartmouth Hall (1784–91); right center, Thornton Hall (1828–29); right, Reed Hall (1839–40). Photograph, c. 1890. Courtesy of the Dartmouth College Library.

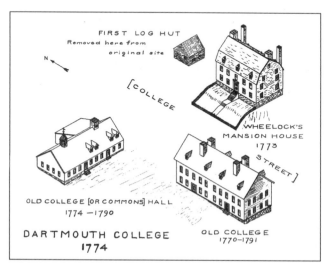

Fig. 2-20. "Dartmouth College—1774." Blueprint drawing, n.d., derived from William W. Dewey sketches. Courtesy of the Dartmouth College Library.

College measured 32 by 80 feet, with its main or east facade facing the Wheelock mansion and what is today College Street, then the main path or road south to Lebanon. Twice the size of Commons Hall, this rude, wooden two-and-one-half-story edifice contained (as completed in 1771) sixteen rooms for student quarters, as well as a library, kitchen, dining hall, and storeroom. A complete remodeling in 1774 resulted in the building being divided into "twenty rooms of equal size, one or two rooms on the ground floor being used by the Moor's Preparatory School, the rest being the students' dormitory, with . . . the library on the second floor."[21] This very basic layout initiated the use at Dartmouth of the "French system" of student housing, which allowed residents private and semiprivate bedrooms and studies connected to separated entryways.[22] Thus, in the same manner as at Harvard, Yale, Brown, and the English universities, Dartmouth offered individual rather than group living along corridors.

Intended for temporary use until the completion of Dartmouth Hall, Old College rested on shallow stone foundations and was unpainted until preservation issues necessitated that it be painted a reddish brown color in 1779. The Dewey sketches (and the blueprint drawing prepared from them) provide the only known surviving view of the highly vernacular exterior. Blockish in shape, the building was surmounted by a pitched roof pierced by dormer windows and large brick chimneys, the only obvious visual accents. Otherwise, Old College was plain, functional, and domestic in appearance, much like most New England farmhouses of the period. After serving as the home of the college for twenty years, it reached such a deteriorated state that it was demolished and its remnants sold for use in the construction of a new building for the Moor's School.

Complementing Old College on Dartmouth's first campus was Commons (College) Hall, raised in 1770. Intended as a replacement for Reverend Wheelock's "log hut," it stood just northwest of and at right angles to Old College. Conceived as a temporary one-story storehouse, it was used until 1773 as a second dwelling for the Wheelock family until the nearby mansion house was completed. Over the next year, it was converted into a commons hall and meeting room with the aid of the citizens of Hanover. To the original 40-by-32-foot structure, a 30-foot addition was appended to the west end, topped by a belfry in which a bell was hung in 1781.[23] The small shed-roof ell on the east end is believed to have accommodated the kitchen. The Dewey sketches indicate that the main roof was pitched and that it was broken by at least one chimney and two sets of paired dormers. According to surviving records, the building was never painted on the inside or outside. Later commons buildings at Yale (1782) and Bowdoin (1829) were of brick construction but in overall form and interior layout were markedly similar.

From the Dewey sketches,[24] it is evident that the eastern one-third of Commons Hall was assigned to the commons department for a dining hall, while the remainder consisted of a large room, used simultaneously by the college and Hanover residents as a chapel, meetinghouse, and public hall. Entered on the south facade, the hall contained a broad aisle, with seats for students on the right side and for townspeople on the left. After two decades of heavy use, including spirited political discussions during the Revolutionary War era, Commons fell into such a deplorable state that the students of Dartmouth, perturbed by the slow progress of

Fig. 2-21. Dartmouth Hall (1784–91, 1904–6, etc.), Dartmouth College. Photograph, 1975.

the college's new main building, vented their frustrations on the decaying old structure: in a "nocturnal visitation" on 3 January 1790 they leveled Commons, piling the wooden siding and support timbers atop its stone foundations.[25] Thus, the first campus on the Hanover green became but a memory, sustained in modern times by its excellent documentary record.

The college's extended and fascinating architectural history next focuses on Dartmouth Hall (1784–91; 1904–6; 1935–36) (fig. 2-21), perhaps its most revered and widely recognized building. Occupying a commanding position on a slight slope to the east of the Hanover town common, it is both the historic and the aesthetic focal point for what is generally regarded as one of the most scenic and well-integrated college campuses in the United States. Flanked by Wentworth and Thornton halls (1828–29) to create the renowned Old Row, it has been the center of college life and activity for over two centuries. Yet it stands dignified and somewhat removed from Dartmouth's more modern buildings, evoking memories of the college's formative years.

Hallowed by use and tradition, and handsome in appearance, Dartmouth Hall ranks among the most significant examples of American higher educational architecture produced in the century before the Civil War. Referencing the English-inspired provincial Georgian vernacular, it displayed in its first form new and distinctively American style features, as well as functional solutions, all with the objective of satisfying a variety of educational demands. Architectural historian Hugh Morrison once referred to the edifice as the "happiest solution of shape and proportion" of its building type.[26] As the multipurpose academic center of one of America's few colonial-era colleges, the building is an important reflection of the late-eighteenth-century commitment to the integration of all educational functions, academic as well as nonacademic.

The first incarnation of Dartmouth Hall was realized over a long time period: more than twenty years passed from its first conception (c. 1770) to its final completion (1791). It had its genesis in the mind of the college's enterprising founder, Reverend Wheelock, who envisioned it as the permanent successor to the initial unrefined structures on the green. In fact, in July 1770, a month before the college was moved to Hanover from its original home in Lebanon, Connecticut, he had written to the Board of Trustees in England that he proposed "to build with bricks, and't is generally thought best that the first building be as large as two hundred [feet] long and fifty wide, and three stories high." Though his plans called for a structure slightly longer than the present Dartmouth Hall, he conceived it along the same general lines. While admitting the economy of wood, he underscored his wish to build in brick or stone, believing it was not feasible to house Native American students, with their supposed carelessness about fire, in a combustible wooden edifice.[27]

While contemplating the ideal structure, Wheelock arrived at the site only to encounter a virtual wilderness and economic limitations. Removed from the source of basic building materials, he managed to acquire from England the necessary glass, nails, paint, hinges, locks, and other items essential for the launching of a successful project. Set back by delays, Wheelock proceeded with the erection of temporary buildings while efforts were undertaken to raise the necessary funds from the citizenry of New England and New York. Although initial subscription efforts failed, and lottery appeals to the New Hampshire provincial government were declined, the indomitable Wheelock moved ahead to amass the required brick, lime, stone, wooden timbers, and so on, secure a labor force, and have the site excavated.[28]

From documents preserved in the Dartmouth College Library, it is apparent that plans for the envisioned building were obtained between 1771 and 1773. Though it cannot be firmly documented, it is possible that President Wheelock sponsored a design competition, for several names have emerged over the years in connection with the design and contracting phases of the project. Comfort Sever, a Stillwater, New York, carpenter; Professor Bezaleel Woodward, the eventual construction supervisor; housewright William Gamble; and Peter Harrison, the prolific master builder from Newport, Rhode Island, are all believed to have been associated with the planning process. Yet even though correspondence, financial records, and original papers exist and serve to validate their involvement, the identity of the principal designer remains uncertain and may never be definitely determined.

The ongoing mystery as to who designed Dartmouth Hall may persist, but provocative fragments of the story can be securely documented. For obvious reasons, Peter Harrison would seem the most likely choice as architect. Perhaps the foremost builder in the colonies at the time, he was credited with several notable structures in Boston, Cambridge, and Newport. In 1769 he made a prolonged visit to his friend Governor John Wentworth at Portsmouth, New Hampshire, and while there assisted in the planning of the governor's summer estate on Lake Wentworth near Wolfeboro in the same state. It is also known that Wentworth recommended Harrison to Eleazar Wheelock as the possible designer for the new main building at Dartmouth, even though the Newport native had no experience in planning educational facilities.[29]

At this point it is apparent that politics influenced the progression of events. According to Harrison's biographer, Carl Bridenbaugh, Reverend Wheelock, while visiting Lebanon Springs, New York, in the summer of 1772, conferred with Comfort Sever, with whom he had communicated in previous years.[30] Anticipating that the college would accept Harrison's plans, he requested that Sever prepare another set of plans. It is further apparent that "with great craft the educator made doubly certain that Comfort Sever would be accommodated with the commission." An equivocal letter, intended to generate a negative response, was sent to Harrison in 1773. The fact that arrangements with Harrison failed to materialize may have resulted from Wheelock's preference for Sever's patriotic and religiously conservative views as opposed to Harrison's (and Wentworth's) advocacy of Tory Anglicanism, though this cannot be concretely ascertained. There exist no plans by Harrison or any response to Wheelock's cryptic letter in the Dartmouth College Archives or elsewhere; therefore, it can be safely concluded that Harrison did not take part in the final design rendering. This may have been most unfortunate from an archi-

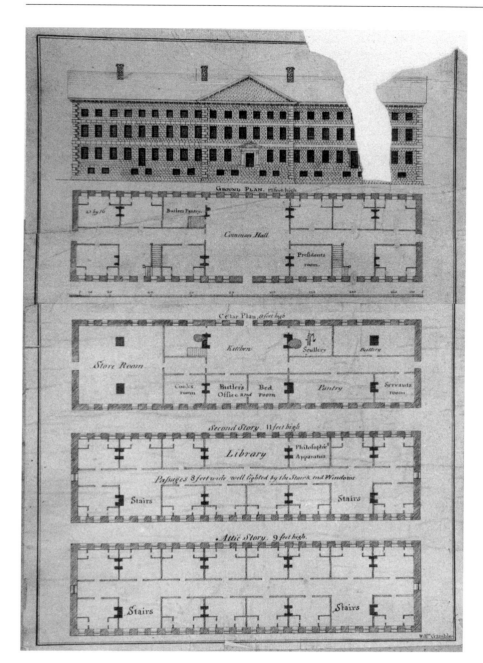

Fig. 2-22. Dartmouth Hall (1784–91), Dartmouth College. Floor plan and elevation drawing, 1773, by William Gamble. Courtesy of the Dartmouth College Library.

tectural vantage point. As Bridenbaugh has noted, despite the positive features of modern Dartmouth Hall, by employing Harrison the college might well have acquired the single most significant example of pre–Revolutionary War American collegiate architecture, possibly inaugurating a new approach to academic building design.[31]

There were several design influences that led to the ultimate building form. A letter from Reverend Wheelock to Comfort Sever in 1771 refers to a plan for the college

building as prepared by William Gamble and acknowledges Sever's role in securing it and sending it to him. To our benefit, this plan (fig. 2-22) has been preserved in the Dartmouth College Library; as the only one known to have survived, it is particularly valuable. Bearing Gamble's name in the lower right corner, it includes a front-elevation view and four floor layouts for an edifice that possesses similarities to the initial version of Dartmouth Hall and to its precursor, Robert Smith's Nassau Hall (1754–56, etc.) at

Princeton University, which set the precedent for New England successors. Though calling for masonry as opposed to wooden construction with differing style elements, the Gamble design features an elongated, three-story rectangular block with pitched roof, a central bay or pavilion with pediment, and three front entrances. The story heights were to be graduated and the interior rooms arranged on either side of corridors extending the length of the building. Though Gamble's proposal was rejected by Wheelock, it is likely that his work did influence the final design. The plan Wheelock requested from Sever has never been found, but in all likelihood it existed at one time. Thus, Morrison's assertion of over fifty years ago that Professor Bezaleel Woodward, the eventual project supervisor, may have arrived at the final design on the basis of the Gamble and Sever plans is difficult to contradict, though we may never have a definitive answer to this lingering question.[32]

By the summer of 1774, the college had obtained a grant of £500 from the provincial assembly, and Eleazar Wheelock had the cellar excavated on his own land "in an elevated situation . . . commanding an extensive and pleasant prospect to the west." Adverse conditions produced by the outbreak of the Revolutionary War, however, intervened and delayed the building project, and in 1779 Reverend Wheelock died "with his dream of a dignified college hall unfulfilled." When the war ended, the building endeavor recommenced, in the face of growing student enrollment and the college's continually decaying physical plant. Adhering to Wheelock's initial guidelines, the Board of Trustees voted in March 1784 to solicit subscriptions and to erect a three- or four-story edifice of brick, sufficient in length for six rooms on each long side, wide enough for two rooms (with two studies each), with ample hallways. At this time, the college committed $9,000, received in subscriptions from a state-sanctioned lottery, toward the final $15,000 cost. At first Professor Woodward worked with a small committee to coordinate the construction project, but the task proved too arduous for him, and he was succeeded by Colonel Elisha Payne, a college trustee, and then by Ebenezer Woodward, who directed the project to completion.[33]

In the spring of 1784 workmen began the slow but continuous process of erecting Dartmouth Hall, other than Brown's University Hall the largest educational structure to be built in New England up to that time. As such, this ambitious project attracted considerable public attention. Set on the location of Wheelock's earlier cellar diggings, now on college-owned land, the stone foundations measured approximately 50 by 150 feet. On these foundations head carpenter John Sprague and his fellow workers, refreshed by prayers and spirits, raised the great interlocked frame of hand-hewn, square wooden timbers, some as long as 75 feet. By 1787, a three-story frame had been completed, and the decision was made to substitute wood for brick siding, as it was less costly and readily abundant due to the proximity of the college's sawmill. During 1787 the workforce covered the frame with clapboards, commenced joiner work, and, under the direction of master builder Israel Parsons of Hatfield, Massachusetts, finished the cupola "with ornaments agreeable to the rules of architecture." By September the project was sufficiently far along to permit commencement exercises to be held on a special stage erected within the vast unpartitioned interior. Following this event, work moved forward again, using chimney bricks from Hanover and nearby Lebanon kilns; lime from Lebanon and Cavendish, Vermont; nails from Grafton and Rowley, Massachusetts; and door handles from a local blacksmith. Finally, in 1791, over two decades after Reverend Wheelock had first brought the college to Hanover, "The College," as the new edifice was called until the late 1820s, was finished.[34]

Fortunately for us today, the first wooden rendition of Dartmouth Hall was thoroughly documented. A late-nineteenth-century photograph (fig. 2-23) from the College Library illustrates its approximate original appearance and was one of several used to reconstruct the building after the fire of 1904. Well-proportioned and architecturally homogeneous, the rectangular block-shaped structure was protected by a low hipped roof with four pairs of massive brick chimneys rising above. The symmetrical, tripartite front facade featured a central three-bay, pitched-roof entrance pavilion with identical flanking wings. The general mass and detailing are strikingly reminiscent of Nassau Hall at Princeton, Hollis Hall (1862–63) at Harvard, and University Hall (1770–71) at Brown, all of which are believed to have been models for their Dartmouth successor. A dentiled cornice was displayed along the full length of the eaves, and five classic entranceways were present on the front facade. Regularly spaced double-sash windows, initially without shutters, created broken horizontal bands across each story level. The graceful, two-stage open cupola, the chief design feature, was likely derived from the builder's guide specifications and relieved the severity of the building, giving it a genuine artistic character. A somewhat different 1845 re-

Fig. 2-23. Dartmouth Hall (1784–91), Dartmouth College. Photograph, n.d., before 1904 fire and restoration. Courtesy of the Dartmouth College Library.

placement was said to have improved further on this grand impression. In the cupola hung the college bell, its clapper periodically removed by spirited students and deposited in the nearby Connecticut River! Yet even though graced by the cupola, the structure was a very functional work of architecture.

Badly divided by intersecting corridors that wasted valuable space, the interior layout of Dartmouth Hall was only moderately successful. Three parallel corridors ran in an east-west direction, with doors at both ends of each, while a single corridor extended the entire length in a north-south axis, bisecting the building. Students and faculty were often critical of this configuration as well as the drafty, dark, and dusty condition of the rooms. Their description of the building as "a great wooden air castle" was not flattering, but characterized well its principal problems![35]

Despite these shortcomings, the venerable edifice served effectively as a multipurpose educational facility for many years, thereby satisfying the philosophical goals of Dartmouth's founders. The structure's thirty-seven rooms were small and intended to meet the needs of the multipurpose academic, residential, and social center. The public rooms — containing the library, the philosophical-scientific apparatus, and a small museum devoted to natural and artificial curiosities — were situated in the central section. In this museum President John Wheelock, Eleazar's brother and successor, kept his prized stuffed zebra, which students delighted in stealing and placing in the top of the chapel belfry tower! Student society libraries and, for a time (until 1811), the medical department occupied the remainder of the interior. Until 1824, when more classrooms were provided, many recitations were held in student dormitory

Fig. 2-24. Interior of the Old Chapel, Dartmouth Hall (1784–91), Dartmouth College. Photograph, n.d. Courtesy of the Dartmouth College Library.

rooms that were heated by open fireplaces and illuminated by glimmering tallow candles. For the recitations, each of the college's four classes was required to furnish a room with a chair and table for the instructor, a blackboard, and a double row of long, rough benches for the students Apparently the cellar was the constant scene of student pranks, and cattle from the town green were occasionally herded into this space and defended against perturbed townspeople, who did not hesitate to wield farm implements and firearms against the building's wooden doors to recover their animals.[36]

Fortuitously, the first Dartmouth Hall escaped major damage from a fire in 1798 and a severe windstorm in 1802 and was largely unaltered until 1828. At this time major renovations were carried out in conjunction with the erection of flanking Wentworth and Thornton halls. At an expense of $3,000, college officials refitted rooms, completed the roof cornices, added the now-familiar green-painted shutters, and installed a clock, repeatedly replaced in later years, in the front pavilion gable. By far the most significant change, however, was implemented on the interior, where a large space in the center pavilion was converted to a chapel (fig. 2-24) two stories in height, containing an encircling balcony and square Doric support columns, and extending the full width of the structure. As a result of these alterations, much space that formerly had been inadequately

used served important religious purposes for many years in the future.[37]

It has been documented without question that the distinguished nineteenth-century designer Ammi Burnham Young, who later became the supervising architect of the U.S. Treasury Department, planned these renovations at the same time that he prepared the plans for Wentworth and Thornton halls. A plan sheet for a chapel room in the College Library, though unsigned, bears a close resemblance to Young's other drawings for the college. Religious services were held in the new room until the construction in 1884–85 of the Romanesque Revival–style Rollins Chapel, slightly to the north of the Old Row. The Dartmouth Hall chapel also accommodated mass gatherings, public speaking events, and occasional classes until disaster struck the college in 1904. In one brief, calamitous hour on the bitter-cold morning of 18 February, fire broke out and reduced the symbolic and physical center of the college to a pile of rubble.[38]

The virtually total destruction of the first Dartmouth Hall, extensively chronicled in photographs (fig. 2-25), removed the last of the Wheelock-era edifices from the campus. This momentary crisis, however, was resolved by a dedicated rebuilding effort that produced the building so many admire today and preserved the balanced panorama of the Old Row. Over the next two years a new structure rose on the same site, some six feet wider and four feet taller than its predecessor. Featuring a new matching east pavilion, it possessed altered window and cupola details and was built of "fireproof" materials. But in all other respects it imitated the first Dartmouth Hall on its exterior, even reusing some of the original materials and details. Under the direction of New York architect Charles Rich (1855–1943), the college expended a total of $101,700 to recreate the original in the safest, most reliable form possible. Contractors employed white-painted brick instead of wood for the outer walls, steel supports in place of cumbersome and flammable timbers for the framing, and copper sheathing instead of wooden shingles and tin for the roof covering. The interior plan bore little resemblance to that of the old structure,[39] as lecture rooms, seminar rooms, and faculty offices were positioned on the floors in a manner still evident today despite damage caused by another, less serious fire in 1935.[40] With interior space now devoted almost entirely to classrooms and offices, the post-1904 rendition of the building abandoned the origi-

1. Massachusetts Hall (1719–21, etc.), The Yard, Harvard University. Photograph, 2009.

2. Harvard Hall III (1764–66, etc.), The Yard, Harvard University. Photograph, 2009.

3. Hollis Hall (1762–63), left, and Stoughton Hall II (1804–5), right, The Yard, Harvard University. Photograph, 2009.

4. University Hall (1813–15), west facade, The Yard, Harvard University. Photograph, 2009.

5. Connecticut (South Middle) Hall (1750–52), east facade, Yale University. Photograph, 2009.

6. Old College Library (Dwight Memorial Chapel; Dwight Hall) (1842–47), Yale University. Photograph, 2009.

7. Manning Hall (1834–35), left, and University Hall (1770–71), right, Brown University. Photograph, 2008.

8. Hope College (1821–22), west facade, Brown University. Photograph, 2008.

9. Old Row and Reed Hall, Dartmouth College. Photograph, 2008.

10. Dartmouth Hall (1784–91; 1904–6, etc.), west facade, Dartmouth College. Photograph, 2008.

11. Shattuck Observatory (1854), Dartmouth College. Photograph, 2008.

12. West College (1791–93), Williams College. Photograph, 2008.

13. Griffin Hall (1828), Williams College. Photograph, 2008.

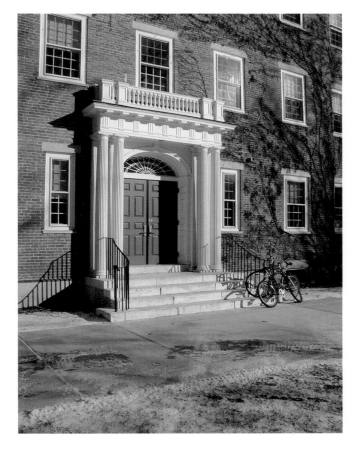

14. Griffin Hall (1828), south porch and doorway, Williams College. Photograph, 2008.

15. Massachusetts Hall (1799–1802), south facade, Bowdoin College. Photograph, 2008.

16. Bowdoin College row. Photograph, 2008.

17. Bowdoin College Chapel (1854–55), west front. Photograph, 2008.

18. The Old Mill (1825–29, etc.), University of Vermont. Photograph, 2008.

19. Painter Hall (1814–16), Old Stone Row, Middlebury College. Photograph, 2008.

20. Old Chapel (1835–36),
Old Stone Row, Middlebury
College. Photograph, 2008.

21. Old Row, north end, Amherst College. Photograph, 2009.

22. Johnson Chapel (1826–27), Old Row, Amherst College. Photograph, 2009.

23. The Octagon (1846–47, etc.), Amherst College. Photograph, 2009.

24. Fenwick Hall (1843–44, etc.), main northwest facade, College of the Holy Cross. Photograph, 2009.

25. Ballou Hall (1852–54), view from southeast, Tufts University. Photograph, 2009.

26. East Hall (1860), view from southwest, Tufts University. Photograph, 2009.

27. South College (Lyceum Building) (1824–25), Wesleyan University. Photograph, 2009.

28. Parker Hall (1856–57, etc.), left, and Hathorn Hall (1856–57), center, Bates College. Photograph, 2008.

Fig. 2-25. Dartmouth Hall (1784–91) during the 1904 fire, Dartmouth College. Photograph, 18 February 1904. Courtesy of the Dartmouth College Library.

nal multipurpose function for one more specialized and primarily academic.

Though it is not a totally faithful reproduction of the original, with somewhat different form, materials, and decorative details, the present Dartmouth Hall remains the focal point of college activities and sentiment and consistently elicits interest for its unpretentious message about early American educational thought and architecture. Visitors to Hanover in the modern era continue to acknowledge its historic significance and take cognizance of what former president Ernest Mark Hopkins once aptly referred to as its "simple dignity and quiet charm." It persists as the symbol of the college.

The completion of the first Dartmouth Hall prompted the removal of the last of the original college buildings from the Hanover green, and the creation of a new, less introverted campus arrangement on the adjacent hillside. Initially, Eleazar Wheelock and the college trustees had hoped

that Dartmouth Hall, on its completion, would be flanked on either side by separate structures housing a library and chapel. Although this idea was never exactly realized (the library remained in Dartmouth), the basic concept was adopted, and two additional structures forming a westward-facing asymmetrical quadrangle were erected between 1789 and 1791.

Beginning steps were taken while the first Dartmouth Hall was in its final phase of construction. In August 1789 the Board of Trustees voted that a new chapel structure be built under the direction of a special committee using funds from the sale of college lands. Soon thereafter, President John Wheelock announced plans for the new facility and signed a contract with Ebenezer Lane, a local carpenter/builder, to complete the project for £300, half paid by the college and half by the town in exchange for use privileges. Completed in five months, New Chapel, as it was termed, was raised, apparently without formal plans,

Fig. 2-26. "A Front View of DARTMOUTH COLLEGE with the Chapel, & HALL." Engraving from *The Massachusetts Magazine or Monthly Museum of Knowledge and National Entertainment* 5, no. 2 (February 1793), opposite p. 67. Courtesy of the Dartmouth College Library.

on a site southwest of Dartmouth Hall (between it and the Wheelock mansion), and extended partially in front of the area where Thornton Hall is now located. The well-known 1793 *Massachusetts Magazine* engraving (fig. 2-26) of Dartmouth College shows the structure on the right side, as does a similar watercolor campus view executed by student George Ticknor in 1803.[41]

Lacking in distinctive architectural details or aesthetic merit, the white-painted, vernacular wooden building was, in the estimate of Dartmouth students, a notoriously cheerless place on the exterior, while others considered it "convenient and well adapted to the objects proposed." As for horizontal dimensions, it measured 55 feet long (east to west) and 36 feet wide. From its stone foundations to the ridgepole of its hipped roof, it measured 20 feet. Plain double-sash windows were set in the side and end walls on two levels, while two unadorned doorways serviced the interior on each long side. The barren, unsophisticated appearance of this structure must have suggested vividly the still harsh, frontier conditions of rural New England life.[42]

Like the exterior, the interior is thoroughly documented, particularly by a scaled floor plan derived from one of the Dewey sketches showing the central, side, and cross aisles and the pew and podium placement. In an 1869 college centennial address, Samuel G. Brown commented on the supposed virtues of the interior:

Its concave roof formed a complete whispering gallery, and from corner to corner, a distance of seventy or eighty feet, the ticking

of a watch, or a whisper inaudible at a distance of a yard from the speaker could be distinctly heard. It was a building without a chimney, and never profaned by a stove, and here before breakfast on cold winter mornings, and in the twilight of evening, muffled in their cloaks, officers and students gathered for prayers with as much punctuality and order as characterize the more comfortable deviations of our own degenerate days.

In addition to religious worship, New Chapel was used for public exercises, orations, senior class recitations, and musical performances. Outmoded by newer edifices and another chapel installed in renovated Dartmouth Hall in 1828, it was displaced by Thornton Hall the same year. Relocated with the aid of forty oxen to the town green for service as a vestry, it was moved again to another location in the village and functioned as a barn until its destruction in 1879.[43]

With the demise of Commons Hall in 1790, the Dartmouth trustees acted quickly to replace the lost dining facilities and contracted with villager Aaron Kinsman to erect a new commons structure at his own expense, and, jointly with James Wheelock (a relative of Eleazar), to assume responsibility for its management. Built in 1791 and known as New Commons Hall, it occupied a site slightly northwest of Dartmouth Hall, near where the Rollins Chapel stands today, facing New Chapel and completing the new open quadrangle scheme. This equally undistinguished vernacular structure served as a commons until 1793, a residence until 1807, a commons again until 1815, and a dormitory until 1827, when it was removed to make way for the new Wentworth Hall.[44]

Our knowledge of New Commons derives largely from old campus views such as the *Massachusetts Magazine* engraving and the Ticknor watercolor drawing and, once again, the invaluable Dewey sketches. In these images the building appears as a two-story, hipped-roof, wooden rectangular block topped by four chimneys, with a western end of three window levels. Dewey's rather rough plan recollections suggest that the length (90 feet) was half that of Dartmouth Hall, and the length (40 feet) approximately two-thirds. The first floor housed a kitchen, a storage room, and a steward's family quarters on the west end and, separated by a large entry hall, a large 40-foot-square dining room with tables, benches, and fireplaces on the east end. The upper floor, not diagrammed by Dewey, may well have contained living quarters. Like New Chapel, New Commons was of limited architectural distinction, but it did clearly express its function as well as the modest circumstances of its creation.

The surviving successors, Wentworth and Thornton halls (figs. 2-27 and 2-28), both erected in 1828–29, were part of a building program intended to create the college's new, renowned Old Row, almost certainly inspired by Yale's Old Brick Row. Flanking and set at right angles to Dartmouth Hall, these two Greek Revival rectangular structures have served the college community in various ways for over a century and a half. The planning process for them, initially as dormitories, commenced in January 1818, when the Board of Trustees, recognizing critical student housing needs, expanded their initial commitment to build one new wooden residence hall, and instead decided to "erect two new buildings of brick, 70 by 50 and three stories high," at a cost of $12,000. The required funds were raised by a subscription campaign instituted by President Bennett Tyler that netted over $25,000, a portion of which was used for Dartmouth Hall improvements and debt settlements.

Work on the nearly identical structures began under the direction of Professor William Chamberlain, a language scholar, who passed away under the strains of his supervisory role prior to their completion. By commencement exercises of 1828, the old chapel had been moved, the ground leveled, and the granite foundations laid for the new buildings. On their completion during the summer of 1829, they were officially named in honor of two important early benefactors of the college—Sir John Wentworth, the colonial war governor of New Hampshire, and John Thornton, a successful Russian trade merchant and the most generous English donor to Dartmouth.[45]

Wentworth and Thornton halls were the first two building commissions of four that architect Ammi Burnham Young, trained as a carpenter in nearly Lebanon, New Hampshire, completed for Dartmouth College. Fortunately, two sets of his signed drawings—one set rejected by the trustees and the other accepted and used—are preserved in the Dartmouth College Library. The rejected set, containing one front-perspective elevation drawing (fig. 2-29), and one drawing of the ground-floor plan, the upper-floor plans, and a longitudinal section, is particularly fascinating for its detail and depiction of a modified open-quadrangle format. But perhaps because of the complexity of the floor plans and the ornate nature of the exterior treatment, this design proposal was regarded as financially impossible at the time. The perspective elevation depicts two temple-

Fig. 2-27. Wentworth Hall (1828–29), by Ammi Burnham Young, Dartmouth College. Photograph, 2008.

Fig. 2-28. Thornton Hall (1828–29), designed by Ammi Burnham Young, Dartmouth College. Photograph, 2008.

like structures similar in form to the current versions but possessing more lavish exterior detail. Possibly inspired by the prior work of Boston's Charles Bulfinch, vertical bands linked by relieving arches embellish the front end walls. Wentworth was to possess four stories and Thornton three, with round-headed windows in the upper stories and main side entrances.

The second and more recent set of drawings is highlighted by a fine front-elevation perspective view (fig. 2-30) illustrating Wentworth and Thornton halls as they were actually raised, lined up in a perfect symmetrical row with Dartmouth. Squatter, less refined, and less detailed than originally planned, they dispense with the engaged-arch motif for more chaste wall surfaces. Like Young's Reed Hall, their close neighbor, they display double-sash windows,

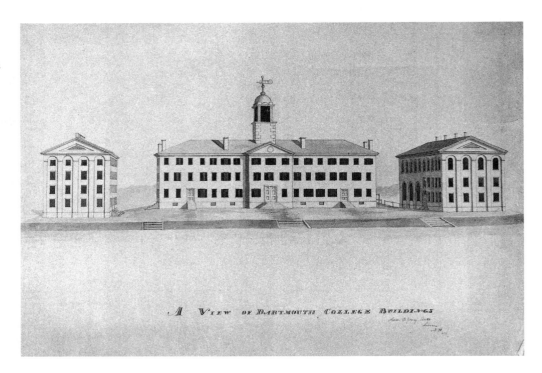

Fig. 2-29. "View of Dartmouth College Buildings." Rejected perspective elevation plan by Ammi Burnham Young, 1828. Courtesy of the Dartmouth College Library.

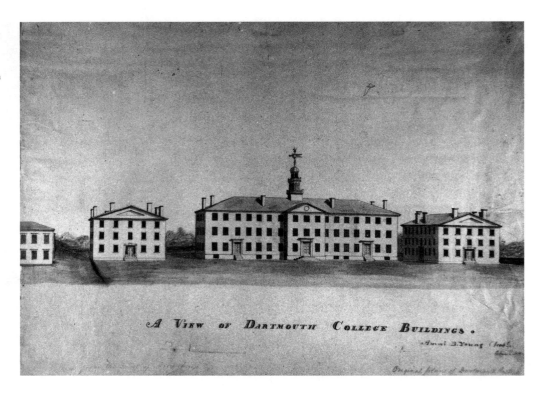

Fig. 2-30. "A View of Dartmouth College Buildings." Elevation drawing by Ammi Burnham Young, 1828. Courtesy of the Dartmouth College Library.

trapezoidal (splayed) granite window lintels, low-pitched roofs atop classic gable pediments, and slightly projecting cornices. Many years after they were built, college officials added dark green shutters to match those of Dartmouth Hall and provide contrasting color accents against the white-painted brick walls. Identical traditional doorway surrounds with glass lights may be seen on the gable end walls of each building, which with the side walls are broad and flat, almost anticipating the simplicity and function of more recent modern architecture.

Without doubt the two designs were strongly influenced by the presence of the central pavilion of Dartmouth Hall and by Young's desire to repeat this dominant form "in good architectural taste." In doing so he departed from the traditional pattern of Yale and other New England college row plans — the Dartmouth buildings flanking the main central edifice presenting their narrow gable-end walls forward, with their longitudinal axes at right angles with the line of the row. Though proportionately short in length, Wentworth (to the north) and Thornton (to the south), when combined with Dartmouth between them, form a trio long recognized as one of the finest early college building groupings in the United States.[46]

Despite the symmetrical perfection of Dartmouth's Old Row, the flanking structures each possessed unique characteristics. Thornton Hall was first arranged internally around a central stairway that extended up through the building and provided circulating space in long "double-loaded" corridors, with rooms on each side. It has retained much the same interior plan to this day. Used exclusively as a residence hall until 1871, it came under student criticism in the 1850s due to its deteriorating condition, with many reluctant to live there due to rooms "dark, cold, dirty and infested with bugs." Some rooms were considered uninhabitable, and students were known to take their hostilities out on the building by chopping wood in the corridors, raising chickens in their rooms, and stripping pieces of plaster and molding strips from the walls for use in playful indoor encounters! Such negative reactions to dormitory conditions were not unusual, however, as evidenced by similar patterns of resident student behavior at other New England colleges then and more recently.

Ultimately, improvements and functional changes were made, and classrooms were placed on the lower floor of Thornton Hall. After a period in Wentworth Hall, the well-known Thayer School of Engineering was relocated to the south side of Thornton in 1874. In 1924 it was totally reconstructed at a cost of $66,000 from plans by the architectural partnership of Larson and Wells so that it could be used entirely for recitation purposes, and its use as an academic facility has continued to modern times. Though the new fire-resistant construction changed the interior appearance and spatial configuration of the building, the exterior has remained unaltered.

Originally Wentworth Hall possessed much the same interior plan as Thornton, but it has undergone a different kind of transformation over the years. It also served as a dormitory until 1871 and was subjected to the same kind of criticism as Thornton. Wentworth, however, was even less popular, primarily because of a deplorable study atmosphere fostered by "noisey and disorderly students [who] tended to congregate there." Classrooms shared the interior until 1911–12, when, following a damaging fire, a complete $40,000 gutting and refurbishing directed by architect Charles A. Rich converted it to the teaching and office facility that it is today. As specified in the Young drawings, interior corridors were reoriented at right angles to their former primary axes and were paneled in oak, and a new central staircase was installed, all supported by a new steel skeleton. These alterations necessitated the relocation of the main entrance to the south-side wall, underneath a new gable. The third floor is especially interesting to examine, for one can still observe there the original pine support trusses exposed during the renovation, as well as an unusual roof skylight.[47]

With the construction of neighboring Reed Hall (1839–40) (fig. 2-31), Ammi Burnham Young was able to realize, at least partially, the concept for the modified open quadrangle, which he had unsuccessfully proposed to the college trustees ten years before. The initial need for Reed, to relieve the overcrowded conditions of Dartmouth Hall's library and classrooms, was realized as early as 1834. At the time the college was graduating more students annually than its principal rivals in the United States, and its physical plant was being subjected to heavy use. Responding to enrollment pressures, the trustees launched a subscription drive in 1836, but this proved unnecessary when news of a generous bequest was made public the following year. William Reed, a former college trustee and successful businessman and judge from Marblehead, Massachusetts, on his death, left a sizable legacy (eventually to reach $19,400) to the college, the major portion of which was set aside for the new edifice.[48]

Fig. 2-31. Reed Hall (1839–40), designed by Ammi Burnham Young, Dartmouth College. Photograph, 2008.

Fig. 2-32. Reed Hall (1839–40), south-end doorway, designed by Ammi Burnham Young, Dartmouth College. Photograph, 1985.

Their confidence raised by this fortuitous development, the trustees decided in October 1838 "that it [was] . . . expedient to proceed and erect two college buildings on the range north and south of the present buildings [Wentworth, Dartmouth, and Thornton halls]." Plans for a second matching building (on the site of the later Rollins Chapel) were dropped during the 1840s due to the depressed state of the national economy. From an architectural perspective this was unfortunate, for had it been built it would have completed the symmetry of Young's enlarged row. But with funding assured, plans for Reed alone were pursued. After the selection of Young as architect, his brother Dyer H. Young, a Lebanon contractor, was awarded the building contract. A second brother, Professor Ira B. Young, a prominent astronomer, was given the task of overseeing the project. In 1839 the impressive structure rose next to Thornton Hall on the raised site formerly occupied by Eleazar Wheelock's mansion house. Positioned slightly southeast and forward from the Old Row, it faced inward (north), with its longitudinal axis parallel to the north-south line formed by the older buildings.[49]

Completed in 1840, Reed Hall, like Wentworth and

The Reed Hall that is admired and used today is the product of an extensive restoration program directed by college architect Jens Fredrick Larson between 1929 and 1932. While preserving the original roof and outer walls, contractors removed the interior fabric of the building and converted it to a modern steel-frame recitation hall with classrooms, conference/seminar rooms, and faculty offices oriented around a central stairwell and long north-south corridor scheme. Despite this reconfiguration of interior space, Reed's architectural charm has been securely retained, and it remains an excellent example of the application of the Greek building ideal to meet modern, multipurpose, utilitarian requirements. On no other early New England college or university campus has a brick Greek Revival structure of such high stylistic quality and importance survived.

The most recent of Dartmouth College's pre–Civil War buildings is the Shattuck Observatory (1854) (fig. 2-34), an important early scientific facility. It was the fifth and last of the observatory building type to be erected at the New England colleges before 1860, with other examples at Williams, Wesleyan, Harvard, and Amherst predating it and discussed in other chapters of this book. Situated on a slight rise behind the Old Row in College Park, this small, white-painted brick structure has continuously served scientific purposes at Dartmouth for over 150 years. The idea behind it originated in the late 1940s, when Professor Ira Young and faculty colleagues expressed interest in such a building. The trustees were informed of their interest and, in 1848, initiated efforts to obtain financial support for the building's design and construction. At first, in 1850, a temporary structure for instruction in astronomy and allied sciences was completed, but it was abandoned and converted to a carpentry shop when the new permanent observatory was completed. Its greatest contribution to the college may have been that it awakened student interest in astronomy and energized the fund drive.[51]

Four more years passed, however, before the structure that we may view today assumed final form. In December 1852, Dr. George C. Shattuck, a Boston physician and 1803 alumnus, made a supporting gift of $7,000, which the trustees promptly accepted, with the understanding that they would provide an additional $4,000 to fully fund the project. Professor Young, working with his brother Ammi, then assumed responsibility for the observatory's completion. With the Young brothers collaborating on the plans and contracting work, the new building was finished and ready for occupancy (at a cost of only $4,500, excluding equipment) in time for the beginning of the 1854 academic year.

As completed, the observatory featured a cylindrical two-story tower, 20 feet in diameter, surmounted by a revolving tin-sheathed dome under which a telescope was mounted on a raised stone pier. Attached to this central core were three modest single-story wings arranged in the form of a Latin cross. The dome was set on six large cannonball bearings and was operated by hand. A library was located on the floor of the tower and was directly accessible from the wings. The sixteen-by-twenty-six-foot east wing contained a transit room, which also served as an entrance hall. The wings to the north and south, both 16 by 20 feet, accommodated an observer's room and a "computer's" room, and featured a meridian circle and other scientific instruments. Making vertical observations possible were slits in the roof, while several rectangular windows (flanked by green shutters) pierced the outer walls. To resist weathering and possible fire, these walls were 15 inches thick, in double layers, and were set on a granite base. Clearly the observatory was the product of the most up-to-date knowledge in structural engineering technology.

Confirming the importance of this undertaking, the full floor plans and a perspective elevation drawing submitted by Ammi Young were reproduced in an 1856 *Harper's Magazine* article (fig. 2-35) and were closely adhered to in the final building form. Since 1854 there have been only a few changes made to the structure—the addition of weather monitoring equipment and two small supplementary buildings, and the replacement in 1959 of the original dome with a new mechanized type. The first dome has since found a useful second home atop an observatory room at the Mid-Fairfield County Youth Museum in Norwalk, Connecticut.[52]

The Shattuck Observatory merits recognition as one of Dartmouth's most significant structures for its utterly functional character and its lack of reliance on previous building models. Ammi Young's prime concern was to emphasize its adaptability to scientific uses, and this, quite understandably, took precedence over expressions of architectural style. Because of this functional orientation, the observatory does not exhibit a specific architectural vernacular(s), and only a few subtle classical details are present on its exterior. Low-pitched roofs on the wings with their gable and cornice moldings echo the rooflines of the other Young buildings nearby. But on its rather secluded and elevated

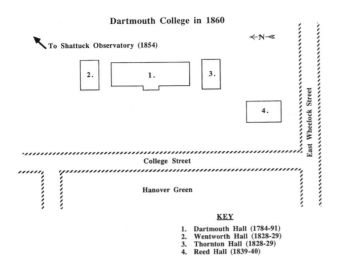

Dartmouth College in 1860

To Shattuck Observatory (1854)

←N—≪

2.   1.   3.

4.

East Wheelock Street

College Street

Hanover Green

KEY

1. Dartmouth Hall (1784-91)
2. Wentworth Hall (1828-29)
3. Thornton Hall (1828-29)
4. Reed Hall (1839-40)

Fig. 2-36. "Dartmouth College in 1860."
Diagram prepared in 1986 by Jon E. Scharf,
graduate student assistant, University of
Delaware.

site, this independent, unpretentious structure forges a successful relationship with the surrounding natural environment and architectural repertoire of the college. A finely proportioned expression of its purposes, the observatory illustrates well the trend in mid-nineteenth-century American public building and commercial-industrial design toward functional, as opposed to artistic, priorities.[53]

When the Shattuck Observatory was completed, Ammi Burnham Young's work for Dartmouth College reached conclusion. With the sole exception of the modernized, reconstructed edition of Dartmouth Hall, every other surviving pre–Civil War Dartmouth building owes its existence to his talented design conceptions and planning skills. The end result is a building grouping (fig. 2-36) that productively blends open quadrangle and row campus planning concepts and that combines, on an even more ambitious scale than Brown University, all educational functions in one higher educational community complex. Dartmouth's early campus remains one of the finest American expressions of Thomas Jefferson's vision of the intellectually and spiritually active, ordered, and eminently practical "academical village."[54]

II

THE COLLEGES BETWEEN THE REVOLUTION AND THE CIVIL WAR

WILLIAMS AND BOWDOIN

Contrasting Planning Theories and the Land

ALTHOUGH THEY WERE developed almost simultaneously beginning in the 1790s, the early campuses of Williams and Bowdoin colleges reflected widely differing planning philosophies and developmental approaches. Committed to the transcendental perceptions and the uplifting impact of the natural world, the founders and first leaders of Williams situated its early buildings randomly on adjacent low hills in Williamstown, a rural western Massachusetts community, initially choosing not to adopt either of the main precedents: the traditional, formalized closed or open quadrangle plans, or the row plan. In contrast, the early leaders of Bowdoin, though they selected a rural location for the college in Brunswick, Maine, situated the campus adjacent to the town center on a flat wooded tract. At first they opted for an open quadrangle plan, which transitioned to a row scheme and became part of an expansive closed quadrangle in the nineteenth and twentieth centuries.

Williams College and the Precepts of Nature

Made possible by the bequest of Colonel Ephraim Williams, Williams College received its charter from the Commonwealth of Massachusetts on 22 June 1793, becoming the second higher educational institution after Harvard to be founded in Massachusetts, and the sixth in New England. Unlike their predecessors at other regional colleges, however, the trustees of Williams, highly influenced by the aesthetic attraction and spiritual and intellectual influence of nature, selected a relatively isolated, countryside site for their new educational venture. In making this critical decision, they anticipated a nineteenth-century pattern: connection with nature and detachment from urban life would soon be of uppermost concern in the location and planning of American colleges. In positioning the first building at Williams and breaking with the more restrictive solutions of other New England higher educational institutions, the trustees opted for an unstructured campus environment. Following this planning philosophy, buildings were situated in relation to each other, the main town road in Williamstown, and, most important, the rolling, scenic, and pastoral landscape of the Berkshires, all with the aim of enhancing the collegiate learning experience.[1]

The initial buildings at Williams College (fig. 3-1) were raised on two "eminences" or hilltops, approximately one-tenth of a mile apart on the western side of Williamstown. The first of these, positioned on the western eminence and originally in the middle of the main road (later Main Street), was West College, approved by the college trustees in 1788 and constructed between 1791 and 1793

Fig. 3-1. "Williams College," Williamstown, Mass. College stationery lithograph, c. 1836, by E. B. and
E. C. Kellogg, Hartford, Conn. Courtesy of Williams College Archives and Special Collections.

at a cost of $11,700. Still the historical symbol of the college, this four-story, 82-by-42-foot edifice (fig. 3-2) was located so that initially the east-west town sidewalk had to be run through a hallway in the center portion. A multipurpose, twenty-eight-room structure originally housing all of the new college's functions, West College contained the president's office and living quarters, and a dining room and kitchen on the first floor. A two-story chapel, used by the president, was on the second and third floors to the south of a central hallway. Occasionally these spaces doubled as classrooms. Above, on the third-floor level, was a room used as a library, so small that it was possible to stand in the middle of the room and reach all the books! The north end of the third floor and the entire fourth floor accommodated student residential quarters, except for one room set aside for bell ringers. Over the years, West College was almost entirely converted to residential use. Some time after West's opening in 1854–55, Williams administrators eliminated the town sidewalk extending through the building, closed the east and west entrances, and installed north and south doorways as part of a general remodeling.

Given that many of the college's first trustees were grad-

uates of Yale, it is not surprising that West College, and other buildings that would soon follow it, resembled older buildings at the New Haven institution in both form and detail. While West is by no means a close reproduction of Yale's larger Connecticut Hall (1750–52), it possesses the same late Georgian/early Federal features and is a similarly uncomplex rectangular brick mass. Like Connecticut, West displays brick stringcourses and evenly spaced, stacked windows on each of its wall surfaces. Variations exist, however, in the location of the doorways, the size of some window apertures, and the roof types: Connecticut is capped by a gambrel roof with dormers, and West by a low hipped roof without dormers. One particularly distinctive feature of West is the central open bell cupola with concave roof cap and finial, positioned in the center of the roof ridgepole and surrounded by four brick chimneys. To quote from an article on the college's architecture from the *Williams Graphic* (1921), "The beauty of the building lies almost wholly in its faithful observance of the laws and canons of proportion." Unfortunately, to date the identity of the designer, if there actually was a professional involved, remains unknown, as is the identity of the master builder.[2]

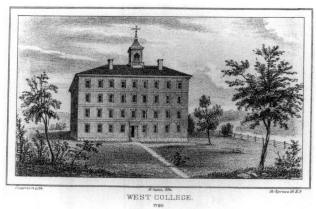

Fig. 3-2. "West College, 1790," view from the east. E. Valor's lithograph, c. 1830, by C. Currier's Lith., New York, from Calvin Durfee, *A History of Williams College* (1860), frontispiece. Courtesy of Williams College Archives and Special Collections.

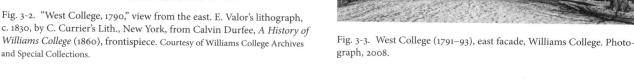

Fig. 3-3. West College (1791–93), east facade, Williams College. Photograph, 2008.

In his book *Williamstown and Williams College* (1884), Nathaniel H. Egleston offered further valuable insights about the architectural significance of West College:

It was a notable structure for the place and time, and compares favorably now with many buildings of more pretentious character and more recent date. It is indeed a marvel that an edifice so solid and impressive in appearance as it is to-day should have been erected nearly a century ago, in what was almost literally a wilderness. Its site overlooks the town and a large portion of the adjacent country, the range of vision limited by the lofty hills and mountains which lift themselves on every side.[3]

Similar complimentary observations have since been made in public statements and a variety of publications.

Since the 1850s, West College has undergone several renovations or reconstructions. In 1904, the north entrance was sealed up and interior refurbishing was implemented. In 1928, the exterior walls were sandblasted to remove paint. A total reconstruction occurred in 1951–52 after a disastrous fire on 2 January 1951, which started in the upper two stories and destroyed the roof, cupola, and entire interior, leaving only the bowed outer brick walls standing. As a consequence of this project, most of the original brickwork was saved, and contractors installed a new reinforced concrete frame and tied the walls to it, resulting in the restored building that we may view today (fig. 3-3). A somewhat questionable but undeniably attractive product of the project was a new east doorway displaying a thick, flat surround with corniced, segmental-arched lintel above. This

doorway was designed by the architectural firm of Perry, Shaw, Hepburn, Kehoe and Dean of Boston, well experienced in the planning of higher educational structures.[4]

Williams College's second building, necessitated by expanding student enrollment, was old East College, approved by the trustees in 1796 and erected in 1797–98 on the eastern eminence of the institutional grounds facing West College. Also constructed of brick and four stories tall, East measured 140 by just 28 feet, contained twenty-eight rooms serving primarily residential but also some recitation purposes, and cost over $11,000 to build. Somewhat larger than West, East had two halls instead of one running through it on an east-west axis. There were two bedrooms associated with each study room, while West had no clearly defined bedrooms. In East, all the major rooms had fireplaces, and student sleeping rooms were placed along the outer walls.

As a result of its destruction by fire in the 1840s, the original East College is visually documented in artistic views, the only ones available in the years predating photography. In the Kellogg lithograph (c. 1836; see fig. 3-1, right side), East appears as a simplified but impressive and massive rectangular block protected by a hipped roof pierced by four brick chimneys, with two entrance doors and evenly spaced windows in its main and side walls. In his book *Reflections on the Architecture of Williams College* (2001), Whitney S. Stoddard appropriately compares East College to South College (Union Hall; 1793–94) in Yale's Old Brick Row, of which it is a near reproduction in terms of size, proportions, and placement of door and window apertures.

Fig. 3-4. South (left) and East (right) Colleges (1841–42), east facades, Williams College. Photograph, c. 1886, by Adams & Aldrich, North Adams, Mass. Courtesy of Williams College Archives and Special Collections.

Fig. 3-5. South (left) and East (right) Colleges (1841–42), east facades, Williams College. Photograph, 1985.

Again, as with West College, the Williams trustees, many of whom had Yale connections, were likely influenced in their planning by a Yale building predecessor.[5]

Vulnerable to fire due to its interior wooden framing and open fireplaces, East College succumbed to a huge conflagration on Sunday, 17 October 1841, while students were attending afternoon chapel services elsewhere in the town. Though the structure was uninsured, the trustees met and acted quickly, raising $9,000 in subscriptions to assist in a rebuilding effort. Due to the need to replace lost student housing, construction moved ahead quickly over the next two years and was completed in 1842. Built on the ruins of its precursor, with its main facade facing east, the new brick-walled East College (fig. 3-4), in contrast, was smaller in all its dimensions, rose three stories instead of four, was topped by a flat roof with brick chimneys, and displayed balustrades atop the long side walls. On the exterior, East looks much the same in the present except for the addition in the early twentieth century (some sources say 1907) of visually attractive, Doric-columned porches in front of the formerly unadorned, twin side-wall entry doorways (fig. 3-5).[6]

At the same time that East College was being rebuilt in 1841–42, the Williams trustees committed to the construction of South College, aligned with East just 75 feet away on a north-south axis. In size, proportions, architectural detail (including Greek-inspired doorway porches), and interior room configuration, it was almost identical to East, and has remained so into this century (see figs. 3-4 and 3-5). At first South also possessed not only dormitory rooms but also a recitation room, the rooms of the Natural History Society (before the erection of Jackson Hall), and space for the Philologian and Philotechnian student societies and their libraries. East and South colleges were rebuilt on their interiors in 1956–57 under the direction of architects Hoyle, Doran and Berry (formerly Cram & Ferguson) at a total cost near $600,000, and today both serve as residence halls. At first comprising a two-building row much like the first two buildings of Brown and Norwich universities, the two structures at Williams now serve as the west wall of a loose open quadrangle (the East Quad), created between 1905 and 1908, with openings between the buildings to allow views of the campus and the nearby hills and mountains.[7]

Chronologically, the third building at Williams College was the Brick Chapel, renamed Griffin Hall in 1859, situated nearby to the north on the other side of Main Street, but on the same eminence as today's open quadrangle (see fig. 3-1).

Erected in 1828 with $10,000 raised by new president Edward Dorr Griffin, the new three-story, multipurpose brick building contained in its west end, on the first two floors, its most important interior space: a new two-story chapel moved from West College. The original chapel pulpit was set high on a platform and, along with faculty pews, was enclosed by a small wooden railing. The main floor contained seats for students, while the small gallery above, supported by wooden piers, was reserved for visitors. In addition to the chapel, Griffin Hall housed the college library (until its 1847 relocation) and recitation, conference, laboratory, and study rooms in its early years.

With good justification, Williams historians have extolled the virtues of Griffin Hall (fig. 3-6), characterizing it as the college's "best" building. It is believed that President Griffin himself, though untrained in architectural design, prepared the plans and that no professional architect was involved with the design process. It has been further conjectured that Griffin was familiar with the work of Sir Christopher Wren, as well as Boston's Charles Bulfinch at the Andover Theological Seminary and elsewhere, and that he closely consulted the illustrated design books of Asher Benjamin, used as guides by many New England master

Fig. 3-6. Griffin Hall (1828), south main façade, Williams College. Photograph, 2008.

Fig. 3-7. Observatory (1836–37), Williams College. Frontispiece engraving, *Catalogue of the Corporation, Officers and Students of Williams College* (1836–37). Courtesy of Williams College Archives and Special Collections.

Fig. 3-8. Hopkins Astronomical Observatory (1837–38), Williams College. Photograph, 1996.

builders at the time. Almost assuredly, the lovely three-stage gold-dome tower at the center of the stately, refined 90-by-38-foot edifice was modeled after a published Benjamin plan. Like Bulfinch (Pearson) Hall (1818) by Charles Bulfinch, now owned by Phillips Academy at Andover, Griffin Hall displays a symmetrical front facade consisting of a central, slightly projecting pavilion with closed triangular pediment and segmental-arched fanlight, flanked by identical wings, all capped by a low hipped roof. Initially there were unobtrusive doors in the facade, positioned to the right and left of the pavilion. In 1904, when the facade was altered, these doors were bricked up and the pavilion received a new central doorway with classical porch, designed by architect John Oakman and similar to the ones added to East and South colleges in around 1907. Perhaps the most visually dominant and attractive feature of Griffin is the Palladian window illuminating the chapel in the west-end wall, a common Federal-style element that is also present in Bulfinch Hall at Andover. In Griffin Hall, this window and the other components are expertly integrated, resulting in a beautifully proportioned, aesthetically appealing collegiate structure, without question one of New England's finest pre–Civil War examples.[8]

Initially situated adjacent to old East College, the Hopkins Observatory (fig. 3-7) was erected in l836–37 under the leadership of Professor Albert Hopkins, the younger brother of President Mark Hopkins. It enjoys the distinction of being the first college or university observatory to be erected in the United States, and the oldest in the country still in operation. In addition to its original site, it has occupied two others: in 1908, it was moved south to the end of the current Berkshire Quad, and in 1960 it was re-

located again to the north end of the same quadrangle. Built at a cost of $2,075, the rubble stone masonry observatory consists of a central octagon (circular on the inside) with two matching square wings, and measures 48 feet long and 20 feet wide. Atop the octagonal section is a white-painted wooden octagon supporting a circular casing for the telescope. Originally, the octagon was surmounted by a revolving dome, 13 feet in diameter (see fig. 3-7), and the wings had openings in their roofs for meridian instruments (which is still the case). The vaulted ceiling of the dome took the form of a hemisphere, painted blue, with gold stars (arranged to form constellations) and the circles of the celestial sphere. The initial entrance to the structure was the north-side doorway, with its flat, Federal-style porch cornice displaying triglyphs and metopes, supported by pairs of thin Doric columns. Since the date of construction, the south door, initially unembellished, has received a porch identical in size, scale, and detail. Long respected for its scientific uses, the Hopkins Observatory has also been admired for its well-integrated geometric forms and its discreet architectural detailing (fig. 3-8).[9]

The next four buildings at Williams College, built during the 1840s and 1850s, were conceived in various expressions of American revivalist architectural styles. The oldest of these was Lawrence Hall (fig. 3-9), erected in 1846–47 adjacent to East and South colleges as the first independent library facility of the institution. Initiated by President Mark Hopkins, the new library project was made possible by previous college benefactor Amos Lawrence of Boston, whose generosity funded the full $7,000 in construction expenses. Consulting on the library design was Charles C. Jewett, the librarian of Brown University, who had traveled in Europe

Fig. 3-9. Lawrence Hall (library) (1846–47), Williams College. "Old Williams" photograph album, n.d. Courtesy of Williams College Archives and Special Collections.

Fig. 3-10. Lawrence Hall (1846–47, etc.), Williams College. Photograph, 2008.

and was able to share his knowledge of French centrally planned libraries. Almost assuredly, Jewett had had contact with the documented architect Thomas A. Tefft (1826–59) of Rhode Island, who during his brief professional career designed more than 150 buildings in variations of the Gothic, Italian, and Romanesque revival styles. On its completion, Lawrence Hall supplanted the library space in Griffin Hall, with shelving initially for 30,000 books. The building's storage capacity grew to approximately 80,000 books after east and west wings were added in 1890 and an ell in 1915. Lawrence served as the college library until 1922, when it was succeeded by the new Stetson Hall. It became the Williams College Museum of Art in 1926 and since then has undergone additional expansion, renovation, and redecoration to accommodate museum and art history department uses (fig. 3-10).

Before it was enlarged, Lawrence Hall, continuing the tradition established at Williams in the central core of the Hopkins Observatory and the tiny Magnetic Observatory (see note 9), was purely octagonal in form, 48 feet in diameter. Topping the low octagonal roof was an octagonal lookout dome with a balustrade. Displayed on the exterior were skillfully integrated classical elements, including brick Doric corner pilasters set on rusticated brick bases and supporting a subtle classical entablature combining an architrave, frieze, and cornice. On the interior, Lawrence possessed components of the Ionic order of the Greek Revival, unquestionably in the eight tall, round, fluted columns with their voluted capitals and round bases, and in a circular entablature supporting a round dome. A surviving interior plan by architect Tefft shows two floors divided into eight

pie-shaped alcoves with bookshelves radiating out from the center, where the librarian was situated, perfectly positioned to monitor book usage. The ground floor was used primarily for book storage, and there were no specifically defined reading areas characteristic of modern libraries except for a periodical room, occasionally used for trustee meetings. While Lawrence Hall served as a library, the spacious, columned rotunda on the second floor was arguably the most distinguished and aesthetically noteworthy interior space in the college's collection of nineteenth-century buildings.[10]

Williams College's next two pre-1860 "revivalist" buildings are no longer in existence. Raised in 1847, Kellogg Hall (fig. 3-11), named after Professor of Languages Ebenezer Kellogg, was formerly situated on low ground in the vicinity of West College, near present-day Jesup Hall. The naming

Fig. 3-11. Kellogg Hall (1846), Williams College. Photograph, c. 1886, by Adams & Aldrich, North Adams, Mass. Courtesy of Williams College Archives and Special Collections.

of this structure was most appropriate, as the land on which it was built was given to the college by Professor Kellogg. Though erected at the height of the revival era in American architecture, Kellogg Hall was virtually devoid of architectural detail on its exterior, assuming the form of an uninspiring, sterile, three-story, rectangular brick box, topped by a low-pitched roof set on a thick cornice. Oriented on an east-west longitudinal axis, Kellogg was roughly one-half the size of East College and was devoted entirely to student housing except early in its history, when there were two recitation rooms on the first floor. In 1900, it was torn down, having outlived its usefulness and considered by many to be visually incompatible with other larger, more attractive, and more serviceable college buildings nearby.[11]

In 1855, Nathan Jackson of New York City donated $2,500 to Williams College to be used to erect a building for the Lyceum of Natural History (Natural History Society), and later, when the final construction costs reached $3,500, he supplemented this gift with another $1,000. Erected during the same year, the new structure was titled Jackson Hall in recognition of his generosity. Located at the southeast corner of the current Berkshire Quad, Jackson Hall (fig. 3-12) was auspiciously introduced in the June 1854 issue of the *Williams Quarterly*:

A plan . . . was resolved upon, and the contracts made for the building, which it is hoped will be completed by the approaching Commencement. The foundation of stone is now in progress. The superstructure is to be of brick, resting upon marble underpinnings. The main building is to be thirty-five feet square by twenty-

Fig. 3-12. Jackson Hall (Natural History Museum) (1855), Williams College. "Old Williams" photograph album, n.d. Courtesy of Williams College Archives and Special Collections.

five feet in height, and lighted chiefly by a large sky-light. On the east side is to be a tower, twenty feet square by forty feet in height, which is to be divided into three stories; the lower two ones to contain specimens, and the upper one to be used for the Society's meetings. In the center of the main building, it is contemplated to place ultimately an ornithological tree, in a glass case, on which the Society's collection of birds shall be mounted. . . . its location is near the brow of the hill south of the Astronomical Observatory, and overlooking the pond below.

In its completed state, Jackson Hall also accommodated cabinets and illustrative collections of the Natural History Society, as well as study rooms and a laboratory and assembly chamber. Over the main entrance door was placed a large bronze eagle presented by the benefactor and resembling one exhibited at the United States Crystal Palace. Considered of insufficiently sound construction and rendered obsolete as a scientific facility, Jackson Hall was razed in 1908, but it still enjoys the distinction of being the first student-conceived and student-built edifice devoted to natural history on an American higher educational campus.

Though Jackson Hall was likely designed by a professional architect, to date no documents have surfaced granting an attribution to a specific individual or partnership. In certain respects (brick Doric corner pilasters; octagonal roof cap; broad roof cornice) it bears a resemblance to Lawrence Hall, so much so that one could logically speculate that Thomas Tefft may have played a role in the design process. Hopefully, it will be possible to make an attribution in the future. Among the most provocative details of this richly embellished structure were the ogee brackets of the thick, hipped main roof and flat tower roof cornices, the octagonal cupola, the metal fencing atop the square tower, and the large ogee brackets supporting the flat roof projection above the main entrance doorway. For many onlookers, Lawrence Hall made a more pronounced mid-Victorian eclectic statement than that of its predecessor, Jackson Hall.[12]

Facing increasingly overcrowded conditions in the Griffin Hall chapel in the 1850s, college trustees and officials budgeted $10,000 (toward a total cost of $13,100) and resolved to construct a new edifice to house a new chapel and an alumni headquarters. Selected as the site was a slight rise between East Hall to the east and the ravine dropping down toward Spring Street. To design the new building the college contracted with Gervase Wheeler (c. 1815–70),

Fig. 3-13. "College Chapel. 1859." Lithograph from Calvin Durfee, *A History of Williams College* (1860), opposite p. 350. Courtesy of Williams College Archives and Special Collections.

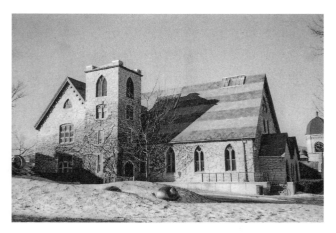

Fig. 3-14. Goodrich Hall (College Chapel) and Alumni Hall (1859), Williams College. Photograph, 2008.

a New York City–based architect and native of England, who also planned alterations to the Bowdoin College Chapel in 1856–57. Erected in 1858–59, the Stone Chapel and Alumni Hall, as the structure was first called, was dedicated on 22 September 1859 and commenced a long, ongoing period of service.

The Stone Chapel, renamed Goodrich Hall when it was remodeled for recitation and seminar purposes in 1905, was a conspicuous Gothic Revival addition to Williams College's growing architectural repertoire (fig. 3-13). Constructed of locally quarried dolomite limestone, the north-facing front facade, set under a steep-pitched slate roof with alternating color strips, features paired main doorways protected by linked, steep-pitched roof porches with segmental-arched openings. The principal side-wall windows continue the segmental-arched form. The tall east-side tower, its steeple spire later removed, was particularly striking, largely due to the broad vocabulary of arches (segmental, slightly pointed, flat) that Wheeler chose to include in the wall surfaces. At the base of the tower, facing north, is the pointed-arched entrance that initially admitted people into both the chapel and alumni hall. The loss of the tower spire was in many respects an injustice, for without it Goodrich Hall appears awkward and poorly proportioned today (fig. 3-14), contrary to how it looked in the nineteenth century. The chapel received a west transept addition in the late 1800s. Today the entire structure is devoted to a reconfigured student-run campus activities center as a result of a total renovation directed by Bruner/Cott Associates in 1998. Despite these changes, the Goodrich Chapel and Alumni Hall building remains an important, represen-

tative chapter in the evolution of Williams College architecture, and a bridge to the post–Civil War development of the campus environment.[13]

Bowdoin College and Traditional Planning Precepts

Between 1798 and 1822, the first trustees and administrators of Bowdoin College developed its initial open quadrangle campus. Facing west like its Harvard and Dartmouth forerunners,[14] it was perceived by many as the most appealing of the three, particularly in a spatial sense. It was situated, as the college is today, east of Maine Street among tall whispering pines on a slight planar eminence just south of the center of Brunswick. Extensive shrub and hardwood plantings, pathways, and wooden fences ordered and beautified the campus scene. Unlike the first two Dartmouth building arrangements, the Bowdoin plan was perfectly symmetrical and was composed of four academic structures. Greater distances were established between the buildings, and the end result was a more open, expansive, and characteristically American collegiate environment. Arguably the most outstanding view of this well-ordered scheme is a lithograph (fig. 3-15) by W. S. and J. B. Pendleton of Boston based on a c. 1822 painting by J. G. Brown, the latter lost for many years, rediscovered in 1960, and now hanging in the college president's office.

Though proving it is difficult, it is quite conceivable that this open quadrangle arrangement at Bowdoin was consciously intended from the time of Maine Hall's completion in 1806–8. It is known that the Bowdoin trustees met in May 1808 and voted to establish an ad hoc committee to ap-

Fig. 3-15. "S.W. View of Bowdoin College, Brunswick, Me." (1825–28). Black-and-white lithograph by W. S. and J. B. Pendleton of Boston, based on c. 1822 painting by J. G. Brown, also of Boston. Left, Massachusetts Hall (1799–1802); left center, Winthrop Hall (1822); right center, Old Chapel (1805); right, Maine Hall (1806–8). Courtesy of the George J. Mitchell Department of Special Collections and Archives, Bowdoin College Library, Brunswick, Maine.

prove and execute a long-range grounds plan and that they contracted for the services of the later well-known Portland and Boston architect Alexander Parris (1780–1852) to prepare the necessary paper renderings. Unfortunately, these have not been seen for over a century, so it is not presently known whether Parris suggested only landscaping improvements or whether his work for the college had a broader influence on the completion of the open quadrangle scheme and later campus development. It is interesting to note, however, that the college treasurer's account book for 1803–21 contains a notation for two payments to Parris totaling $28 for "planning [the] college yard."[15] Although the debate will doubtless continue as to how this information should be interpreted, it is evident that Bowdoin's building planners were properly concerned with the broad educational environment of the college in its infancy.

With the similar square appearance of an urban, Federal-style domestic dwelling, Massachusetts Hall (1799–1802; fig. 3-16), the first structure in the open quadrangle at Bowdoin College, is as significant for its architecture as for the varied educational role it has played for over two centuries. Though a somewhat atypical and monumental example of early collegiate building design, it has occupied a vital, functional place in Bowdoin's long and distinguished history. The records of the Boards of Trustees and Overseers relate the complete story of Massachusetts's planning

and construction. On 18 July 1796, the trustees assembled in Brunswick "to agree upon a spot . . . whereon to erect suitable buildings for the College." The next day this same group voted to raise a structure of brick 100 feet long, 40 feet wide, and four stories high, with a cellar. The approved plan, regarded as overly ambitious and expensive, was soon dismissed, but it was revived ten years later in conjunction with the planning of a subsequent building, Maine Hall. Another year passed, and a less ambitious conception took its place. After some disagreement between the trustees and overseers, it was resolved on 7 November 1797 "that a brick building be erected, 50 feet by 40, three stories high, with a cellar under the whole, for the President's House, and to accommodate a few students, before the College is erected."[16] At the same time, a committee was charged with the responsibility of soliciting donations and initiating building plans.

A sum of $2,300 was raised and appropriated for the project, but financial difficulties soon made it impossible for the college to direct this money toward construction. Nonetheless, by the spring of 1799, walls of Portland brick had been raised above the stone foundations, with graduated stories of ten, nine, and seven and a half feet. Funds become exhausted, however, and in this unfinished state there was no recourse but to suspend the work, provide a temporary roof, and finish the outside to protect the interior

Fig. 3-16. Massachusetts Hall (1799–1802), Bowdoin College. Photograph, c. 1968.

from the effects of harsh weather. The building remained incomplete and unused for two more years, "an empty shell, with its windows boarded up, standing on the sandy plain" among tall pine trees in an area that is still part of the Bowdoin campus. But in the spring of 1801, the state of the college treasury had improved enough that the agent chosen to erect the new edifice was instructed to "cause it to be completed in a plain manner according to the finishing of Hollis Hall [Harvard], and that he make all his contracts both for labor and materials, for payment in cash only, in order that the building be finished in the cheapest manner." With an additional $2,000 committed toward the total cost of $5,100, work resumed the ensuing summer, with gratifying results:

within a year from that date [1802], the lower two stories of the house were finished;—the eastern portion in a manner clearly denoting the domestic uses originally contemplated, viz., with chambers above, and with a parlor in the southwest corner below, a kitchen in the northeast corner, and a pantry in the projection;— the western portion, with two rooms below thrown into one for a chapel and hall, and two rooms in the second story for the occupation of students.

When the college opened in the fall of 1802, these rooms, as well as the third floor (reserved for students), and space for a library and recitations—twelve rooms altogether—

had been efficiently provided within this single compact edifice. By September 1802, enough of the work was sufficiently finished that the trustees were able to meet at "the College House" and vote to christen it Massachusetts Hall.[17] The newly inaugurated President Joseph McKeen, his family, two faculty, and eight students took up residence soon after as the first of a long list of tenants.

For many years, the question of who prepared the designs for Massachusetts Hall remained open to conjecture. The minutes of the boards' meetings of 25 May 1801 state that Captain John Dunlap, a wealthy Brunswick lumberman and merchant, was appointed to serve as the college's contracting supervisor. There is no evidence that Dunlap actually drew up formal plans, though the trustee records indicate that he was compensated for materials and labor and that in later years he informed President Leonard Woods of his role in the erection of the building. The same trustee records, however, reveal that two local carpenter/builders, Aaron Melcher and Samuel Melcher III (1775–1862), participated in the work and were granted substantial compensation for their efforts.[18] In fact, Dunlap actually chaired the building committee that apparently hired the Melcher brothers to participate in the building project. Further evidence of their involvement are the stylistic and technical similarities between Massachusetts Hall and other documented Melcher structures at Bowdoin and elsewhere in Brunswick. Although irrefutable documentation is lacking, it appears safe to assume that the Melchers, in whole or in part, prepared the final designs and carried out the construction. Samuel Melcher's involvement was to lead to other significant building commissions at the college.[19]

Although its uses have varied over the years, Massachusetts Hall has served consistently as a multipurpose building and the historic center of the college. After President McKeen departed with his family for a separate house in 1803, their former quarters were transformed into a laboratory and a room for minerals and philosophical apparatus. When Professor Parker Cleaveland came to Bowdoin from Harvard to occupy the chair of Mathematics and Natural Philosophy, a large lecture room and laboratory were formed on the first floor, accommodating his experiments and classes for over fifty years. On the completion of Melcher's separate wooden chapel in 1805, the chapel in Massachusetts became the treasurer's office. The second and third stories were left vacant in 1807 by the removal of

Fig. 3-17. Massachusetts Hall (1799–1802), south front doorway, Bowdoin College. Photograph, 2008.

the students living there to a new dormitory, Maine Hall, opened in that year. Employed briefly for classrooms and a painting gallery, this space was turned over to the new Medical School of Maine in 1820, which remained there until the completion of Seth Adams Hall, its long-term and more spacious home, in 1861.

For the next decade, the battered old edifice stood neglected. Then, in 1872–73, it received a magnificent new lease on life when Peleg W. Chandler, a college trustee and Boston lawyer, underwrote the costs to create in Massachusetts a scientific museum in memory of the prolific Professor Cleaveland. Under the direction of Boston architect Abel C. Martin (1835–79) and builder Richard T. D. Melcher, the son of Samuel III, the so-called Cleaveland Cabinet was placed in the upper two stories under a slightly raised roof, with a story added on top of the former easterly pantry projection to provide special access from the outside. Crammed with cases displaying minerals and shells, the 20-foot-high room was surrounded by a gallery reached by a spiral staircase. As an exhibition hall, it was indeed admirable, but as a teaching facility it was said to have had severe limitations. Fortunately, the exterior of the structure remained relatively unchanged by this Victorian-era conversion. The interior continued in this form until renovations in 1936 and 1941, when the cabinet was removed and the building restored to its original form and turned over to administrative and faculty offices and classrooms. A walk through the interior utilizing its graceful spiral staircase gives the modern-day visitor a clear impression of what the inside of Massachusetts must have been like in the days of President McKeen and Bowdoin's first faculty members.[20]

The unadorned exterior of Massachusetts Hall conveys a strong sense of restraint and honesty, reflecting the economic and aesthetic characteristics of the time when it was built. It has proven to be as durable and as fitting for its environment as other Bowdoin structures of superior size, grace, and proportion. The structure is capped by a hipped roof with four brick chimneys and features a narrow cornice and a south main doorway (fig. 3-17) crowned by a charming fanlight and framed by wooden pilasters and a plain entablature. This entrance, coupled with rectangular window framings, juxtapose their white painted surfaces against the deep red of the brick walls. Twin roof pediments originally planned for the building fail to appear in later printed and photographic views, but these may well have existed when it was built. A two-story eastern projection, once the beautiful porticoed entrance to the Cleaveland Cabinet, deprives the edifice of otherwise perfect front-facade symmetry.

It is apparent from the Pendleton lithograph of the campus (see fig. 3-15) that Massachusetts Hall, shown on the left, was initially capped by a ponderous, oversized Georgian-style bell cupola. Though for some years there was much controversy and mystery about its existence, this cupola finally was satisfactorily documented. Plans for its removal are first alluded to in the trustee records for 19 May 1818, when it was voted to relocate the college bell from the roof of Massachusetts to the tower of Old Chapel. While this occurred, the cupola remained. Eleven years later, in 1829, this vote was reaffirmed by the college's Visiting Committee, this time with specific mention of the cupola, and during the next year the trustees followed suit. Views of the structure after 1830 fail to show the cupola; thus, it may be safely assumed that its removal indeed did occur about that time.[21] While it was present, though, the cupola must have lent considerable nobility to Bowdoin's first multipurpose home.

A plain, vernacular wooden building like Dartmouth College's New Chapel (1790) before it, Old College Chapel, the second building in the former open quadrangle, proved to be an equally workable architectural solution for educational demands. Like its older counterpart, it successfully combined modest styling and function, while simultaneously speaking for the often-harsh climatic conditions of its locale, and the solid values of the people who frequented it. Located on the south end of the open quadrangle (see fig. 3-15), it stood opposite Massachusetts Hall and directly adjacent to Maine Hall, where today walkways from the present chapel and the north end of the campus intersect.

Soon after its opening, it became obvious that Massachusetts Hall, crowded with classroom and chapel facilities, was inadequate for housing the full range of college functions. In response to this reality, it was decided at the May 1805 meeting of the governing boards "that a building forty feet long, twenty-five feet wide and two stories high, the lower story to be twelve feet and the upper story nine feet in the clear for the purpose of a chapel and place of deposit for the library and philosophical apparatus, be erected of wood . . . and that the sum of twelve hundred dollars be appropriated to that purpose." As agent for the construction of the chapel, President McKeen negotiated a contract with Samuel Melcher III to undertake the project. Melcher's ledger book, in the possession of the college, contains men-

tion of this agreement, as well as building measurements, total costs, and the various wood materials employed. A conscientious businessman and gifted craftsman, Melcher called on his shipwright experience to construct the new edifice so skillfully that it long outlasted its expected lifetime. Though conceived as a minor, temporary facility, it was not razed and sold for materials until 1847, following an impressive forty-two years of service.

At first facing the west side of the open quadrangle, Old College Chapel contained on its first floor a room for religious, academic, and public uses that was furnished with cold benches facing an enclosed bench and center desk. An area for deposit of the 1,500-volume library collection and the philosophical apparatus was located on the second floor. Because there are no floor plans, little else is known about the interior layout. Like its Dartmouth equivalent, it rested on stone underpinnings, was lighted on the inside by unadorned rectangular window portals, and was protected by a low hipped roof, except where a pediment and cornice were situated above the main doorway. Only its trimmings were painted. In 1818, by trustee action, the chapel received a new modicum of proportion and style when it was turned to face Massachusetts Hall to the north, painted a straw color, and fitted with a tower and Georgian open cupola in which the college bell (shifted from the top of Massachusetts) was hung. Efforts were made seven years later to improve the chapel's spatial accommodations by enlarging the building mass 18 feet in a southerly direction, but apparently, with funds lacking and ideas for a newer and grander religious structure circulating, this project never came to fruition. Cramped, poorly arranged, and unheated, it restricted the normal growth of the library collection and was "in every way unsatisfactory." But despite its critics, while it existed Old College Chapel was a favorite campus landmark for Bowdoin faculty, students, and alumni.[22]

Maine Hall (1806–8 and 1836–37; fig. 3-18), the third Bowdoin College building, was the first bona fide permanent dormitory edifice erected for a northern New England higher educational institution. Distinguished by the former presence of such notable personages as Franklin Pierce and Nathaniel Hawthorne during their student years, it has come down the years greatly altered, once totally rebuilt, but still a vital part of the institutional physical plant. It was during President Jesse Appleton's term of office that the building was made possible by the first of a long line of bequests to the college—a grant in 1806 from the State

Fig. 3-18. Maine Hall (1806–8; 1836–37), Bowdoin College. Photograph, 2008.

of Massachusetts in the form of the township of Etna in Maine. From the proceeds of the ensuing land sales from this bequest, $11,300 was appropriated, and the old plans for a brick dormitory structure — hopes that had been nurtured since 1798 — were finally realized.[23]

Directly following the news of the grant, the trustee building committee, appointed in 1804, issued the following encouraging report in September 1806:

The Committee who were appointed to make an estimate . . . of a building to be erected of brick, one hundred feet long, forty-two feet wide, and four stories high, by leave to report, that they have made inquiry of the most eminent carpenters and masons in this vicinity.

There seems to be little doubt that the successful bidder of the "carpenters and masons" was Samuel Melcher III, cobuilder (with his brother Aaron) of Massachusetts Hall, and that he was contracted by the college to implement the project plans. The completed building was unquestionably in the Melcher vein and resembled certain works of architecture that he had likely seen on prior trips to Boston. Early historians of Bowdoin grant him the attribution without question, and Melcher's own ledger books and the college treasurer's account books indicate that he performed extensive work on the structure in 1808. Former Bowdoin professor William D. Shipman, in his book *The Architecture of Bowdoin College and Brunswick, Maine* (1973), convincingly asserts that the first rendition of Maine Hall was definitely of Melcher's authorship.[24]

Situated in the open quadrangle east of Old College

Chapel and Massachusetts Hall, Maine Hall — or Old College, as it was called until Maine statehood[25] — was initially a handsome and imposing structure. From what is evident in the early Pendleton lithograph of the college (see plate 15), Maine Hall, which appears on the right side, initially possessed considerably more detail than the later Bowdoin residence halls and in this respect was decidedly more provocative. It was protected by a balustraded hipped roof from which several tall chimneys projected, and each of the long sides was broken by a subtly projecting bay in the middle, capped by a low triangular pediment enclosing a delicate semicircular fanlight. The principal entrances were on the campus facade, not, as today, in the end walls. Thirty-two rooms were located in two separate entryways, an arrangement inherited from buildings at Harvard and Yale and at English universities before them. Four rooms, containing at least two students each, were situated on each story of both entries. Wood holes and study closets, evident still in old Harvard Yard dormitories, were present in each room in Maine. It appears, therefore, that the total capacity of this first version of the building must have been at least sixty-four students. A library and classrooms were also present at various times in its history.

The resemblance between this first form and Harvard's Hollis Hall (1762–63), still standing in the Yard in Cambridge, immediately strikes the appreciative eye. In the estimate of Shipman, the design could well have been taken from any number of older building examples in the Boston area, or from one of the builders' handbooks (i.e., William James Pain, *The Practical House Carpenter* [Boston, 1796]), then circulating in the New England region. The most sought-after of Bowdoin's early dormitories, the edifice "seems to have attracted students for their good morale and piety, probably members of the praying circle, since its two ends were nicknamed 'Paradise' and 'Zion.'" Other students, however, complained that the rooms were barren, harsh, and cold.[26]

Maine Hall, in contrast to its neighboring structures, has twice been the serious victim of the ravages of fire, which has resulted in the transformed building we may view today. The first fire of 4 March 1822 was said to have started in the attic while Maine's residents were absent attending a lecture elsewhere. Fortunately, the walls of the dormitory were not badly damaged, but the roof and the entire interior had to be replaced, at a staggering cost to the college. Contributions of $8,000 from Congregational churches in Maine and Massachusetts graciously alleviated the funding problem, however, and the college remained in solvent condition.[27] Subsequently, under Samuel Melcher's guidance, the battered structure reassumed its nicely proportioned original form, but with a fireproof roof installed and lightning rods added, wood holes removed, and special stoves provided so as to minimize the possibility of a reoccurrence. Some first-story rooms were devoted to recitation, a change from the pre-fire interior plan.[28]

From the second disastrous fire of 17 February 1836, caused by the ignition of dry wood in the cellar, Maine Hall did not emerge in redeemable condition. In the words of an undergraduate observer, nothing was left of "the great building but the blackened, windowless, doorless, roofless walls." Its remains declared structurally unsound, it was leveled to its foundations and raised anew in 1836–37 under the direction of builder Anthony Coombs Raymond for $10,800. Raymond, under the guidance of the president and the boards, apparently reused Melcher's design for Winthrop Hall and did not reproduce the distinguished elements of the first design for Maine. It appeared, therefore, as a rather plain rectangular block, free from any other real stylistic adornment except for another roof balustrade, later removed. Once more, fireproofing features were optimistically added. Though supposedly rebuilt with better accommodations for its "inmates," and literary and scientific societies in two separate entryways, the new Maine was considered "less pleasing," lacking its former front pediment and entrances.[29] The new elliptically arched, deeply recessed side entrances and eight relocated chimneys are

marked features of the present-day edition of the building, which in its simplicity still makes a strong architectural statement (see fig. 3-18).

Maine Hall's altered form, influenced by its unfortunate history and circumstances, is perhaps attributable more to national economic conditions of the times than to any other single factor. For better or worse, though, a pattern of simple, direct, and utterly functional residential architecture was established, one that determined the designs of Bowdoin's next three dormitories and influenced the planning of comparable buildings at other institutions. Renovated again in 1892 and 1964–66, Maine has doggedly carried forward a respected tradition of refined and flexible design.

Although they were built twenty years apart, Bowdoin's next two dormitory structures, Winthrop (1822–23) and Appleton (1842–43) halls (figs. 3-19 and 3-20), have so much in common that they should properly be discussed together. Both also bear a striking resemblance to the surviving 1836–37 version of their quite bleak predecessor, Maine Hall. Among the features that the three buildings have in common are materials (brick, timber, tin, and glass); stone foundation measurements (100 by 42 feet); brick bond (English common, with Flemish variation); number of stories (four); type of roof style (low hipped); number, size, and positioning of the brick chimneys (eight tall, set in and flush with the walls); window detail (limestone lintels, and end flat Palladian motifs) and type (six-over-six double-sash on first, second, and third stories; three-over-six double-sash on the fourth-story level); and floor plan (end doorways, twin entries of sixteen rooms each). The only ob-

Fig. 3-19. Winthrop Hall (1822), Bowdoin College. Photograph, 2008.

Fig. 3-20. Appleton Hall (1842–43), Bowdoin College. Photograph, 2008.

vious variation between the three is in the doorway framing, essentially classical in conception in each instance.

There are several reasons for this overall similarity. First, as college and personal records have established, in their original versions all three structures were designed and constructed by master builder Samuel Melcher III, alone or in partnership with another professional. Therefore, the presence of common style features and construction techniques is not surprising. Second, the same geographic, climatic, and local economic considerations that played a role in the realization of Maine also affected the shapes and details of both Winthrop and Appleton. Third, there was a desire on the part of the Bowdoin trustees and officials to erect a continuous, balanced row of compatible buildings on a north-south axis across the campus, in the manner of Yale's eighteenth-century Old Brick Row. By the early 1840s it was determined that two structures would flank a new, dominant chapel on each side in order to present the onlooker with a symmetrical arrangement from either a westerly or easterly direction.[30]

Winthrop Hall had its origins during the early stages of President William Allen's administration, when the increase in the number of enrolled students at Bowdoin made additional living accommodations a high priority. In September 1821 the trustees authorized the expenditure of $10,000 (final cost, $9,550) and appointed a small committee from its membership to raise the requisite funds, assemble materials, and direct construction. After a delay due to the lack of monetary resources, Samuel Melcher was hired to execute his own plans, an arrangement affirmed by the trustee meetings minutes and by his personal journal, now in the possession of Brunswick's Pejepscot County Historical Society. Work commenced in April 1822 and continued until August 1823. Placed 100 feet north of Maine, for over two decades the building was recognized as New College or North College, until in 1848 it was officially named for John Winthrop, the first governor of the Massachusetts Bay Colony. Recitation rooms occupied the lower floor, with student double rooms in the stories above.[31] Completely stripped on its interior in 1964–65 and further renovated in recent years, it houses only students today.

As it was a new dormitory, Winthrop Hall was considered cleaner and better equipped than its forerunner, Maine Hall, and therefore had a tendency to attract Bowdoin's more affluent students. According to college historian Louis C. Hatch, its north end quickly became the "aristocratic quarter," but "aristocracy and propriety do not always go together and the conduct of students rooming in Winthrop soon became so disorderly as to gain for its 'ends' the nicknames of Sodam and Gamorrah." Such conditions were gradually alleviated; by 1853 the Visiting Committee was able to submit the uplifting report about Winthrop that "the bad reputation of certain localities … had in great measure passed away and that students of irreproachable moral character were willing to live in it." Nevertheless, bad habits returned, and the North Winthrop entry had to be closed and repaired before it could be reopened four years later in 1868. In 1926, after a long period of hard use, the entire interior had to be reconstructed, to the tune of $20,000.[32] A similar interior refurbishing project took place in 1964–66. Such a history illustrates the constantly changing esteem in which early college dormitories were held, as well as the continual problems that faced higher educational administrators in keeping them serviceable. The proper maintenance of dormitory structures still poses challenges to administrators as they seek to provide students with successful living/learning environments.

The building of Winthrop Hall's successor, Appleton Hall (see fig. 3-20), signaled Bowdoin's departure from the original open quadrangle to a new, expanded row plan. Though anticipated as early as 1808, the fully developed row scheme, now the west side of the college's large main quadrangle, was possibly the brainchild of President William Allen. With full appreciation of the need for proper building separation and the future growth of the college, he persuaded the Board of Trustees to adopt and enlarge upon a "three-college plan" discussed by this body some years before. In his 1835 annual report he spoke of the advantages of fire security and uniformity of arrangement and advised that a "new college should be placed at least 300 feet south of Maine Hall, leaving room for a central Chapel with a space of 100 feet on either side of it." In the 1866–67 edition of the college catalogue, a Joseph Griffin engraving (fig. 3-21) depicts the early open quadrangle design, deprived of Old College Chapel, and stretched into a long impressive line of four buildings by the addition of Appleton Hall and Richard Upjohn's College Chapel (1844–55). With the subsequent construction of a fifth structure, Hyde Hall, similar in form to Appleton on the south end in 1917, the perfect symmetry of Trumbull's Yale row model, in enlarged form, was guaranteed for the modern generation. An inspection of this pleasant building group today, New England's largest

Fig. 3-21. "Bowdoin College, Brunswick, Me." Frontispiece engraving, c. 1865, by Brunswick printer Joseph Griffin from the *1866–67 Catalogue of the Officers and Students of Bowdoin College and the Medical School of Maine*. From left to right: Seth Adams Hall (1861–62); Massachusetts Hall (1799–1802); Winthrop Hall (1822); Maine Hall (1806–8; 1836–37); College Chapel (1844–55); Appleton Hall (1842–43). Courtesy of the George J. Mitchell Department of Special Collections and Archives, Bowdoin College Library, Brunswick, Maine.

and finest historic row exemplar, gives one an excellent idea how Yale's pace-setting plan must have appeared before its highly debatable destruction.

Prospects for Maine Hall's other twin, Appleton Hall, first entered into official discussions in 1835, a full eight years before its completion and formal opening. At that time, the trustees acted to set up a special committee "to consider the subject of a new College Building for the residence of students and to take the opinion of an Architect as to plan for the same and estimate of expense." Delayed by the lack of funds and a lag in enrollment, deliberations continued over the next few years until the middle of 1842, at which time the trustees voted that "the building committee be directed to purchase materials and contract for the erection of a new College Hall the next year." Again Samuel Melcher III, assisted by his sons, performed the necessary design and contracting tasks, at a cost of $9,100. A lengthy contractual agreement, in the possession of the college archives, not only identifies Melcher as the principal party for the erection of the structure, but also contains full materials and building specifications, which relate the story of how Appleton was assembled.[33]

For two years, this building was known as South College, but in 1847 it received the new name of Appleton Hall in honor of Reverend Jesse Appleton, Bowdoin's second president. Today it still occupies the site originally specified by President Allen, some 100 feet south of the College Chapel. Appleton has had a rather uneventful and charmed history; it has neither been burned, like Maine, nor temporarily closed, like Winthrop. In fact, for a long time it was regarded so highly that it was nicknamed New Jerusalem, an uncharacteristic accolade for most dormitory structures! But then again, its existence has not been a wholly atypical or abnormal one in student affairs. For example, in 1860, festive activity in its north division brought it to the scornful attention of the campus temperance society.[34] In the twentieth century, Appleton continued to maintain a record of productive usefulness. The many dollars expended for the complete replacement of its interior in 1964–66 is testament to its ongoing importance and effective service as a college community residence hall.

Initially intended solely for dining purposes, Commons Hall (1829; fig. 3-22), located at the north end of the extended row opposite Massachusetts Hall on Bath Street, has served a variety of functions over the years. Much needed after the failure of a dining arrangement with a local inn, a separate college-owned commons building was approved in concept by the Board of Trustees at their September 1828 gathering. On this occasion, Joseph McKeen, Bowdoin's treasurer, was entrusted with the responsibility of supervis-

Fig. 3-22. Commons Hall (1829), Bowdoin College. Photograph, c. 1968.

ing the procurement or erection of a suitable structure, setting student board stipulations, and appropriating $1,750 to cover costs. When it was subsequently resolved to proceed with new construction, a suitable location was selected for the initial excavations on what was then the Bath turnpike. Nearly a year later, in August 1829, the Visiting Committee proudly reported:

Since the last Commencement, a neat and convenient building has been erected for a commons hall, fitted up with all the necessary apartments for cooking, store rooms too, and with sleeping rooms for the persons working as the cooks. In this building the students provide commons for themselves of a good quality at a very economical rate.

After a few years of student-managed dining service for boarding students, the distinctive brick structure was used for medical lectures by the mid-1840s, converted to a gymnasium in 1860 and then to an analytical chemistry laboratory and classroom and office building during the 1870s, and thereafter it housed a carpentry shop and provided storage space. Sadly, the lack of floor plans and written descriptive accounts prevent even guesses as to early interior layouts, though we do know that while Commons served as a dining facility, the lower half story was used as a kitchen and service area, and the upper main story as a dining hall. In recent times, Commons, now physically linked to neighboring Rhodes Hall, has taken on a new function as headquarters for the college maintenance and campus security departments. Although its architectural dignity has been somewhat compromised by such varied use, the building

has passed to the current generation in an excellent state of preservation.

Much is unknown about the interior operations of Commons Hall, but direct observation of its thought-provoking exterior may provide sufficient compensation. Roughly 18 by 50 feet in dimensions, this modest-sized structure possesses many features of Samuel Melcher III's previous work for Bowdoin, as well as more modern qualities of the Greek Revival. In fact, though it has yet to be substantiated, one might reasonably speculate that Melcher himself executed the design. However, as Patricia Anderson notes in her 1988 book on Bowdoin College architecture, a more likely possibility is Anthony Coombs Raymond, the builder of the 1836–37 edition of Maine Hall. Present in the college's special collections is an estimate from Raymond to erect Commons Hall for the sum of $1,775.[35]

Solid and quite inelaborate, the building displays delicate linear moldings along the gables and eaves of its low-pitched roof, and light wooden frames around its windows and doorways. Plain, parallel brick pilasters break the flatness of the long sides and create a refreshing staccato effect. The south end underscores the fine scaling of the whole structure, with its three, small double-sash windows set above two thin rectangular door portals topped by horizontal glass lights and white, splayed stone lintels, similar to those above the larger side-window apertures. From what we may witness today about building shape and detailing, as well as natural lighting potential, it is apparent that Commons Hall more than likely satisfied dining needs with success and aesthetically complemented the larger college structures of its period situated just to the south.

Financed largely by the proceeds of the $300,000 James Bowdoin estate, the Bowdoin College Chapel (fig. 3-23) was conceived as the monumental, Romantic-era, centerpiece edifice of President William Allen's five-building row. It assumed its present form over a long and trying eleven-year period, from 1844 to 1855. Of unusual German Romanesque Revival eclectic styling and one of the earliest of its vernacular, the chapel has long been regarded by architectural historians and others as one of the country's most notable church structures of its time. In addition, it merits recognition along with the most outstanding higher educational facilities of pre–Civil War America. Yet the hesitation with which the Bowdoin Board of Trustees approached the construction project seems rather ironic in today's light. It was, without question, extremely ambitious and expensive

($46,800). Nevertheless, even before this was apparent, opposing factions of the board were forced to compromise so that the final design drawings could be accepted. In return for supporting the appointment of Henry Wadsworth Longfellow, a liberal Unitarian, as professor of languages at the conservative Congregational institution, the trustees unsympathetic to the chapel undertaking agreed to alter their views and back approval of the innovative plan.[36]

Inspired by this sanction, President Leonard Woods was able to pursue the dream of his youth—a structure that was inspired by the ecclesiastical architecture of the English colleges, subservient to the law of optics, "eloquently building itself into an expressive cross and lifting up its spires to heaven as accompaniments of prayers rising from the morning and evening, day and night." Beauty, freely expressed and divorced from utility, was the chief aim. Seeking an architect with knowledge of sophisticated European architecture, the college contracted with Richard Upjohn (1802–78) of New York City, highly regarded in the field of ecclesiastical design, who had helped inaugurate the Gothic Revival in America with Manhattan's famous Trinity Church (1833) and with other churches that followed.[37]

A reference to the need for a new religious structure appears in the official records of Bowdoin College as early as 1825, at which time "a chapel of brick" was considered. In 1834, the possibility of such a project was still under scrutiny:

The chapel [1805] is not what it used to be, and the Boards of Trustees and Overseers have no place in which they can conveniently meet to transact the business of the corporation—so as soon as the funds of the college will justify the measure, . . . a building [must be provided] for a chapel, sufficiently large for that object, & for the accommodation of the College & society libraries, the Gallery of Paintings, the meetings of the boards, and as many lecture and recitation rooms as can be had in it.[38]

The need for such a versatile, multipurpose facility continued to be expressed throughout the college community until authorization was given in 1842 for the collection of subscriptions, the purchase of building materials, the selection of an architect, and the drawing up of contracts. Finally, after Upjohn was officially hired, it took the trustees two more years to resolve "that the plan for the proposed Chapel drawn by Mr. Richard Upjohn be adopted, and that the building committee be authorized to proceed immediately to the erection of the same according to such a plan."

Fig. 3-23. Bowdoin College Chapel (1854–55), designed by Richard Upjohn. Photograph, c. 1969.

Delays occasioned by the lack of funding and certain design obstacles hindered the completion of the new edifice. But eventually the stone exterior was raised by New York workmen, and the interior finished in magnificent black walnut wood by Samuel Melcher III and his son Richard, and in May 1855 the chapel was finished and dedicated.[39]

The following lengthy but provocative description (1894) of the interior (fig. 3-24) of the Bowdoin College Chapel, as prepared by faculty member George T. Little, has on many past occasions been cited as invaluable documentation:

The main walls are equal in length to the height of the towers and shut off the nave, which forms the chapel proper, from the aisles. These, thus converted into separate rooms, together with the choir in the rear, make a home for the library. The transepts break the long reach of the low roof of the aisles and afford entrances and office rooms. It is the nave that especially illustrates the aesthetic views of President Woods. On passing through the vestibule, one finds himself in a broad aisle, on either side of which are five forms running lengthwise with three rows of seats, each behind and above the other. These are occupied by the students, the lower classes sitting nearer the entrance, while members of the

Fig. 3-24. Bowdoin College Chapel (1844–55), interior. Photograph, n.d. Courtesy of the George J. Mitchell Department of Special Collections and Archives, Bowdoin College Library, Brunswick, Maine.

faculty occupy seats between the forms, or on the platform which occupies the entire end of the room. High above the platform is the gallery which affords admission to the room lately used for the art collections. The entrance to it is so arranged that the large rose window in the east end pours a flood of light into the chapel in the morning. Directly opposite is the organ with a gallery for the choir, and a tasteful organ, the gift of a recent graduate and his wife. The woodwork, all of black walnut, has designs in relief in harmony with the architecture of the building [fig. 3-25]. The smooth walls rise nearly forty feet above the wainscoting before they are broken by the clerestory windows. This space is divided by decorative frescoing, into twelve large panels for as many paintings. On the north side are scenes from New Testament history, viz., the annunciation, the adoration of the magi, the baptism, the transfiguration, Peter and John healing the cripple, and Paul and Mars Hill. Opposite are St. Michael and the dragon, Adam and Eve, and Moses giving the law. The ceiling, which is open to the roof, is painted blue with golden stars.[40]

Chimes were installed in the southwest tower in 1924, and a complete organ console was introduced in 1927. Flags of the original thirteen colonies plus that of the State of Maine hung from poles projecting from the walls of the nave under an open-timbered pitched roof. With its 90-by-28-foot nave as the core of its English cruciform (or Latin cross) floor plan, the chapel broke with New England church tradition, but also served well its intended purposes.

To the rear of the chapel, the library, or Bannister Hall (fig. 3-26), as it was named, extended originally for the full width of the structure and contained octagonal piers on each side, supporting an arcade holding a clerestory wall at this location. The piers were painted marbleized yellow with black veins, and a section of the ceiling, apparently original, has small arabesques in the corners of the square panels. The whole effect was pointedly religious. Many contemporary observers, full of praise for the spacious chapel hall, overlooked the artistic attributes of the library and labeled it unsatisfactory in a functional sense. It was also said to lack sufficient study and shelf space, adequate light and ventilation, and an atmosphere conducive to academic activity. The painting gallery in the north wing and Overseers' Hall (for a time the home of the Maine Historical Society)

Fig. 3-25. Bowdoin College Chapel (1844–55). Interior rear wall elevation drawing, signed by "R. Upjohn, 64 Broadway, N.Y., 4 August 1851." Courtesy of the George J. Mitchell Department of Special Collections and Archives, Bowdoin College Library, Brunswick, Maine.

Fig. 3-26. Bowdoin College Chapel (1844–55). Interior of the College Library, Bannister Hall. Photograph, c. 1880. Courtesy of the George J. Mitchell Department of Special Collections and Archives, Bowdoin College Library, Brunswick, Maine.

above the library have generated more positive assessments over the years.[41] For most, the library's replacement in 1903 by a specialized building, Hubbard Hall, was extremely welcome. Today, continuing the tradition of early multipurpose buildings, this area contains faculty and administrative offices and a lecture room.

Constructed of gray, undressed Brunswick granite, the chapel was for a brief period named in honor of Governor William King in recognition of his bequest to Bowdoin. When King's estate proved insufficient to the commitment, his heirs asked that the name William King Chapel be dropped. The choice of German Romanesque styling for the building is regarded as most unusual, for as far as is known, Upjohn had not been to Germany before he was awarded this commission. In the estimate of his grandson and biographer, Everard M. Upjohn, it is quite probable, in view of the restricted detailing on the exterior, that he

took his cue from illustrated books. As shown in a rear view (fig. 3-27), the windows and doors possessed semicircular headings, with "a complete avoidance of even moldings to soften the austere lines." The windows in most instances are paired. Such round-headed openings, more versatile than the square-headed Georgian apertures, were hallmarks of the period, were found on all types of buildings, and were incorporated into other style vocabularies.

Primarily responsible for the German quality of the structure are the slender, 120-foot, steep-gabled twin towers with their four-sided spires, the lines and planes of which are marked by vertical rows of four narrow inset arched windows topped by gables with stepped corbels. These towers seem to compress the front facade into a tall, narrow mass and contribute to excellence in proportion. Yale art historian Carroll L. V. Meeks held that the towers' smooth shafts indicate southern Rhenish German in-

Fig. 3-27. Bowdoin College Chapel (1844–55), rear east-end view. Photograph, c. 1969.

fluence and that their possible reference was the Cathedral of Speyer, much abridged. The chapel edifice is not wholly medieval Romanesque in feeling and really looks like "a Gothic formula with slightly modified trimming." Upjohn was certainly not an all-out Lombard and was powerfully influenced, as evidenced by the Bowdoin plan, by his English background. An absence of lighter elements, coupled with cold, heavy stone walls, produces a foreboding impression, one quite out of harmony with the surrounding English-influenced New England environment. Nevertheless, despite this shortcoming, the library's modest failings, and the fact that interior function is largely determined by exterior artistic concerns, the facility as a whole has demonstrated its educational value for over a century and a half.[42] In the Bowdoin College Chapel, function is perhaps too much the servant of form. Yet the building conveys a sense of how, during the Romantic era, America's search for cultural significance was expressed architecturally. Like the mid-nineteenth-century revival-style buildings at Williams College, it presents an enlightening and intriguing contrast to the neighboring older, traditional classic structures of its formalized campus environment.[43]

THE VERMONT INSTITUTIONS

University of Vermont, Middlebury, and Norwich University

DESPITE THE PRESENCE of only a few buildings, the rich and all-encompassing legacy of pre–Civil War higher educational architecture and campus planning in Vermont merits our close, critical attention within the broader New England context. Traditional as well as innovative in form as well as function, the first structures at the University of Vermont, Middlebury College, and Norwich University all offer provocative responses to the challenges posed by early higher educational life and learning. At these three institutions, campus plans were centered on building rows following the precedent set at Yale in the eighteenth century.

The University of Vermont and Its Historic Main Buildings

The College Edifice and the Old Mill at the University of Vermont, Burlington, may be rightfully considered two of New England's most outstanding early-nineteenth-century higher educational structures.[1] The quality and importance of the first of these was recognized in 1806, when President Timothy Dwight of Yale visited Burlington on one of his many journeys throughout New England. During a brief visit to the university, the distinguished educational leader offered a provocative observation about the College Edifice (1801–7), the institution's first home: "The college is a copy of those at Princeton, Providence and Dartmouth, but is handsomer than either of them."[2] If, as Dwight suggested, this building indeed surpassed in excellence such outstanding early architectural monuments as Princeton's Nassau Hall (1754–56), Brown's University Hall (1770–71, etc.), and Dartmouth Hall (1784–91, etc.), then architectural historians to date have overlooked a structure of considerable merit and significance. Consequently, there has been little or no mention of it in published literature, and there exist only a small number of building images.

The fact that the College Edifice has received little attention (other than my 1972 published article in *Vermont History*; see note 1) may in part be a result of its loss to fire in 1824, and its replacement soon afterward on the same site by the venerable Old Mill (1825–29), in Victorian eclectic altered form most often associated today with the university's founding and early history.[3] Fortunately, by making use of views, published references, and manuscript sources, it is possible to relate the story of the creation of what clearly was a strikingly beautiful, discreetly conceived, and well-proportioned work of architecture. Plans for this structure can be traced to 1791, when the university's Board of Trustees, led by founder and benefactor Ira Allen, voted "to provide means for erecting as soon as may be a commodious building or buildings, for the reception and accommodation of Students, Officers and Servants."[4] A year later the trustees agreed that land just above the present College Green, on the hillside to the east of downtown Burlington, should be cleared, donations sought, and materials collected on the appointed spot.[5] Due to adverse local economic conditions, however, these steps were not undertaken successfully for nine years.

Finally, in 1800 the trustees acted under the inspiration of a $2,300 grant from the citizens of Burlington, and then officially authorized construction in spring 1801. By two separate resolutions, Mr. David Russell was designated as agent to initiate contracting, and Governor Isaac Tichenor as representative to procure and transmit a suitable plan.[6] On Tichenor's unexplained failure to provide an acceptable scheme, newly elected President Daniel Clarke Sanders banded together with Russell and another trustee, William C. Harrington, to complete this task and to get the actual building project under way. Ironically, when the final result was considered, the design proposals met with widespread trustee opposition; however, this resistance was quickly dissipated by persuasion from the president's committee.[7] During the spring and summer of 1801, once the forest was felled and the site prepared, the long-awaited building began to rise.[8]

In his written correspondence President Sanders described the slow but discernible progress of the College Edifice as it was erected:

In 1800, about 300,000 bricks were burned, and timber contracts made. Stone were drawn this winter in immense quantities. In the spring of 1801, the building was commenced in good earnest. . . . The President laid the first stone in the foundation, S.W. corner. Pine planks were laid at the bottom of the whole trench in order that the walls might settle equally. . . . The first year, it was carried up to the 3rd story. The work was renewed with the same persevering spirit in 1802; when the brick part was completed and the roof covered. It took one day to each story to lay the [supporting] timbers and five days to raise the roof and tower; all effected without one man being wounded. In 1803, 16 rooms, 8 at each end of the building, were completed, so that they were occupied in the season of 1804.[9]

It has been said that the president himself, a powerful and energetic man, participated in the project by personally cutting trees, laying bricks, and sharing in the direction of the job along with other members of the community.

In July 1805, the *Vermont Sentinel* reviewed the brief history of the university, discussed its financing, and described the College Edifice:

4 stories high; 45 feet wide at each end, 75 in the middle, formed by a projection of 15 feet in the front, 15 in the rear, 100 feet long [most sources say 160], built of [unpainted] brick, of durable materials and excellent workmanship.[10]

On the inside of the building, a chapel, a philosophical room, two society halls, a medical hall, a library, a mineral museum, a recitation hall, and forty-six rooms for students were fitted out as quickly as funds, weather conditions, and labor supply permitted. On all four floors of the cruciform plan, rough unplaned corridors ran the entire length of the edifice on a north-south line and on an intersecting east-west line as well, undoubtedly creating the same space-consuming layout as existed in its predecessor, Dartmouth Hall (see fig. 2-21).[11] Despite this shortcoming, the overall interior design seems to have been extremely well received by the faculty and students. Virtually all functions of the university were combined under one roof. Such a design philosophy is evident in nearly all American college architecture dating from the colonial or early national periods, and it has had an influential impact on higher educational planning ever since.[12]

By the middle of 1805, the College Edifice was still unfinished. At that time, Captain Daniel Hurlburt of Burlington was contracted by the trustees to complete the work project.[13] Following commencement exercises on Friday, 23 August, the *Vermont Sentinel* was able to announce that "the chapel of the spacious College Edifice being completed, was on Sunday evening preceding Commencement, solemnly consecrated."[14] After another year passed, President Sanders, in a letter to Reverend Leonard Worcester of Peacham, Vermont, could proudly proclaim:

The College Edifice is nearly glazed. The [40-foot] tower is finished and painted on the dome. The vane and the lightening rod are up. The bell proves a good one. The masons are at work, and all the [twelve] chimneys will probably be finished before Commencement. The 16 end-rooms are completed; and more are

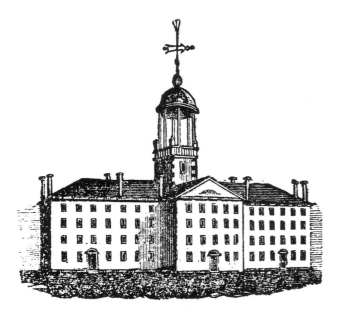

Original University Building.

Fig. 4-1. The College Edifice (1801–7), University of Vermont. Woodcut engraving from Zadock Thompson, *History of Vermont, Natural, Civil and Statistical* (1842), p. 144. Courtesy of Special Collections, University of Vermont Libraries.

nearly ready for lathing and plastering. All parts of the work progress well, and all in a way to be soon finished.[15]

According to historian Zadock Thompson, the total costs approached $35,000, an astoundingly large sum for a structure of its type, size, and time.[16] Of course it is possible that this figure represents an error, or a cumulative amount including furnishings and building repairs over many years. It can be safely assumed, nonetheless, that the expense is indicative of the quality and quantity of craftsmanship that went into the College Edifice. It also reflects the strong sense of commitment by local subscribers who struggled to meet their obligations by means of cash payments, land sales, and gifts of cattle, produce, and building materials.

We are fortunate today to have ready access to a small number of excellent early views of the University of Vermont's stately original headquarters. Perhaps the most valuable of these is an informal woodcut engraving (fig. 4-1) published in Zadock Thompson's *History of Vermont, Natural, Civil and Statistical* (1842).[17] Though a somewhat misleading representation, with the seemingly oversized central tower, this view distinctly reveals effective detail-

ing, including round-arched doorways with fanlights; a boxed and pedimented front pavilion gable with segmental-arched window; a long hipped roof broken by vertical chimney accents; and the tower, topped by a dome with massive weathervane and incorporating an open belfry with balustrade set on a cubical base displaying corner quoins. A small reverse painted view on a Lemuel Curtis banjo clock in the collections of the university's Fleming Museum captures most of these same features, though with less accuracy, and adds surrounding Lombard poplar trees and a front wooden fence that was destroyed by mischievous students in 1808. Another quite intriguing illustration appears on an 1806 commencement ball ticket (fig. 4-2), copies of which are preserved in the university library's Special Collections and Archives. Although some style details are absent because of the center oblong cutout, most of the features exhibited in other views are repeated, and the structure's proper scale is conveyed. To be sure, an examination of different views reveals certain discrepancies, but a sufficiently accurate impression is established for making critical assessments.[18]

For additional insight about the general configuration of the College Edifice we may turn to comparable earlier extant models in New England, such as Dartmouth Hall (see fig. 2-21), Brown's University Hall (see fig. 2-3), and Harvard's Hollis Hall (see fig. 1-8). Pronounced similarities appear in the general outlines and in such details as the central projecting bays with pediments, three front-facade entranceways, hipped roofs, tall brick chimneys, and, with

Fig. 4-2. The College Edifice (1801–7), University of Vermont. Engraved view on 1806 Commencement ticket. Courtesy of Special Collections, University of Vermont Libraries.

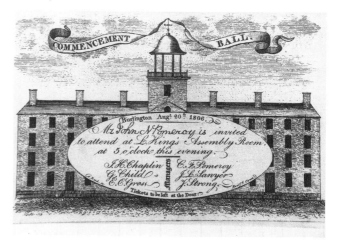

the exception of Hollis, Georgian cupolas. Starting with the Nassau Hall precedent at Princeton, there seems to be little question that institutional building planners were influenced by design projects that preceded their own. The end result in Burlington was a reasonably homogeneous and integral structure displaying most of the best qualities of its forerunners.

As to the architect of the College Edifice, it is possible to offer a certain attribution. It is evident from President Sanders's papers that Abraham Bethrong was the "Chief Mason," but it may be assumed that this same individual, because of his area of specialization, was unlikely to have prepared the designs. In these same papers John Johnson (1771–1842) of Essex, Vermont, is identified as "Carpenter."[19] Another source, based on the written recollections of Charles Adams, Class of 1804, specifically refers to Johnson as "architect" as well as "practical builder."[20] His association with the project is also validated in a 1922 *Burlington Free Press* article that describes his role in a local professional organization, "The Architectural Society in the County of Chittenden," and credits him with the design of the dome. Additional, irrefutable evidence further supporting the attribution is a contract between Johnson and the university dated 18 August 1801 and contained in the Johnson Papers at the university's library.[21] Chiefly known for his land-surveying activity (he served as surveyor-general of Vermont, 1813–28 and 1832–38), Johnson was also well respected as a planner and contractor of bridges, dams, forges, and all types of mills, many examples of which were located in northern Vermont and New York State.[22] It is quite evident that Johnson's mathematical and engineering skills contributed significantly to his design of the university's first monumental main building. An examination of the original version of the Old Mill, the successor to the College Edifice and a documented Johnson building, reveals the same crisp purity and simplicity in aesthetic appearance, as well as excellence in structural planning.

The premature demise of the College Edifice was brought about by two unfortunate episodes. During the War of 1812, soldiers and arms belonging to the U.S. Army were deposited there without the consent of the university trustees or faculty. In 1814, the building was formally rented to the army as an arsenal and barracks, but only under the threat of forcible possession if the trustees did not agree to the arrangement. Consequently, the regular course of instruction was suspended for a year, at which time the structure was

evacuated and repaired at a cost of $4,500. Damage, however, had been excessive and lasting. The final tragedy occurred on 27 May 1824, when this fine multiusage facility was reduced to ashes by fire, caused accidentally by sparks falling on the roof from one of the tall chimneys.[23] Thus one cannot personally experience the College Edifice as Timothy Dwight had the pleasure of doing in 1806, but we can still admire other older American college buildings to which John Johnson's creation was so favorably compared. Without exception, these examples, like the College Edifice, were forceful, symbolic representations of their respective institutions — honest, uncomplicated, and versatile architectural statements reflecting an unpretentious yet productive and resourceful early American society.

The successor to the College Edifice, the Old Mill, built on the same site between 1825 and 1829, is the University of Vermont's oldest surviving building. Hidden behind its deceiving Victorian eclectic outer brick shell is the substance of a structure dating back a century and a half, to the institution's formative years. Few people who visit the campus today and walk along University Place on the College Green are aware of the age, design, and construction of this complex, or of its original function and appearance. Attired in the garb of the region's traditional Federal-style architecture and surmounted by a magnificent dome, the Old Mill — in a form very different from what one may currently see — dominated the center of Burlington for over fifty years, from its elevated location on the ridge to the east. Even after it was subjected to radical alterations in 1882–83, it retained its stately and imposing physical presence, as well as its prominence as an early functioning example of American multipurpose higher educational architecture. Despite major renovation, it did not lose its significance as the first instance of architectural master planning implemented for a northern New England college or university.

Planning for the Old Mill was brief and efficient. On 1 June 1824, five days after the College Edifice was lost to fire, the university trustees, united in purpose by the emergency, gathered in Burlington and called for plans for a complex of buildings to replace the initial edifice:

Resolved: As the Sense of the Corporation, we deeply feel that calamity which has befallen us, . . . but seriously impressed with the importance of public instruction, and [having] perfect confidence in the spirit and liberality of the citizens of this, and the neighboring towns, and of the State, consider it important that measures should be immediately taken to erect suitable buildings, and to raise the necessary funds for that purpose, and that a committee of seven be appointed to prepare an address to the public, and to make all the necessary arrangements, to solicit and raise subscriptions for that purpose.[24]

On this occasion President Nathan B. Haskell and the faculty were asked "to report a plan for a College Building at the next Commencement," and the university building inspector was requested "to take all the necessary care of the materials for the College" in readiness for the new construction.[25]

In response to the trustees' pleas for aid, the residents of Burlington and vicinity came to the assistance of the financially starved institution and, during the summer after the fire, pledged the generous sum of over $8,000 toward the rebuilding effort.[26] To disburse these funds and to initiate construction, the trustees appointed two friends of the university, Luther Loomis and George Moore, as project superintendents.[27] In lieu of tuition for his sons, Jonathan Ferris returned lands once part of the original university tract, a gracious gesture that made it possible for the trustees to consider a larger physical plant than the institution had possessed before the College Edifice burned.[28] Within three months, plans for the new complex were approved and the contracts for construction of the university's second home were awarded.

For a long time it was not known whom the trustees had selected as architect and contractor for the new buildings, though it had often been speculated that John Johnson, the designer and master builder of the College Edifice,[29] was the logical choice for the commission. Verification of Johnson's association with the Old Mill construction project came in the late 1970s, when the university's Bailey/Howe Library acquired over five hundred of Johnson's survey sheets, engineering drawings, sketches, maps, business papers, and architectural plans. Contained in this manuscript treasure trove, the record of Johnson's distinguished career as civil engineer, surveyor, architect, and public official,[30] were plan sheets for portions of the original Old Mill. This exciting discovery eliminated for all time any doubt that Johnson was the trustees' choice to complete another building project for the university.

The task facing Johnson and his subordinates was lengthy and fatiguing and began with still-sobering memories of the 1824 fire. Professor George W. Benedict later described what he remembered about May 1825, the beginning of his faculty appointment at the university: "The ruins of the fire had been cleared away, but not a building was to be seen—only preparation for the north part of the present structure. Its foundations had been laid only a few days before."[31] Literally, the only physical evidence of the university that existed on Benedict's arrival in Burlington was the old foundation, a few baskets of books, and philosophical apparatus in a nearby storehouse. But work proceeded apace, and within another month the foundations for the north end of the complex were in place. Blessed with this good timing and seizing on a fortuitous opportunity, university officials persuaded the Marquis de Lafayette, then touring the United States, to lay the cornerstone. This he did with much pomp and ceremony on 29 June 1825, thereby setting a tone of optimism for the university as it rose again, both physically and figuratively, from the ruins of the College Edifice.[32]

Largely as a fire prevention measure, three unconnected brick-walled and tin-roofed sections, conceived by Johnson to look like a single building, were erected separately, with gaps of approximately seven feet. What was in reality a symmetrical three-building row scheme was without doubt inspired by the oldest portion of the Old Brick Row at Yale (see fig. 1-31): the central structure, its gable end forward, was flanked on either side by rectangular block buildings with their longitudinal axes at right angles. A scaled schematic wall plan (fig. 4-3) for the Vermont complex from the Johnson Papers shows the three components placed in harmonious relationship with each other, as had been done first at Yale. Despite poor communications and travel connections, ideas passed readily between the New England colleges; President Haskell, a Yale graduate (Class of 1802), surely recalled Yale's appearance and very likely played a role in determining the configuration of the Old Mill.

In an 1837 issue, the *American Magazine of Useful Knowledge* published a front-elevation view (fig. 4-4) of the "Old Mill" as it appeared after the first stage of its construction. Even the wooden fence, main entrance gate, and turnstile, the gift of the Class of 1837, are present. This printed view illustrates the remarkable similarity between this work of architecture and the textile mills erected during the same era in Waltham, Lowell, Manchester, and other New England industrial cities and towns. Given this fact, as well as Johnson's experience as a designer and builder of factory struc-

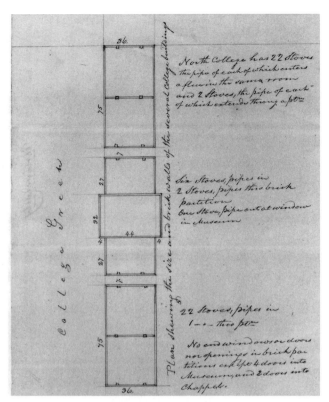

Fig. 4-3. Foundation wall plan for the Old Mill (1825–29), University of Vermont. Courtesy of Special Collections, University of Vermont Libraries.

Fig. 4-4. The Old Mill (1825–29), University of Vermont. Woodcut engraving from *The American Magazine of Useful Knowledge* 3 (1837), p. 273. Courtesy of Special Collections, University of Vermont Libraries.

tures in Vermont, it should be no mystery why the Old Mill received its popular name early in its history.

The two rectangular wings, long referred to as North College and South College, were completed by August 1826. Each was three stories tall, 75 by 36 feet, and protected by a moderately pitched roof. Six slender brick chimneys protruded above each of the two roofs. Bricks salvaged from the remains of the College Edifice were reused in the new complex, which limited total expenses to about $10,000. Each wing contained twenty-four rooms, most of which were used for student housing, and was divided into two entryways by an inner partition wall, a system employed widely in early collegiate residence hall design in the United States. There were no halls running lengthwise in either building. Each separate entryway had its own entrance and central stairwell, which proved inconvenient for students and faculty, who were forced to go outdoors to pass from one to the other.[33] Twelve rooms were present in each of the four entries, with four rooms per story, a pattern fairly common in dormitory structures of the period. The Old Mill could accommodate nearly one hundred students, a number that increased after renovations in the early 1860s. During the 1830s the space not used for housing on the lower floor of South College was taken over by the chemistry department for a laboratory, lecture hall, and assaying rooms.[34]

At their January and August meetings in 1828 the trustees resolved to proceed with the erection of the main or central section of the Old Mill, to be known, appropriately, as Middle College.[35] With Burlington's Osias Buel serving Johnson as principal contractor,[36] $9,000 more, generated through subscriptions, was expended to complete the third and final unit, and hence the entire complex, by the end of 1829. As the aesthetic focal point for the Old Mill, as well as the functional locus of all university affairs, Middle College was notably successful. A beautifully rendered elevation drawing (fig. 4-5) by Johnson provides the best extant representation of this handsome and well-proportioned structure. Three stories high, 36 feet wide at its ends (the same as North and South colleges), and 86 feet long, with gabled two-story pavilion projections in both the front and the rear, it was capped by a large rounded dome (with an open cupola above), "whose glistening surface formed a notable beacon for the whole [Lake Champlain] valley above where it stood." Charles Bulfinch–inspired blind arcades defined the arched windows in each pavilion wall surface.

The great tin-roofed dome, for which some sources

Fig. 4-5. Middle College (1828–29), Old Mill, University of Vermont. Front-elevation drawing by architect John Johnson. Courtesy of Special Collections, University of Vermont Libraries.

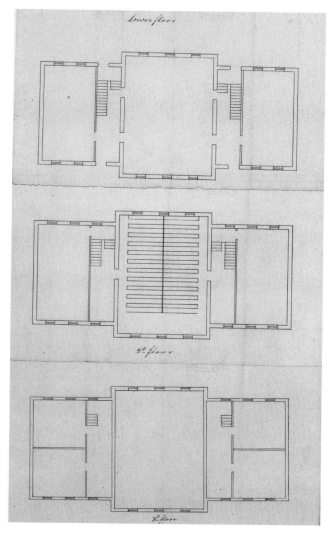

Fig. 4-6. Middle College (1828–29), Old Mill, University of Vermont. "Lower Floor, 2nd Floor, and 3rd Floor Plans" by architect John Johnson. Courtesy of Special Collections, University of Vermont Libraries.

suggest Professor Benedict prepared the working plans (although the form and structural work were probably conceived by Johnson),[37] was not only the primary visual attraction for the Old Mill and the symbol of all university interests, but also served as a superior observation tower with breathtaking views of the Green Mountains to the east and Lake Champlain and the Adirondack Mountains to the west. Its dark windowless interior, which students called the Black Hole, was used for the study of astronomy, as well for occasional secret society initiations, according to university lore. But, most significantly, it was the dome that lent a proper architectural scale and organization to what, lacking its presence, would have been an overly elongated and awkward block.[38]

Fortunately, the Johnson collection contains plans (fig. 4-6) for all three floors of Middle College. These docu-

ments plus written descriptions of the interior indicate that there were two (some sources say four) recitation rooms on the north and south ends of the ground floor, with a museum in the two-story central pavilion. Above the museum on the second floor of the pavilion was the old chapel, illuminated by three lovely, tall round-arched windows. Facing the edifice to the left on this floor was the library (until 1863), and to the right a room for lectures in natural philosophy. On the third floor, on either side of the pavilion chapel, were two rooms assigned to the rival debating societies—the Phi Sigma Nu and the University Institute—for their meetings and library collections.[39] Such a floor scheme allowed for an effective blending of instructional, religious, and extracurricular facilities and expressed well the prevailing American educational philosophy of the day, encouraging the combination of all facets of college/uni-

Fig. 4-7. The Old Mill (1825–29, 1846–48), University of Vermont. Photograph, c. 1875. Courtesy of Special Collections, University of Vermont Libraries.

versity life in single main buildings or closely integrated building groups.

Since it was first raised, the Old Mill has undergone two renovations—the first not inconsequential and actually quite flattering, and the second broad, sweeping, and somewhat controversial. In 1846 the end walls of North and South colleges were raised above the roof cornice lines, and the paired end chimneys were joined in brick, much in the fashion of a Boston townhouse or industrial community housing block of the same time. Simultaneously, North, Middle, and South colleges were united to form a single 250-foot-long building. A c. 1875 photograph (fig. 4-7) from the university library's archives shows the Old Mill in its revised state, with the two gaps that had formerly separated the units replaced by welcome additional interior space. Two years later, alterations were completed when the original tin roof was replaced by one of Welsh slate.[40] In 1861–64, repairs were made to the north and south wings, the chapel was enlarged, and, through subdivision, additional rooms were provided for students. However, the monu-

mental, strongly horizontal mass, anchored by the great central dome, remained unchanged on the exterior.[41]

The building complex continued in this state—a serviceable, crisply delineated, and well-detailed expression of New England's Federal-era architecture—until 1882, when John P. Howard, a wealthy philanthropist and generous university benefactor, donated $50,000 to subsidize a total internal and external modernization of the edifice. Such efforts to "improve" or "upgrade" plain and traditional examples of pre–Civil War buildings were common on American college and university campuses during the Victorian era. Based largely on reconstruction plans supplied by J. J. R. Randall of Rutland, greater height was given to each story, and the ends and the center pavilion were raised and brought forward by the addition of new frontal pavilion projections, resulting in a depth at the center of 65 feet and at the end of 42 feet. A fourth attic story was created at the ends of what were once North and South colleges. Formerly blank walls on either end of the building were furnished with narrow, raised central pavilions and pierced by new window and door apertures. In terms of architectural style, the renovated Old Mill was given both Gothic Revival and Romanesque Revival features (the resulting combination was commonly called "U.S. Grant–type architecture") by the use of high projecting gables and steep-pitched roofs (including dormers), rounded and segmental recessed window and door arches, recessed wall panels and blind arcades, false buttresses, and a tall central pointed spire (its gilded finial 150 feet above ground level) incorporating an elaborately detailed closed belfry. It is this greatly transformed version (figs. 4-8 and 4-9) of John Johnson's original Old Mill that we may see on the university campus today, comfortably situated south of Williams Science Hall (1896) and Henry Hobson Richardson's Billings Student Center (1886), formerly the library, both distinctively Romanesque Revival stylistic interpretations. On 26 June 1883, as part of the commencement program, the cornerstone initially laid by Lafayette in the southeast corner of South College was repositioned on the southwest corner of the center pavilion, thereby signaling completion of the massive project.[42]

The interior of the Old Mill may have been functionally enhanced, though there is only fragmentary evidence to suggest that this was actually the case. A sufficient number of changes, however, further moved the building toward the preponderantly academic uses that it accommodates today. The chapel and the principal lecture rooms were made larger, administrative offices expanded, and the museum converted to a drill hall and gymnasium. A modern chemistry laboratory was installed and, through the addition of the extra attic story, the number of student rooms increased from forty to sixty. These attic rooms remained in use until 1918, when a fire caused by a lightning strike prompted further renovations: the attic story was closed, the dormer windows largely removed, and most dormitory rooms eliminated, all but negating the multipurpose nature of the Old Mill as envisioned by its first planners. As a result of twentieth-century modifications and modernization (including the addition of a contemporary-style ell connector to Lafayette Hall to the rear), the complex is currently devoted to classrooms and to administrative and faculty offices for the arts and science departments.[43]

Perhaps the most controversial result of the 1882–83 reconstruction was the removal of the dome, made necessary by the increased elevation of the altered building. This resulted in mass protests from alumni, for whom the uni-

Fig. 4-8. The Old Mill (1825–29, 1846–48, 1882–83, 1918, etc.), west main facade, University of Vermont. Photograph, 2008.

Fig. 4-9. The Old Mill (1825–29, 1846–48, 1882–83, 1918, etc.), south end and east rear walls, University of Vermont. Photograph, 1988.

versity seemed to lose its physical identity when the new square tower with spire roof was erected. Many ridiculed this replacement (from which the view in all directions was still outstanding), referring to it as a "bird-cage" and harshly criticizing President Matthew H. Buckham and the trustees for their decision to accept the terms of the Howard gift. In architectural as well as engineering terms, however, had the dome been retained, it would have been in direct conflict with the proportions and embellishment of the building as we know it today. Perhaps in some ways, as alumnus Joseph Lawrence Hills argued, "the face lifting of the mid-eighties was faulty"; nonetheless, the University of Vermont is today blessed with a structure that, with other distinguished nearby campus buildings, accurately and imaginatively reflects the aesthetic preferences and values of American Victorian culture. In the modern era the Old Mill has remained at the center of campus life and an important physical manifestation of the university's long and eventful history.[44]

The Old Stone Row at Middlebury College

The legendary Old Stone Row at Middlebury College, Middlebury, is renowned in the architectural repertoire of New England higher education for its aesthetic virtues, unusual solid granite-block construction, and scenic location on a slight wooded rise just to the west of the village center and Otter Creek. For the first sixteen years of its history, however, the college, chartered by the Vermont legislature in November 1800, was housed in another building formerly located at the junction of South Main and Center streets below and east of the future campus site. It had its origins with the local townspeople, who petitioned the legislature in November 1797 for the authority to erect a structure to house the new Addison County Grammar School and the anticipated higher educational institution. With subscription proceeds from Middlebury and surrounding communities, a rectangular-shaped wooden edifice, to be known as the Academy and ultimately as East College, was raised in 1797–98 for approximately $1,000 on a sizable fenced plot deeded to the corporation by villager Seth Storrs.[45]

Fig. 4-10. East College (1797–98), Middlebury College. Sketch, n.d. Courtesy of the Henry Sheldon Museum of Vermont History, Middlebury.

Two surviving sketches prepared by Middlebury College students in the mid-1800s offer valuable insight as to the original external appearance of East College. The most detailed of these, in the manuscript collections of the town's Sheldon Museum, provides particularly vital documentation (fig. 4-10).[46] This attractive view depicts a tasteful and nicely proportioned building, three stories high, set on stone foundations, 80 feet long and 40 feet wide. Atop the timber-frame block covered with white-painted clapboards was a low hipped roof, punctured at its four corners by brick chimneys, and surmounted at its center by an unostentatious open hexagonal cupola containing a large bell. The structure possessed east and west entries, a circumstance that quite defied anyone from being able to tell which was the front and which the rear![47] Style details were restrained but included a plain cornice embellished with dentil molding along the eaves, suggestions of corner pilasters, and a small pitched-roof porch with narrow round support columns protecting the front doorway. Perhaps the most noticeable feature of the building, however, was the great number of windows on all four walls. This fact was noticed by college historian W. Storrs Lee, who observed in his 1936 institutional history that the planners were obviously "obsessed with letting more than one kind of light into the school."[48]

Originally, the interior of East College was configured to meet all the assorted requirements of a secondary school as well as a college. Although the exact sizes and locations of the rooms are unknown, it is evident from written descriptions that the first floor contained classrooms, a laboratory, and a library; the second, dormitory rooms with space for two to three students per room; and the third, additional dormitory rooms around a central chapel.[49] Student rooms were unfurnished, and the residents had to supply their own beds, bedding, desks, chairs, and chests and a bucket for the water pump outside the west entrance. On the completion of the college's next building, Painter Hall, in 1816, all living areas were converted to academic uses. Additional changes occurred on the opening of Old Chapel in 1836, at which time interior renovations were made, the chapel was shifted to the Old Stone Row structure, and all other space was returned to residential purposes.[50] Originally known to many as the Addison County Grammar School, the building shed that appellation after 1805 when the grade school moved to other quarters in the town.[51] Finally, a victim of its economical construction, East College was abandoned by the college in 1864 and demolished, and the land was taken over for a new local graded-school building in 1867.[52] Its seventy-year presence, however, established a pattern of refined, functional architecture that Old Stone Row and subsequent Middlebury campus structures have creatively adopted.

One who visits the hillside campus of Middlebury College today can only be impressed by the Old Stone Row, a balanced trio of structures erected between 1814 and 1836. Hamilton Child's *Gazetteer . . . of Addison County, Vermont for 1881–82* contains a highly accurate steel-plate-engraving view of how it looked before subsequent minor face-lifts and internal rearrangements over the next century (fig. 4-11). We cannot be certain about the origins of its planning, but the concept behind the scheme probably originated with Yale's highly influential Old Brick Row. In fact, it may have directly resulted from the well-publicized visit of Yale president Timothy Dwight to the then-remote rural institution in 1811, only a few years before the construction of the first row building. With Painter Hall (1814–16) flanking Old Chapel (1835–36) to the north, and Starr Hall (1859–61 and 1865) to the south, the arrangement faces eastward to the Green Mountains and presents the onlooker with a superb, homogeneous architectural impression. The parklike campus potential initiated at Middlebury by the creation of the Old Stone Row and adjacent buildings has long been regarded as a particularly outstanding example of the adaptation of natural beauty to challenges of higher educational campus planning.[53]

The row's first structure, and the oldest college/university structure still in use in Vermont, is Painter Hall (or "West College," as it was originally titled), constructed of gray granular limestone in 1814–16. It had its origins, however, in 1810, a full six years before its completion. Soon after Henry Davis was inaugurated as president of the college, the corporation began to feel the need for a new building for the housing of students and other needs to supplement East College.[54] On 1 October, the Middlebury trustees, after a dispute over the site, voted "to erect a new college edifice on the ground lately conveyed to the President and Fellows of Middlebury College by Col. Seth Storrs."[55] Located behind East College, this thirty-acre parcel of land covered what was appropriately called Storrs Hill, the core of the modern Middlebury campus. It was agreed that the new edifice would be situated in the northeast corner of the tract, with an easterly orientation.[56] Toward the building goal, the cit-

Fig. 4-11. Old Stone Row, Middlebury College. Left, Starr Hall (1859–61; 1864–65); center, Old Chapel (1835–36); right, Painter Hall (1814–16). Engraving from Hamilton Child, *Gazetteer and Business Directory of Addison County, Vermont for 1881–82*, opposite p. 35. Courtesy of College Archives, Special Collections, Middlebury College, Middlebury, Vt.

izens of the town subscribed $8,000,[57] a sum that went a far way toward meeting the $15,200 in total contracting expenses. In 1814, contributions of local stone, lumber, nails, glass, and roofing materials were collected on the selected site, and the skeleton of what would become a new multi-purpose dormitory slowly began to form.[58]

Sturdy in appearance, practical, and master of its surroundings, Painter Hall (fig. 4-12), under the supervision of trustee Rufus Wainwright, was raised four stories high on block granite foundations measuring 106 by 40 feet. Flat townhouse-type end walls with no window or door apertures bound the mill-like structure, and virtually no stylistic elements were present. As completed in 1816, it contained thirty-six rooms for student housing, a 1,500-volume library, and academic offices in three separate entryways.[59] Yale president Timothy Dwight's 1811 visit to Middlebury may well have been influential in determining the internal floor layouts of the building. Arranged in the fashion of Yale's Old Brick Row dormitories, each of Painter's entries was subdivided into sixteen rooms arranged around a central stairway core. As first conceived, each room had its own fireplace for heating, which accounts for the eight large chimneys that still rise impressively above the building's slightly pitched roof. College and personal records indicate that Gamaliel Painter (for whom the building was later named)—town leader, successful businessman, and college fellow—was charged with the supervision of con-

Fig. 4-12. Painter Hall (1814–16), Old Stone Row, Middlebury College. Photograph, 2008.

struction, and he may well have been responsible for the preparation of designs to the extent that formal plans were used.[60] But whatever the nature of the specifications, the architectural outcome has been a unified aesthetic and functional asset to the college.

In the same manner as its predominantly dormitory counterparts at other institutions, Painter Hall has met nonresidential demands and has undergone substantial renovation during its long lifetime. Just before the Civil War, the two upper floors of the south entry were transformed into a gymnasium where ropes, rings, parallel bars, rowing machines, and exercise pulleys were utilized for physical fitness.[61] By 1900 the structure had been deprived of all student living quarters; a reading room had been installed in the south entry, and an expanded library in the north. Soon afterward, however, the gym was removed, and the transition back to dormitory usage commenced. In 1936 Painter became almost entirely residential again when it was completely stripped down to its bare exterior walls. Even its old heavy support timbers were disassembled and removed, and modern steel and masonry were introduced to guarantee structural soundness. New corridors were installed linking the three entryways, but the bearing-wall chimneys were preserved. A suggestion of the classical revival was introduced by the addition of three handsome entrance porches with round Doric support columns sup-

porting closed pediments on the front facade, a change that is both visually and functionally successful.[62] These and more recent alterations have both prolonged Painter's educational relevance and sustained its highly positive architectural impact.

The central edifice of Middlebury College's Old Stone Row, Old Chapel (1835–36; fig. 4-13) is a quite imposing, nicely proportioned work of transitional architecture. While it exudes the formal simplicity and delicacy of earlier decades, it also displays the aesthetics of the mid-stage Greek Revival, whose bold forms and open interiors nearly created a nineteenth-century national style. Exhibiting Greek-inspired detailing in its cupola, it adapts the traditionally tall New England meetinghouse massing to the pitched-roof Greek temple building mass. Composed of rough gray granular limestone (like Painter Hall), red-clay brick, and hardwood framing and boarding, Old Chapel accurately reflects the unpredictable climate, rugged terrain, geographical remoteness, and economic limitations of the nineteenth-century western Vermont farm country of which it was a part. With one of its narrow pedimented ends forward in characteristic Greek fashion, it continues to act as the principal ordering point for the modern Middlebury campus.

A full five years before the completion of Old Chapel, steps were taken to provide Middlebury with a long-needed

Fig. 4-13. Old Chapel (1835–36), Old Stone Row, Middlebury College. Photograph, 2008.

general-use facility comparable to those at the University of Vermont, Dartmouth, and other New England institutions at the time. On 18 August 1831, President Joshua Bates and the Fellows of Middlebury College assembled together and resolved:

That the President and the three Professors of the College be a committee to make inquiry and report . . . as to a plan of a Building for a chapel and public rooms which in the opinion it may be expedient to adopt and ascertain and report whether funds can be raised for the erection of such a Building and to take such steps to procure funds for that purpose as they may deem proper.[63]

Sufficiently organized by 1833, the designated committee conducted an ambitious and successful subscription drive. Trips undertaken to Boston, New York, and other locations produced a level of generosity unprecedented in the college's history. Instead of the usual farm produce and building materials, committee members netted $30,000 in cash, half of which was earmarked for the pending construction project.[64] Encouraged by this pleasant development, and oblivious to the national economic chaos just ahead, the trustees met again and drafted and approved the following motion:

that in consideration of the Present State of the College, and the increased numbers of students and the demand for greater accommodations for students this corporation deem it to be their duty

to proceed immediately to the erection of an additional building for a chapel with suitable public rooms.[65]

In 1835, the noises of construction once more echoed across the sylvan hillside campus. By the following summer, Old Chapel stood silent and inactive as college officials finished preparing it for a demanding lifetime of varied educational service.

Available documentary sources indicate that President Joshua Bates himself acted as the principal instigator and designer of the building. The story behind this revelation is quite fascinating. In 1939, photostatic copies of a letter and plan, which had made their way westward at some point, were presented to Middlebury's special collections by the director of the William L. Clements Library at the University of Michigan. Dated 1 September 1834, these two items were sent by Bates to his Harvard College classmate of 1800, Loammi Baldwin, Jr. (1780–1838), of Charlestown, Massachusetts. Renowned for his ambitious canal, harbor, dam, and railroad planning, Baldwin is regarded by many as the father of American civil engineering. Having designed Holworthy Hall (1811–12) at Harvard, he also had experience with academic building. Unfortunately, a reply to Bates's letter has yet to be found, so it is not known to what degree Baldwin may have influenced the Old Chapel planning process. In the text of his letter, Bates refers to the plan as

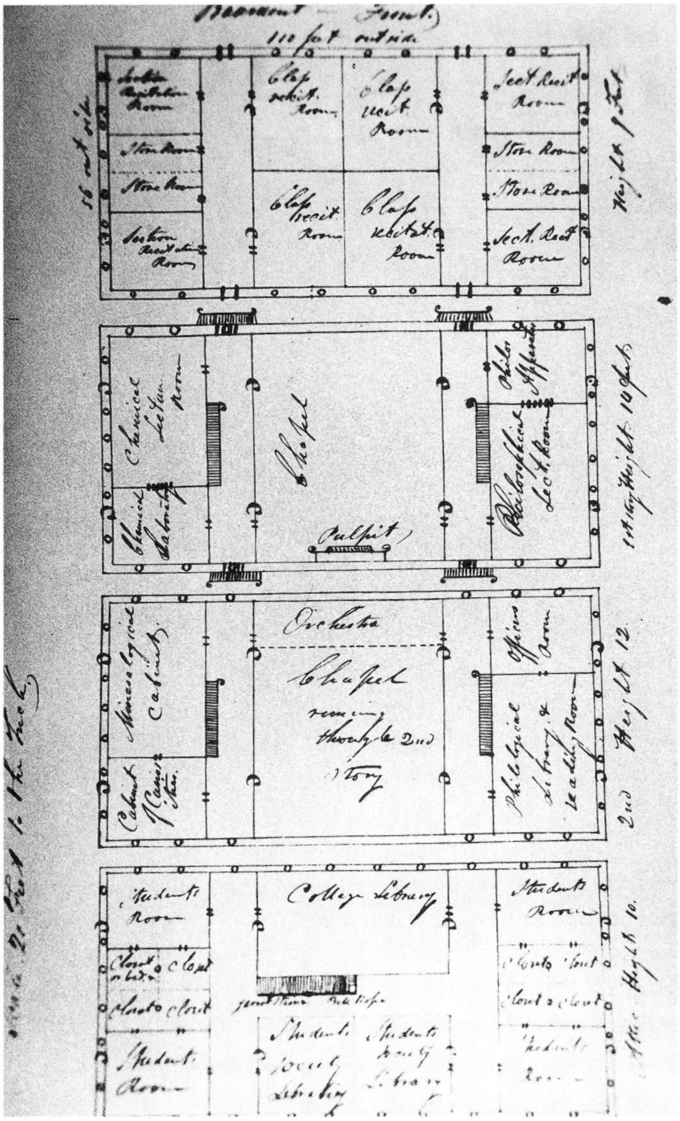

Fig. 4-14. Old Chapel (1835–36), Old Stone Row, Middlebury College. Sketch floor plans (1834) attributed to Joshua Bates. Courtesy of the William L. Clements Library, University of Michigan, Ann Arbor.

framing system offers at least one hint that Baldwin may indeed have responded to the president's inquiries.

Although they were somewhat altered in the final plan for Old Chapel, Bates's floor layouts provided a model from which contractors were able to work. Under the direction of local entrepreneur Ira Stewart,[68] two library rooms and a mineralogical museum were placed on the first floor, and class and lecture rooms on the second. With a long balcony on the south side, the chapel rose two stories from the third floor. The president's office and small faculty offices occupied the remaining space on the third and fourth floors.[69] High above in the front-tower belfry was a modest astronomical observatory. It is obvious that the Bates plan was far more ambitious than the final interior arrangement, as certain student rooms, laboratories, and other spaces that he had hoped for apparently could not be squeezed into the new building along with everything else. His scheme does reveal, however, the continuing importance then attributed to the integration or consolidation of all of the college's educational functions within a single building unit. This heritage of varied utility remained unbroken until a total interior remodeling in 1941, when Old Chapel became the college's administrative center, like other structures of its period and building type elsewhere, housing the offices of the president, vice presidents, deans, and financial staff. The multiuse tradition has been continued, however, by the presence of two large seminar rooms for academic purposes.[70]

As one views Old Chapel in the current era, it is impossible not to be impressed by its solidity, its conservative, strongly stated style details, and its blockish form, which recalls the largely bygone New England textile mills. Its 75-by-55-foot outer shell rises majestically some 50 feet above ground level.[71] Two rectangular frontal entrances, one above the other, penetrate the thick square stone projecting tower facade, the lower almost hidden within the base of a graceful double stairway, unusual for this period in the region. A simple round aperture containing a clock may be observed at the top of the stone tower. Above this is a striking three-stage, white-painted wooden upper section, the top portion a graceful octagonal cupola contained within a square balustrade, capped by a dome with weather vane, and containing a bell that for generations has sounded across the campus to mark college events. Though Georgian in style, the cupola displays Roman Doric pilasters and architrave bands, nineteenth-century additives to

"his own" and asks a series of questions that indicate not only his knowledge of structural design but also his wariness in taking on such a large building project.[66] It seems, though, that the president was being unduly humble when he stated, "I have no skill as an artist, and not much taste in architecture."[67] The floor-plan sketches (fig. 4-14) reveal in tangible form Bates's true skill, if not as an exemplar of style, then at least as a master of logical interior arrangement. The heavy wooden supportive framing, expertly prepared and joined, illustrates the hand of a knowledgeable and skilled structural planner. Furthermore, the excellent an eighteenth-century, English-inspired architectural vocabulary. Like Painter and Starr halls on either side, Old Chapel stands as a physical monument to the philosophical ideals of Middlebury's early educational leaders and their successors.

On the critical date of 10 August 1858, efforts were launched to create the fourth of Middlebury College's structures, Starr Hall, on the south end of the Old Stone Row. At their summer meeting, President Benjamin Labaree and the college fellows committed themselves to the undertaking and established a special committee to raise subscriptions, adopt a plan, make personal contacts, and supervise construction.[72] After a year of unproductive fund-searching by the committee, three private benefactors—Charles J. and Peter Starr, both trustees, and Egbert Starr—donated the $15,500 needed to carry out the project.[73] Immediately, the fellows reaffirmed their original intentions, and at a 5 October 1859 meeting they approved this motion:

That the paid President and Fellows shall erect or cause to be erected a substantial and convenient edifice for the accommodations of at least sixty students. . . . That said edifice shall be ready for the occupation of students on or before the 1st day of September, 1861.[74]

With the chairmanship of the building committee assumed by the president (a practice peculiar to Middlebury),[75] the new structure was raised on schedule and, at its dedication, took the name of the family whose financial support had made it possible. An 1898 alumni publication observed that "its completion marked a great revival for the college, and it seemed as if she were once more truly prosperous."[76]

Initially, the interior of Starr Hall consisted of two separate sections, according to the long-successful pattern of the vertical dormitory entryway, and contained only residential quarters. Thirty-two student suites were placed in the building: sixteen per entry, with two people assigned to each (therefore, eight people on each level), for a maximum capacity of sixty-four. This plan survived the disastrous fire of Christmas night, 1864, and comprehensive renovations were implemented in 1905 and 1946.[77] Today, Starr Hall serves exactly the same dormitory functions as it did originally, a circumstance that speaks positively for the practical and future-oriented thinking of its planners.

The 1864 conflagration, the product of a faulty clean-out door in a south entryway chimney, completely destroyed the interior of the building, and seriously threatened the rest of the Old Stone Row as well.[78] President Labaree, who had been trying to resign his position for several years, again consented reluctantly to head the building committee.[79] With an $8,000 subscription from the town citizenry,[80] and more aid from the Starr family, the dormitory rose again within its old walls by the end of 1865, assuming its original appearance. Though college records and personal correspondence offer no definite clues, it is evident that Labaree played an extensive role in the preparation of the initial as well as reconstruction plans. His financial notebook, contained in the college's library holdings, refers to his responsibility "to devise plans";[81] hence, it is conceivable that he acted in the capacity of architect and that no outside professional designer was employed.

Looking at Starr Hall today, one sees substantially the same structure as was first built and then re-erected in the mid-1860s (fig. 4-15). Four stories in height and 120 feet long, it was constructed with the same rough gray granular limestone as its Old Stone Row precursors, Painter Hall and Old Chapel. Narrower than Painter, the building mass is covered by a low-pitched roof penetrated by brick chimneys and marked by gable roofs above each of the front entry doorways. Protecting the doorways are flat-roofed classical porches supported by round Doric columns, added in 1946. White-painted wooden eaves and gable moldings, window framings, and semicircular end pediment windows provide linear contrasts to the stolid, rustic, ivy-clad wall surfaces. Well-proportioned and assertive of its function, Starr Hall is positively integrated with the balance of the cam-

Fig. 4-15. Starr Hall (1859–61, 1864–65), Old Stone Row, Middlebury College. Photograph, c. 1969.

Fig. 4-16. Starr Hall (1859–61, 1864–65), left, and Old Chapel (1835–36), right, Old Stone Row, Middlebury College. Photograph, c. 1885. Courtesy of College Archives, Special Collections, Middlebury College, Middlebury, Vt.

pus structures and comfortably relates to the natural environment by virtue of the materials of which it is composed. Though configured slightly differently than Painter Hall, its balancing counterpart to the north of Old Chapel, it successfully completes Middlebury College's historic and charismatic Old Stone Row (fig. 4-16).

Norwich University's First Campus

An abbreviated version of the row plan was employed with quite effective results at the Norwich, Vermont, campus of the American Literary, Scientific and Military Academy (later Norwich University). Unlike most other row examples at early New England educational institutions, the Norwich scheme consisted of just two buildings and therefore lacked any central organizational focal point. Despite these shortcomings, this row plan encouraged positive site

relationships and, because of comparable building massings, displayed excellent balance. In an unusual sketch (fig. 4-17) of the academy as it appeared in the early 1830s, South Barracks (1819–20) to the right and North Barracks (1831–32) to the left are partially obscured by Ammi Burnham Young's Congregational Church (1817), which in 1853 was moved from the town common (known locally as the Norwich Plain) across one of the bordering streets, where it stands today. Providing an unobstructed and landscaped expanse before it, the academy grouping must truly have been a fascinating relic of pre–Civil War collegiate planning (fig. 4-18), and it is to be regretted that it no longer exists to convey its formerly rich sociocultural message.

Although its first buildings are no longer standing, and it relocated to Northfield, Vermont, in the 1860s, Norwich University once played an important role in the history of the town of Norwich and in nineteenth-century American education. The oldest civil engineering college in the country and, with the exception of West Point, the senior military institution, it was founded by Captain Alden T. Partridge (West Point, Class of 1806) in 1819 under its somewhat cumbersome academy title. This title, however, reflected its combined military, classical, and technological curriculum. At its current location, the university has continued to practice Partridge's cardinal educational precepts—the training of young men for effective service in times of peace as well as war. Such a philosophy was clearly expressed in the two structures that comprised the original academy campus in Norwich. In the tradition of their counterparts elsewhere, both were multipurpose academic facilities conceived primarily for student quarters, but also for all associated educational functions.[82]

In preparation for the academy's September 1820 opening, plans were set in place during the preceding year for the completion of its original home. Most significantly, Partridge and the trustees established guidelines for the construction of a substantial brick structure four stories tall, 100 feet long, and 50 feet wide.[83] To realize this objective, the board contracted with a well-respected and accomplished master builder: Joseph Emerson, a native of Norwich and a former store owner and general merchandise trader.[84] The terms of the academy's legal agreements with Emerson outlined contractual obligations and the materials to be employed and stipulated the external and internal features of the contemplated edifice. These documents,[85] presently in the Norwich University Archives and Special

Fig. 4-17. "Old Norwich Academy Buildings, 1820," Norwich University, Norwich, Vt. Left, North Barracks (1831–32); center, Congregational Church (1817); right, South Barracks (1819–20). Reproduced conjectural sketch from William A. Ellis, *Norwich University* (1898), opposite p. 1. Courtesy of Norwich University Archives and Special Collections, Kreitzberg Library, Northfield, Vt.

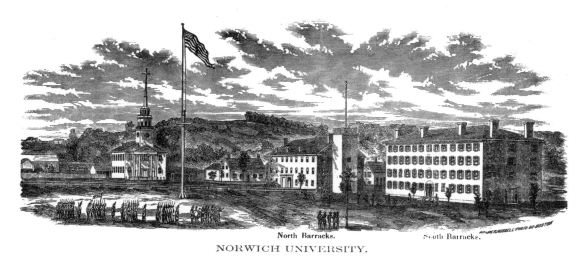

Fig. 4-18. "Norwich University," stationery letterhead, c. 1860. Left, North Barracks (1831–32); right, South Barracks (1819–20). Courtesy of Norwich University Archives and Special Collections, Kreitzberg Library, Northfield, Vt.

Fig. 4-19. "Norwich Cadets Polka," sheet music, composed by P. S. Gilmore. Lithograph by J. H. Bufford's Lith., published by Russell & Richardson, Boston (1857), depicting South Barracks (1819–20), Norwich University. Courtesy of Norwich University Archives and Special Collections, Kreitzberg Library, Northfield, Vt.

Collections, are exceedingly valuable for what they tell us about building techniques of the day. Their existence also makes possible a comparison between original specifications and the final building outcome, which is clearly evident in an enlightening and appealing 1857 J. H. Bufford sheet music lithograph (fig. 4-19) of the venerable edifice and associated military life.

On the exterior of South Barracks, little adornment was present. A low hipped roof was topped by eight tall brick chimneys set along the side and end walls. A surprising fifty-one double-sash windows were arrayed across the main west facade. The only valid style details displayed were rectangular white stone lintels over the window apertures, a plain cornice running just under the eaves, and small fanlight windows above each entrance.[86] Closely resembling contemporary dormitory designs at Bowdoin, Colby, and other New England institutions, the structure rested comfortably and securely on a spacious parade ground and, early in its history, was set within an 8-foot-tall

wooden fenced enclosure, broken only by a gate and flanking twin wooden guardhouses on the west side.[87] Though it was physically separated from the village and surrounding countryside, South Barracks related well to its rural environment and expressed the unpretentious and direct qualities of its design.

The interior of South Barracks was divided into a lecture room, two recitation rooms, an armory, a library, and forty-two student rooms arranged on either side of long floor corridors.[88] The presence of main entrances on three outside walls suggests that stairwells were present in the building and connected all stories. Such a layout would seem to possess poor acoustical qualities, but reactions by students and faculty were quite positive.[89] A lengthy description from the pen of Colonel H. O. Kent, Class of 1854, provides insight as to the basic functions of the structure:

The room on the right of the entrance, in front, was the library, while those in the rear were the cabinet and Professor Averill's recitation room. Professor Jackman's room was on the second passage, immediately over the entrance. The large recitation room was over this, and in it were read morning and evening prayers. The armory was over the center room on the fourth passage. Roll-calls were had in the second passage, the right resting on the north. The rooms were practically alike; numerous chimneys provided each pair of adjoining rooms with fireplaces or later with an opportunity for stoves, and space between chimney, passage, and outer wall for closets, thus offered one unbroken side to each apartment. These rooms were all "white-washed" with a tint, known by cadets as "brindle." There were no bedsteads, mattresses, or carpets. A wooden bunk, three feet wide, with slat bottom held the blankets and sheets and recumbent cadet, and was turned up against the wall before morning inspection. Over the bunk was the gun rack, with wooden pegs on which were suspended the musket and equipment.[90]

An unfortunate chimney defect within the interior brought about an end to South Barracks: on 14 March 1866 it burned to the ground in a spectacular fire,[91] thus making the move to Northfield inevitable. On the site today, a simple granite and brick centennial monument, erected in 1919 with materials from the destroyed building, commemorates the establishment of the now almost forgotten academy.[92] Though long departed, South Barracks has made a lasting statement on behalf of workable, economical, and refined design for a building used predominantly as a residence hall.

Fig. 4-20. "Old Norwich Buildings," Norwich University. Left, North Barracks (1831–32); right, South Barracks (1819–20). Photograph, 1862, from William A. Ellis, *Norwich University* (1898), opposite p. 2. Courtesy of Norwich University Archives and Special Collections, Kreitzberg Library, Northfield, Vt.

The second academy building was constructed in 1831–32 on a piece of land slightly north of South Barracks, where today the local public elementary school stands. Dedicated as North Barracks, it appears on the left of an old photograph (fig. 4-20), next to its predecessor behind a group of cadets under inspection. Though also designed by Joseph Emerson, it has a decidedly different appearance than his initial effort for the academy. Smaller in size, it rose three stories above ground level and was covered by a pitched roof, punctured intermittently by thin chimneys. A square, balustraded stair tower, similar to those found in industrial architecture of the time, was appended to the south end wall. At the front central doorway, a classic porch with balustrade acted as the chief focal point and broke the monotonous flatness of the redbrick facade. The three levels of windows were graded in size: the tallest were in the ground story, the medium-sized in the second story, and the smaller, square windows in the upper story. Such a window configuration was later employed by architect Ammi Burnham Young in Reed Hall at Dartmouth, and by building planners at other institutions.[93]

It is known that North Barracks contained many rooms for student living, and probably also a public room, commons, recitation rooms, and faculty offices.[94] Otherwise, it is difficult to determine anything else about the interior layout and usage due to the lack of original data concerning the academy for the years 1829–34, those immediately following the move back from Connecticut (see note 82). After the university departed for Northfield, the empty, primarily dormitory structure was sold to the Norwich Classical and English Boarding School, established in November 1867, and was repaired and refurnished at a cost of $3,000.[95] On the failure of this educational venture in 1877, North Barracks was taken over by the town to satisfy public school needs, and finally met the same unfortunate fate as South Barracks. On 13 October 1897, it was destroyed by fire, thus permanently depriving the community of its last physical connections with Norwich University.[96] It is to the University of Vermont and Middlebury College, therefore, that one must now look for surviving examples in Vermont of pre–Civil War higher educational architecture and campus planning.

5

THE CONTINUING
MASSACHUSETTS LEGACY

Amherst, Holy Cross, and Tufts

THE EARLY CAMPUSES of Amherst College, the College of the Holy Cross, and Tufts University (College) reflect varying planning philosophies and implementation practices. While Amherst's first leaders were committed to the row plan precedent initiated at Yale, those at Holy Cross emulated the single multipurpose complex of other older Roman Catholic higher educational institutions in the country. The initial decision makers at Tufts took a totally different planning approach, adapting a campus scheme then unique to New England colleges/universities—a mall with parallel rows of buildings facing each other on either side. Individual building designs at the three institutions imaginatively combined diverse educational functions with a variety of architectural styles, ranging from the late Federal and Greek Revival to the burgeoning Italian Revival and Second Empire (Mansard) of the mid-nineteenth century.

Amherst College: Traditional and Eclectic Architecture

Amherst College, located in central Massachusetts in the town of Amherst, is fortunate to possess one of the most outstanding and varied collections of early higher educational architecture in the New England region, rivaling that at Harvard. Of the eleven major buildings erected there before the Civil War, nine are extant and have continued to serve the myriad needs of the institution to this day. Like the campuses at Williams and Tufts, Amherst's first structures were positioned on a hilltop site or sites but were configured differently in relation to the natural environment. The initial expression of the Yale-inspired row plan at Amherst (fig. 5-1), highly formalized, stands in stark contrast to the more informal building arrangement at Williams, or the innovative mall scheme at Tufts.[1]

Founded in 1821, the college was named for Lord Jeffrey Amherst, a British general in the French and Indian War. As an outgrowth of Amherst Academy, which commenced operations in 1814 (though it was not chartered until 1816), the new institution was the product of fortuitous circumstances. Responding to the academy's immediate success, the trustees, in an effort to extend its positive impact, made the decision to raise a charity fund to help educate the promising and to endow a new institution of higher learning "for the classical education of indigent young men, of piety and

Fig. 5-6. Johnson Chapel (1826–27), interior of main chapel, Old Row, Amherst College.
Photograph, 1885, by W. H. Barker, Saratoga Springs, N.Y. Courtesy of Archives and Special Collections,
Amherst College Library.

it is a spireless two-stage square tower — a feature charac-teristic of Damon's many church designs. Defined by flat, paneled corner pilasters, the lower stage of the tower con-tains a belfry, while the upper stage, also with flat corner pilasters and topped by a balustrade, houses a clock with round time faces on all four sides. The view of the Connect-icut River valley and the Holyoke mountain range from the 96-foot-tall tower has long received accolades and is exten-sively described in nineteenth-century college literature.

On the interior, the Old Chapel (fig. 5-6), with its su-perbly refined Greek Revival detailing, occupied the two upper stories in the rear of the building mass. Other spaces in what, despite its name, was a multipurpose edifice ini-tially accommodated an additional small chapel (later divided for the president's offices), classrooms in the base-ment and on the first floor, libraries on the third floor, and elsewhere a museum (philosophical and natural history) and scientific offices and laboratories. Later in the nine-teenth century, and more recently, many of these functions have been relocated to other campus structures, so today the Johnson Chapel continues to house the Old Chapel as well as administrative office space.

Over the course of the building's history, the constantly changing requirements of the college, as well as expected wear and tear, have necessitated periodic repairs and spatial modifications on the interior. In 1863–64 the chapel build-ing, which had deteriorated from heavy use, was remodeled on the inside under the direction of William A. Dickinson, requiring the use of nearby Williston Hall as a temporary place of worship. At this time, rooms were "refitted, fres-coed and furnished," but there were no major changes to the floor plans. Extensive repairs were made to Johnson Cha-pel in around 1872 for $15,000 (ironically, the cost of the original building), but these also left the structure basically intact. In 1933–34, however, under the direction of archi-tect and Amherst alumnus James Kellum Smith of McKim, Mead and White, Johnson Chapel underwent a major trans-formation when the east (rear) facade was extended and re-built, structural members were strengthened, and interior spaces were reformatted to house the president's office and other administrative offices and enlarge the Old Chapel be-hind the pulpit. From the front, though, the building pos-sesses the same striking appearance that it did nearly two centuries ago, when it was created as the central focal point of the original Old Row (sometimes called College Row or Chapel Row).[5]

Fig. 5-7. "View of Amherst College, Mass. — From the President's House." Left, North Hall (1827); left center, North (Middle) College (1822–23); center, Johnson Chapel (1826–27); right center, South College (1820–21); right, unrealized dormitory. Color lithograph, c. 1829, signed by J. C. Kidder, pinxt." Published by Pendleton, Boston. Courtesy of the Boston Athenæum.

As early as the late 1820s, Amherst College officials became committed to expanding the original three-building campus composition to a five-building row. Their intention is well documented in printed views from that time (fig. 5-7). At their annual meeting in August 1827, the trustees charged the Prudential Committee with the responsibility of erecting Amherst's fourth major structure, to be similar in plan to those previously built, on a site (today occupied by Williston Hall) at the north end of the original row. Erected under the direction of Amherst contractor George Guild, this plain, pitched-roof brick edifice, known as North College or North Hall, was completed in 1827–28 at an expense of $10,000 to serve as a student residence. Though a favorite dormitory for its entire history, the building, in the view of many, had the disadvantage of an east-west instead of a north-south axis (at right angles to the longitudinal axis of the original row), so that rooms on its north side never benefited from direct sun exposure. Nevertheless, many students and alumni considered it better designed than its predecessors, with bedrooms that were ample in size, generally well lighted, and supplied with closets. North College met student residential needs for just three decades, until it was totally destroyed by a large conflagration in January 1857 due to the carelessness of a student occupant. Soon thereafter, Samuel Williston of Northampton visited the fire site, saw the damage, and, subject to certain conditions, offered the college funds for the erection of a replace-

ment building on the site. Thus began the Williston Hall construction project.[6]

Chronologically, Amherst College's next major building was College Hall (fig. 5-8), opposite the Old Row at the intersection of South Pleasant and College streets. It was constructed in 1828–29 at a cost of $7,000 to serve as a meetinghouse for the First Congregational Parish, replacing an older church on College Hill. The college did not actually own this structure for a long period, in fact, but did donate the land on which it was built, along with $7,000, with the understanding that commencement exercises and other public exercises and events could be held there. Finally, after using the building for nearly forty years, Amherst purchased it for $12,000 (including repairs) in 1867 and continued to use it primarily as an auditorium. More recently, as a result of 1980 and 2005 remodelings, it has been converted to administrative office space.

As conceived by architect/builder Warren S. Howland of Amherst, the templelike church structure was intended to mimic the early Greek Revival style, especially on its front (east) facade, of the nearby Johnson Chapel. Until 1861, when it was removed, College Hall displayed a four-column Doric portico, with plain entablature and closed pediment above. Positioned on the roof ridgepole was a well-articulated, concave-domed, octagonal belfry set on a square base, which, judging from visual documentation, appears unchanged from the original. When the building was remodeled in 1905 for $15,000, architect William R. Mead (Class of 1867) of the renowned New York firm of McKim, Mead and White facilitated the interior refurbishing as well as the enlargement and restoration of the portico

Fig. 5-8. College Hall (1828–29), Amherst College. Photograph, 2009.

end, but with six columns instead of four, as we view it presently. Allen Brothers of Amherst served as contractors for the project, which produced, in the popular estimate, "one of the loveliest buildings on campus."[7]

Following the leadership of Edward Hitchcock, beginning in the late 1840s Amherst College changed course architecturally and erected several intriguing, nonclassical, revivalist-style structures. In doing so, the expanding institution departed from the early Old Row building tradition that Hitchcock candidly characterized as a nondescript line of "parallelepipeds," lacking in design spirit! The first of these structures, the sixth of the college's pre-1860 collection, was the Woods Cabinet and Lawrence Observatory, put up in 1847–48 on a slight knoll on the hill northwest of the Old Row, overlooking South Pleasant Street. Quite appropriately, it was named in honor of Enfield, Massachusetts, manufacturer Josiah B. Woods, a college benefactor who spearheaded the $9,000 fundraising effort, and Abbott Lawrence of Boston, a wealthy mercantilist who was the largest contributor. Following the intentions of the college board of trustees and architect/contractor Henry A. Sykes of Springfield, Massachusetts, the innovative new "fire-proof" edifice was planned to serve as a study and exhibition center for natural history, as well as an astronomical observatory and college museum. It was dedicated on 28 June 1848 at formal ceremonies led by President Hitchcock.

Characterized by some as an asymmetrical "picturesque reaction against a doctrinaire Greek Revival," the new structure (fig. 5-9) ultimately assumed its current name, The Octagon. This was due to the octagonal form of its main central portion as well as the attached observatory tower, originally capped by a dome protecting a telescope and other scientific equipment and possessing a small transit-room wing. While the exact inspiration behind Sykes's design is not known, it is possible that the plan had Amherst origins: the most influential and widely distributed book treating octagonal plans was compiled by Orson Squire Fowler, Amherst Class of 1834, under the title A Home for All, and was published in 1849, soon after the dedication event. Built of brick and wood, the new structure featured Italian Revival decorative elements (cornices, support brackets, etc.), and specially treated wall surfaces, plastered, painted, and scored to resemble stone.

The principal Woods Cabinet space, inside the octagon proper, was initially devoted to a collection of geological specimens of the Western hemisphere on the first floor, the

Fig. 5-9. Woods Cabinet/Lawrence Observatory (The Octagon) (1847–48, etc.), Amherst College. Photograph, 2009.

Fig. 5-10. Interior, Woods Cabinet, The Octagon (1847–48, etc.), Amherst College. Photograph, from 1877 Album by Lovell, Photographer, Amherst, Mass. Courtesy of Archives and Special Collections, Amherst College Library.

Shepard collection of meteorites and books on the second floor, and, in the gallery above, a collection representing the geology of the Eastern hemisphere (fig. 5-10). To the original building, the Geological Lecture Room was added on the northwest corner in 1855, followed in 1857 by the Dickinson Nineveh Gallery at the opposite end, displaying Assyrian sculptured stone artifacts. Since then the Octagon has been used for various other purposes, starting in 1903, when the college completed and opened a new observatory. In 1908, all collections were relocated to other campus structures, and it became the headquarters of the Department of Music. In 1934–35, the large second-floor space was remodeled as the Frank L. Babbott meeting room, with James Kellum Smith as the architect. Since the late 1960s, the Octagon has been home to the Black Culture Center

Fig. 5-11. "New Library at Amherst College." Printed view from *Ballou's Pictorial Drawing-Room Companion* 8, no. 11 (17 March 1855), p. 169. Courtesy of Archives and Special Collections, Amherst College Library.

and, as envisioned by its creators, continues to attract notice for its innovative geometrical design.[8]

Located on South Pleasant Street between College Hall and the president's house is the Morgan Library, the next of Amherst's early buildings, the first section (fig. 5-11) of which was raised in 1852–53 in the then highly fashionable Italian Villa style. Like the Octagon, it was designed and built by architect/contractor Henry A. Sykes and was positioned on a tract purchased by the board of trustees from Reverend David Parson utilizing funds donated by friends of the college. The successful completion of the new $10,000 building introduced a new era in the college's architecture through the use of Pelham gneiss (granite) for the exterior walls, instead of the brick employed in earlier campus structures. Marked by its off-center, square, flat-roofed tower with Italianate cornice brackets, and round-arched double windows and apertures, the appropriately asymmetrical, two-story first section contained archives, pamphlet, catalogue, and other workrooms on the first floor, and a reading and book storage room above (fig. 5-12).

In 1882–83, from plans drafted by Arthur Kenway and Francis R. Allen of Boston, the Morgan Library, in need of greater book storage capacity, received a major granite addition to the southwest corner and west rear, as shown in an outstanding 1885 photographic view (fig. 5-13) in the collections of the Amherst College Archives. The largest gift for this addition was from the estate of Henry T. Morgan of New York, in whose memory the fully developed edifice

Fig. 5-12. Morgan Library (1852–53), interior, Amherst College. Photograph, 1880. Courtesy of Archives and Special Collections, Amherst College Library.

Fig. 5-13. Morgan Library (1852–53, 1881–83), Amherst College. Photograph, 1885, by W. H. Baker, Saratoga, N.Y. Courtesy of Archives and Special Collections, Amherst College Library.

was officially dedicated in 1884. Perpetuating the Italianate character of the first section, the addition was devoted to a librarian's office and other rooms at the southwest side and to six levels of book stacks in the rear, dramatically increasing book storage space to over 120,000 volumes. At the same time, the original section was renovated, the cost of the entire project reaching just over $48,000. The building continued to meet the library demands of the college until the erection of the Converse Library in 1916–17, after which time, as Morgan Hall, it has been used by the buildings and grounds division, the college physician, the Faculty Club, the Department of Fine Arts, and other academic units, and for general recitation rooms and other purposes. Additional interior space remodelings were implemented in 1935 under the direction of architect James Kellum Smith, and a planetarium was installed in 1960. Though partially concealed today by trees, shrubs, and utility poles and wires,

it has largely retained its appealing exterior appearance of over a century ago.[9]

The third of Henry A. Sykes's designed buildings for Amherst College, and the eighth of the institution's pre–Civil War structures, was the Appleton Cabinet, constructed in 1855. Positioned on College Hill at the south end of the Old Row to balance North Hall, it completed the five-unit configuration envisioned by college officials over three decades before and illustrated in early printed views. Erected by Easthampton contractor George P. Shoals, it was intended primarily to house the college's zoological collection, which included President Edward Hitchcock's gift of his superlative personal collection of fossilized footprints. The $10,000 cost was covered by funds from the estate of Samuel Appleton, a Boston manufacturer, importer, and philanthropist; consequently, the new museum building was named in his honor.

Fig. 5-14. Appleton Cabinet (1855), Old Row, Amherst College. Photograph, c. 1892, by Lovell, Photographer, Amherst, Mass. Courtesy of Archives and Special Collections, Amherst College Library.

Fig. 5-15. Adams Zoological Museum, second floor, Appleton Cabinet (1855), Old Row, Amherst College. Photograph, c. 1885. Courtesy of Archives and Special Collections, Amherst College Library.

Fig. 5-16. Appleton Cabinet (Hall) (1855, 1925, etc.), Old Row, Amherst College. Photograph, 2009.

Displaying the influence of the Italian Revival style, the original Appleton Cabinet was a two-story rectangular block of "fire-proof" brick (fig. 5-14) with a low-pitched roof and a modest one-story ell to the rear, raised to two stories in 1892. There were two rows of round-arched windows on each long side and, on the projecting west facade, a single arched doorway framed by stacked masonry blocks and topped by a molded stone rectangle under a flat stone lintel. Decorating the overhanging, molded roof cornices were a series of modillions, while the wall corners displayed white-painted, alternating brick quoins. On the interior of this well-integrated architectural composition in around 1875 were the Hitchcock Ichnological Cabinet and the Gilbert Museum of North American Indian Relics on the first floor; the Adams Zoological Museum on the second floor (fig. 5-15); and a zoological lecture and recitation room and laboratories in the ell. Over the following years there were changes in the museum's contents, including the addition of the Audubon Collection of Birds, which the college received from E. E. Farnam in 1886, and the inclusion of an enlarged college herbarium.

In 1925, under the direction of architects McKim, Mead and White, the collections were relocated elsewhere, and the entire interior was renovated to accommodate offices, lecture halls, and classrooms on three as opposed to the original two stories. On the exterior, two rows of flat-headed windows replaced those of the original first story, the pitched roof and cornices were reconfigured, and three rounded-headed windows were installed in the blank wall surface above the main west-facade doorway (fig. 5-16). At this time, the building was given its present name, Appleton Hall. As a result of a sweeping interior remodeling carried out in 1998, it was converted to a student housing facility.[10]

Following the loss of North College (Hall) (1822–23) to fire in the winter of 1857, Samuel Williston, an Easthampton button manufacturer and Amherst trustee, came forward and made a generous offer to the college. In addition to endowing a professorship, he pledged funds for a general-purpose structure to replace North College (Hall), with the provision that the trustees use the fire insurance proceeds, as well as additional subscriptions and a loan, for the construction of a new dormitory. The resulting $15,000 building, situated behind and northeast of the Old Row, was East College (Hall) (fig. 5-17), built in 1857–58 from designs drafted by architect Charles E. Parkes of Boston, with George P. Shoals of Easthampton as the chief contractor.

Fig. 5-17. East College (Hall) (1857–58; demolished, 1883), Amherst College. Photograph, from *1877 Album* by Lovell, Photographer, Amherst, Mass. Courtesy of Archives and Special Collections, Amherst College Library.

Dedicated on 19 May 1858, with an address by theologian Henry Ward Beecher, the new four-story brick East College was the largest residence hall (fig. 5-18) on campus, of traditional rectangular block form with a hipped roof and tall brick chimneys. With the exception of slight five-bay projections on the south and north ends of the west-facing front facade, it closely resembled its neighboring predecessors, South and North colleges. The object of campus criticism and occupying a highly desirable elevated site, East had a relatively brief lifetime, was razed in 1883, and has since been replaced by other Amherst buildings.[11]

Also constructed in 1857–58, and again utilizing the talents of Charles E. Parkes and George P. Shoals, was multipurpose Williston Hall, named for Samuel Williston, the funder and project supervisor of the new $16,000 building. Dedicated on 19 May 1858, the same day as East College, this intriguing edifice (fig. 5-19) initially contained the Department of Chemistry on the first floor, while the second floor was used for undergraduate society libraries, and the third floor for Alumni Hall and also occasionally for student examinations. Within a few years, at a $12,000 expense, the third floor was converted to accommodate the 80-by-40-foot Mather Art Gallery (1874; fig. 5-20) for plaster casts, and then a freshman reading room, while the two lower floors took on new roles for recitation rooms and the headquarters of the Christian Association. In the mid-twentieth century, Williston, while continuing to house the association, was largely converted to a classroom and faculty office facility, its primary function until 2002–3, when it was renovated for student housing.

Fig. 5-18. Interior of student study 18, East College (Hall) (1857–58; demolished, 1883), Amherst College. Photograph, 1879. Courtesy of Archives and Special Collections, Amherst College Library.

Fig. 5-19. Entrance to the main campus of Amherst College, looking southeast. Left, East College (1857–58); left center, Williston Hall (1857–58); center, North College (1822–23); right center, Johnson Chapel (1826–27); right, South College (1820–21) and the Octagon (1847–48). Photograph, c. 1875. Courtesy of Archives and Special Collections, Amherst College Library.

Fig. 5-20. Interior, Mather Art Gallery (1874), Williston Hall (1857–58), Old Row, Amherst College. Photograph, c. 1885. Courtesy of Archives and Special Collections, Amherst College Library.

Situated at the north end of the Old Row, its front facade facing north, Williston Hall has had its supporters as well as its detractors during its 150-year history. College President William A. Stearns glowingly characterized East College and Williston as the "great blessing" resulting from the "great [fire] catastrophe," with Williston "so comely in appearance, so convenient in arrangement, so generously bestowed and so full of invitation." Others, including later architectural critics, saw Williston as awkward and undistinguished in its design and only moderately successful in its function. Conceived in what Paul F. Norton has called the "Collegiate Italian Villa" style, the building did aesthetically balance, if it did not exactly replicate, Appleton Cabinet (Hall) at the south end of the row. With a formidable presence, the three-story brick edifice, topped by a hipped roof, possessed an eye-catching square tower with concave roof cap and finial; set front and center, the entire mass successfully counterbalanced the older two-stage tower atop nearby Johnson Chapel. Its roof cap and upper stage reconstructed in 1880 and again in 1924, this tower was removed in 1950–51, when Williston underwent major alterations on

Fig. 5-21. Williston Hall (1857–58, 1950–51), Old Row, Amherst College. Photograph, 1985.

simplicity." Based on traditional classical design but exhibiting the impact of the then-popular Italian Revival in its modest embellishment, Barrett possesses segmental-arched windows on the first story and round-arched windows on the second, with a heavy cornice under its pitched-roof eaves, stone block quoining on all four corners, and a stone horizontal band between the stories. On its perfectly symmetrical, west-facing facade is a round window set within a triangular pediment with returns, below which is a Palladian window above a round-arched main entrance. Barrett Hall is predicated on coherency and efficiency in form as well as function, perpetuating the design precedent of Amherst's first Old Row buildings.[13]

its exterior as well as interior. At this time, the entire design was "classicized" under the direction of James Kellum Smith of McKim, Mead and White, the firm that had similarly transformed the Appleton Cabinet (Hall) in 1925. As a consequence, Williston (fig. 5-21) now relates well to its other traditional Old Row neighbors.[12]

Amherst College's eleventh and last major pre–Civil War building is Barrett Hall (Gymnasium) (fig. 5-22), named for Dr. Benjamin Barrett of Northampton, the largest contributor toward its $15,000, fully equipped project cost. Designed by Boston architect Charles E. Parkes and erected in 1859–60 by Northampton contractor R. R. Myers, this two-story, 70-by-50-foot, Pelham gneiss stone (granite) edifice is situated in the quadrangle behind the Old Row, north of the former site of East College (Hall). First serving as a gymnasium, it had bowling alleys, an office, and a dressing room on the first level, and gymnastic apparatus in a "drill hall" on the second (fig. 5-23). Believed to be the first American college gymnastic building supervised by an appointed professor, it housed the Department of Hygiene and Physical Education from 1859 to 1884, when it was replaced by the Pratt Gymnasium. Scarcely used for many years, in 1907 it was renovated at a cost of $11,000 for use as a recitation and office building for the modern languages departments under the new name of Barrett Hall. Currently, it serves similar purposes.

Over time, Barrett Hall has received generally positive architectural assessments. In his 1895 history of the college, William S. Taylor described it as one of the finest buildings on the campus, with "the beauty of fitness and . . . of a severe

Fig. 5-22. Barrett Hall (Gymnasium) (1859–60), Amherst College. Photograph, 2009.

Fig. 5-23. Barrett Gymnasium (1859–60), interior, second level, Amherst College. Photograph, c. 1879. Courtesy of Archives and Special Collections, Amherst College Library.

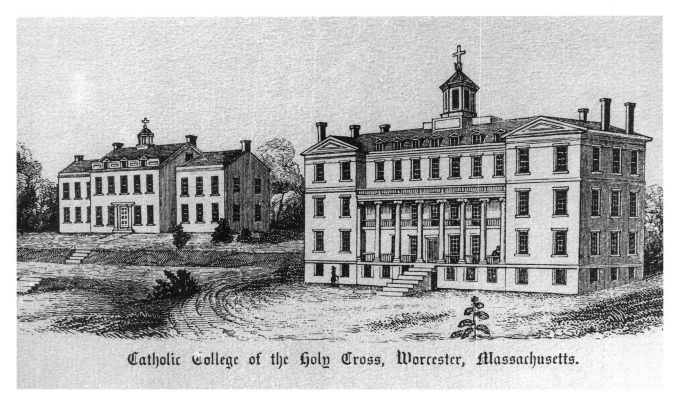

Catholic College of the Holy Cross, Worcester, Massachusetts.

Fig. 5-24. "Catholic College of the Holy Cross, Worcester, Massachusetts." Left, Mount St. James Academy; right, original College building (1843). Head of promotional/informational broadside, 1845. Courtesy of Archives and Special Collections, Dinand Library, College of the Holy Cross.

The College of the Holy Cross:
The Single Complex Concept

Set on a pronounced, north-facing hillside site overlooking the downtown section of Worcester, Massachusetts, the buildings of the College of the Holy Cross, in their interrelationships and individual designs, reflect a somewhat different planning heritage than Amherst College and other pre–Civil War New England higher educational institutions. Like the founders of other Roman Catholic colleges/ universities in the United States, those who established Holy Cross adopted traditions and practices that generally were more European than English or Anglo-American in their origins. Consequently, following the pattern of Georgetown University and other Roman Catholic predecessors in the country, urban-based Holy Cross grouped its buildings randomly and closely together adjacent to a main multipurpose structure. In time, this initial central edifice evolved into a massive complex of connected components distinguished by eclectic detailing and dominated by tall towers

with spire roofs. In implementing such planning, the college's founders departed from the formalized, systematic closed and open quadrangle and row campus schemes embraced by their New England counterparts, commencing at Harvard and Yale, with their inclusion of multiple-function as well as single-purpose buildings.[14]

The oldest Catholic and Jesuit religious order college in the New England region, the College of the Holy Cross was founded in 1843 at the instigation of the Right Reverend Joseph Benedict Fenwick (1781–1846), the second bishop of Boston, and was named after his cathedral church in that city. Of invaluable assistance to Bishop Fenwick in this pioneering educational venture was Reverend James Fitton, the first priest in the Worcester section of the diocese, who in 1836 had erected on the future college site (traditionally called Pakachoag Hill) a single edifice for the Academy (Seminary) of Mount St. James. In 1842, Father Fitton had deeded this unassuming, wooden, two-story structure (fig. 5-24), along with approximately sixty acres of land, to the bishop for the new institution. The first classes and administrative functions at Holy Cross were located in the former main building of the academy from November 1843 until early in the following year.[15]

On 21 June 1843, prior to the beginning of classes, the initial incarnation of Fenwick Hall, the college's first building, was commenced with the ceremonious and official laying and blessing of its cornerstone. Named for founder Bishop Fenwick and situated slightly northwest of the academy building (see fig. 5-24), it represented the first of several phases through which the building would evolve to the present expanded and updated complex. Erected under the direction of Tobias Boland (1795–1886), a well-known Worcester contractor who constructed buildings for the academy, the new edifice was officially completed on 13 January 1844 at a cost of $19,000, funded entirely by Bishop Fenwick. To date, the identity of the architect remains unknown, though it is conceivable that Boland himself, working with college officials, may have prepared the designs. Serving, as intended, all of the college's administrative, academic, and residential functions, Fenwick Hall was initially 108 feet in length and 48 feet in width and stood four stories high, the upper three stories with brick walls set on granite basement-story foundations. As an architectural composition, it was notably successful, its symmetrical front facade framed on each end by slightly projecting pavilions and graced by a picturesque, two-story, balustraded portico with Greek Ionic order columns. Set atop the low-pitched roof at its center was an octagonal cupola crowned by a distinctive six-foot-tall gilt cross. This imposing structure was undoubtedly an asset to the college in its efforts to establish its reputation and recruit faculty and students during its formative years.[16]

The next stage in the development of Fenwick Hall, initiated in August 1846, was an 80-by-47-foot extension to the east of the original building. Completed and opened on 27 March 1847, the new three-story wing was the work of the firm of Gower and Raymond and was funded for under $9,000. The successful realization of this project provided the now-expanding college with additional dormitory rooms, a chapel, and a dining room as well as a study hall. Although there was discussion about a possible matching west wing, and the college actually published engravings (c. 1850 and later) showing Fenwick with two wings, there is no convincing evidence in college documents or published sources that such a project was implemented at that time.[17]

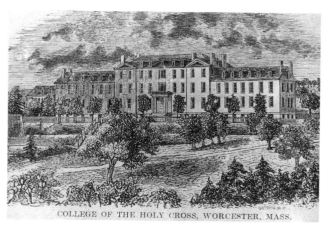

Fig. 5-25. "College of the Holy Cross, Worcester, Mass." Woodcut engraving (with east and proposed west wings) from *Catalogue of the College of the Holy Cross* (1858–59), frontispiece. Courtesy of Archives and Special Collections, Dinand Library, College of the Holy Cross.

Disaster struck the College of the Holy Cross on the afternoon of 14 July 1852, when a fire broke out on the third floor of the original building, resulting in major damage. Only the added east wing was left unaffected and standing, saved through the valiant efforts of the local firefighters. This unfortunate event had a severe financial impact on the college: the loss of the building and most of its contents (estimated at $40,000) was nearly complete, and there was no insurance coverage. As a result of the fire, the college was forced to close temporarily, but it reopened in early October 1853, utilizing the undamaged east wing and the old main academy building. Immediately after the fire, college officials commenced reconstruction of the original structure under the direction of Captain Edward Lamb, a Worcester contractor. This critical project proceeded slowly: the brick work was completed by December 1853, but the interior remodeling was extended for an additional two years to avoid increasing the college's debt. While it closely resembled the pre-fire edifice, the four-story replacement structure (fig. 5-25), with an attached east wing, possessed a small, projecting porch instead of the original grand portico, and lacked a roof cupola. With a floor plan closely resembling that of its predecessor, rebuilt Fenwick Hall contained forty-two rooms, with a chapel, a refectory, a study room, two student common dormitories, and a basement furnace room that provided the beginnings of central heating.[18]

Fenwick Hall remained essentially unchanged on its exterior for the next twelve years, at which time growing student enrollments and budget surpluses led to the decision to further enlarge the complex. At the end of 1867, the col-

Fig. 5-26. "Proposed Alteration of the College of the Holy Cross, Worcester, Mass." By "E. Boyden & Son, Architects." Architectural drawing, c. 1868. Courtesy of Archives and Special Collections, Dinand Library, College of the Holy Cross.

Fig. 5-27. "College of the Holy Cross, Worcester, Mass." Engraving from *Catalogue of the College of the Holy Cross* (1875–76), frontispiece. Courtesy of Archives and Special Collections, Dinand Library, College of the Holy Cross.

Fig. 5-28. Fenwick Hall (1843–44, etc.), study hall, first floor, College of the Holy Cross. Photograph, c. 1880. Courtesy of Archives and Special Collections, Dinand Library, College of the Holy Cross.

lege trustees, working with then-president Father Robert Brady, authorized loans totaling $46,000 (the final cost was around $50,000) to further reconstruct and modify Fenwick Hall. Carried out in 1868–69, this ambitious project resulted in a new five-story west wing (one story higher than the main section of the building), an added story, and an enlarged Corinthian-columned porch in the main section, and two identical, imposing square towers with tall spire roofs flanking the main section. A new mansard roof broken by stylized dormers and paneled chimneys topped the full complex. As a consequence of these extensive alterations, Fenwick continued as an unbalanced architectural composition (fig. 5-26), the older east wing somewhat overwhelmed visually by the massive new wing addition on the west side. Responsible for generating the plans for this phase of the structure's development was Elbridge Boyden (1819–96), a Worcester-based architect who, during his fifty-year career, designed numerous churches, hotels, and private residences in the region.

In 1875, under the direction of the next Holy Cross president, Father B. O'Hagen, and funded by an additional loan of $30,000, the east wing, which had survived the 1852 fire, was extended by over 30 feet (producing "the annex") and was raised two stories with embellished mansard roof to closely match the exterior appearance of the west wing (fig. 5-27). The total length of the expanded wing was 112 feet, with an east frontage of 90 feet. The major spaces of the revised interior layout were refectories, a study hall (fig. 5-28), and a third-floor chapel (fig. 5-29), with its stylized Gothic Revival pointed-arched windows, wooden pews, and frescoed, paneled ceiling. Credited with the design work for the new east wing was P. W. Ford, a relatively unknown but clearly accomplished Boston architect.[19]

Over the years since these major alterations, there have been additional interior reconfigurations, exterior detail modifications, and ell additions to Fenwick Hall, but these have not substantially changed the overall appearance of its historic front facade, over 300 feet in length (fig. 5-30). In 1888, minor renovations included the creation of a new laboratory for applied chemistry. In 1901 college officials opened a new infirmary in the east wing and permanently replaced gas lighting with electricity. In 1906, the Boston architectural partnership of Maginnis and Walsh redesigned the basement for the kitchen and refectory. Between 1891 and 1895, the first of two major appendages to the building (arguably "ells"), five-story O'Kane Hall (fig.

Fig. 5-29. "The College Chapel," Fenwick Hall (1843–44, etc.), College of the Holy Cross. Photograph, c. 1880. Courtesy of Archives and Special Collections, Dinand Library, College of the Holy Cross.

Fig. 5-30. Fenwick Hall (1843–44, etc.), main northwest facade, College of the Holy Cross. Photograph, 2009.

Fig. 5-31. O'Kane Hall ell (1891–95), Fenwick Hall (1843–44, etc.), College of the Holy Cross. Photograph, 2009.

5-31), was attached to the end of the west wing, adding a large gymnasium, swimming pool, museum, auditorium/theater, dormitory rooms, scientific laboratories, and lecture rooms to the college's growing physical plant facilities. The local architectural firm of Fuller and Delano drafted the plans for the central-tower structure that is so compatible architecturally with Fenwick Hall. In 2000, a long annex known as Smith Hall was attached to the back (south) wall of the central section for additional office and classroom space. Responsible for the design was the distinguished architectural firm of Graham Gund Associates.

As it is currently configured, Fenwick Hall has continued its multipurpose tradition, accommodating offices for the president, senior vice president, admissions, development, grants and research, and academic departments, as well as space for the Brooks Music Center, the music library, and computer technology and department seminar rooms. Named to the National Register of Historic Places in 1980 along with O'Kane Hall, Fenwick Hall continues to occupy a major place in the history of American Roman Catholic as well as New England regional higher education and its architecture.[20]

Tufts University and the Hilltop Mall

Like the founders of Williams College in western Massachusetts, the founders of Tufts College (Tufts University after 1955) selected a site for their new institution that possessed unusual and appealing natural features, including good viewpoints, that they believed would enhance the higher educational learning process. As Paul Venable Turner observed in his classic work *Campus: An American Planning Tradition* (1984), it was during the early to mid-nineteenth century, or in some instances earlier, that, as a reflection of the desire to connect with nature, the "image of the 'college on the hill' became a common ideal." In New England there is no better example of an institution that fulfilled this ideal and also creatively related to nature than the original core (fig. 5-32) of the current Tufts Medford-Somerville campus. Furthermore, this core, departing from the prevailing open quadrangle and row plans in the region, is unique in New England as the only pre-1860 example of a mall plan (fig. 5-33), in all likelihood inspired by Thomas Jefferson's distinctive mall configuration (1817–26) at the University of Virginia at Charlottesville. At Tufts, as at Virginia, parallel rows of buildings face each other across the central mall space (often referred to today as The Green), which serves as the main axis of the hilltop campus.[21]

Crowning tree-bedecked College Hill (formerly Walnut Hill) at the center, the original core is the first structure erected at Tufts College, in recent years increasingly recognized for its architectural merit and historical significance.[22] Named in honor of Hosea Ballou II, the institu-tion's first president,[23] Ballou Hall (1852–54) has served as the physical and academic heart of the college/university ever since its formal establishment in 1852 as the first institution of higher learning founded by the Universalist denomination in the United States.[24] Beyond this distinction, the building has achieved recognition as one of the most expertly designed and best-preserved surviving examples of nineteenth-century Italian Renaissance Revival architecture in New England. Credited with the design of Ballou is Boston's celebrated mid-Victorian designer Gridley James Fox Bryant (1816–99), also known for his campus plan and individual building conceptions for the Maine State Seminary (Bates College) at Lewiston, Maine, in the mid-1850s. The attribution of Bryant as Ballou's architect is further reason for directing major attention to what is still Tufts's principal landmark and symbol of institutional aspirations and accomplishments.

Initially referred to as the College Building or College Hall,[25] Ballou Hall was conceived by the institution's founders during the late 1840s. It was not until the summer of 1852, however, that sufficient funds were raised and land located so that formal action could be taken to initiate the construction project. At a meeting on 21 July of that year, the newly constituted Board of Trustees voted to create a building committee and instructed this body "to devise a plan for College buildings with all consistent dispatch, and . . . to report, to call a meeting of the Board to hear the report, and act on the same." Two months later a verbal report was presented to the trustees, and votes were taken to enlarge the building committee, to "proceed immedi-

Fig. 5-32. "Tuft's College." Engraving by A. L. Rawson from Charles Brooks, *History of the Town of Medford* (1855), opposite p. 296. Courtesy of Digital Collections and Archives, Tufts University.

Fig. 5-33. College Hill mall (The Green) from the west. Photograph, c. 1890. Courtesy of Digital Collections and Archives, Tufts University.

Fig. 5-34. "Tufts College, Somerville, Massachusetts" (Ballou Hall, 1852–54). Engraving from *Ballou's Pictorial and Drawing-Room Companion* 11, no. 15 (11 October 1856), p. 225. Courtesy of Digital Collections and Archives, Tufts University.

Fig. 5-35. Ballou Hall (1852–54), view from southeast, Tufts College. Photograph, c. 1862. Courtesy of Digital Collections and Archives, Tufts University.

ately to erect a Building for the use of the College," to complete the foundation the ensuing fall, and "to expend a sum, not exceeding $20,000."[26] The figure budgeted proved all too modest, but additional subscriptions were raised, and the project moved forward. In the end, the new facility cost $38,000.[27]

Under the direction of a trustee, the Reverend Otis Skinner, construction was initiated in November 1852, only to be interrupted by the harsh weather of the winter months. The following spring, work was energetically resumed on the then nearly barren eminence at the center of the original pastoral twenty-acre tract of land granted to the college by Somerville farmer Charles Tufts, for whom the college was subsequently named.[28] Sufficient progress was made on the project so that gala cornerstone-laying ceremonies for Ballou Hall were held on 19 July 1853. This occasion was vividly recounted in the *Trumpet and Universalist Magazine*, a leading Universalist Church publication:

The Corner-Stone of Tufts College was laid with appropriate religious services on Tuesday forenoon last. A special train left Boston at 9 o'clock. On arriving at the hill it was found that Mr. Yale of Boston (one of our brethren of the faith) had spread a very large awning, under which seats were prepared for the ladies. Three American ensigns were floated from the top at proper distances from the canvas, and equidistant from each other. A part of the wall of the college had been built; and a section of the freestone laid, at one of the corners, some fifteen feet in height. The day was delightful—balmy—and the tent screened the people from the rays of the sun, and no one suffered from the heat. The people kept

coming until the services were half through; and we are confident there were upwards of a thousand present.[29]

Inspired by this momentous event, the contractors completed the walls and roof by November, and hastened to finish the interior in preparation for the fall session of 1854. Readied for academic use, Ballou Hall must have looked much the same as it does in an 1856 woodcut engraving of the south-facing facade from *Ballou's Pictorial* (fig. 5-34).[30]

In his history of the college to 1952, former Professor Russell E. Miller aptly observed that the exterior of Ballou Hall (fig. 5-35) presented a "more imposing appearance than its surroundings" during the earliest years of the institution.[31] While under construction, it was described thus by the *Trumpet and Universalist Magazine*:

The principal college building . . . is designed in the Italian [Renaissance Revival] style, being a parallelogram in outline, measuring 100 by 60 ft., and 3 finished stories [60 ft.] in height, . . . the exterior construction to be faced [red] bricks, with [Connecticut brown] sandstone basement story, corner quoins, and window and door dressings. The whole crowned with an enriched bracketed cornice, and balustrade around the roof. The main entrance to the building is to be arched and covered by a Roman Ionic portico, surmounted with a balustrade.[32]

Six paneled brick chimneys rose above a slate truncated roof, two at each end wall, and two atop the roof plane of the north or rear facade. Enclosed within a wooden balustrade was the cast-iron college bell, used to sound emergencies and to call students and faculty to lectures, chapel

Fig. 5-36. South main porch, Ballou Hall (1852–54), Tufts University. Photograph, c. 1975.

Fig. 5-37. Ballou Hall (1852–54), view from southwest, Tufts University. Photograph, 2009.

services, and special events. Broad, brown sandstone belt courses extended around the entire structure at the second- and third-floor levels. Apart from the belt courses and rusticated corner quoins, the brick wall surfaces were smooth and plain and served as an effective neutral background for the double-sash, wood-framed windows, doors, and south porch. First brown, then white paint was used on all exterior woodwork. The window lintels varied, with plain block and bracketed entablatures displayed at the second and third stories, and the segmental-arched variation featured at the first. Highlighting the entire edifice was the tall south porch (fig. 5-36), with its beautifully proportioned entablature and graceful fluted Ionic columns. Centered above it was a flat-headed Palladian window that repeated the tripartite effect created by the paired porch columns flanking the central entrance space.

We are fortunate today to be able to view Ballou Hall in much the same form externally as it appeared during the 1850s (fig. 5-37). Thanks to over a half million dollars in restoration work completed by the New York architectural firm of McKim, Mead and White in 1955–56,[33] the building

is little altered from the original version except for the absence of the south porch balustrade, the presence of paired dormer windows in the east and west roof planes, and the addition in 1939 of the Eugene B. Bowen Porch, closely matching the south porch, to the formerly unadorned north entranceway.[34] A stylistic rarity for its building type and locale, Ballou reproduces the basic form of the astylar Italian palazzo of High Renaissance Rome and Florence in Italy, first revived in England by Charles Barry in the late 1820s, and introduced to this country during the 1840s. In contrast to the popular and adaptable Italian Villa mode of the same era, the Renaissance was essentially nonpicturesque, monumental, and symmetrical. In the manner of Ballou, buildings designed in this style were restrained and dignified freestanding blocks that possessed stylistic decor but lacked noticeable diversions in style and shape. Emphasis was placed on "correctness" and on balanced and unified composition. Despite heaviness in form conditioned by its elevated site, Ballou Hall adheres well to the stylistic principles that inspired its conception. Elsewhere in New England, other than Bryant's own Hathorn Hall (1856–57) at Bates College, it has no stylistic rivals among higher educational structures. In fact, it is more comparable to certain civic structures, most notably those erected under federal government auspices from the designs of Ammi Burnham Young when he was serving as supervising architect of the U.S. Treasury Department in the 1850s.[35]

Unlike the still relatively intact exterior, the interior of Ballou Hall has been renovated and rearranged on several occasions since 1854, appropriately changing its character and purposes with each passing generation of students. The most sweeping of the alterations were those implemented under President Nils Y. Wessell's administration in 1955–56, when the building was totally gutted, new steel-reinforced walls and floors inserted, and conversion to a modernized, exclusively administrative facility realized.[36] Today it houses the offices of the president, trustees, vice presidents, provost, deans, and university counsel, and equal opportunity, information technology, and other administrators. As initially planned, however, Ballou was intended to serve as the multipurpose academic center of Tufts College. In the fashion of its counterparts at other New England colleges, it was built as the educational as well as architectural focal point of its institution—an object of reference in relation to which a full campus plan could be, and has subsequently been, developed.

The original interior of the edifice was characterized by broad functional flexibility and versatility. Classrooms, laboratories, a library, a chapel, student living quarters, administrative and faculty offices, and even bathing facilities were combined under one roof. But such a scheme was hardly novel, as we can observe at other older New England colleges and universities discussed in earlier chapters of this book. At these institutions, educational leaders had long been professing the advantages of intimately associating all facets of student higher educational life so as to widen knowledge, deepen experience, and promote personal growth and individualism. In the years just before the Civil War, American educators, including those at Tufts, continued to subscribe to these long-standing principles and practices, following the example of the first English universities, whose physical plants were configured to encourage the implementation of such thinking. Actual extant structures such as Ballou are physical testaments to this powerful and enduring ideal.

While it appears that the original floor-plan drawings for Ballou Hall no longer exist, the Rollins notebooks in the Tufts archives contain an indispensable record of the building's initial interior layout.[37] From these notebooks we know that the top floor was first utilized for student dormitory rooms, but within a few years it was altered and refurbished to accommodate faculty offices, a literary society room, the college library, a mineral cabinet (museum), and classrooms. The second floor was intended to be the main floor of the building and was reached by a broad stairway extending up from the porch entrance on the south facade. The principal room on this floor was the Large Chapel, the somber and formal appearance of which is conveyed in a c. 1885 photograph contained in the Tufts archives (fig. 5-38).[38] This space required enlargement in around 1861 but later was partitioned for classrooms after the construction of the Goddard Chapel (1882–83) just to the east of Ballou. Also present were a smaller chapel room, a recitation room, and the president's office. Designated as "service space," the first floor was given over to offices and classrooms and featured a lower ceiling than was present in the upper two stories. When the engineering school was founded in 1865, laboratory space was created in the cellar that provided areas for a dynamo room, a battery room, a laboratory for electrical measurements, a workshop, a furnace room, a coal bin, and a deep well from which water was pumped by hand. Most of the interior wall surfaces were plain, with the exception of those in the library and Large Chapel, on which decorative stucco was spread. Certain details of the external pilasters and cornice were repeated in stucco in the hall and staircase spaces inside. On all floor levels the rooms were conveniently arranged in relation to the central stairwell and corridors and were close enough in proximity to allow the interrelationship of all college programs and activities.[39]

Surviving college documents in manuscript form provide irrefutable evidence that Gridley J. F. Bryant was the architect of Ballou Hall. Although Bryant's drawings and professional papers appear to be beyond recovery, it is possible to grant a conclusive attribution on the basis of 1855 and 1857 entries for $950 in fees in the Tufts College treasurer's case and ledger books, and the presence of Bryant's signature on a college legal document.[40] Furthermore, in a June 1853 article, the *Trumpet and Universalist Magazine* identifies Bryant as architect and names Boston contractors Joseph W. Coburn, Wyatt Richards, and S. C. Felton as the builders.[41] Indeed, the college was very fortunate in attracting a professional with Bryant's structural engineering knowledge and architectural planning skills. As noted in the discussion of Bryant's Maine State Seminary (Bates College) master plan in chapter 7, he maintained a large and influential architectural practice in Boston commencing in the late 1830s and extending for several decades, and amassed a distinguished group of commissions, a high percentage of which were in Boston itself. Providing services to Tufts at the midpoint of his career, Bryant was a master of aesthetically attractive as well as utilitarian architecture

Fig. 5-38. Ballou Hall (1852–54), large chapel interior, Tufts College. Photograph, c. 1885. Courtesy of Digital Collections and Archives, Tufts University.

and deserves notice as "a stabilizing force in an architecturally uncertain age."[42]

Despite an extensive listing of known commissions, Gridley Bryant prepared very few designs for higher educational institutions in the United States.[43] Comparable in overall quality, form, and stylistic detail is the aforementioned Hathorn Hall, which he conceived in the mid-1850s as the central building focal point of a symmetrical three-building master plan for the Maine State Seminary (Bates College) in Lewiston, Maine.[44] The Bates structure displays the same powerful three-story block mass, dentiled cornices, varied window treatments, and front Roman entrance porch as Ballou Hall. Like Ballou, Hathorn conveys a feeling of functional simplicity, handsome proportion, and discreet detailing present in the majority of Bryant's buildings. Although he was later to make his reputation through applications of the French Second Empire style in his numerous commissions, one could justifiably argue that Bryant was even more successful, if not more productive, with his earlier efforts in versions of the Italianate. Ballou Hall, as well as Hathorn Hall at Bates, offers visible support for such a contention.

The architectural and historical significance of Ballou Hall will doubtless continue to interest scholars and critics of higher educational architecture in the years to come. Like most of its counterparts at other New England institutions, it has remained and will likely continue to remain secure in the care of respectful and appreciative trustee and administrative leaders. The focal point of a modern, bustling academic community, its current role is as viable now as it was over a century and a half ago, when an infant college staked an uncertain future within its stolid walls and commenced the development of the mall plan on College Hill.

Other buildings would soon follow the Ballou precedent on the opposite side of the mall. The second of Tufts University's major pre-1860 buildings, also extant, is Packard Hall, situated directly across the mall to the north of and directly facing Ballou Hall (see fig. 5-32). Although it lacks the monumental presence and architectural distinction of Ballou, it too has served a variety of instructional, administrative, and residential purposes, and hence has played a significant role in the life of the institution since its first years in the 1850s.

Soon after the completion and opening of Ballou Hall, as student enrollments grew, the college's Board of Trustees,

Fig. 5-39. Middle (Packard) Hall (1856), left, and East Hall (1860), right, Tufts College. Photograph, 1875. Courtesy of Digital Collections and Archives, Tufts University.

committed to a residential student community, recognized the need for a new, separate, predominantly dormitory structure. Consequently, at a meeting held on 29 May 1855, they voted to authorize the Building Committee to erect such an edifice for a "boarding house." By May of the following year, at a total cost of $9,715.93, the committee was able to report that the college had "erected a boarding house of brick, three stories high, 57 x 39 ft., having accommodations for the family in charge of it, [lower-level kitchen and dining facilities], and twenty-six students" (fig. 5-39). Known briefly as Building A, the new structure assumed the name West Hall from its 1856 completion to 1872 (when the present mid-Victorian Gothic Revival West Hall was completed on the mall slightly to the west), and subsequently Middle Hall from 1872 to 1885. In that year the name "Library" appeared carved in stone over the front central main entrance, signifying a change in function when the college library was moved to Middle Hall from Ballou. For a time

the first-floor rooms accommodated reading spaces, and a half-hexagonal addition topped by a finial was attached to the rear to house book stacks. In 1908, the library was relocated to the new Eaton Memorial building nearby. Two years later, Middle Hall assumed its current name, Packard Hall, in honor of a generous deceased benefactor, Sylvanus Packard of Boston.[45]

A suitable chronicle of the architecture and related history of Packard Hall would be seriously deficient if it did not include an abbreviated summary of its continuing multiple uses as well as its structural problems. The college's second president, A. A. Miner, reluctantly had to deal with building defects such as bulging walls (stabilized by the insertion of iron tie-rods), as well as moisture seepage through the walls, which necessitated a series of additional repairs and interior redecoration. Students continued to reside on the upper two floors until 1901, but then had to be removed as their woodstoves and fireplaces (predating central heat-

Fig. 5-40. Packard Hall (1856, etc.), Tufts University. Photograph, 2009.

ing) posed a potential fire-damage threat to the library. In 1910, after two years of vacancy, the versatile structure became the headquarters of the Crane Theological School; subsequently, it was assigned to the Department of English. Packard continued to be threatened when in the mid-1930s the trustees considered moving the building back to make way for two new larger academic structures, or demolishing it or replacing it with or incorporating it into a new student/alumni center. None of these projects were realized, however, largely due to conflicting ideas and the lack of financial resources during the Great Depression years. In the late 1970s, Packard Hall was again remodeled, this time for the use of development office and other administrative functions. In 2008-9, with William Rawn Associates of Boston as architects, it underwent a complete exterior restoration and interior refurbishing. Major changes included the addition of a square, four-story tower on the west side containing a second stairway, elevator, and elevator lobby, and the replacement of older windows with new glass windows. On the completion of this project, the building was totally devoted to the political science department.[46]

As constructed (see fig. 5-39), Packard Hall, on its sloping site, was a plain, uninspiring, primarily unembellished brick structure, protecting by a pitched roof broken by dormer windows and three tall, thin brick chimneys rising above each side wall. The only evidence of decorative detail was the dentil cornices under the side-wall roof overhangs. In 1885, when the library was moved to Packard, the building (fig. 5-40) became aesthetically more compelling when the tall brick chimneys were removed, and the severity of the front facade was alleviated by the addition of brick corner quoins, pediment detail including cornice molding, and

an enlarged main entrance topped by a segmental-arched fanlight and contained within a small brick porch with heavy cornices and engaged, flat pilasters.[47] The building has largely retained this exterior appearance to this day, despite the tower addition, the window reconfigurations, and the refinishing of the brick surfaces. In retrospect, multipurpose Packard Hall has been a lesson in survival, change, and adaptability for its entire history.[48]

Situated directly east of Packard Hall, its main facade facing southward on the north side of the mall, is East Hall, erected in 1860 after several years of deliberations by the Tufts Board of Trustees. At their annual meeting of 13 January 1857, the trustees authorized the Executive Committee "to cause to be erected such additional house or houses, on the College land, as they may judge necessary for the fit accommodation of the students." The same year, this was reaffirmed at a 26 May meeting of the board, with an estimated expense of $10,000. Two years passed, however, before the Executive Committee, at its 24 May 1859 meeting, voted "to proceed at once to the erection of a new Boarding Hall which has become a positive necessity." Almost exactly one year later, the trustees, at their meeting on 29 May, reported that they had contracted with Boston's Thomas W. Silloway (1828–1910), an ordained Unitarian clergyman converted to architectural work, to prepare the plans and specifications for and oversee the erection of the new edifice. Primarily known for his designs of numerous churches in New England, Silloway also secured commissions for public and higher educational buildings during his productive career. Working with Silloway as chief contractor was Griswold S. Adams, also based in Boston. At the trustee meeting of 28 May 1861, the Executive Committee was able to report that East Hall had been completed on schedule at a total cost of $19,191.90 and was already occupied by students. Fortunately for the college, this larger-than-expected expense was funded from a $50,000 state pledge made in 1859, even though the entire amount was not received until 1864 due to the dislocation caused by the Civil War and its economic impact on state finances.[49]

It is evident from photographs (see fig. 5-39 and fig. 5-41) and comments by past students and faculty members that during its early years East Hall was a somewhat bland, if not even grim-looking, three-story rectangular-block brick structure. One, however, could argue the contrary in today's perspective. Topped a low-pitched roof pierced by brick chimneys, and possessing on its front symmetrical facade a slight projection capped by a closed triangular pediment, the building displayed an array of Italianate elements, including segmental-arched window headings, heavy dentiled cornice molding and paired support brackets under the roof eaves, and a central, segmental-arched front doorway with thick brownstone molding incorporating a keystone. Initially, this successful design articulation was compromised by the presence of somber brown mastic (stucco) covering the rough brick walls, which, after the mastic partially peeled off, were significantly improved in appearance over the years by repeated paintings and sandblastings. In the twentieth century, the window sashes and frames, windowsills, and cornice moldings and decorative details were painted white, enhancing East Hall's aesthetic character. In addition, over the years college officials have bricked up the east-end doorway (1883), removed most of the chimneys, and applied white ornamental scrolls on either side of the window centered in the front pediment gable. Today, East is a distinctive visual asset to the hilltop campus and its diverse architectural repertoire (fig. 5-42).[50]

When East Hall opened, it contained a central stairwell from which double-loaded corridors extended north and south on each of the three main floors. These corridors contained suites and single rooms capable of housing fifty students. A dining facility, moved from Middle (Packard) Hall and known as The Dive, was installed on the basement level (along with a kitchen and washroom), which had the advantage of windows on three sides because of the grade of the hill. Used as the Commons dining hall for the entire campus, it was converted to additional dormitory space when multipurpose Commons Hall (now Curtis Hall) was put up in the early 1890s. Subjected to hard use over many years, as is typical of college/university residential buildings, East has been remodeled on its interior several times, including 1937, 1945 (following World War II military use), and 1966. In the latter year, after 106 years as a men's dormitory, the building underwent total interior reconstruction and changed roles, becoming a predominantly academic building for the Departments of English, German, and Romance Languages, with the computer processing center in

Fig. 5-41. East Hall (1860), Tufts College. Photograph, 1874, by Edwin B. Rollins. Courtesy of Digital Collections and Archives, Tufts University.

Fig. 5-42. East Hall (1860), Tufts University. Photograph, c. 1968.

the basement. Currently it continues to house English, in addition to the Department of History, with faculty and administrative offices, classrooms, and an all-purpose lounge. Like so many of New England's pre–Civil War higher educational structures, including multipurpose Fenwick Hall at Holy Cross and buildings at Amherst College, East Hall has served its institution in a variety of roles during its highly serviceable lifetime and maintains a positive architectural presence on the College Hill mall portion of the Tufts University campus.[51]

6

TRINITY AND WESLEYAN
IN CONNECTICUT

THE FIRST ROW plan campuses occupied by Trinity (Washington) College in Hartford and Wesleyan University in Middletown were derivatives of Yale's Old Brick Row in New Haven, also located in Connecticut. Erected at the same time, the intended symmetrical three-building rows at the first Trinity campus, no longer in existence, and the one at Wesleyan, never completed as conceived, expressed historic New England planning principles in both their composition and individual building designs. The row at Wesleyan, though limited to two original structures, ultimately grew to become a picturesque, unbalanced five-unit axial composition, combining classical and Victorian eclectic design styles spanning over half a century of American historical and architectural development.

The "College Hill" Campus of Trinity (Washington) College

Long envisioned,[1] Washington College originated through the efforts of Episcopalians in Connecticut to create a second higher educational institution in the state. In December 1822, at a meeting of Connecticut Episcopal clergymen in New Haven led by Bishop Thomas C. Brownell, a memorial document was prepared for the state legislature "to grant an act of incorporation for a college with power to confer the usual literary honors, to be placed in either of the cities of Hartford, Middletown or New Haven." The memorial also specified that incorporation should officially occur as soon as $30,000 in subscription funds had been raised and that the new college take the name Washington in honor of America's first president.

Stipulating that the new institution was to be nondenominational, the charter for the college was approved by the Connecticut house, the senate, and the governor and granted on 16 May 1823. In May 1824, the newly appointed board of trustees voted to locate the college in Hartford after the required sum of $30,000 (later increased to $50,000) had been raised from a general subscription drive, Hartford goods and services with monetary value, pledges from Hartford residents, and an appropriation by the Hartford Town Meeting. Promptly, for the sum of $4,000, the trustees acquired a superb fourteen-acre hilltop tract adjacent to the South Meetinghouse near West and Buckingham streets, known traditionally as the Whitney-Seymour property. As the site of the new institution, it soon assumed the name of College Hill, well positioned approximately one-half mile from the historic downtown center of Hartford. Overlooking the scenic Park or Hog River, the wooded, raised site in many respects was ideal for the location of a higher educational institution.[2]

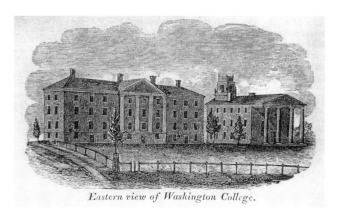

Fig. 6-1. "Eastern View of Washington College." Left, Jarvis Hall (1824–25); right, Seabury Hall (1824–25). Engraving from John Warner Barber, *Connecticut Historical Collections* (1836), p. 88. Courtesy of Trinity College Archives, Trinity College, Hartford, Conn.

Fig. 6-2. Solomon Willard's plan (c. 1824) for Washington College. Courtesy of Trinity College Archives, Trinity College, Hartford, Conn.

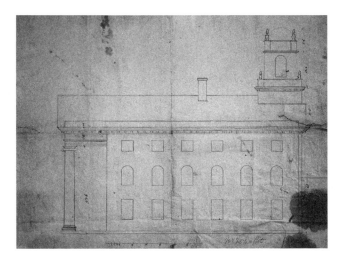

Fig. 6-3. Solomon Willard's north-side elevation plan (c. 1824) for Seabury Hall (1824–25), Washington College. Courtesy of Trinity College Archives, Trinity College, Hartford, Conn.

In June 1824, within a month after the acquisition of the Hartford property, the trustees commenced the construction of the first two buildings (fig. 6-1) of the newly formed Washington College. Built quickly and efficiently, they were ready for occupancy by the autumn of 1825. The new Greek classical structures—in 1845 named Seabury Hall after Samuel Seabury, the first Episcopal Bishop of Connecticut, and Jarvis Hall after Abraham Jarvis, Seabury's successor—were clearly conceived to comprise two units of an eastward-facing, symmetrical, three-building row inspired by the original Yale row scheme and implemented by other pre–Civil War colleges and universities discussed in this book. The fact that all three buildings constituting the row were not erected simultaneously was in all likelihood due to limited financial resources and the lack of additional spatial needs during the college's initial years. A front-elevation drawing (fig. 6-2), prepared in around 1824 by the noted Boston architect, sculptor, and teacher Solomon W. Willard (1783–1861), depicts the row as it was initially planned for completion and irrefutably links Willard with the overall project.[3]

Anchoring the row at the center, with its main end facade facing eastward, was Seabury Hall (see fig. 6-7), a nicely proportioned three-story, pitched-roof brownstone edifice distinguished at the front by its four-column, Ionic portico with plain entablature and closed pediment above, and at the rear by its two-stage, square bell tower with corner finials on two levels. According to Trinity tradition and repeatedly mentioned in older published sources, the versatile Samuel F. B. Morse (1791–1872), known primarily as the inventor of the telegraph and a portrait painter, exe-

cuted the designs for the new building. Such an assertion, however, seems doubtful, as convincing documentation of an attribution to Morse is lacking in his published biographies and in his personal papers housed at Yale University's Sterling Memorial Library and at the Library of Congress. Furthermore, there exists in the Trinity College Archives a north-side elevation drawing (fig. 6-3) by Solomon Willard, raising the distinct possibility that he may have drafted the complete plans for Seabury Hall simultaneous with his work on Jarvis Hall.

Referred to as College Chapel during its first twenty years, the 87-by-55-foot structure contained as its largest room the chapel, along with a five-thousand-volume "library, mineralogical cabinet, philosophical chamber, laboratory and recitation rooms." Soon growing to about twelve thousand volumes, the library quickly became one of the

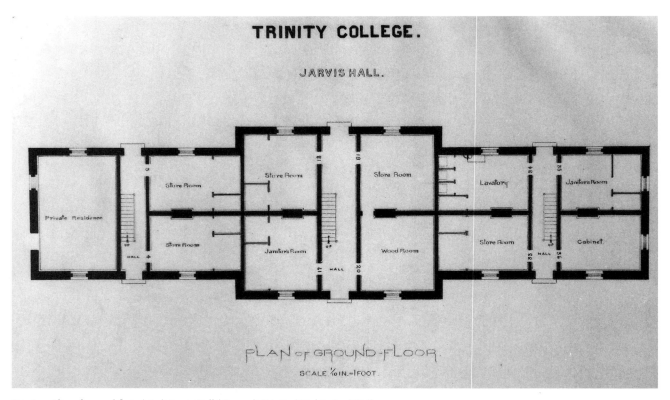

Fig. 6-4. Plan of ground floor (1871), Jarvis Hall (1824–25), Trinity (Washington) College.
Courtesy of Trinity College Archives, Trinity College, Hartford, Conn.

most outstanding in New England higher education, with its rich holdings in Latin classics and religious/ecclesiastical works. The cabinet was said to contain an extensive collection of minerals, geological specimens, and shells, gaining it considerable respect in the scientific community. After a half century of service to the college, Seabury Hall was demolished in the summer of 1878 as part of the process of relocation of Trinity College to its current site at Rocky Ridge in Hartford.[4]

Erected in the same time frame as Seabury Hall was Jarvis Hall (see fig. 6-1), a dormitory known initially as The College containing rooms for approximately one hundred students. Situated just to the south of Seabury, its main front facade also faced eastward, its longitudinal axis at right angles to the longitudinal axis of Seabury, emulating the Yale row model. Also built of brownstone masonry and displaying the Greek Ionic order in its detailing, Jarvis was an equally functional, imposing, well-scaled structure, four stories in height, 148 feet long and 43 feet wide at its midpoint, and contained forty-eight rooms, including a resident faculty suite (fig. 6-4). Student rooms, the largest measuring 12 by 20 feet, were considered spacious and even

luxurious compared with the off-campus, temporary quarters first occupied by Washington College students. Over the years, however, the building, like so many residence halls at other New England colleges, showed the effects of intensive use, requiring the constant attention of college officials. Like Seabury, Jarvis was torn down in the summer of 1878, when the first campus was in the process of being abandoned.[5]

Manuscript and published sources convincingly document that Solomon Willard was the architect of Jarvis Hall. Perhaps best known for the design and construction of the Bunker Hill Monument (1825–42) in Charlestown, Massachusetts, he initially specialized in forms of carpentry and mastered the art of wood carving, preparing capitals and other architectural features for Boston churches and other building types, as well as figureheads for sailing ships. A keen student of architecture and a practicing architect, Willard prepared plans for several well-known Boston buildings, including the United States Branch Bank (1824), the Suffolk County Court House (1825), and the Boston Court House (1832). The validity of his Jarvis Hall commission for the college is assured by the presence of his signed

Fig. 6-5. Solomon Willard's front-facade elevation plan (c. 1824) for Jarvis Hall (1824–25), Washington College. Courtesy of Trinity College Archives, Trinity College, Hartford, Conn.

front-elevation plan (c. 1824; fig. 6-5) in the Trinity College Archives.[6]

As an expression of early-nineteenth-century New England college dormitory design, Jarvis Hall, as seen in a c. 1870 photograph (fig. 6-6), was exemplary. The central ordering focal point of the tripartite building was a pitched-roof front projection or pavilion, its front wall surface placed approximately 5 feet in front of the main facade extensions. Consistent with those of Seabury's front facade, Jarvis's major features included four flat Ionic columns in relief set on a one-story base and supporting a flat entablature. Above was a closed pediment with dentiled cornice. The entablature and cornice were continued around the entire building under a main hipped roof penetrated by four tall brick chimneys. Aesthetically, the building was a gem, clearly the work of a skilled architect thoroughly familiar with Greek classical design principles and their application to mid-Victorian American architecture.

In 1845, two important events took place—a change in the college's name, and the construction of a third major building, which resulted in the completion of the original row plan. On 8 May 1845, the trustees, concerned that the

Fig. 6-6. Jarvis Hall (1824–25), Trinity (Washington) College. Photograph, c. 1870. Courtesy of Trinity College Archives, Trinity College, Hartford, Conn.

Fig. 6-7. The Old Campus, Trinity (Washington) College. Left, Jarvis Hall (1824–25); center, Seabury Hall (1824–25); right, Brownell Hall (1845). Photograph, c. 1870. Courtesy of Trinity College Archives, Trinity College, Hartford, Conn.

Fig. 6-8. Student room, Brownell Hall (1845), Trinity (Washington) College. Photograph, c. 1870. Courtesy of Trinity College Archives, Trinity College, Hartford, Conn.

name of Washington College was becoming too prevalent in the United States, voted to request that the Connecticut legislature approve the new name of Trinity College following the example of Trinity College at Cambridge University in England. The legislature promptly granted approval, and the governor signed the act on 24 May of the same year. Also in 1845, under the presidency of Silas Totten, the citizens of Hartford provided $15,000 in funding for a second dormitory (fig. 6-7), which took the name Brownell Hall in honor of Trinity's first president, Thomas C. Brownell. At the same time, The College and the College Chapel received their more familiar names.[7]

Assumed from the beginning as a component of the campus master plan, Brownell Hall occupied a site balancing that of Jarvis Hall, just north of Seabury Hall. Like Jarvis, Brownell faced east, its longitudinal axis at right angles to that of Seabury. On the exterior, it was a precise duplicate of Jarvis, identical in dimensions, constructed of the same materials and adorned with the same Greek Ionic order details. Plans for the new edifice are believed to have been prepared by President Totten, and while this may be true, one may speculate that they were directly inspired by the work of Solomon Willard on the full row plan, specifically his design for Jarvis Hall. Construction was implemented at a rapid pace, and Brownell was ready for service in just over a year.

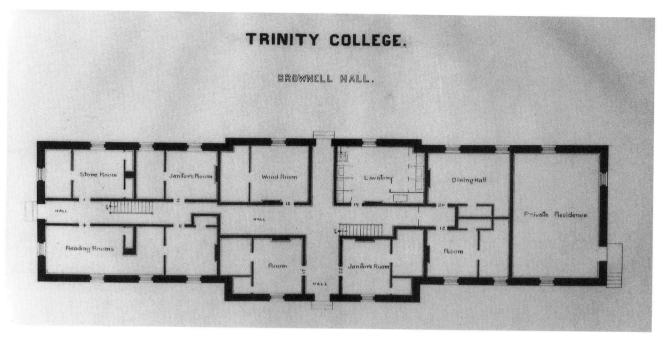

Fig. 6-9. Plan of ground floor (1871), Brownell Hall (1845), Trinity (Washington) College. Courtesy of Trinity College Archives, Trinity College, Hartford, Conn.

Although Brownell Hall was a mirror image of Jarvis Hall on its exterior, the interior layout was different. Brownell contained a smaller number of rooms, with thirty-eight for student housing (fig. 6-8), an apartment for the occupancy of a faculty member and family, and a recitation hall. Unlike Jarvis, which had entryway corridors, Brownell possessed a central entry and long corridors extending the length of each floor (fig. 6-9). The Brownell interior plan is believed to have improved illumination of the interior rooms by natural lighting through the windows. This likely encouraged occupants to view the impressive outside grounds, with their variety of trees and shrubs, as well as a nearby formal garden with a greenhouse.[8]

The completion of Brownell Hall, and concurrently the three-unit row, created a 450-foot frontage of college buildings intentionally placed within an attractive natural setting (fig. 6-10). This undoubtedly enhanced the learning experience in ways consistent with the philosophy of the founders of Williams College. Unfortunately, unlike Williams, Trinity's first campus did not survive, particularly because the campus and adjacent park were considered the most desirable site in the City of Hartford. For many years, Hartford and New Haven had vied to see which would become the permanent capital of Connecticut. In 1871, Hartford officials extended an offer to the state of a new site for the capitol building and approached the Trinity College trustees with a proposal to purchase the College Hill campus for that purpose. At first the trustees, taking into account the negative sentiment of faculty, student, and alumni, rejected the purchase offer, but after further negotiations, on 21 March 1872 the trustees voted to proceed with the sale. On 15 April, the deed for the property was signed, and the City of Hartford compensated the college trustees with $100,000 in cash as well as a bond for the $500,000 balance. In addition, the college reserved the right to occupy and utilize the buildings and grounds of the campus until April 1877. Seabury and Jarvis halls succumbed to the wrecking ball in summer 1878, while Brownell Hall was demolished in stages between spring 1873 and summer 1877. The first Trinity College campus thus met the same fate as the first Colby (Waterville) College campus would in the mid-twentieth century.

Replacing the Trinity row was Richard M. Upjohn's majestic and eclectic Victorian masterpiece, the Connecticut State Capitol (1872–79), which to this day visually dominates the center of downtown Hartford. Utilizing the proceeds from the sale, the college trustees, after considering several sites, acquired the present Trinity campus, located just over a mile to the southwest at Rocky Ridge. In 1875–78, based on designs by the British architect William Burges,

Fig. 6-10. "Trinity College about 1850." Left, Jarvis Hall (1824–25); center, Seabury Hall (1824–25); right, Brownell Hall (1845). Lithograph, c. 1894, Case & Green, Lith., Hartford Conn. Courtesy of Trinity College Archives, Trinity College, Hartford, Conn.

as adapted by the American supervising architect Francis H. Kimball (1868–1948) of New York, a three-quadrangle master plan was approved, and the western side of the central quadrangle was constructed, combining elements of the "French" Gothic and Romanesque revival styles. In implementing this ambitious project, later known as the Long Walk, the tradition of superlative architectural creativity and practicality established at the initial College Hill campus was perpetuated.[9]

The A.L.S.&M. Academy and the Old Campus of Wesleyan University

The first two buildings of Wesleyan University's nineteenth-century "College Row," South College and North College (fig. 6-11), predate the official founding of the institution and were the creation, under different names, of Wesleyan's forerunner, the American Literary, Scientific and Military Academy. Originally opened in Norwich, Vermont, in 1820 under the leadership of Captain Alden T. Partridge, the academy, in need of a better location to expand, was

moved to Middletown, Connecticut, in 1825 in response to a generous offer by the local citizenry. In August of the preceding year, a special promotional committee had been formed to secure the required funds for purchasing the land

Fig. 6-11. "Wesleyan University, Middletown, Conn." Lithograph by Endicott, B. Tharp, Pinxt, c. 1836. Courtesy of Special Collections and Archives, Wesleyan University.

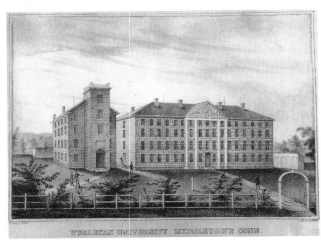

WESLEYAN UNIVERSITY MIDDLETOWN CONN.

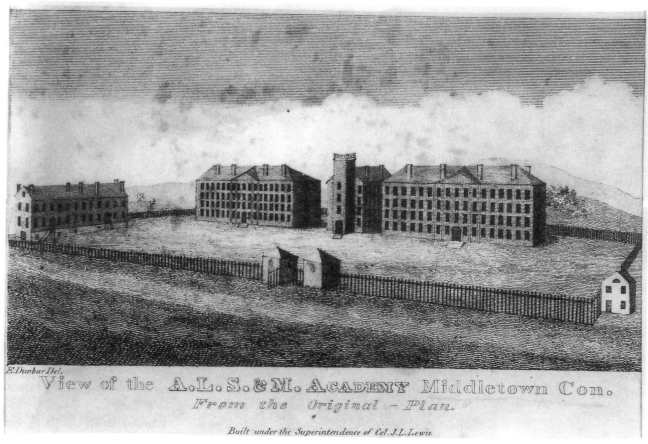

Fig. 6-12. "View of the A.L.S.&M. Academy, Middletown, Con. From the Original Plan. Built under the Superintendence of Col. J. L. Lewis." Signed "E. Dunbar, del." Frontispiece of J. Holbrook, *Military Tactics* (Middletown, Conn.: Printed by E. & H. Clark, 1826), p. 344. Courtesy of Special Collections and Archives, Wesleyan University.

and erecting the buildings. On raising over $30,000 for the project, the committee acquired twelve acres of prime land for $3,000 on the hillside above High Street overlooking the downtown district and the Connecticut River to the east. After the academy stockholders received a charter from the Connecticut Assembly in May 1825, the promotional committee transferred title for the land and buildings to the newly formed academy corporation, and the official opening followed in September.

Although the relocated academy attracted large enrollments and maintained high visibility from the onset, it soon encountered financial difficulties and was unable to procure additional funds from the local community or the legislature. In response, Partridge reopened the previous Norwich, Vermont, campus, supposedly as a preparatory school for the Middletown institution, but it soon became Norwich University. By the spring of 1829, the academy buildings had been vacated, and local leaders commenced

the process of establishing a new college in Middletown to be affiliated with the Methodist church. Finally, on 3 September 1829, a special joint Methodist committee of the New York and Connecticut conferences, created to review proposals for a new denominational college, made the decision in favor of Middletown, which provided fifteen acres of land, the two academy buildings and secondary structures, academic materials, and $18,000 in subscriptions (of a total of $40,000 being raised) to buy stock in the new collegiate venture. Named in honor of John Wesley, the primary founder of Methodism in England in the mid-1700s, Wesleyan University was officially chartered in May 1831, and, under the presidency of Wilbur Fisk, the new college officially opened to students the following September.[10]

As conceived, the principal physical plant inherited by Wesleyan from the academy was intended to be a symmetrical three-building row (fig. 6-12) following Yale's Old Brick Row precedent in much the same configuration as

Fig. 6-13. South College (Lyceum Building) (1824–25), Wesleyan University. Photograph, c. 1880. Courtesy of Special Collections and Archives, Wesleyan University.

Fig. 6-14. South College (Lyceum Building) (1824–25), Wesleyan University. Photograph, 2009.

the row at Trinity (Washington) College in Hartford, commenced at the same time. The central focal point of the unrealized row was South College (fig. 6-13), built by the academy in 1824–25. Known as the Lyceum to 1862, it was designated as the College Building from 1862 to 1871, then assuming its current and most common name. The oldest surviving structure on the Wesleyan campus, South College was designed by architects Edward Hine and Merrill Ward and constructed under the direction of contractor John L. Lewis. Long the center of the educational life of the academy and then the university in the nineteenth century, South initially accommodated an arsenal and laboratory in the basement, and classrooms on the first and second floors. On the third floor was the Hall of the Lyceum, used as a chapel, drill room, and meeting space. After its acquisition by the university, the hall housed only a chapel facility, which was relocated to the basement in 1835. At the same time, the hall was converted into a library and a museum (then referred to as "cabinets"), which remained there until 1868 and 1871, respectively. In addition, recitation rooms, offices, and student rooms occupied the structure until 1906, when it was remodeled and assumed its current role as an administrative facility for the president's and associated offices. It has been remodeled several times since.

Constructed of random rubble brown limestone from Portland, Connecticut, South College (fig. 6-14) has dimensions of 45 by 56 feet. The basement level of the three-and-one-half-story, pitched-roof block is partly above ground. Positioned at the center of the front facade is a 14-by-16-foot tower, approximately 75 feet tall. It is topped by a flat roof with molded cornice, above which is a balustrade and octagon-shaped, enclosed belfry cupola with round cap topped by a finial. Designed by the renowned New York City architect Henry Bacon (1866–1924), the present cupola, added in 1919, replaced an older wooden bell structure and contains a chime of eleven bells cast in England. Pairs of tall side-wall chimneys pierce the south and north roof planes. The current raised, segmental-arched main entrance in the tower facade replaced the original ground-level entrance. Plain, with modest classical detail, South College closely resembles the central row buildings at other early New England higher educational institutions, particularly that at Middlebury College in Vermont.[11]

North College (fig. 6-15)—known until 1871 as the Old Academy Barracks or the Dormitory—was erected in 1824–25, during the same time period as the Lyceum (later South

Fig. 6-15. North College (The Dormitory) (1824–25), Wesleyan University. Photograph, c. 1880.
Courtesy of Special Collections and Archives, Wesleyan University.

College), some 20 feet to the north on the line of the College Row. Like South College, North was planned by architects Edward Hine and Merrill Ward and was built by contractor John L. Lewis. Also constructed of random rubble brown limestone from Portland, Connecticut, it measured 150 feet in length and 53 feet in width, with four stories and an attic set on cellar foundations, and a hipped roof penetrated by eight tall chimneys. Serving as a residence hall (fig. 6-16) for its entire history, North initially possessed long corridors that ran north-south through the center of each floor level, but in 1832 two partitions were constructed separating the interior into north, middle, and south sections. The sectional partitions were subsequently pierced with doorways at an unknown time, but they were restored in 1893 as a result of a $26,500 gift for remodeling from alumnus John E. Andrus. Accessed by a central stairwell, the building contained sixty-four rooms on either side of the corridors.

The principal architectural feature of North College was its front central projecting pavilion, recalling earlier examples adorning Nassau Hall at Princeton, University Hall at Brown, Hollis Hall at Harvard, and Dartmouth Hall. Perfectly symmetrical, the pavilion displayed Federal-style details, including fanlights above the front central doorway

Fig. 6-16. Student room, North College (The Dormitory) (1824–25), Wesleyan University. Photograph, c. 1870. Courtesy of Special Collections and Archives, Wesleyan University.

Fig. 6-17. North College (1907–8), Wesleyan University. Photograph, 2009.

and in the closed pediment above, and a modillioned cornice. Supporting the cornice on the left and right were pairs of tall, flat, brown limestone pilasters with Doric capitals, a reflection of the early Greek Revival influence. These various components were masterfully integrated, creating a nicely proportioned front wall surface. Sadly, on 1 March 1906, the building was totally destroyed by fire, and the New England region lost one of its most outstanding early-nineteenth-century collegiate dormitories.

In response to this unfortunate event, Wesleyan trustees and administrators approved and financed a reconstructed version of North College (fig. 6-17) begun in March 1907 and ready for student occupancy in January 1908. Designed by the New York architectural firm of Albro and Lindeberg, the replacement structure was built very much along the lines of its predecessor on the same site, preserving the integrity of the expanded College Row. Major differences of the new North College, however, included greater overall height; the placement of a pronounced cornice between the third and fourth stories; an entrance portico with evenly spaced, round columns; an entrance stairway and terrace; tightly jointed, cut-brownstone construction; and a greater reliance on neoclassical design detail. Containing 104

rooms, the reconstructed North College was used largely as a dormitory until 1966, but after 1955 it had begun a gradual metamorphosis to an office building. At present, most of Wesleyan's administrative offices are located there, including those of the provost, vice presidents, and deans. Despite this functional change, and the structural and design differences cited above, the current edifice visually perpetuates the legacy of the original North College.[12]

A third Wesleyan University pre–Civil War building, first known as the Old Boarding Hall (see fig. 6-12), was constructed and operated as a private enterprise to serve the academy and then the university. Raised in 1825, in April 1833 it was purchased for $2,000 at auction by the trustees and thereafter became the institutional commons under the name College Hall. Set back from High Street adjacent to the row and facing north, it opened in April 1834 and continued in service until a new boarding hall was erected in 1839. A rather plain, nondescript edifice, it was constructed of brick with dimensions of 150 by 50 feet. Two stories tall, College Hall was capped by a pitched roof with tall brick chimneys, like its row neighbors, and possessed a main unembellished entrance at its north end. At first the basement was used as a kitchen, the first story as a dining hall, and the second story as residential quarters. The building was almost totally devoid of architectural detail; the only evidence of stylistic influence were the Federal-era fanlights set in the closed pediments of the east and west ends of the building. By the summer of 1846, College Hall had outlived its usefulness, was sold for $500, and was demolished over the next two years by new private owners.[13]

While it was not a major component of the campus architecturally, Captain Partridge's gun-house, put up with his own funds in 1826, served a variety of functions after Wesleyan purchased it from him in 1835 for a mere $175. Situated on flat ground just behind the Old Academy Barracks (North College), this unembellished, two-story, pitched-roof brick structure was 55 feet long and 30 feet wide, with its main entrance facing east. Under the name of Old Laboratory, it served as a chemical laboratory to 1871, a commons for nonfraternity men from 1872 to 1875, an icehouse and carpentry shop from 1876 to 1890, an electrical laboratory from 1891 to 1905, and a bacteriological laboratory until 1907, when it was razed, its reputation as an important collegiate scientific facility secured.[14]

The university's last early major building was the Boarding Hall (later Observatory Hall), which was in the planning stages for several years, commencing in 1834. Over a nearly five-year period, discouraged by the national economic Panic of 1837, the Board of Trustees and Prudential Committee initiated strategies, adopted plans, and secured estimates for a new commons hall, part of which was to be used as a chapel. It was originally to be located south of the Lyceum (South College), roughly the same distance away as the Dormitory (North College) to the north. As built it was not incorporated into the row; rather, it was situated over 100 yards to the southwest. Finally, on 31 July 1838, Wesleyan's joint board recommended that the trustees secure a loan of $10,000 and proceed with construction. Fortuitously, early in 1839 the Connecticut General Assembly appropriated $10,000 to the university, and the Boarding Hall was completed before the end of the year. The final cost was approximately $8,000.

A bland, awkward, three-story, pitched-roof brick edifice, the new 100-by-40-foot structure (fig. 6-18) initially housed pantries and a kitchen on the first floor, a large dining room in the middle of the second, the infirmary and, later, society rooms on the third, and the steward's family quarters in the south rooms on all three floors. After the dining commons closed in 1846, the interior was gradu-

ally converted to dormitory use. On the front center of the building was an enclosed stairwell fabricated of wood and displaying classical details, including four flat pilasters with Doric capitals, with an entablature and a closed pediment above. The presence of this configured, albeit scaled-down form effectively repeated the classical composition of the front projection of North College.

In 1839, the university constructed its first observatory, a small, octagonal, white wooden structure on Cross Street. In the fall of 1868, to house a new Alvan Clark & Sons 12-inch refractor, the wooden stairwell addition was removed from the front of the Boarding Hall and was replaced by a new brick stairwell tower with front entrance and porch. At the top of this tower was a cubical wooden stage supporting a cylindrical observatory facility, which replaced the earlier, freestanding observatory. The presence of the new tower, with its Italianate corner pilasters, cornice, balustrade, and porch details, substantially upgraded the aesthetic appearance of the Boarding Hall, now retitled Observatory Hall (fig. 6-19). When the current Van Vleck Observatory was erected in 1914–16, the tower was no longer needed and was removed. In 1927, the main building block was leveled to make way for a new dormitory, Harriman Hall (1928), which occupies the site today. By this action, Wesleyan

Fig. 6-18. Boarding Hall (1839) before renovation, Wesleyan University. Photograph, from Class of 1865 album. Courtesy of Special Collections and Archives, Wesleyan University.

Fig. 6-19. Observatory Hall (Boarding Hall) (1839, etc.). Photograph, n.d. Courtesy of Special Collections and Archives, Wesleyan University.

University lost a structure rich in history but of questionable architectural merit.

At about the same time that the Boarding Hall transitioned to Observatory Hall, President Joseph Cummings led a movement in the late 1860s to abandon the three-building row idea so well articulated at Trinity (Washington) College and to place a new church edifice at the center of a longer row. Following Cummings's successful appeals to Methodist supporters for donations, three new brownstone buildings were successfully financed and erected in a line south of North and South colleges. Completing the revised five-building row were the Gothic Revival Memorial Chapel (1871), the planned central focal point; Rich Hall (1868), the new library, also in the Gothic Revival style; and, at the south end, mansard-roofed Judd Hall (1871), one of the first structures in this country designed exclusively for undergraduate science education. While the expanded row lacked the perfect balance of Bowdoin College's five-building row, its similar configuration reflected a major commitment to the row plan concept dating from the era of Captain Partridge's American Literary, Scientific and Military Academy and the first years of Wesleyan University.[15]

COLBY AND BATES IN MAINE

THE FIRST PRE-CIVIL WAR examples of multifaceted higher educational architecture and concerted campus planning at Colby and Bates colleges in Maine, while exemplary, achieved varying historical/architectural results and legacies. Each campus building configuration, however, drew its inspiration from the traditional New England row plan, initiated at Yale and subsequently adopted by other New England institutions. Integrating a variety of educational objectives, individual buildings displayed similar as well as differing stylistic idioms and were, by and large, functionally successful expressions of the evolving educational philosophies of the New England region.

The Bricks at Colby (Waterville) College

For well over a century, the former three-building row at Colby (initially Waterville) College, locally known as The Bricks, was one of New England's handsomest and most imposing higher educational building groups.[1] Situated in downtown Waterville in central Maine, on the west side of and parallel to the Kennebec River, this "simple symmetrical trinity" of structures once dominated the rolling valley terrain adjacent to its peaceful, wooded campus site. Over time, however, this once-unspoiled rural environment underwent dramatic change, and today these fine early specimens of collegiate architecture no longer stand. Circumscribed by the river, the growing industrial town, a new highway, and the Maine Central Railroad tracks, the small, elongated fifteen-acre campus was replaced in the 1950s by a new, expansive complex planned by Jens Fredrick Larson on rural Mayflower Hill, a mile west of Waterville.[2] For many people, especially the college's alumni, the decision to demolish the original buildings and relocate the campus was met with feelings of regret and nostalgia. At the same time, they realized that the college could progress and achieve its historic mission only in a more suitable setting where there was room for future educational innovation and physical expansion.

Development of The Bricks articulated the prevailing higher educational philosophy of early-nineteenth-century America. In the full building group, as well as the individual structures, the college's early planners combined all of the components of the undergraduate educational experience — academic, religious, social, cultural, recreational, dining, and residential — rather than segregating them into separate campuses or buildings, as was ultimately the case at most institutions after the Civil War. This philosophy, which encouraged the integration of formal as well as informal learning, was directly reflected in campus plans and interior building layouts at the pre-1860 New England colleges. Thus the entire academic and living environment of The Bricks was condi-

Fig. 7-1. The Bricks, detail from the "Northwest View of Colby College." From left to right: North College (1822); Recitation Hall (1836); South College (1821). Lithograph after Esteria Butler oil painting, c. 1836, Colby College Art Museum, by Thomas Moore, Boston. Courtesy of Colby College Special Collections, Waterville, Maine.

tioned by broadly embraced educational principles and the architecture they inspired and brought to fruition.

Fortunately for those who wish to study the first Colby campus, sufficient source materials exist. In addition to detailed references in published works, several valuable manuscript citations survive, as do a number of nineteenth-century printed views and photographs of the campus and its buildings. One may gain an accurate impression of how the row buildings appeared in their parklike surroundings in a detail (fig. 7-1) from Thomas Moore's c. 1836 lithograph, derived from Esteria Butler's painting of the young college.[3] Commanding foremost attention in the middle of the view is Recitation (Champlin) Hall (1836–37), with its tall, imposing chapel tower a fitting symbol of the college's chartered role as a training school for Baptist clergymen. This monumental edifice was the last of The Bricks group to be constructed, fulfilling the original trustee plan for a symmetrical three-building row on the model of Yale (see fig. 1-31) and other early New England colleges.[4] In the Butler view, two earlier, virtually identical structures, South (1821)

and North (1822) colleges, occupy flanking positions in the row scheme, equidistant from Recitation. A highly functional and aesthetically pleasing arrangement, Colby's row made a powerful, unified architectural statement without compromising the virtues and qualities of its separate components.

Conceived primarily as dormitories, South and North colleges possessed the same simple and direct qualities as their New England predecessors. Ideas circulated freely among college institutions in the region, and it is probable, though undocumented, that the design concepts for these buildings originated with older, similar residential structures at Yale, Andover Theological Seminary, Harvard, Bowdoin, and so on. Given its proximity to Waterville, Maine Hall (1807–8, etc.) (see fig. 3-18) at Bowdoin College in Brunswick, Maine, appears to have had the most direct and pronounced influence. Large, adorned rectangular blocks, South and North were strikingly similar in size, scale, and most stylistic features. This is hardly surprising given that they were both designed and erected by local master builders Peter Getchell and Lemuel Dunbar. A rare 1857 daguerreotype (fig. 7-2) of the row shows the two buildings on either side of Recitation Hall nearly a century before they were lost to the Mayflower Hill campus development.

Planning for South and North colleges began in 1819, when a Waterville College trustee resolution called for the construction of a wood-frame house for the president and a larger brick building.[5] The latter structure, to be known as South College, was delayed until 1821 due to the lack of funding, a common problem among educational institutions of the era. As a result, construction did not occur until the trustees persuaded a sufficient number of subscribers to commit their support to the building effort.[6] An 1822 publicity leaflet offers descriptive information and critical commentary about the new structure:

The Trustees . . . during the present year (1821) . . . have erected a brick edifice 80 by 40, and four stories high, for the use of Students. This . . . building is calculated to contain thirty-two rooms, and, when completed, will accommodate sixty-four students. It is considered by good judges a fine building, and does honour alike to the workmen employed upon it, and to the gentlemen who superintended the erection of it. A Hall intended to answer the purposes of a temporary Chapel, and eighteen rooms for Students are already finished.[7]

A double-entryway plan accommodated a variety of educational facilities — recitation rooms, a mineral exhibit, a philosophic society, and a library (until 1836) in interior spaces not utilized for residential quarters.[8] With credits due Getchell for his masonry work and Dunbar for his carpentry,[9] the new building was dedicated in an impressive ceremony at which college officials placed candles behind each of the thirty-two panes of glass in every window on the west facade and south end. Superimposed against the trees and darkness behind, the scene must have been memorable.[10]

Fig. 7-2. The Bricks, Colby (Waterville) College. From left to right, North College (1822); Recitation Hall (1836); South College (1821). Daguerreotype, 1856. Courtesy of Colby College Special Collections, Waterville, Maine.

Fig. 7-3. "Colby College—South College and Row." Photograph, c. 1880. Courtesy of Colby College Special Collections, Waterville, Maine.

Fig. 7-4. "North College (Chaplin Hall)," Colby University. Photograph, c. 1870. Courtesy of Colby College Special Collections, Waterville, Maine.

The Colby College Special Collections possesses only a few visual images depicting the nineteenth-century South College. A photograph (fig. 7-3) from about 1880 shows the college physical plant in a state quite altered from the earlier daguerreotype view, the results of a sweeping 1873 renovation. A small, square wooden cupola containing the college bell (cast at the Paul Revere Foundry in Massachusetts in 1824) sits astride the ridgepole of South College's low hipped roof. An unflattering but functional wooden porch was attached to the south end. Wooden Italianate support brackets were positioned under the eaves along the cornice line. Inside, student accommodations were enlarged to suites of two rooms to create bedroom/study combinations as in other New England college dormitories of the period.[11] In other respects South College remained unaltered. The crisply delineated outlines of the roof and walls and the sharp accents of its chimneys and white stone window lintels continued to reflect the precision, economy, and provinciality that went into its making.

North College, younger than its twin by one year, conveyed a similar visual impression and is of equal architectural and historic significance. Another early photo (fig. 7-4) from the archives shows the building prior to its 1872 renovation. Evident are paired double-sash windows and arched entry doorways with semicircular fanlights, an obvious vestige of the Federal style. In dimensions and virtually every architectural detail it was identical to South College. The building originated with a trustee Prudential Committee resolution in May 1822:

Voted—That the Prudential Committee be authorized to erect another college building this present season . . . Voted—That the Prudential Committee be instructed & authorized to complete the contract they have informally entered into with Peter Getchell for a new brick College building eighty by forty, four stories high for the sum of three thousand dollars, the building to be erected . . . similar in style to the College Edifice already built . . . Lemuel Dunbar . . . doing the carpentry work of the outside of the building.[12]

Typical of its time, the structure combined several educational functions, initially containing thirty-two rooms for student living, a cellar that accommodated a chapel until 1836, and a spacious dining and commons hall for large college functions.[13] To commemorate the 1872 renovation, the trustees renamed the building Chaplin Hall after the college's first president, Reverend Jeremiah Chaplin.

Experiencing almost as harrowing an existence as Bowdoin's Maine Hall (which suffered major fires in 1822 and 1836), North College burned on three separate occasions but each time was rebuilt and put back into service, virtually unchanged. After the initial fire in 1902, a special $15,000 grant from the Maine legislature funded the necessary repairs, along with new suite-type rooming arrangements. In 1911, after another serious blaze, $25,000 was required to rebuild the entire interior, as well as the roof on the south entry.[14] Yet the greatest tragedy for the college lay ahead: on 4 December 1922 a fire broke out in the north entry, killing four students and ruining all four floors.[15] For an additional sum of $15,000, the old dormitory was restored and returned to use for the final time. Thirty years later it would be subjected to the terminal poundings of the wrecking ball. In retrospect, it seems unfortunate that the money repeatedly expended to rebuild North College could not have made possible its long-term survival and continued use.

Nearly fifteen years after the completion of South and North colleges, Recitation Hall assumed its place as the dominant center structure in Colby College's trio of row buildings. A block-shaped, multipurpose edifice, it embodied the same educational philosophy and possessed many of the same traditional Federal-style features as its predecessors. On the brick-walled exterior certain innovative Greek Revival elements were also introduced, principally in the panel brick treatment and in the lofty triple-stage tower, which rose high over the primary building mass, endowing it with monumental scale. Due to the tower it became a local legend that Recitation was the tallest extant building in the State of Maine. Throughout its existence it took on different visual personalities, evidence of which can be seen in printed views and photographs.

Recitation Hall, the dream of President Rufus Babcock, was authorized in 1835 when the college trustees designated a sizable portion of an anticipated $25,000 fund "to erect a building for general classroom purposes in which a large and well equipped chapel should be arranged."[16] Determined that their Baptist college have a respectable chapel facility, the trustees, with the aid of Dr. Babcock, developed an innovative means to raise the needed money by issuing scholarship certificates to contributors. The wording of these certificates reflects the trustees' financial acumen:

This certifies that _____ has paid into the treasury of Waterville College $600 towards erecting a chapel. Thereby he and

Waterville College.

Fig. 7-5. "Waterville College," engraving from Austin J. Coolidge and J. B. Mansfield, *A History and Description of New England* (1860), vol. 1, p. 345. Courtesy of Colby College Special Collections, Waterville, Maine.

his assigns forever are entitled to enter and have one student in the college, free of all bills for room, rent, tuition, lectures, and library; but no assignment shall be recognized by the College as valid unless the same shall be made by the donor to some incorporated body in the trust or otherwise. Provided that, if the College shall at anytime hereafter pay the donor, his trustees or assigns, the sum of $600, the scholarship shall cease.[17]

Restricting the number of scholarships to twenty-five to prevent oversubscription, the trustees next approved the preparation of lumber and masonry materials for the building project, a task carried out in large part by students of the college.[18] During the summer of 1836 the college commenced the construction of what was to be an $8,000 structure, the entire funding provided by the ingenious scholarship scheme.[19] Recitation Hall was completed in early 1837. Measuring 65 by 40 feet at its stone foundations, it was originally just two stories high and was covered by a hipped roof. Positioned atop the roof was the tall wooden tower, which gave the appearance of graduated, stacked shoe boxes (fig. 7-5), causing some to question its aesthetic merit. Classical Greek-inspired pilasters were present on the sides of the tower sections (the lower of which contained the college bell), and at the corner intersections of the four main brick walls. Otherwise Recitation was quite stark and plain, like South and North colleges, and consequently blended effectively with the two older buildings.

The interior of Recitation Hall was also multipurpose, devoted to academic as well as ecclesiastical functions. The

main story was raised several feet above ground level, creating a basement story with a substantial number of windows for the admission of natural light. Located here were four recitation rooms. While these were much needed by the college, they were received with little enthusiasm, as they were regarded as damp, dreary, and generally unappealing by the faculty and student body.[20] Situated in the main story above was the new college chapel (relocated from North College), high above ground level, and hence accessible only by an exterior flight of stairs. Above the chapel on the north side of the second story was the library (transferred from South College), and on the south side a philosophical (physical science) apparatus room and classroom for natural philosophy (natural science).[21] Sometime before the mid-1850s, a third story was added for recitation rooms, a modification that improved the building both visually and functionally. Like the central main structures of other New England college row groupings, Recitation was the hub of the Colby academic community, serving a myriad of needs for faculty and students.

The identification of the architect of Recitation Hall has long eluded scholars. Curiously, in official college correspondence and records where one might expect to find references, there is no mention of a specific name. Until recently there was only one solid lead: in his *History of Higher Education in Maine*, Edward Winslow Hall, the librarian of Colby College in the 1890s, attributed the design to Philadelphia's Thomas Ustick Walter (1807–87), one of this country's most esteemed pre–Civil War architects. Walter was an avid exponent of the Greek Revival style and the designer of the national Capitol's dome and its extensions (1851–65).[22] Furthermore, he is possibly the only American architect of his era to travel to Europe specifically to study higher educational architectural design.[23] Presumably Hall, who had easy access to college archival materials, based his attribution on documents that have been misplaced or no longer survive. Of this, however, we cannot be certain. It stands to reason, though, that Walter, who had strong Baptist convictions, would have drawn the attention of the college trustees as they sought a designer for the new main building of their fledgling Baptist institution. In the early history of American higher education there are many instances of colleges selecting an architect in part for religious reasons.

One can speculate further about a possible attribution. Although the standard published materials treating Walter's early career fail to cite any associations with the college dur-

Fig. 7-6. "Champlin Hall—Recitation," Colby University. Photograph, c. 1880. Courtesy of Colby College Special Collections, Waterville, Maine.

ing the 1830s (the first decade of his professional practice), it is conceivable, based on architectural style alone, that Recitation Hall was a Walter design. In several obvious respects, it resembled some of his well-documented commissions of the time. It is known that he worked throughout the northeastern United States, particularly in Pennsylvania, where he produced some landmark educational complexes. The most widely recognized of these were the Girard College for Orphans (1833–47) in Philadelphia, and a portion of the University of Lewisburg (later Bucknell University) complex (1848–59).

Fortunately, we now have reliable confirmation of the Hall attribution. In the late 1970s, in conjunction with the Walters Papers publication project, one of the editors carefully inspected a manuscript journal covering the years 1834–36. Contained in the journal is an entry dated 9 January 1836 indicating that Walter had indeed "made [the] design for Waterville College, Me." This valuable document was initially discovered in a large collection of Walter materials owned by his descendants in Colorado. This collection was subsequently acquired by The Athenaeum of Philadelphia and is now available to researchers.[24] Thus, we may be assured that, while it stood, the first Colby College possessed one of the few pre–Civil War higher educational

buildings in New England to be designed by a major American architect.

In the summer of 1872, after several decades of hard use, Recitation Hall was totally remodeled under the direction of Boston architect Alexander R. Esty (1826–81), the designer of Memorial Hall (1869) at Colby, as well as buildings at other New England colleges and universities. At an expense of $6,000 donated by benefactor and college namesake Gardner Colby of Boston, the old chapel was removed and the resulting space converted to new classrooms and a lecture hall. From that time until its destruction, the building was employed exclusively for academic and extracurricular activities.[25] At the same time, the exterior of Recitation was also transformed (fig. 7-6). Since the outer walls were in danger of collapsing from the weight of the central tower, college officials reluctantly decided to have the tower removed.[26] Concurrently, the building assumed an Italianate look through the addition of heavy decorative window and door moldings, limestone horizontal belt courses, and a series of wooden brackets along the broad cornice under the roof eaves. In its size and proportions, as well as specific ornamental features, the revised version of Recitation resembled Gridley J. F. Bryant's Ballou Hall (1852–54) at Tufts College near Boston. Esty may well have been familiar with

Coburn Hall. Gymnasium. Chaplin Hall. Champlin Hall. South College. Memorial Hall. Library.

COLBY UNIVERSITY, WATERVILLE, ME.

Fig. 7-7. "Colby University, Waterville, Me." Engraving from Rodney H. Howard and Henry C. Crocker, *A History of New England* (1880), vol. 1, p. 71. Courtesy of Colby College Special Collections, Waterville, Maine.

the Tufts building, given that he served as a draftsman in Bryant's office early in his career.[27]

In its altered but improved state, Recitation Hall was re-titled Champlin Hall in honor of James T. Champlin, the president of the college from 1857 to 1873.[28] An engraving (fig. 7-7) from Howard and Crocker's *History of New England* (1880) shows this pivotal structure at the center of The Bricks, which itself is flanked by later nineteenth-century buildings.[29] This pleasant composition, though supplemented by additional, more modern architecture in the twentieth century, remained little changed until the destruction of the first Colby campus in the 1950s.

By eliminating its original buildings, Colby joined a group of other New England colleges and universities whose early row plans were victims of change and advancement in higher education—Yale, Trinity, the University of Vermont, and Norwich University (initially the American Literary, Scientific and Military Academy). To gain a current critical appreciation of early row plans, however, one may still view extant examples in each of the six New En-

gland states, as discussed and illustrated in this book. Like The Bricks, these early core building groups perform diverse but integrated educational functions, expressing current educational philosophy while perpetuating architectural legacies and historical memories.

Bates College and Antebellum Architectural Master Planning

Boston architect Gridley J. F. Bryant's campus design for the Maine State Seminary (Bates College after 1863–64) in Lewiston is one of two documented examples of comprehensive architectural master planning at a pre-1860 northern New England higher educational institution.[30] The other, John Johnson's Old Mill (1825–29; fig. 4-4) at the University of Vermont, although historically significant and architecturally meritorious, is eclipsed by the seminary scheme in several key respects. From its inception Bryant's plan was more ambitious in scope and elaborate in detail, incorporating sound construction technology and flexible, functionally successful interior spatial principles. Furthermore, unlike its Vermont predecessor, it was the brainchild of a major nineteenth-century American building designer. It also commands the attention of architectural historians and others because the total concept, unlike earlier recorded planning efforts by John Trumbull at Yale and Charles Bulfinch at Harvard, was approved in its entirety by the institution's governing board before a single building was erected. While earlier New England college campuses had evolved over many years, like Colby, the seminary was intended to assume form as a single integrated complex within a strictly defined period.

Bates College is the direct outgrowth of the Maine State Seminary, a Free Baptist educational institution established in 1855–56, and its forerunner, Parsonfield Academy in Parsonfield, Maine. It acquired its corporate status as a liberal arts college with its 1864 charter, and its present name was adopted in recognition of a $200,000 gift from textile magnate Benjamin E. Bates of Boston. The founder of the seminary, and the man who oversaw its quick transition to college status, was Reverend Oren B. Cheney (president of Bates College from 1863 to 1894), and the new curriculum reflected his vision and aspirations for the institution. In fact, Cheney had envisioned a college right from the beginning but for reasons relating to the finances and political considerations had at first opted for an advanced seminary preparatory school. From its inception the college was co-educational; it is now free of denominational control, and has long specialized in the training of elementary and secondary school teachers.[31]

The idea of an entirely planned campus at the new seminary was in keeping with the college's location in Lewiston, a comprehensively planned mid-nineteenth-century textile manufacturing center. Largely the creation of Boston-area financial interests previously responsible for the origins and development of Lowell and Lawrence in Massachusetts and Manchester in New Hampshire, Lewiston is similarly located at a rural site adjacent to a great waterpower resource. Gridley J. F. Bryant, by 1850 the leading architect in Boston, was likely known to Lewiston's financiers and was therefore a logical candidate for the preparation of site and building plans for the fledgling educational institution.

Bryant, the son of the noted local engineer, railway pioneer, and builder Gridley Bryant, had been born in Boston in 1816. After an apprenticeship with Alexander Parris and Loami Baldwin, he opened his own office in his native city in 1837. Subsequently he carried out what became the largest, most lucrative, and most efficiently organized architectural practice in New England. Bryant designed scores of public buildings, commercial and institutional structures, and churches, many of them in Boston and more than 150 of them destroyed in the great Boston fire in 1872. Still, many fine and varied examples of his work survive in that city and elsewhere in New England, among them the structures on the Bates College campus.

In their selection of Bryant as architect, the Maine State Seminary trustees were most assuredly influenced by their familiarity with his work in Boston as well as by his building designs for other educational institutions—Ballou Hall (1852–54) for Tufts College and the Fryeburg Academy complex (c. 1852) at Fryeburg, Maine. Perhaps even more compelling to the trustees was their knowledge of Bryant's design of the Androscoggin County courthouse and jail in Auburn, just west across the Androscoggin River from Lewiston. This project was also launched in 1856, at just the time that construction for the seminary was beginning. One design commission may have led to the other, although it is uncertain which the architect secured first.[32]

Fortunately for students of Victorian-era institutional architecture, Hathorn and Parker halls (1856–57), the two realized buildings of Bryant's seminary plan, have survived and constitute a vitally important physical record. Furthermore, substantial published and manuscript material treating the origins and development of the project is available for study. The Bryant scheme is fully documented in seminary trustee meeting notes, in the architect's drawings now in the Bates College Archives, in *The Seminary Advocate* (the institution's first newspaper), and in a manuscript list of the architect's plans and specifications housed at the library of the University of Oregon at Eugene.[33]

The 1856 issues of the *Advocate* contain evidence of the trustees' initial thinking—a description and an artist-rendered woodcut engraving (fig. 7-8) of a conjectural first stage, a Greek Revival–inspired, three-building layout with narrow building ends facing forward. After Bryant was officially commissioned as architect, the scheme assumed a more precise and detailed form in design drawings and published engravings that illustrated adjustments made in building placement, interrelationships, orientation, and Italianate stylistic features. Perhaps the finest of the engravings (fig. 7-9), by Bryant and published in the seminary catalogue of 1860, shows Hathorn Hall in the center;

Fig. 7-8. Artist's rendering of the Maine State Seminary campus plan, showing Parker Hall (left), Hathorn Hall (center), and a proposed dormitory (right). Engraving from *The Seminary Advocate* (1856). Courtesy of the Edmund S. Muskie Archives and Special Collections Library, Bates College.

Fig. 7-9. Gridley J. F. Bryant, "Maine State Seminary, Lewiston, Me." Frontispiece engraving from the *Catalogue of the Officers and Students of the Maine State Seminary, Lewiston* (1860). Courtesy of the Edmund S. Muskie Archives and Special Collections Library, Bates College.

Parker Hall, the men's dormitory, to the left; and a building intended as a women's dormitory to the right. This last building was never built due to the lack of adequate student enrollment and construction funds.[34] Arranged on a longitudinal axis, this row grouping of buildings was unquestionably inspired by earlier compact tripartite row plans at Yale, neighboring Colby College, and other New England institutions. The engraving shows Parker Hall and the proposed matching dormitory, with their long sides rather than their ends serving as front facades, flanking and equidistant from Hathorn, and reflects the trustees' interest in campus landscaping and an interlocking system of walking pathways.

A later unexecuted plan by Bryant provided for the enlargement of the first-stage layout to a single complex of five connected buildings, in the tradition of older campus schemes by Thomas Jefferson at the University of Virginia (1817–26) and Joseph-Jacques Ramee at Union College

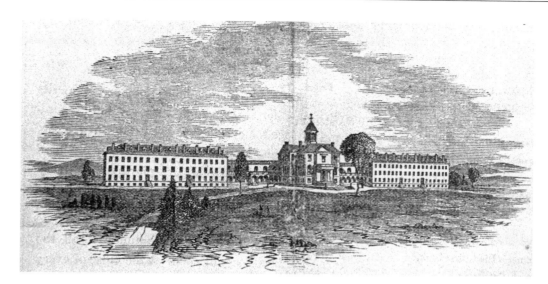

Fig. 7-10. Bates College row with connector buildings. Engraving from *The College Crescent*, April 1864, p. 1. Courtesy of the Edmund S. Muskie Archives and Special Collections Library, Bates College.

(1813) in New York State. The April 1864 issue of *The College Crescent*, Bates's student newspaper, contains the only known illustration of the expanded plan (fig. 7-10). The dormitory wings were to be physically linked to the central structure, Hathorn Hall, by means of 84-by-54-foot, two-story connector units with arcaded porch passageways. The total length of the complex would have reached 513 feet.[35] Such a conception broke with the practice established by earlier New England colleges of consciously organized campuses comprised of separate, freestanding buildings; indeed, connected institutional complexes did not appear in New England until the 1870s, when insane asylums, such as those at Worcester, Massachusetts, and Augusta, Maine, were constructed. As a prototype, Bryant's second-stage plan anticipated the larger university campus plans conceived throughout the United States after the Civil War. Because of its significance as an early documented example of collegiate master planning, it is unfortunate that Bryant's full plan for the Maine State Seminary was never totally realized; nonetheless, even in its incomplete state one can get a valuable idea of how it might have appeared.

Like the central main buildings of earlier New England college row schemes, Hathorn Hall (fig. 7-11) was intended to accommodate a wide variety of educational and administrative functions. It is deserving of notice and recognition for several reasons. First, in purely aesthetic terms, the building is illustrative of the then-popular and innovative application of Italianate style elements to higher educational architecture, thereby departing from the predominantly Greek Revival influence of the 1830s and 1840s. Second, it

originated as the primary focal point for a pioneering campus master plan. Third, Bryant, by the time that he had prepared the plans for Hathorn, had established himself as an esteemed commercial and public building designer.

In 1855 and 1856, founder Oren Cheney and the trustees of the Maine State Seminary carefully considered their first rough planning ideas for the new campus and its centerpiece, Hathorn Hall. A trustee building committee was formed in June 1855, and later that month the full board passed a formal resolution to proceed with the construction project.[36] Presumably the trustees hired Bryant as architect about this time, but trustee records and correspondence do not indicate the precise date of his contract. With Bryant definitely engaged in the design process by February 1856, the building committee selected the site, contracted for site preparation and materials, and designated Alvin Fogg of Augusta, Maine, as project supervisor.[37] Contrary to customary practice, the structure was graced with a name before construction got under way; in May the trustees voted to title the new edifice in honor of Mr. and Mrs. Seth Hathorn of Woolwich, Maine, whose gift of $5,000 provided half of the eventual building expenses. Seminary representatives collected the remaining funds through subscriptions from the citizens of Lewiston.[38]

Construction proceeded in a timely fashion. On 26 June 1856, gala ceremonies, including a parade of enthusiastic local schoolchildren, accompanied the laying of the cornerstone of Hathorn Hall. In July, Bryant submitted a full set of plans, for which he subsequently billed the seminary $150. By October work had advanced so far that Ebenezer

Fig. 7-11. Hathorn Hall (1856–57), view from southeast, Bates College. Photograph, c. 1985.

Knowlton, a member of the building committee, offered an encouraging report:

Sunday morning I went to Lewiston—Found Hathorn Hall fast going up, the frame and boarding of the roof being done, and the slating being done this week. The building makes a fine appearance, and it seems to advantage from various parts of village, and when completed will compare with any building in the state or even in all New England. There is a neatness, finish and taste about it, which is not extravagant, is truly beautiful and inviting; as such a building, in such a place, for such a purpose, and built for such people ought to be.[39]

By December work had ceased for the winter months, but *The Seminary Advocate* offered additional good news about the impressive structure: "The outside of Hathorn Hall is completed, the windows are in, and the building is closed up."[40] The workmen were back on the job in May

1857, and the interior finishing was well along by the end of the summer. At a delayed matriculation on 1 September, 115 students were formally enrolled for academic study in the new facility. Two weeks later, peals from a recently cast one-thousand-pound bell in the cupola officially proclaimed the successful opening of the new building.[41]

Although Bryant's plans for Hathorn have yet to be found and may no longer exist, printed sources describe the appearance and interior floor configuration of the building on its opening. In its early years the edifice contained six recitation and two literary rooms on the third floor, and the president's office, a chapel, a library, and scientific rooms on the first floor or half-basement level. For thirteen years the second floor remained unfinished as college officials awaited sufficient funding to complete the building project.[42] The library was at first viewed as "a modest room" and "a quiet place," but it was subjected to overcrowding and soon lost its positive reputation. By 1873 all available shelf space had been filled, and books had to be stacked in piles on the floor or placed elsewhere in inaccessible storage spaces. This shortcoming was not rectified until the opening of the Corum Library at Bates in 1902.[43]

Ultimately, when the second floor received its final finish, chapel services were moved there, and the first chapel below was converted to more recitation rooms and a physics laboratory. The new chapel room—shown in an old photograph (fig. 7-12) decorated for commencement exercises in 1896—was completed and opened in 1870, but, as with the library, its history became somewhat clouded. Several years later its ceiling was declared structurally unsound and had to be repaired. This repair effort upgraded an interesting but unsuccessful space-maximizing structural engineering solution that Bryant had personally devised. So that the chapel would not have pillar obstructions, the ceiling had been suspended from the upper-floor support beams by long iron tie-rods, which themselves proved to be of insufficient strength.[44] Though the concept behind the ceiling was deemed faulty, it anticipated modern hung-ceiling design. Despite this flaw and other minor functional deficiencies, Hathorn Hall continues to serve the same broad purposes for which it was originally intended.

Although it is not widely known by students of architecture, Hathorn Hall should be recognized as one of the best surviving examples of Italianate college design in the United States. Its listing in 1970 on the National Register of Historic Places underscores this assertion. In its initial rejected plan form (see fig. 7-8), the structure embodied a neoclassical design tradition characterized by refinement and excellence in proportions and detail. In its final realized form (see fig. 7-11), Hathorn's large 86-by-50-foot mass is distinguished by a tasteful selection of white-painted classical elements (perhaps originally covered with stone-colored paint) effectively set off against redbrick outer walls.[45] Above most of the third-story windows are bracketed flat lintels surmounting plain Tuscan Italian entablatures. In the second and third stories of the side pavilions are long, narrow, round-arched windows, many of which are capped with bracketed hoodmolds enclosing semicircular fanlights. The segmental arches employed as window headings in the first story add variety in the window framing. Capping the low-hipped roof is a large, ornamented, open octagonal cupola with a dome, the chief focal point of the edifice. The closed pavilion pediments (one of which is set above a stair tower added in the 1960s) are embellished with heavy, protruding molding strips and cornice brackets. Another eye-catching feature of the building is the tall four-column Corinthian portico (fig. 7-13) shielding a large, round-arched main entrance on the south facade. Today, visitors looking across the original campus, with its

Fig. 7-12. Hathorn Hall (1856–57), interior of the chapel, Bates College. Photograph, 1896. Historic Photograph, Collection #080-D-010. Courtesy of the Edmund S. Muskie Archives and Special Collections Library, Bates College.

Fig. 7-13. Hathorn Hall (1856–57), front (south) porchway, Bates College. Photograph, 2008.

remarkable stand of great elm and maple trees, are immediately struck by the grandeur and near-perfect proportions of this porchway. In Hathorn Hall, Bryant produced a work of architecture that expresses well the flexible and imaginative Italian classicism of the American Romantic era. While somewhat less common in public, ecclesiastical, and institutional building design, this style was frequently employed in New England residential architecture of the 1850s and 1860s.

Parker Hall is unique among pre–Civil War New England dormitory structures because it is the only one for which a comprehensive set of original architectural drawings exists. Named for Judge Thomas Parker of Farmington, Maine, the largest individual contributor, this $11,000 facility was positioned approximately 100 feet west (left) of Hathorn Hall in Bryant's original scheme (see fig. 7-9).[46] As a single architect designed these two buildings, it is hardly surprising that the first version of Parker conveyed the same forcefulness and sharply defined detail as Hathorn. Both featured qualities—among them the rectangular-block form, thick

masonry or brick construction, and heavy cornice molding—present in Bryant's Boston commercial structures and other commissions. Unlike Hathorn, however, Parker has been completely transformed in the twentieth century; hence, only older visual sources convey a sense of its first appearance.

A set of thirteen Bryant drawings at the Bates College Library fully documents the original plan of Parker Hall.[47] These drawings are particularly valuable for their representations of Italianate stylistic elements as well as their structural engineering detail. The first-floor plan sheet (fig. 7-14) provides an accurate idea of the room configurations on all floors of the three-and-a-half-story building. Measuring 44 by 147 feet at its stone foundations, Parker was divided crosswise into two entries separated by a thick, load-bearing firewall.[48] At various times in Bates College history men and women have occupied these adjacent living quarters, with occasional humorous consequences that have added to institutional lore.[49] Each entry was arranged to take fifty students in double rooms (approximately 14 by 16 feet each) situated on either side of L-shaped corridors.[50] During the 1860s, all rooms were furnished with bedsteads, spring beds, mattresses, stoves, bookcases, wardrobes, chairs, sinks, woodboxes, washbowls, water pails, and other articles, some of which the students supplied themselves.[51] Suites could be created by joining together a series of rooms, a foresighted, flexible feature that worked so well that the entire interior was permanently rearranged along such lines in 1896.[52] The half-basement was appropriated exclusively for a dining hall, kitchen, and storage areas,[53] and it served as the college's coeducational food service facility for many years. Parker was an unusually versatile and functionally successful building, and as initially constructed it anticipated many of the best features—finely proportioned building masses and efficient, flexible floor plans—of late-nineteenth-century New England dormitory design found at Harvard, Yale, Bowdoin, Amherst, Trinity, Tufts, and other regional institutions.

Bryant's front-elevation view (fig. 7-15) provides the most accurate indication of how Parker Hall looked at the time of its dedication. To provide more attic space, the final rendition altered only the roof: formerly hipped, it was changed to a flat mansard type with dormer windows, as shown in engravings published during the 1860s (see fig. 7-9). Only in this respect does the building display evidence of the Second Empire style—a popular design idiom that came

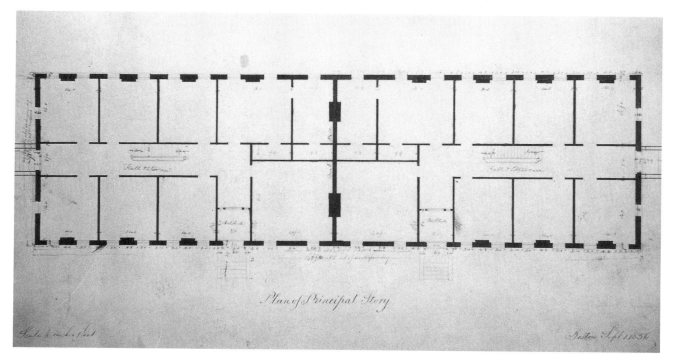

Fig. 7-14. Gridley J. F. Bryant, "Plan of Principal Story," Parker Hall (1856–57), Maine State Seminary, 1 September 1856. Architectural Plans and Drawings, CA07.05, V.P. for Finance and Administration and Treasurer, Physical Plant Records. Courtesy of the Edmund S. Muskie Archives and Special Collections Library, Bates College.

Fig. 7-15. Gridley J. F. Bryant, "Front Elevation," Parker Hall (1856–57), Maine State Seminary, 30 October 1856. Architectural Plans and Drawings, CA07.05, V.P. for Finance and Administration and Treasurer, Physical Plant Records. Courtesy of the Edmund S. Muskie Archives and Special Collections Library, Bates College.

Fig. 7-16. Parker Hall (1856–57, etc.), Bates College. Photograph, 2008.

to dominate Bryant's work, particularly in Boston, in the 1860s and later.[54] Despite this French-originated influence, Parker was very American in its overall simplicity and in the economical and sensible way in which its materials, all of local origin, were combined. While heavily framed Italianate doorways were located on the main south facade and on the end walls, the window and cornice moldings were flat and unembellished, and virtually no other style elements were present. Unpretentious, solid, and balanced, Parker was a monument both to utilitarianism and to conservative aesthetic taste.

In its present-day, neo-Federal form (fig. 7-16), Parker Hall bears only slight resemblance to Bryant's original conception on the exterior. Yet the interior has retained the best qualities of the original plan. In 1926 a front piazza, still very much in evidence, was attached to the main facade.[55] During 1967–68 the college undertook a near-total renovation. A pitched roof replaced the original mansard roof, dormers, and balustrade (removed in the 1860s), and the installation of long, monitor-like, shed-roof dormers extending nearly the entire length of the building created a fourth residential floor. For reasons of safety as well as convenience, stairwells were added by expanding the end walls 12 feet eastward and westward. To complement the main piazza, small classical porches were erected in front of each end door. This wholesale redesign of Parker was predicated on the desire to modernize the building functionally and to create a harmonious relationship with the predominantly neo-Federal character of much of the present Bates physical plant.

Gridley J. F. Bryant's master plan for the Maine State Seminary represents one of the earliest and most unusual efforts in the United States at planning an entire educational campus at a single point in time. Conceived with highly ambitious intentions, this row scheme had the potential to be one of New England's most outstanding pre–Civil War collegiate building groupings. The fact that Bryant's vision for the seminary, unlike that implemented for Colby, was never fully realized is in many ways regrettable; however, Hathorn and Parker halls and surviving sources assure the plan's significance in the annals of architectural design. The story and product of Bryant's initial planning efforts, subsequently the historic and physical core of Bates College, constitute a compelling episode in nineteenth-century New England educational and architectural history.

Productively combined in open, extroverted campus building groupings such as that at Bates, the majority of pre–Civil War New England collegiate structures forcefully projected their separate identities and clearly expressed the factors that influenced their architectural form. Uncomplicated, functional, and generally tasteful designs, these buildings accurately reflected the educational philosophies of their respective planners and the intellectual, social, cultural, economic, and geographical conditions of their region and times. In the modern era, when college and university architecture has recurrently assumed a variety of structural forms and campus planning schemes, often vast and unsystematic, the many traditional buildings that have survived continue to offer an ordering dignity to the higher educational settings of which they are a vital part. By virtue of their successful presence, they encourage the retention of the concept and the spirit behind Thomas Jefferson's exemplary "academical village" ideal, and in doing so, they foster the practice of clairvoyant building design, as well as coherent, visually attractive master planning. In the majority of buildings discussed and illustrated in this book, stability, utility, and aesthetic virtue have been combined to create bona fide works of architecture, as distinguished from certain more recent, sterile products of the college/university building trade. Though often in altered form, those early New England structures that remain continue to meet ever-changing higher educational needs. At the same time, they serve as inspiring and enlightening reminders of the still-viable heritage of pre–Civil War higher education in New England—as surviving expressions of the fertile relationship between architecture and academe.

Notes

Introduction

1. In the preparation of this section of the book, the following sources were consulted: Bush-Brown, "College Architecture: An Expression of Educational Philosophy," *Architectural Record* 122 (1957), pp. 156–57; Dober, *Campus Planning*, pp. 17–23, 120; Wertenbaker, *Princeton, 1746–1896*, pp. 3, 78; Rudolph, *The American College and University*, pp. 3–22; Bailyn, *Education in the Forming of American Society*, pp. 22, 36, 49; Works Progress Administration, *New Hampshire*, p. 94; Dean, "Early College and Educational Buildings in New England," *Pencil Points* 20 (1934), p. 602; Hamlin, *The American Spirit in Architecture*, p. 236; Kimball, *American Architecture*, p. 37; Morrison, *Early American Architecture*, p. 469; Thwing, *A History of Higher Education in America*, pp. 404, 406; Schuyler, "The Architecture of American Colleges: VIII — The Southern Colleges," *Architectural Record* 30 (1911), pp. 57–84; Willard, "The Development of the College in America," *New England Magazine* n.s. 16 (1897), pp. 520–21; Turner, *Campus*, introduction and chaps. 1, 2, and 3, pp. 9–127.

Chapter 1: Harvard and Yale

1. Bunting and Floyd, *Harvard*, pp. 1–12; Cambridge Historical Commission, *Survey of Architectural History in Cambridge. Report Four: Old Cambridge*, p. 149; Morison, *The Founding of Harvard College*, pp. 270–89; Morison, *Three Centuries of Harvard University*, pp. 13, 17, 82–84; Vaille and Clark, eds., *The Harvard Book*, vol. 1, p. 19; Morison, *Harvard College in the Seventeenth Century*, vol. 1, pp. 43–47. Harvard College was officially renamed Harvard University in 1781.

2. Bunting and Floyd, *Harvard*, pp. 13–14; Morison, *Harvard College in the Seventeenth Century*, vol. 1, pp. 342–44; Cambridge Historical Commission, *Survey of Architectural History in Cambridge. Report Four: Old Cambridge*, p. 149; Morison, *Early American Architecture*, p. 87; Morison, *Three Centuries of Harvard University*, pp. 21, 38; Vaille and Clark, eds., *The Harvard Book*, vol. 1, p. 21; Morison, "A Conjectural Restoration of 'Old College' at Harvard," *Old-Time New England* 23, no. 4 (April 1933): 130–58.

3. Bunting and Floyd, *Harvard*, pp. 16–21; Cambridge Historical Commission, *Survey of Architectural History in Cambridge. Report Four: Old Cambridge*, p. 150; Vaille and Clark, eds., *The Harvard Book*, vol. 1, pp. 72–75; Andrews, ed., *A Prospect of the Colledges in Cambridge in New England*, pp. 11, 12, 16; Morison, *Harvard College in the Seventeenth Century*, vol. 2, pp. 423–30; Morison, *Early American Architecture*, pp. 38, 72, 85–87; Morison, *Three Centuries of Harvard University*, pp. 16, 21.

4. Morison, *Early American Architecture*, p. 88; Bunting and Floyd, *Harvard*, pp. 21–22; King, *Harvard and Its Surroundings* (1882), p. 31; Cambridge Historical Commission, *Survey of Architectural History in Cambridge. Report Four: Old Cambridge*, p. 150; Morison, *Harvard College in the Seventeenth Century*, vol. 2, pp. 518–21; Vaille and Clark, eds., *The Harvard Book*, vol. 1, pp. 79–80; "Stoughton Hall," *Harvard Bulletin*, 2 June 1909.

5. Shand-Tucci, *The Campus Guide: Harvard University*, pp. 31–33; Bunting and Floyd, *Harvard*, pp. 22–23; Cambridge Historical Commission, *Survey of Architectural History in Cambridge. Report Four: Old Cambridge*, pp. 150–51; Palfrey, "A Study of Massachusetts Hall," *Harvard Register* 3 (1881): 222–25; Vaille and Clark, eds., *The Harvard Book*, vol. 1, pp. 53–57; Morison, *Early American Architecture*, p. 463; Morison, *Three Centuries of Harvard University*, p. 22; Chamberlain and Moffat, *Fair Harvard*, p. 15; "Massachusetts Hall," *Harvard Alumni Bulletin* 10 (19 February 1908); "Double Centenary of Oldest American College Building," *Harvard Crimson*, 20 January 1920.

6. Cambridge Historical Commission, *Survey of Architectural History in Cambridge. Report Four: Old Cambridge*, p. 152; Batchelder, "The Singular Story of Holden Chapel," *Harvard Alumni Bulletin* 23, no. 18 (3 February 1921); Vaille and Clark, eds., *The Harvard Book*, vol. 1, pp. 57–60; Shand-Tucci, *The Campus Guide: Harvard University*, pp. 36–38; Bunting and Floyd, *Harvard*, pp. 25–27; Morison, *Early American Architecture*, p. 465; "Holden Chapel," *Harvard Crimson*, 23 November 1934; Morison, *Three Centuries of Harvard University*, p. 94; "Harvard's First Chapel," *Harvard Bulletin*, 31 March 1909; Plan Book, Harvard University Archives.

7. Bunting and Floyd, *Harvard*, pp. 27–28; Shand-Tucci, *The Campus Guide: Harvard University*, pp. 36, 39; Cambridge Historical Commission, *Survey of Architectural History in Cambridge. Report Four: Old Cambridge*, pp. 152–53; Vaille and Clark, eds.,

The Harvard Book, vol. 1, pp. 61–71; King, *Harvard and Its Surroundings* (1882), p. 33; Morrison, *Early American Architecture*, p. 466; Morison, *Three Centuries of Harvard University*, p. 94; "Hollis Hall," *Harvard Bulletin*, 17 June 1908; "Hollis Hall, 1763–1913," *Harvard Alumni Bulletin*, 12 March 1913; "Hollis Hall," *Harvard Bulletin* 15 (17 March 1909): 395–98.

8. Bunting and Floyd, *Harvard*, pp. 28, 30–35; Vaille and Clark, eds., *The Harvard Book*, vol. 1, pp. 75–78; Cambridge Historical Commission, *Survey of Architectural History in Cambridge. Report Four: Old Cambridge*, pp. 153–55; Shand-Tucci, *The Campus Guide: Harvard University*, pp. 33–36; Morrison, *Early American Architecture*, p. 465; "Historic Preservation" column, *Newsletter of the Society of Architectural Historians* 12, no. 6 (December 1968): 4; Morison, *Three Centuries of Harvard University*, pp. 95, 97; "Harvard Hall," *Harvard Bulletin*, 5 May 1909.

9. Bunting and Floyd, *Harvard*, p. 35; Vaille and Clark, eds., *The Harvard Book*, vol. 1, pp. 80–81; Shand-Tucci, *The Campus Guide: Harvard University*, p. 41; Cambridge Historical Commission, *Survey of Architectural History in Cambridge. Report Four: Old Cambridge*, p. 154; Morison, *Three Centuries of Harvard University*, p. 173; Kirker, *Bulfinch's Boston*, pp. 61, 88; Ware, "Stoughton Hall," *Harvard Register* 3 (1881): 72–74; "Stoughton Hall," *Harvard Bulletin*, 2 June 1909; Kirker, "The Architect of Stoughton Hall," *Harvard Alumni Bulletin* 68, no. 2 (9 October 1965): 64–65, 67; Kirker, *The Architecture of Charles Bulfinch*, pp. 216–17.

10. Cambridge Historical Commission, *Survey of Architectural History in Cambridge. Report Four: Old Cambridge*, pp. 154–55; Vaille and Clark, eds., *The Harvard Book*, vol. 1, pp. 82–83; Bunting and Floyd, *Harvard*, pp. 40–41; King, *Harvard and Its Surroundings* (1882), pp. 30–31; Shand-Tucci, *The Campus Guide: Harvard University*, p. 41; Works Progress Administration, *Massachusetts*, pp. 197–98; Morison, *Three Centuries of Harvard University*, p. 215; "Holworthy Hall," *Harvard Bulletin*, 16 June 1909; "Holworthy Hall," *Harvard Alumni Bulletin* 14 (1 May 1912).

11. Bunting and Floyd, *Harvard*, pp. 41–43; Shand-Tucci, *The Campus Guide: Harvard University*, pp. 42–46; Cambridge Historical Commission, *Survey of Architectural History in Cambridge. Report Four: Old Cambridge*, pp. 155–56; Vaille and Clark, eds., *The Harvard Book*, vol. 1, pp. 84–108; "University Hall," *Harvard Bulletin*, 8 April 1908; "The Faculty Room in University Hall," *Harvard Alumni Bulletin*, 12 February 1913; Morison, *Three Centuries of Harvard University*, p. 215; Works Progress Administration, *Massachusetts*, p. 196; Kirker, *Architecture of Charles Bulfinch*, pp. 273–80; King, *Harvard and Its Surroundings* (1882), p. 27.

12. Bunting and Floyd, *Harvard*, pp. 43–46; Cambridge Historical Commission, *Survey of Architectural History in Cambridge. Report Four: Old Cambridge*, pp. 156–57; Vaille and Clark, eds., *The Harvard Book*, vol. 1, pp. 112–21; Ware, "The Harvard College Li-
brary. No. 2," *Harvard Register* 1–2 (1880): 201–4; Quincy, *History of Harvard University*, vol. 2, pp. 599–601; Morison, *Three Centuries of Harvard University*, pp. 266–67; King, *Harvard and Its Surroundings* (1882), pp. 24–26; "The Passing of Gore Hall," *Harvard Alumni Bulletin* 15, no. 16 (15 January 1913): 260–64; Withey, *Biographical Dictionary of American Architects (Deceased)*, p. 65; Shand-Tucci, *The Campus Guide: Harvard University*, pp. 151–52. Although they do not meet the guidelines established for this book, three Harvard buildings erected just prior to Gore Hall are worthy of mention. The first is Dane Hall, a T-shaped brick Greek Revival structure with a two-story front portico, raised in 1832 to house the new Law School, and located south of Massachusetts Hall until it was destroyed by fire in 1918. On the west side of Harvard Square, a brick dormitory for law students with the name Graduates' Hall (later College House) was constructed in 1832, repeatedly enlarged and remodeled, and then partially demolished in the twentieth century, leaving in place the north portion of the original block. The third building, the Divinity School, was put up in 1825 under the direction of Boston architect Solomon Willard (see chap. 6) and Thomas W. Sumner, and, with its original form largely preserved, is still standing on Divinity Avenue in the North Yard. It was the first major Harvard building to be located outside the old Yard. This plain, rather austere, three-story, symmetrical structure is highlighted by its front projection with closed pediment and tall, round-arched windows, and the front columned entrance porches in the wings (see Bunting and Floyd, *Harvard*, pp. 43, 51, 52–53).

13. Bunting and Floyd, *Harvard*, pp. 54–55; Cambridge Historical Commission, *Survey of Architectural History in Cambridge. Report Four: Old Cambridge*, p. 158; Withey, *Biographical Dictionary of American Architects (Deceased)*, pp. 521–22; Bond, "Description of the Observatory at Cambridge, Massachusetts," *Memoirs of the Academy of Arts and Sciences* n.s. 9 (1849): 177–88; Quincy, *History of Harvard University*, vol. 2, pp. 566–68; Vaille and Clark, eds., *The Harvard Book*, vol. 1, pp. 143, 303–8; Placzek, *Macmillan Encyclopedia of Architects*, vol. 3, pp. 599–601; Morison, *Three Centuries of Harvard University*, p. 265; King, *Harvard and Its Surroundings* (1882), pp. 59–60.

14. Cambridge Historical Commission, *Survey of Architectural History in Cambridge. Report Four: Old Cambridge*, p. 158; Bunting and Floyd, *Harvard*, pp. 55–56; Vaille and Clark, eds., *The Harvard Book*, vol. 1, pp. 279–82; *Education, Bricks and Mortar*, pp. 15, 76; Eustice, "The Lawrence Scientific School," *Harvard Register* 3 (1881): 375–78; King, *Harvard and Its Surroundings* (1882), p. 40.

15. Bunting and Floyd, *Harvard*, pp. 46, 48–49; Cambridge Historical Commission, *Survey of Architectural History in Cambridge. Report Four: Old Cambridge*, p. 159; King, *Harvard and Its Surroundings* (1882), p. 30; Withey, *Biographical Dictionary of*

American Architects (Deceased), p. 542; Vaille and Clark, eds., *The Harvard Book,* vol. 1, pp. 122–24; Chamberlain and Moffat, *Fair Harvard,* p. 32. The distinguished architect Richard Upjohn also submitted plans for the chapel, but they were not accepted by Harvard officials.

16. Bunting and Floyd, *Harvard,* pp. 49–50; Cambridge Historical Commission, *Survey of Architectural History in Cambridge. Report Four: Old Cambridge,* pp. 159–60; *Education, Bricks and Mortar,* pp. 15, 56; King, *Harvard and Its Surroundings* (1882), pp. 23–24; Shand-Tucci, *The Campus Guide: Harvard University,* pp. 150–51.

17. Bunting and Floyd, *Harvard,* pp. 56, 93–96; Cambridge Historical Commission, *Survey of Architectural History in Cambridge. Report Four: Old Cambridge,* p. 170; Morison, ed., *The Development of Harvard University,* pp. 400–403; King, *Harvard and Its Surroundings* (1882), p. 46; *Building Harvard* (1975 ed.), "Agassiz's Dream" section; Withey, *Biographical Dictionary of American Architects (Deceased),* pp. 251, 563; Shand-Tucci, *The Campus Guide: Harvard University,* pp. 226–27.

18. Cambridge Historical Commission, *Survey of Architectural History in Cambridge. Report Four: Old Cambridge,* p. 160; Bunting and Floyd, *Harvard,* p. 57; Gardiner, *Harvard,* pp. 256–58; Placzek, ed., *Macmillan Encyclopedia of Architects,* vol. 1, p. 363; Withey, *Biographical Dictionary of American Architects (Deceased),* pp. 102–3.

19. Vogt essay from Scully et al., *Yale in New Haven,* pp. 53–54; Isham, "The Original College House at Yale," *Yale Alumni Weekly* 25, no. 5 (20 October 1916): 115–20; Works Progress Administration, *Connecticut,* pp. 78, 289, 291; Morrison, *Early American Architecture,* p. 467; [Belden], *Sketches of Yale College,* pp. 24–25; Kingsley, *A Sketch of the History of Yale College,* p. 8; Barber and Punderson, *History and Antiquities of New Haven* (1856 ed.), pp. 13–15; Seymour, "Henry Caner, 1680–1731," *Old-Time New England* 15, no. 3 (January 1925): 98–124; Oviatt, *The Beginnings of Yale (1701–1726),* pp. 338, 344–45, 353–56; Seymour, *New Haven,* pp. 366–70. Yale College officially became Yale University in 1887 by state charter. Also erected by Henry Caner in 1722 was a nearby house for the college rector (president).

20. Vogt essay from Scully et al., *Yale in New Haven,* pp. 55–56; Pinnell, *The Campus Guide: Yale University,* pp. 11–12; Morrison, *Early American Architecture,* pp. 467–68; Holden, *Yale,* plate 16 caption; Tucker, *Puritan Protagonist,* pp. 75–76; Kingsley, *Yale College,* vol. 1, pp. 441–50; Brown, *New Haven,* p. 122; Steiner, *History of Education in Connecticut,* pp. 105–8; Works Progress Administration, *Connecticut,* p. 241; Cuningham, *Timothy Dwight, 1752–1817,* p. 185; Kingsley, *A Sketch of the History of Yale College,* p. 13; "The Restoration of University Hall," *Brown Alumni Monthly* 6, no. 3 (October 1905), p. 53; Heintz, "Old Yale: Doubling the College," *Yale Alumni Magazine* 50, no. 2 (November 1986): 40–42.

21. Vogt essay from Scully et al., *Yale in New Haven,* pp. 56–57, 79; Holden, *Yale,* plate 20 caption; Milham, "Early American Observatories," *Popular Astronomy* 9 (November 1937), pp. 21–22; Tucker, *Puritan Protagonist,* pp. 75–76; Kingsley, *A Sketch of the History of Yale College,* p. 13; Steiner, *History of Higher Education in Connecticut,* p. 108; Kingsley, *Yale College,* vol. 1, pp. 451–52; Decrow, *Yale and "The City of Elms,"* p. 13.

22. Vogt essay from Scully et al., *Yale in New Haven,* pp. 57–58; Morgan, *The Gentle Puritan,* pp. 423–24; Keith and Warren, "Peter Banner, a Builder for Yale College. Part II. Berkeley Hall," *Old-Time New England* 47, no. 2 (Fall 1956): 51–53; Pratt, "John Trumbull and the Brick Row," *Yale University Library Gazette* 9, no. 1 (July 1934): 11–20; Brockway, "John Trumbull as Architect of Yale," *Magazine Antiques* 28 (September 1935): 114–15; Turner, *Campus,* pp. 38, 41, 42, 43.

23. Vogt essay from Scully et al., *Yale in New Haven,* pp. 67–69; Holden, *Yale,* plates 21 and 22 captions; Kingsley, *A Sketch of the History of Yale College,* p. 27; Morgan, *The Gentle Puritan,* p. 423; Steiner, *History of Higher Education in Connecticut,* pp. 131–32; Kingsley, *Yale College,* vol. 1, pp. 457–62; Decrow, *Yale and "The City of Elms,"* pp. 11–12.

24. Vogt essay from Scully et al., *Yale in New Haven,* pp. 69–76; Withey, *Biographical Dictionary of American Architects (Deceased),* p. 34; Kingsley, *A Sketch of the History of Yale College,* pp. 33, 37; Holden, *Yale,* plates 25, 26, and 27 captions; Cuningham, *Timothy Dwight,* p. 185; Keith and Warren, "Peter Banner, a Builder for Yale College. Part II. Berkeley Hall," *Old-Time New England* 47, no. 2 (Fall 1956): 49–53; Keith and Warren, "Peter Banner, a Builder for Yale College. Part III. The Lyceum," *Old-Time New England* 49, no. 4 (Spring 1959): 104–10; Steiner, *History of Education in Connecticut,* pp. 139–40; Kingsley, *Yale College,* vol. 1, pp. 465–71; Shumway and Hegel, *New Haven,* p. 131; Decrow, *Yale and "The City of Elms,"* pp. 15–17.

25. Vogt essay from Scully et al., *Yale in New Haven,* pp. 76–79; Holden, *Yale,* plate 30 caption; Kingsley, *A Sketch of the History of Yale College,* p. 37; Withey, *Biographical Dictionary of American Architects (Deceased),* p. 24; Kingsley, *Yale College,* vol. 1, pp. 474–84; Decrow, *Yale and "The City of Elms,"* pp. 18–19.

26. Vogt essay from Scully et al., *Yale in New Haven,* p. 79; Holden, *Yale,* plates 28 and 29 captions; Kingsley, *A Sketch of the History of Yale College,* pp. 3, 7; Kingsley, *Yale College,* vol. 1, pp. 485–87; Decrow, *Yale and "The City of Elms,"* pp. 17–18. Divinity Hall, the first home of the Yale Divinity School, was erected in 1835 at the north end of the Old Brick Row next to Elm Street, leaving the requisite gap for another chapel type, this one never realized. In its brick, rectangular block form and limited details, Divinity Hall mimicked the other, older residence halls in the row. The divinity school was founded in 1827 as the Theological Department,

independent of Yale College. The building was removed in 1869 to make way for Durfee Hall. The architect has not yet been identified (see Vogt essay from Scully et al., *Yale in New Haven*, pp. 79, 81).

27. Vogt essay from Scully et al., *Yale in New Haven*, p. 76; Holden, *Yale*, plates 36 and 37 captions; Cuningham, *Timothy Dwight*, p. 186; Kingsley, *Yale College*, vol. 1, pp. 453–56; Baldwin, *Annals of Yale College*, pp. 236–37; Decrow, *Yale and "The City of Elms,"* pp. 30–31.

28. Vogt essay from Scully et al., *Yale in New Haven*, p. 67; Holden, *Yale*, plate 35 caption; Withey, *Biographical Dictionary of American Architects (Deceased)*, pp. 290–91; Placzek, ed., *Macmillan Encyclopedia of Architects*, vol. 2, p. 396; Kingsley, *Yale College*, vol. 1, pp. 472–73; Kingsley, *A Sketch of the History of Yale College*, p. 37; Decrow, *Yale and "The City of Elms,"* pp. 29–30; [Belden], *Sketches of Yale College*, pp. 107–9; Steiner, *History of Education in Connecticut*, p. 154.

29. Vogt and Lynn essays from Scully et al., *Yale in New Haven*, pp. 81, 109; Holden, *Yale*, plate 40 caption; Shumway and Hegel, *New Haven*, p. 128; Kingsley, *A Sketch of the History of Yale College*, pp. 37–38; [Belden], *Sketches of Yale College*, pp. 103–6; Sizer, "The Trumbull Gallery, 1832–1932," *Yale Alumni Weekly* 42 (28 October 1932): 143–46; Decrow, *Yale and "The City of Elms,"* pp. 26–27.

30. Vogt essay from Scully et al., *Yale in New Haven*, pp. 88–89; Works Progress Administration, *Connecticut*, pp. 93, 241; Holden, *Yale*, plates 42, 43, and 44 captions; O'Gorman, *Henry Austin*, pp. 125–31; Pinnell, *The Campus Guide: Yale University*, pp. 14–16; Brown, *New Haven*, p. 123; Withey, *Biographical Dictionary of American Architects (Deceased)*, p. 26; Placzek, ed., *Macmillan Encyclopedia of Architects*, vol. 1, pp. 117–18; Seymour, *New Haven*, pp. 219–33, 726–29; Decrow, *Yale and "The City of Elms,"* pp. 27–29. Though architect Alexander Jackson Davis (1803–92) had also prepared plans for the library project, these were not formally accepted by Yale officials. Austin likely saw them, however, and they may have impacted his final design renderings and the overall library composition.

31. Vogt essay from Scully et al., *Yale in New Haven*, p. 90; Holden, *Yale*, plates 46 and 48 captions; Works Progress Administration, *Connecticut*, p. 242; Placzek, ed., *Macmillan Encyclopedia of Architects*, p. 512; Withey, *Biographical Dictionary of American Architects (Deceased)*, pp. 162–63, 603–4; Kingsley, *Yale College*, vol. 1, pp. 488–89; Decrow, *Yale and "The City of Elms,"* pp. 24–25.

32. Lynn and Goldberger essays from Scully et al., *Yale in New Haven*, pp. 110, 265, 366; Withey, *Biographical Dictionary of American Architects (Deceased)*, p. 577.

33. Vogt essay from Scully et al., *Yale in New Haven*, pp. 91–99; Pierson, *Yale*, vol. 1, pp. 29–31, and vol. 2, p. 401; Turner, *Campus*, p. 41; Guilbert, "Something That Loves a Wall: The Yale University Campus, 1850–1920," *New England Quarterly* 68, no. 2 (June 1995):

257–77; Whitlock, "Who Killed the Old Brick Row?" *Yale Alumni Magazine* 38, no. 4 (January 1975): 25–29.

Chapter 2: Brown and Dartmouth

1. Brown University, founded as Rhode Island College in 1764, was initially located at Warren, Rhode Island. It was moved to Providence, Rhode Island, in 1770.

2. Jordy, *Buildings of Rhode Island*, p. 97; Placzek, ed., *Macmillan Encyclopedia of Architects*, vol. 1, p. 297; Miller, *The Architects of the American Colonies*, p. 140; Wroth, "The Construction of the College Edifice, 1770–1772," chap. 3, pp. 16–18.

3. Guild, *History of Brown University*, pp. 229–36; Mitchell, *Encyclopedia Brunaniana*, pp. 550–51; Freiberg, "Brown University's First 'College Edifice,'" *Old-Time New England* 50, no. 4 (April–June 1960): 85–90; Bronson, *History of Brown University, 1764–1914*, pp. 55–57; Kenny, "How the College Edifice Was Built," *Brown Alumni Monthly* 72, no. 1 (October 1871): 26–31.

4. Freiberg, "Brown University's First 'College Edifice,'" p. 85; Jordy, *Buildings of Rhode Island*, pp. 97–98; Hitchcock, *Rhode Island Architecture*, pp. 22–23; Morrison, *Early American Architecture*, pp. 468–69; "National Historic Landmark," *Brown Alumni Monthly* 50, no. 9 (July 1963): p. 17.

5. Mitchell, *Encyclopedia Brunaniana*, pp. 551–54; Bronson, *History of Brown University, 1764–1914*, pp. 68, 72–74, 392–93, 473; *Exercises Commemorating the Restoration of University Hall, Brown University*, pp. 44–48; Guild, *Early History of Brown University*, pp. 332–38; Guild, *History of Brown University*, pp. 245–46; Brown, ed., *Memories of Brown*, p. 321.

6. Mitchell, *Encyclopedia Brunaniana*, pp. 554–55; "Restoration of University Hall," *Brown Alumni Monthly* 5, no. 7 (February 1905): 135; "The Restoration of University Hall," *Brown Alumni Monthly* 6, no. 3 (October 1905): 49–50; Jordy, *Buildings of Rhode Island*, pp. 98–99; "The Restoration of University Hall," *Brown Alumni Monthly* 39, no. 8 (March 1939): 220; "Campus Revisions," *Brown Alumni Monthly* 40, no. 3 (October 1939): 60; "The New U.H.," *Brown Alumni Monthly* 40, no. 5 (December 1939/ January 1940): 115; "Rededicating the 'College Edifice,'" *Brown Alumni Monthly* 40, no. 8 (April 1940): 199–200; "In Homage to University Hall," *Brown Alumni Monthly* 51, no. 1 (June 1940): 7–8.

7. Schuyler, "Architecture of American Colleges — VII. Brown, Bowdoin, Trinity and Wesleyan," *Architectural Record* 29 (January–June 1911): 148; *Old Providence*, p. 23; Guild, "Brown University," *New England Magazine* 1, no. 1 (January 1886): 1; Bronson, *History of Brown University, 1764–1914*, pp. 171–73; Guild, *Historical Sketch of Brown University*, p. 8; Jordy, *Buildings of Rhode Island*, p. 99; Mitchell, *Encyclopedia Brunaniana*, pp. 288–89; Iselin, *Ivied Halls*, p. 3.

8. Cady, *The Civic and Architectural Development of Providence, 1636–1950*, p. 87; Turner, *Campus*, pp. 21, 41, 51.

9. Mitchell, *Encyclopedia Brunaniana*, p. 289; *Hope College . . . for the Promotion of Virtue, Science and Literature*, pp. 2–3; Brown, *Memories of Brown*, pp. 323–24; Munro, "The Old Back Campus II: Concerning Hope College," *Brown Alumni Monthly* 28, no. 5 (December 1927): 119–20.

10. "Hope College," *Brown Alumni Monthly* 57, no. 5 (February 1957): 6; Bronson, *History of Brown University, 1764–1914*, p. 459.

11. Iselin, *Ivied Halls*, pp. 3–4; *Hope College . . . for the Promotion of Virtue, Science and Literature*, pp. 1–3; "Restoring Hope College," *Brown Alumni Monthly* 57, no. 2 (November 1957): 20; "For the Reconstruction of Hope College," *Brown Alumni Monthly* 41, no. 8 (April 1941): 221; "Hope College," *Brown Alumni Monthly* 59, no. 9 (July 1959): 28, 29, 54; "Hope College—'Go Ahead,'" *Brown Alumni Monthly* 58, no. 5 (February 1958): 18; "Of National Importance," *Brown Alumni Monthly* 58, no. 6, p. 19.

12. Mitchell, *Encyclopedia Brunaniana*, p. 357; Barry and Mitchell, *A Tale of Two Centuries*, p. 39; Locke, *Brown University*, p. 38; Bronson, *History of Brown University, 1764–1914*, p. 222; Guild, *History of Brown University*, pp. 265, 266, 268; Report of the President and Faculty to the Corporation, 5 September 1833.

13. Wayland, *The Dependence of Science*, p. 35.

14. Placzek, ed., *Macmillan Encyclopedia of Architects*, vol. 1, pp. 315–20; Withey, *Biographical Dictionary of American Architects (Deceased)*, pp. 88–89, 635–36; Clancey, *Exterior Paint Survey*, p. 1.

15. Mitchell, *Encyclopedia Brunaniana*, p. 358; Bronson, *History of Brown University, 1764–1914*, p. 334; Faculty Records, 18 February 1873, 24 September and 26 November 1878; Brown, ed., *Memories of Brown*, pp. 327–29; Cady, "Manning Hall, Centenarian," *Brown Alumni Monthly* 34, no. 9 (April 1934): 209–11; "Where a Man May Worship," *Brown Alumni Monthly* 58, no. 6 (March 1958): 3–5; Annual Report of the President, 21 June 1888, 20 June 1895, 17 June 1897, 22 June 1899; Jordy, *Buildings of Rhode Island*, p. 99.

16. Mitchell, *Encyclopedia Brunaniana*, p. 466; Jordy, *Buildings of Rhode Island*, p. 99; Cady, *The Civic and Architectural Development of Providence, 1636–1950*, p. 109; Guild, *Historical Sketch of Brown University*, p. 8; Richardson and Clark, *The College Book*, p. 138; Bronson, *History of Brown University, 1764–1914*, p. 389; Specifications for a New Edifice for Brown University, 25 May 1839; Corporation Records, 8 September 1836 and 3 September 1873.

17. King, *King's Pocket-Book of Providence, R.I.*, p. 15.

18. Mitchell, *Encyclopedia Brunaniana*, p. 460; Guild, *History of Brown University*, pp. 271–74; letter, Nicholas Brown to Moses Brown Ives, 18 March 1839.

19. Most of the content of this section of chapter 2 derives from my illustrated article, "The Evolution of a Campus: Dartmouth College Architecture Before 1860," *Historical New Hampshire* 42, no. 4 (Winter 1987): 329–82. Containing similar content is Scott Meacham's excellent architectural guide, *The Campus Guide*, which cites the article as a major source.

20. Chase, *A History of Dartmouth College and the Town of Hanover*, p. 223; Dewey, "Reminiscences of Hanover." Chronologically, the "log hut," as it has traditionally been termed, was the first Dartmouth College building, but as a solely residential structure, it does not qualify for treatment in this study. Used for only a brief period, this 18-foot-square cabin housed President Eleazar Wheelock and his family, and a few students. Moved to a second site, it was demolished in 1782. See Hill, ed., *The College on the Hill*, p. 34.

21. Dewey, "Reminiscences of Hanover," sketches; Chase, *A History of Dartmouth College and the Town of Hanover*, p. 222; Lenning, "A History of Dartmouth Hall," p. 2. The Moor's Preparatory School was founded by Eleazar Wheelock at Lebanon, Connecticut, in 1735, and was the forerunner institution to Dartmouth College. Intended for the religious training of Native American boys, it was moved to Hanover when the college was established there. It prepared many students for admission to Dartmouth until its closure during the Civil War.

22. Lenning, "A History of Dartmouth Hall," p. 2; Norton, "Latrobe and Old West at Dickenson College," *Art Bulletin* 33 (1951): 128.

23. Chase, *A History of Dartmouth College and the Town of Hanover*, pp. 22, 268, 585.

24. Dewey, "Reminiscences of Hanover," sketches.

25. Chase, *A History of Dartmouth College and the Town of Hanover*, p. 269; Richardson, *History of Dartmouth College*, pp. 53, 212.

26. Morrison, *Early American Architecture*, p. 469.

27. Childs, "Dartmouth Hall—Old and New," *Dartmouth Alumni Magazine* 28 (1936): 7; Richardson, *History of Dartmouth College*, p. 131.

28. Chase, *A History of Dartmouth College and the Town of Hanover*, p. 271; Patrick, "The Dartmouth College Green," p. 62.

29. Richardson, *History of Dartmouth College*, p. 131; Lenning, "A History of Dartmouth Hall," p. 3; Childs, "Dartmouth Hall—Old and New," p. 7; Morrison, *Early American Architecture*, p. 459.

30. A letter from Comfort Sever to Eleazar Wheelock, December 1868, Albany, New York (Rauner Special Collections, Dartmouth College Library), mentions Wheelock's promise to allow him to design and build the new edifice. Other correspondence between the two men is present in the archives and spans the years 1768 to 1773, when Sever relocated to Hanover under Wheelock's patronage.

31. Bridenbaugh, *Peter Harrison*, pp. 151, 153–54; Eleazar Wheelock to Comfort Sever, Hanover, 9 July 1773, and Eleazar Wheelock to Peter Harrison, Hanover, 28 June 1773, Rauner Spe-

cial Collections, Dartmouth College Library. Bridenbaugh further observes that the Dartmouth rejection may partially explain "the eclipse of Peter Harrison's forms and status as the foremost American architect" of his time.

32. Eleazar Wheelock to Comfort Sever, Hanover, 20 May 1771, Rauner Special Collections, Dartmouth College Library; Morrison, *Early American Architecture*, p. 471.

33. Belknap, *History of New Hampshire*, vol. 3, p. 222; Childs, "Dartmouth Hall—Old and New," p. 7; Dartmouth College Board of Trustees Records, Meeting of 31 March 1784, Annual Meeting of 1784, Meeting of September 1786 and Meeting of September 1788, Rauner Special Collections, Dartmouth College Library; Chase, *A History of Dartmouth College and the Town of Hanover*, pp. 574–75; Childs, "Dartmouth Hall—Old and New," p. 7.

34. Morse and Parish, *A Compendious-History of New England*, p. 338; Farmer and Moore, *A Gazetteer of the State of New Hampshire*, p. 32; Hill, ed., *The College on the Hill*, p. 52; Morrison, *Early American Architecture*, p. 471; Lenning, "A History of Dartmouth Hall," p. 10; Chase, *A History of Dartmouth College and the Town of Hanover*, pp. 576–79.

35. Morrison, *Early American Architecture*, p. 471; Lord, *A History of Dartmouth College (1815–1909)*, p. 285; Patrick, "The Dartmouth College Green," pp. 67–68; Richardson, *History of Dartmouth College*, p. 213; "A Brief Account of Dartmouth College in New England," *American Museum* 2 (1787): 344.

36. "Brief Description of Dartmouth College with a View," *Massachusetts Magazine* 5 (1793): 68; Merrill, *Gazetteer of the State of New Hampshire*, p. 142; Dwight, *Travels in New England and New York*, vol. 2, p. 115; Lord, *A History of Dartmouth College (1815–1909)*, pp. 205, 507; Hill, ed., *The College on the Hill*, pp. 52, 109; Childs, "Dartmouth College—Old and New," p. 9; Richardson, *History of Dartmouth College*, p. 251; Lenning, "A History of Dartmouth Hall," p. 16.

37. Lenning, "A History of Dartmouth Hall," p. 15; Childs, "Dartmouth Hall—Old and New," pp. 11–12; Richardson, *History of Dartmouth College*, p. 277; Lord, *A History of Dartmouth College (1815–1909)*, pp. 223–24; Bartlett, "Pen and Camera Sketches of Hanover and the College Before the Centennial: IV—The Old Chapel," *Dartmouth Alumni Magazine* 13 (1921): 444.

38. Lenning, "A History of Dartmouth Hall," p. 19. See notes below for Wentworth and Thornton halls. Hopkins, ed., *Exercises and Addresses Attending the Laying of the Cornerstone of the New Dartmouth Hall . . . October 25 and 26, 1904*, p. 4; Lord, *A History of Dartmouth College (1815–1909)*, p. 419. In around 1840, college administrators relocated the museum, art gallery, and society libraries to newly constructed Reed Hall.

39. One of the most momentous events in the college's history, the 1904 fire was caused by defective electrical wiring. Starting early in the morning while students were attending religious ser-

vices at Rollins Chapel, it raced through the dry wooden timbers of the structure, creating such an inferno that all hope of saving it passed within a few minutes. See Bramen, "The Fated Morning," *Dartmouth Alumni Magazine* 56, no. 5 (1964): 28–30; Hill, ed., *The College on the Hill*, p. 297; Childs, "Dartmouth Hall—Old and New," pp. 14–16; Lord, *A History of Dartmouth College (1815–1909)*, pp. 489–91; Dartmouth College Board of Trustees Records, Meeting of 20 February 1904; Lenning, "A History of Dartmouth Hall," p. 29; Richardson, *History of Dartmouth College*, p. 680; Childs, "Dartmouth Hall—Old and New," pp. 15–16.

40. Of unknown origins, the 25 April 1935 fire started in the cellar and rose up through the building, destroying the belfry and a portion of the roof but causing little additional damage. Subsequently, reconstruction architect Jens Fredrick Larson directed the remodeling of the interior and the restoration of the two-story Young chapel, omitted when the structure was rebuilt in 1904–6. The current building contains seminar rooms, faculty offices, and lecture rooms on all three floors. Eliminating as much wood as possible, Larson introduced several safety features, such as concrete floors, steel staircases, fireproof partitions, and a copper-covered gypsum roof. See Lenning, "A History of Dartmouth Hall," p. 33, and Childs, "Dartmouth Hall—Old and News," pp. 16–17.

41. Lenning, "A History of Dartmouth Hall," p. 42; Younger, "Dartmouth Hall (1784–1984): A Bicentennial Tribute," *Dartmouth Alumni Magazine* 77, no. 4 (December 1984): 44–47; Dartmouth College Board of Trustees Records, Annual Meetings of August 1789 and March 1790; Chase, *A History of Dartmouth College and the Town of Hanover*, p. 581. The original Ticknor watercolor drawing, the basis for modern reproductions, is owned by Dartmouth College. See *Antiques* 46, no. 3 (September 1944), frontispiece and accompanying essay.

42. Richardson, *History of Dartmouth College*, p. 213; Chase, *A History of Dartmouth College and the Town of Hanover*, p. 581; Wheelock, *Sketches*, p. 32.

43. Dewey, "Reminiscences of Hanover," sketches; Brown, "Historical Address," from the *Centennial Celebration of Dartmouth College, June 21, 1869*, pp. 6–41.

44. Dartmouth College Board of Trustees Records, Meeting of August 1790; Richardson, *History of Dartmouth College*, p. 214; Chase, *A History of Dartmouth College and the Town of Hanover*, p. 582; Robert L. Fletcher, "Table," from Hapgood, ed., *Echoes from Dartmouth*, p. 148; Farmer and Moore, *A Gazetteer of the State of New Hampshire*, p. 36.

45. Dewey, "Reminiscences of Hanover," sketches; Richardson, "Brief Biographies of Buildings: I—Wentworth and Thornton Halls," *Dartmouth Alumni Magazine* 35 (1942): 11–12; Lord, *A History of Dartmouth College (1815–1909)*, pp. 221–22; Dartmouth College Board of Trustees Records, Meeting of January 1828; Richardson, *History of Dartmouth College*, p. 395; Dartmouth

College President's Report for 1828 (Bennett Tyler), College Archives, Dartmouth College Library. The actual cost of the project was $16,200, including expenses for the concurrent restoration of Dartmouth Hall.

46. Kenney, "The History of Wentworth and Thornton Halls," pp. 8, 12–14. Both buildings possessed either unfinished brick or whitewashed walls until 1868 when, along with other Dartmouth buildings, they were painted yellow in preparation for the college's centennial celebration. In subsequent years they were painted white. See Lord, *A History of Dartmouth College (1815–1909)*, p. 268.

47. Richardson, *History of Dartmouth College*, pp. 415, 541, 775; Richardson, "Brief Biographies of Buildings: I—Wentworth and Thornton Halls," p. 12; Kenney, "The History of Wentworth and Thornton Halls," pp. 1, 2, 21.

48. Benezet, "The History of Reed Hall," pp. 1, 6–7; Richardson, "Brief Biographies of Buildings: II—Reed Hall," *Dartmouth Alumni Magazine* 35 (1942): 21; Dartmouth College Board of Trustees Records, Meeting of 29 July 1835. The bequest that was supposed to have covered the expenses of Reed Hall's construction was unavailable for over twenty years due to the restrictive terms of Mr. Reed's will. During this period, the building cost was carried as a loan against the general funds of the college.

49. Dartmouth College Board of Trustees Records, Meeting of October 1838; Benezet, "The History of Reed Hall," p. 2; Lord, *A History of Dartmouth College (1815–1909)*, p. 259; Richardson, *History of Dartmouth College*, p. 401. The building contract with Dyer Young called for an expenditure of $11,000, but the final cost exceeded the original estimate. This led to a dispute, which was resolved by arbitration in 1843. The total expense was greater than the combined costs for Wentworth and Thornton halls a decade before. In 1838 the Wheelock mansion was moved across the Hanover green to Wheelock Street, where today, in modified form, it serves as a portion of the town library.

50. Patrick, "The Dartmouth College Green," pp. 110–11; Benezet, "The History of Reed Hall," pp. 5–9, 16, 26, 31; Dartmouth College Board of Trustees Records, Annual Meeting of June 1839; Richardson, "Brief Biographies of Buildings: II—Reed Hall," p. 211; Lord, *A History of Dartmouth College (1815–1909)*, p. 260. About the same time that Young designed Reed Hall for the college, he prepared plans for two other buildings in New Hampshire that were strikingly similar—Seminary Hall (1839–40) for the Gilmanton Theological Seminary, Gilmanton, and an addition (1839–40) to the main building of Kimball Union Academy, Meriden. Both no longer exist. See Bryant F. Tolles, Jr., "Ammi Burnham Young and the Gilmanton Theological Seminary," *Old-Time New England* 61, no. 2 (Fall 1970): 47–54, 56.

51. Benezet, "The History of Reed Hall," pp. 1, 14, 26; Larson and Palmer, *Architectural Planning of the American College*, p. 112; Donnelly, "Astronomical Observatories in New England," *Old-Time New England* 50 (1960): 72–75; Dartmouth College Board of Trustees Records, Annual Meeting of 1848; Williams, "The Architectural History of the Observatory," pp. 5–7. This 28-by-13-foot, two-room temporary building was located where South Massachusetts Hall stands today. It was made larger than originally planned in hopes that it might be moved across the green and used as the east wing of the permanent observatory, but this never occurred. The total cost was a mere $250.

52. Lord, *A History of Dartmouth College (1815–1909)*, p. 288; "Observatories in the United States," *Harper's New Monthly Magazine* 13 (1856): 44–45; Williams, "The Architectural History of the Observatory," p. 10; Ammi Burnham Young, Drawings for the Shattuck Observatory, Rauner Special Collections, Dartmouth College Library; *New York Times*, 16 and 18 November 1958; *Bridgeport* (Conn.) *Sunday Post*, 19 July 1959.

53. Morgan, "A Case for the Permanent Preservation of the Dartmouth College Observatory," pp. 1–3.

54. Williams, "The Architectural History of the Observatory," pp. 21, 24, 25; Turner, *Campus*, p. 3. Not included in this section of the study (see the preface) is the original, bland, three-story rectangular Dartmouth Medical School building (1811; enlarged, 1873; demolished, 1961), formerly located north of the Old Row to the east of College Street.

Chapter 3: Williams and Bowdoin

1. Turner, *Campus*, pp. 52, 101; Stoddard, *Reflections on the Architecture of Williams College*, pp. 13, 30; Davis, "Williams College in 1845," University of California *Chronicle* 14, no. 1 (c. 1911); Brooks, *Williamstown*, pp. 23–24; Field, *A History of the County of Berkshire, Massachusetts*, pp. 166–67. It is interesting to note that almost all of the early trustees of Williams College were graduates of Yale, yet they departed from the organized, strict planning of the Old Brick Row. See Ballinger, "Williams College," *New England Magazine* n.s. 42, no. 2 (April 1910): 146.

2. "Our Campus Architecture," *Williams Graphic* 1, no. 2 (1921): 10; Stoddard, *Reflections on the Architecture of Williams College*, pp. 16–18, 30; Durfee, *A History of Williams College*, pp. 56–62, 83, 344–45; Spring, *A History of Williams College*, pp. 37–38; Smith and Cushing, *History of Berkshire County*, vol. 2, p. 684. West College was originally planned for and used by the Academy and Free School, which was, by act of incorporation in 1793, changed to Williams College. There are numerous examples of buildings, mostly residential, at other pre–Civil War American higher educational institutions that were called "colleges," a practice initiated at Harvard.

3. Egleston, *Williamstown and Williams College*, p. 25.

4. Stoddard, *Reflections on the Architecture of Williams College*, pp. 18, 108; Sawyer Library, Williams College, catalogue.

5. Stoddard, *Reflections on the Architecture of Williams College*, pp. 22–23, 190; Spring, *A History of Williams College*, pp. 50–51, 260; Durfee, *A History of Williams College*, pp. 345–46; Perry, *Williamstown and Williams College*, pp. 260, 262. Early in their respective histories, East and West colleges were connected by a straight avenue of Lombard poplar trees, at the time the sole embellishment of the college grounds.

6. Stoddard, *Reflections on the Architecture of Williams College*, pp. 22, 190; Durfee, *A History of Williams College*, pp. 250–51, 356; Wells and Davis, *Sketches of Williams College, Williamstown, Mass.*, p. 41; Perry, *Williamstown and Williams College*, pp. 263, 267. The 1841 fire is thoroughly described in student letters contained in the Williamsiana Collection, Williams College Archives and Special Collections.

7. Durfee, *A History of Williams College*, p. 346; Salisbury, *In the Days of Mark Hopkins*, pp. 66–67; Stoddard, *Reflections on the Architecture of Williams College*, pp. 34–35, 174–76; Perry, *Williamstown and Williams College*, p. 528; Department of Buildings and Grounds records, Williamsiana Collection. The total cost of the East and South colleges project was $11,000 (see Durfee, *A History of Williams College*, p. 251). South College was renamed Fayerweather Hall after a remodeling and expansion to the south in 1905–6 directed by Allen & Collens of Boston and made possible by a $275,000 bequest by businessman Daniel Fayerweather (see Sawyer Library catalogue). It goes by the name of South College as well as Fayerweather Hall today.

8. Stoddard, *Reflections on the Architecture of Williams College*, pp. 26–28; Smith and Cushing, *History of Berkshire County*, vol. 2, p. 685; "Three Chapels," *The Argo* 2, no. 2 (20 May 1882): 20; Durfee, *A History of Williams College*, pp. 195–96, 201, 346–47; Spring, *A History of Williams College*, pp. 131–32; Perry, *Williamstown and Williams College*, pp. 456–58; "The Story of a College Building," *Williams Literary Monthly* 17, no. 9 (April 1902): 438–41; Sawyer Library, Williams College, catalogue; Field, *A History of the County of Berkshire, Massachusetts*, p. 168; "Williams College," *American Advocate* 2, no. 75 (10 September 1828): 90–91. Griffin Hall underwent an interior remodeling in 1860–61 (see the *Williams Quarterly* 9, no. 1 [August 1861]: 65). The chapel room was converted to a library in 1904 but was restored close to its original state in the late 1900s. Griffin Hall originally was situated almost flush with Main Street but was moved to its present location in 1904 in preparation for the building of Thompson Memorial Chapel. In 1972 Griffin Hall underwent a $28,000 restoration directed by architect Peter F. Welanetz.

9. Stoddard, *Reflections on the Architecture of Williams College*, p. 32; Durfee, *A History of Williams College*, pp. 248, 347–48; Salisbury, *In the Days of Mark Hopkins*, pp. 70–71; Wells and Davis, *Sketches of Williams College, Williamstown, Mass.*, pp. 40–41; Milham, *The History of Astronomy at Williams College and the Founding of Hopkins Observatory*, pp. 9–12. In his book on Williams College architecture, Whitney Stoddard also briefly comments about the Magnetic Observatory, or The Hermitage, another Albert Hopkins–inspired structure built near the Hopkins Observatory in 1842 and near the location of the current Driscoll Dining Hall. Part of the "philosophical" apparatus on the campus, it housed scientific instruments, and later in the 1870s was used as a dormitory space for one student! A small, one-story brick octagon with windows and a single doorway, it was torn down in 1905 when Berkshire Hall was built.

10. Stoddard, *Reflections on the Architecture of Williams College*, pp. 38–41; Placzek, ed., *Macmillan Encyclopedia of Architects*, vol. 4, p. 189; Durfee, *A History of Williams College*, pp. 261–62, 348; Department of Grounds and Buildings records, Williamsiana Collection; Rudolph, *Mark Hopkins and the Log*, pp. 175–77; Malmstrom, "Lawrence Hall at Williams College," pp. 1–10. The building was named Lawrence Hall by vote of the Board of Trustees to recognize Amos Lawrence's donation. Four drawings of Lawrence Hall by Thomas Tefft exist in the Tefft Papers at the John Hay Library, Brown University, Providence, R.I.

11. Stoddard, *Reflections on the Architecture of Williams College*, p. 190; Durfee, *A History of Williams College*, pp. 266, 268, 349. Two "gymnasium" structures, no longer extant, were modest-sized wooden vernacular buildings situated southwest of South College. The first, erected in 1851, burned just a year later and was replaced on the same spot by a second, which also burned in 1858. Their successor, a small, uninspiring brick structure once located at the corner of Spring and Main streets, was completed in 1859, was soon converted into a service and storage building and was leveled in 1928 (see Stoddard, *Reflections on the Architecture of Williams College*, p. 191).

12. Stoddard, *Reflections on the Architecture of Williams College*, p. 191; Durfee, *A History of Williams College*, pp. 272–73; "Nathan Jackson, Benefactor," *Williams Alumni Review* 29, no. 8 (June 1927): 354–56; Rudolph, *Mark Hopkins and the Log*, pp. 145, 147–48; *Williams Quarterly* 2, no. 4 (June 1855): 382; Sawyer Library catalogue; Spring, *A History of Williams College*, p. 256.

13. Stoddard, *Reflections on the Architecture of Williams College*, pp. 46–47, 178–79; Placzek, ed., *Macmillan Encyclopedia of Architects*, vol. 4, pp. 388–89; Durfee, *A History of Williams College*, pp. 302–303; 349–51; Rudolph, *Mark Hopkins and the Log*, p. 205; Department of Grounds and Buildings records, Williamsiana Collection; Salisbury, *In the Days of Mark Hopkins*, pp. 67–68. The chapel interior of the building consisted of a main aisle culminating with an altar and organ above. The entire hall was finished in dark wood, originally with pews to seat the entire student body. The chapel was contained in the main building, with outside dimensions of 44 by 61 feet. The rear building was 36 by 56 feet and housed Alumni Hall with a speaker's platform and desk, and seats

for three hundred persons. The lower story of the rear building was devoted to two large recitation rooms.

14. There seems to be no obvious rationale as to why most of the early New England open quadrangle and row plans were situated on a north-south axis and faced west. One would expect campus planners to have oriented such building arrangements southward to take advantage of the prevailing heat and light provided by the sun in favorable weather conditions. Furthermore, such schemes were exposed to prevailing western winds so common to all sections of New England.

15. Slattery, "Brunswick and Bowdoin College," *New England Magazine* n.s. 5 (1891): 455; "Domestic Correspondence from Bowdoin College," *The World* (New York), 9 August 1860, p. 2; Cleaveland and Packard, *History of Bowdoin College*, p. 26; Brault, "A Checklist of Portraits of the Campus of Bowdoin College Before the Civil War," pp. 1–4; Brault, "The Earliest Painting of the Bowdoin College Campus," *Old-Time New England* 51 (1961): 101–103; Tolles, "College Architecture in New England Before 1860 in Printed and Sketched Views," *Magazine Antiques* 103, no. 3 (March 1973): 503–4; Records of the Board of Trustees of Bowdoin College, Meetings of 17 May and 5 September 1808; Bowdoin College Treasurer's Account Book (1803–21), Statement for 16 May 1809.

16. Records of the Board of Trustees of Bowdoin College, Meeting of 18 and 19 July 1796; Woods, *Address on the Opening of the New Hall of the Medical School of Maine*, pp. 5–6; Howell, Jr., "Evidences of the Massachusetts Hall Cupola," *Bowdoin Alumnus* 33 (1959): 13; Hatch, *The History of Bowdoin College*, p. 9; Records of the Board of Overseers of Bowdoin College, Meeting of 7 November 1797.

17. Records of the Board of Trustees of Bowdoin College, Meetings of 15 May 1799, March 1800, 20 May 1801, 1 September 1802; Woods, *Address on the Opening of the New Hall of the Medical School of Maine*, pp. 7–8; Hatch, *The History of Bowdoin College*, pp. 10, 104; Dwight, *Travels in New England and New York*, vol. 2, p. 212; Calhoun, *A Small College in Maine*, pp. 40–42.

18. Records of the Boards of Overseers and Trustees of Bowdoin College, Meeting of 25 May 1801; Woods, *Address on the Opening of the New Hall of the Medical School of Maine*, p. 5; Records of the Board of Trustees of Bowdoin College, Annual Statement of 1805.

19. Anderson, *The Architecture of Bowdoin College*, p. 10; Shipman, *The Early Architecture of Bowdoin College and Brunswick, Maine*, pp. 13–16. Samuel Melcher III was born on 8 May 1775 and died on 3 March 1862. During his lifetime, he established a reputation as a careful and artful designer and builder of residential, ecclesiastical, and educational structures, though he was not an architect in terms of professional training. Many of his lovely Federal-style residences are still standing in Brunswick, Topsham, and vicinity. They reveal a delicacy in Adamesque taste and fa-

vorably compare with those by Samual McIntire in Salem, Massachusetts. Melcher's best-known works are the Parker Cleaveland, Upham, Gilman, and Dunlap houses in Brunswick, the King House and the Frost Mansion in Topsham, the old Congregational Meeting House in Wiscasset, the Spite House and the Kavanaugh Mansion at Damariscotta Mills, and the several buildings he was associated with at Bowdoin College.

20. "Old Massachusetts," *Bowdoin Orient* 13 (1883): 156–58; Cleaveland and Packard, *History of Bowdoin College*, pp. 26, 95; Hatch, *The History of Bowdoin College*, pp. 58, 461; Little, "Historical Sketch of the Institution During the First Century," *General Catalogue of Bowdoin College and the Medical School of Maine*, p. xxxviii; Anderson, *The Architecture of Bowdoin College*, p. 11; Works Progress Administration, *Maine*, p. 146; *Bowdoin College Bulletin, Catalogue Sessions for 1968–69*, p. 31.

21. Shipman, *The Early Architecture of Bowdoin College and Brunswick, Maine*, p. 18; Records of the Board of Trustees of Bowdoin College, Meetings of 16 May 1799, 19 May 1818, 31 August 1830; Howell, "Evidences of the Massachusetts Hall Cupola," *Bowdoin Alumnus* 33 (February 1959): 13; Minutes of the Visiting Committee of the Boards of Trustees and Overseers of Bowdoin College, Report of 1829; Anderson, *The Architecture of Bowdoin College*, p. 11. It has been suggested by some that the re-creation of the cupola atop Massachusetts Hall would be an exciting restorative exercise.

22. Records of the Board of Trustees of Bowdoin College, Meetings of 15 May 1805, 19 May 1818, 3 September 1825; Samuel Melcher III Ledger Book (1805), entry of 13 July 1805, pp. 35–36; Shipman, *The Early Architecture of Bowdoin College and Brunswick, Maine*, pp. 25–26; "The Old Chapel and the New," *Bowdoin Orient*, 3 February 1873, p. 180; Hatch, *The History of Bowdoin College*, pp. 414–15; "The Old Chapel," *Bowdoin Orient*, 5 March 1884, p. 214.

23. Hawthorne, "Nathaniel Hawthorne at Bowdoin," *New England Quarterly* 13 (1940): 263; Hatch, *The History of Bowdoin College*, pp. 41–42; Little, "Historical Sketch of the Institution During the First Century," p. xliv; Records of the Board of Trustees of Bowdoin College, Meetings of 4 September 1804 and 3 September 1805.

24. Records of the Board of Trustees of Bowdoin College, Estimate of the Committee for Building a College, September 2nd, 1806; Cleaveland and Packard, *History of Bowdoin College*, p. 93; Little, "Historical Sketch of the Institution During the First Century," p. xliv; Samuel Melcher Ledger Books; Bowdoin College Treasurer's Account Books (1803–21); Shipman, *The Early Architecture of Bowdoin College and Brunswick, Maine*, pp. 25, 27.

25. Records of the Board of Trustees of Bowdoin College, Prudential Committee, Meeting of 21 August 1822. At this meeting a vote was passed to rename the dormitory structure Maine Hall.

26. Shipman, *The Early Architecture of Bowdoin College and Brunswick, Maine*, pp. 27–28; Little, "Historical Sketch of the Institution During the First Century," p. xliv; Hatch, *The History of Bowdoin College*, p. 403; Hawthorne, "Nathaniel Hawthorne at Bowdoin," p. 403.

27. Cleaveland and Packard, *History of Bowdoin College*, p. 12; Hatch, *The History of Bowdoin College*, p. 406. The college, lacking insurance coverage for Maine Hall, had only this means at its disposal to finance the restoration. Contributions actually exceeded the $6,500 in costs by $3,500, giving Bowdoin an unexpected profit from the ordeal.

28. Records of the Board of Trustees of Bowdoin College, Report of the Committee to Rebuild Maine Hall, 1 September 1823, and Meetings of 27 March 1822 and 1 September 1824; Anderson, *The Architecture of Bowdoin College*, p. 13.

29. Little, "Historical Sketch of the Institution During the First Century," p. lxxi; Anderson, *The Architecture of Bowdoin College*, pp. 14–15; Minutes of the Visiting Committee of Bowdoin College, Report of 9 March 1836; Records of the Board of Trustees of Bowdoin College, Meeting of 6 September 1836; Hatch, *The History of Bowdoin College*, p. 13; Cleaveland and Packard, *History of Bowdoin College*, p. 13.

30. Minutes of the Visiting Committee of Bowdoin College, Exhibit A of Report of August 1825. The final dormitory of the four in the row, Hyde Hall, was not constructed until 1917, but when completed it was observed to be a close copy of Melcher's 1836–37 rendition of Maine Hall. The design was prepared by the Boston architectural firm of Allen and Collens.

31. Hatch, *The History of Bowdoin College*, p. 408; Records of the Board of Trustees of Bowdoin College, Meeting of 5 September 1821, Building Contract Report of 1 September 1823, Meetings of 3 August and 1 September 1847; Samuel Melcher III Day Book (18 September 1811 to 21 November 1818); Anderson, *The Architecture of Bowdoin College*, pp. 17–18; Clayton, *History of Cumberland Co., Maine*, p. 244.

32. Hatch, *The History of Bowdoin College*, pp. 408–9, 411; Minutes of the Visiting Committee of Bowdoin College, Meeting of 1853.

33. Hatch, *The History of Bowdoin College*, p. 409; Anderson, *The Architecture of Bowdoin College*, pp. 19–21; Records of the Board of Trustees of Bowdoin College, Meetings of 2 September 1835, 6 and 7 September 1842, and 3 and 4 September 1844; Joseph McKeen to Hon. Judge Weston, 2 September 1843; Articles of Agreement made and concluded by and between . . . Samuel Melcher and sons . . . and the President and Trustees of Bowdoin College (1843).

34. Records of the Board of Trustees of Bowdoin College, Meetings of 31 August and 1 September 1847; Hatch, *The History of Bowdoin College*, p. 409.

35. Records of the Board of Trustees of Bowdoin College, Meeting of 2 September 1828; Minutes of the Visiting Committee of Bowdoin College, Report of 13 August 1829; Hatch, *The History of Bowdoin College*, pp. 344, 350; Wheeler, *History of Brunswick, Topsham and Hartswell, Maine*; Anderson, *The Architecture of Bowdoin College*, p. 123.

36. Minutes of the Visiting Committee of the Boards of Trustees and Overseers of Bowdoin College, Annual Meeting of 1852; conversation with Robert L. Volz, then Curator of Special Collections, Hawthorne-Longfellow Library, Bowdoin College, Brunswick, Maine, July 1969. This story may be verified in the trustee records for the 1840s.

37. Hatch, *History of Higher Education in Maine*, p. 72. One of America's most distinguished mid-nineteenth-century architects, Richard Upjohn was an exponent of a purer and more artistic form of the Gothic Revival than had hitherto prevailed. He is also remembered as the originator and first president (1857–76) of the American Institute of Architects. Born in Shaftesbury, England in 1802, Upjohn emigrated to the United States in the 1820s, settled in New Bedford, Massachusetts, and then relocated to Boston, opening a small practice and completing the Trinity Church design. He continued as a Gothic Revival specialist in church planning, designing numerous ecclesiastical structures in New York City, New York State, New Jersey, and New England, among them the First Parish Church and St. Paul's Episcopal Church, both also in Brunswick. Upjohn's civic architecture revealed many of the same characteristics as his churches, while his domestic commissions were customarily in the Italian Renaissance vernacular.

For Upjohn, the Bowdoin College Chapel represented a stylistic departure from his customary commitment to the Gothic Revival for ecclesiastical design. See Withey, *Biographical Dictionary of American Architects (Deceased)*, pp. 611–12; Everard M. Upjohn, *Richard M. Upjohn*.

38. Records of the Board of Trustees of Bowdoin College, Meeting of 28 February 1825; Minutes of the Visiting Committee of the Boards of Trustees and Overseers of Bowdoin College, Meeting of 12 August 1834.

39. Cleaveland and Packard, *History of Bowdoin College*, p. 24; Hatch, *The History of Bowdoin College*, p. 418; Records of the Board of Trustees of Bowdoin College, Meetings of 6 and 7 September 1842, and Meetings of 3 and 4 September 1844. Other documentation in the college archives of Upjohn's relationship with Bowdoin includes entries in the Minutes of the Visiting Committee; letters to Upjohn duplicated in the Letter Copy Book of Joseph McKeen, College Treasurer from 1837 to 1863; and certain letters of President Leonard Woods.

40. Little, "Historical Sketch of the Institution During the First Century," p. lxxvii.

41. Upjohn, *Richard Upjohn*, pp. 80–81; Rush, *History of Maine*

College Libraries, p. 16; "The Old Chapel and the New," *Bowdoin Orient*, 3 February 1873, p. 181; Anderson, *The Architecture of Bowdoin College*, p. 27.

42. Records of the Board of Trustees of Bowdoin College, 31 August and 1 September 1852; Upjohn, *Richard Upjohn*, p. 80; Meeks, "Romanesque before Richardson in the United States," *Art Bulletin* 35 (1953): 23–24; Anderson, *The Architecture of Bowdoin College*, p. 26; Hatch, *The History of Bowdoin College*, p. 420.

43. The next major building constructed for Bowdoin College, excluded from discussion in the text because of its dating and its primary function, is Seth Adams Hall (1861), designed by the highly regarded architect Francis H. Fassett (1823–1908) of Brunswick and then Portland, Maine. This striking, sophisticated Italian Revival masonry structure was initially utilized as the primary facility for the Medical School of Maine and as a laboratory for the undergraduate science curriculum. The first totally instructional building at Bowdoin, it was built at the north end of the old row (near Massachusetts Hall) at Bath and Harpswell streets. See Anderson, *The Architecture of Bowdoin College*, pp. 29–32, and Calhoun, *A Small College in Maine*, pp. 113–17.

Chapter 4: The Vermont Institutions

1. The content of this section of chapter 4 is a revised version of two illustrated articles previously published by the author— "The 'College Edifice' (1801–1807) at the University of Vermont," *Vermont History* (Vermont Historical Society) 40, no. 1 (Winter 1972): 1–9; and "The 'Old Mill' (1825–29) at the University of Vermont," *Vermont History* 57, no. 1 (Winter 1989): 22–34.

The University of Vermont was chartered as a private college in 1791, the same year in which Vermont achieved statehood. The individual deserving of principal credit for its establishment was Ira Allen, the brother of the legendary Ethan Allen. Academic sessions commenced in 1800. In 1865, the university became a national land-grant institution under the terms of the Morrill Act and was incorporated as the "University of Vermont and State Agricultural College," still its formal title.

2. Dwight, *Travels in New England and New York*, vol. 2, p. 424.

3. Lindsay, *Tradition Looks Forward*, p. 122.

4. Minutes of the Board of Trustees of the University of Vermont, Meeting of 3 November 1791, Special Collections, University of Vermont Libraries, Burlington.

5. Minutes of the Board of Trustees of the University of Vermont, Meeting of 16 June 1792.

6. Minutes of the Board of Trustees of the University of Vermont, Meetings of 17 January and 18 October 1800; Lindsay, *Tradition Looks Forward*, p. 34; Daniels, *The University of Vermont*, p. 29.

7. Minutes of the Board of Trustees of the University of Vermont, Meeting of 13 January 1801; Lindsay, *Tradition Looks Forward*, pp. 59–62.

8. Lindsay, *Tradition Looks Forward*, p. 46; Wheeler, *A Historical Discourse*, p. 11.

9. Lindsay, *Tradition Looks Forward*, pp. 58–59.

10. "University of Vermont at Burlington," *Vermont Sentinel*, 24 July 1805, p. 2.

11. Bush, *History of Education in Vermont*, p. 158; Thompson, *A Gazetteer of the State of Vermont*, p. 36; Goodrich, "One Hundred Years Ago: The Beginnings of the University of Vermont," *The Ariel* 18 (1905): 214; Rann, *History of Chittenden County*, p. 206.

12. See Thwing, *A History of Higher Education in America*, pp. 406–7, and Bush-Brown, "College Architecture, an Expression of Educational Philosophy," *Architectural Record* 122 (1957): 154–57.

13. Schedule of Payments payable to the Committee for finishing the College Edifice in Burlington in the County of Chittenden, State of Vermont, September 1805, Special Collections, University of Vermont Libraries.

14. *Vermont Sentinel*, 23 August 1805.

15. Daniel Clarke Sanders to Reverend Leonard Worcester, 24 June 1806, Special Collections, University of Vermont Libraries.

16. Thompson, *A Gazetteer of the State of Vermont*, p. 36.

17. Thompson, *History of Vermont, Natural, Civil and Statistical*, p. 144.

18. Goodrich, "One Hundred Years Ago," p. 215; "The Clock Maker of Old Burlington," *Vermont Life* (Fall 1966): 43; Thomas, *University of Vermont*, p. 9.

19. Lindsay, *Tradition Looks Forward*, p. 58.

20. Allen, "Early History of the University of Vermont and the First Graduating Class," *Burlington Free Press*, 2 July 1904. Based on the handwritten "Recollections of Charles Adams, Class of 1804," Vermont Historical Society, Montpelier.

21. "Early Architecture of Vermont," *Burlington Free Press*, 12 July 1922; John Johnson contract with the University of Vermont to erect college building, 18 August 1801, Johnson Collection, Special Collections, University of Vermont Libraries.

22. Hemenway, ed., *Vermont State Historical Gazetteer*, vol. 1, p. 597. John Johnson was among the earliest and best-known citizens of Burlington, Vermont. A prominent surveyor, he laid out many townships in the northern sector of the state. He also wrote extensively on aspects of civil and mechanical engineering and did much practical design work in this field. The Johnson arch truss for long bridges was employed all over New England and Lower Canada at the time. After 1808 he lived on the hill near the university, held civic offices, and planned and was head contractor for several large buildings in the Burlington region. See also Child, *Gazetteer and Business Directory of Chittenden County, Vermont for 1882–83*, pp. 751–53; *The National Cyclopedia of American Biog-*

raphy, vol. 17, pp. 290–91; and J. Kevin Graffagnino, "John Johnson," *Vermonter*, magazine section of the *Burlington Free Press*, 6 July 1980, pp. 3–4.

23. Thompson, *History of Vermont, Natural, Civil and Statistical*, p. 145; Daniels, *The University of Vermont*, pp. 15, 41.

24. Minutes of the Board of Trustees of the University of Vermont, Meeting of 1 June 1824.

25. Ibid.

26. Minutes of the Board of Trustees of the University of Vermont, Meeting of 10 August 1824.

27. Minutes of the Board of Trustees of the University of Vermont, Meeting of 12 August 1824.

28. Lindsay, *Tradition Looks Forward*, p. 122.

29. John Johnson, contract with the University of Vermont to erect a College building, 18 August 1801, Johnson Collection, Special Collections, University of Vermont Libraries.

30. Johnson's maps and surveys became the basis of land records for substantial areas of northern Vermont.

31. Lindsay, *Tradition Looks Forward*, p. 126.

32. Ibid., p. 127; Thompson, *History of Vermont, Natural, Civil and Statistical*, p. 147; Hills, "UVM History," p. 6, Joseph Lawrence Hills Papers, Special Collections, University of Vermont Libraries.

33. Tolles, "College Architecture in New England Before 1860 in Printed and Sketched Views," *Magazine Antiques* 103, no. 3 (March 1973): 505–6. The names "North College" and "South College" were derived from English universities and were used at numerous other New England colleges. Lindsay, *Tradition Looks Forward*, p. 127; Rann, ed., *History of Chittenden County*, p. 207; *Catalogue of Officers and Students of the University of Vermont for 1825*, p. 8; Hills, "UVM History," pp. 5–7.

34. Rann, *History of Chittenden County*, p. 207.

35. Minutes of the Board of Trustees of the University of Vermont, Meetings of 3 January and 5 August 1828.

36. Minutes of the Board of Trustees of the University of Vermont, Treasurer's Statement, Meeting of 4 August 1831.

37. Poole, "Vermont Campus Tradition Centers About Venerable 'Old Mill,'" *Vermont Alumnus* 7 (8 February 1928): 231; Hills, "UVM History," p. 5.

38. Thompson, *History of Vermont, Natural, Civil and Statistical*, p. 147; Auld, *Picturesque Burlington*, pp. 110–12.

39. Thompson, *History of Vermont, Natural, Civil and Statistical*, p. 147; Lindsay, *Tradition Looks Forward*, Old Mill plate.

40. Lindsay, *Tradition Looks Forward*, Old Mill plate; Rann, *History of Chittenden County*, p. 207; Hills, "UVM History," p. 5.

41. Poole, "Vermont Campus Tradition Centers About Venerable 'Old Mill,'" p. 231.

42. Rann, *History of Chittenden County*, p. 208; Auld, *Picturesque Burlington*, pp. 112–13; Allen, *About Burlington, Vermont*, p. 45; Hills, "UVM History," p. 8; Poole, "Vermont Campus Tradition Centers About Venerable 'Old Mill,'" p. 231.

While the west or front facade was completely reconstructed, the east or rear wall surface has remained partially intact (see fig. 4-9). It is still possible to see flat expanses of the original brickwork, original fenestration, and distinct lines of demarcation between the original and more recent brickwork. Apparently, either due to preference or the need for economy, it was decided not to "Victorianize" the less conspicuous side of the building.

43. Hills, "UVM History," pp. 8, 12, 13, 14, 18; Gayer, "UVM's 'Old Mill' Enters 21st Century," *AIA Vermont Report* (June 1997): 1.

44. Hills, "UVM History," pp. 8–9. Nearby the Old Mill overlooking the College Green at the south end is the first Medical College (1828–29, etc.), now Pomeroy Hall, which is not discussed in this chapter, as the building type is not included in the subject definition for this book.

In 1975, the Old Mill was placed on the National Register of Historic Places as a part of the University of Vermont Historic District.

45. Swift, *History of the Town of Middlebury*, pp. 372–79; Andres, *A Walking History of Middlebury*, p. 49.

46. Letter, W. Storrs Lee to Bryant F. Tolles, Jr., 15 July 1969, in the author's possession. The other sketch, rather roughly drawn, was done by student Samuel Everts in 1828. Reproductions of the two sketches have appeared with published writings about the college on several occasions. As examples, see Bain, *The College on the Hill*, p. 5, and Stameshkin, *The Town's College*, p. 25.

47. Lee, *Father Went to College*, p. 155; Hendrie, "History of Middlebury College," p. 2; Andres, *A Walking History of Middlebury*, p. 49.

48. Lee, *Father Went to College*, p. 155.

49. Ibid.; Swift, *History of the Town of Middlebury*, p. 372; Hayward, *The New England Gazetteer*, appendix, p. 8; Smith, *History of Addison County, Vermont*, p. 344.

50. Hendrie, "History of Middlebury College," p. 2; Merrill, *Semicentennial Sermon Containing a History of Middlebury, Vermont*, p. 70; *Middlebury College*, p. 7; Andres, *A Walking History of Middlebury*, p. 49.

51. Swift, *History of the Town of Middlebury*, pp. 373–74. In 1844 the grammar school returned to its original home on a space-sharing basis with the college. Part of the lower story was altered and equipped for this purpose. The school remained there until the 1860s.

52. *Middlebury College: A Souvenir Published by the Class of '98*, p. 7; Prentiss, "Middlebury College," *University Magazine* 1 (1904): 18.

53. Tolles, "College Architecture in New England Before 1860

in Printed and Sketched Views," *Magazine Antiques* 103, no. 3 (March 1973): 509; Wright, "A Sketch of Middlebury College," *Education* 19 (1859): 598; Connell, "Middlebury—The Beauty of Variety," *American Landscape Architect* 11 (1932): 24.

54. Swift, *History of the Town of Middlebury*, p. 381; Andres, *A Walking History of Middlebury*, p. 56.

55. Middlebury College President and Fellows Minutes of the Annual Meetings, Meeting of 1 October 1810.

56. Prentiss, "Middlebury College," *University Magazine* 1 (1904): 11.

57. Dwight, *Travels in New England and New York* 1, p. 419; Swift, *History of the Town of Middlebury*, p. 381; Hemenway, ed., *The Vermont State Historical Gazetteer*, vol. 1, p. 55.

58. Lee, *Father Went to College*, p. 69.

59. Hoskins, *History of the State of Vermont from Its Discovery and Settlement to the Year 1830*, p. 310; Thompson, *History of Vermont, Natural, Civil and Statistical*, p. 132; Hayward, *The New England Gazetteer*, appendix, p. 8; Bain, *The College on the Hill*, p. 22. Sources are confusing as to the number of rooms in the original building. For the most part, older published sources state forty-eight.

60. Middlebury College President and Fellows Minutes of the Annual Meetings, Meeting of 1 October 1810; Gamaliel Painter's Day Book for "Stone College" (1811–16).

61. Lee, *Father Went to College*, p. 157.

62. Bush, *History of Higher Education in Vermont*, p. 182; "Painter Hall," *Vermonter* 41 (1936): 118; Renovation Plans for Painter Hall, 1936; "Painter Hall" brochure, President's Historical Commission of Middlebury College, 1988; brochure, "The Rededication of Old Stone Row," Middlebury Bicentennial Office, 1999.

63. Middlebury College President and Fellows Minutes of the Annual Meetings, Meeting of 18 August 1831.

64. Middlebury College President and Fellows Minutes of Annual Meetings, Meeting of 3 September 1833; Swift, *History of the Town of Middlebury*, p. 382; Thompson, *History of Vermont, Natural, Civil and Statistical*, p. 157; Lee, *Father Went to College*, p. 119.

65. Middlebury College President and Fellows Minutes of the Annual Meetings, Meeting of 21 August 1834.

66. *Dictionary of American Biography*, vol. 1, pp. 540–41; Joshua Bates to Loami [Loammi] Baldwin, 1 September 1834, William L. Clements Library, University of Michigan, Ann Arbor; Bain, *The College on the Hill*, p. 45.

67. Joshua Bates to Loami [Loammi] Baldwin, 1 September 1834, William L. Clements Library, University of Michigan, Ann Arbor.

68. Fowler, "Historical Sketch of Middlebury College," *American Quarterly Register* 9 (1837): 227; Stameshkin, *The Town's College*, p. 66.

69. Thompson, *History of Vermont, Natural, Civil and Statistical*, p. 157; Lee, *Father Went to College*, p. 119. In 1881 the library was moved to Painter Hall and it remained there until the Starr Library was erected in 1900.

70. Brochure, "Old Chapel, 1836," Middlebury College, Middlebury, Vermont, 1988; *Middlebury College Bulletin, Catalogue Number, 1969–70*; Andres, *A Walking History of Middlebury*, p. 57. The chapel room was completely remodeled in 1891. During the 1890s, biology and chemistry laboratories, and recitation rooms were placed on the first floor, and a physics laboratory on the third floor.

71. Fowler, "Historical Sketch of Middlebury College," p. 227.

72. Middlebury College President and Fellows Minutes of the Annual Meetings, Meeting of 10 August 1858.

73. Middlebury College President and Fellows Minutes of the Annual Meetings, Meeting of 10 August 1859; Prentiss, "Middlebury College," p. 18; Bain, *The College on the Hill*, p. 85; Stameshkin, *The Town's College*, p. 150. The building assumed its long-term name specifically in honor of Peter Starr a year after his death, though the entire family's role was recognized.

74. Middlebury College President and Fellows Minutes of the Annual Meetings, Meeting of 5 October 1859.

75. Benjamin Labaree, "Outline History of His Several Endeavors to Obtain Funds for Middlebury College from 1840 to 1868," p. 9.

76. *Middlebury College: A Souvenir Published by the Class of '98*, p. 9.

77. Renovation Plan for Starr Hall, 1945.

78. Lee, *Father Went to College*, pp. 148–50; Bain, *The College on the Hill*, p. 115.

79. Labaree, "Outline History," p. 49; Smith, "The Burning of Starr Hall," *Undergraduate* (April 1899): 48–49.

80. Swift, *History of the Town of Middlebury*, p. 377.

81. Labaree, "Outline History," pp. 31–33. The chief builders of Starr Hall were I. Morse & Bros., and I. W. Course.

82. White and Johnson, *Early Houses of Norwich, Vermont*, p. 41; *"Know Your Town"—The 1940 Survey of Norwich, Vermont*, p. 54. In 1824, Captain Partridge transferred the original academy to Middletown, Conn., in response to a liberal subscription. Here a new row-scheme campus was laid out, the buildings later purchased by Wesleyan University on its establishment. In 1828, after failure to receive a charter for his school from the Connecticut legislature, Partridge acted to move the academy back to Norwich and its original physical plant. In the fall of 1829, classes were resumed in the first academy barracks, which, in the interior, had accommodated a male seminary, set up as a preparatory school for Partridge's college. In 1834, under Universalist auspices, a charter was obtained from the Vermont legislature changing the name

of the institution to Norwich University and defining its degree-granting powers. After a disastrous fire in South Barracks in 1866, and continuing competition from Dartmouth College just across the Connecticut River to the east, the university accepted an offer of land from the town of Northfield, Vermont, facilitated the move there, and created the extensive physical plant that is there today. During its history, the university has also been known as Lewis College and the Military College of the State of Vermont. For a full treatment of its early history, consult Ellis, *Norwich University*, pp. 3–9, and appropriate parts of Ellis and Dodge, *Norwich University, 1819–1911*, 3 vols.

83. Hayward, *The New England Gazetteer*, appendix, p. 11; Ellis and Dodge, *Norwich University, 1819–1911*, vol. 1, p. 4.

84. Joseph Emerson and two brothers, Elihu and Thomas, were Norwich's chief housebuilders in the early nineteenth century. Specifically to Joseph's credit is the Emerson-Douglas House on Main Street and several other domestic structures on which he collaborated with his brother Thomas. The buildings for the academy were his foremost commissions. More a sound builder than an architect, he lived in Norwich until his death in 1857. See White and Johnson, *Early Houses of Norwich, Vermont*, pp. 33–34; Goddard and Partridge, *A History of Norwich, Vermont*, p. 204.

85. Articles of Agreement made, entered into and agreed upon between Pierce Bouton, Alden Partridge and Thomas Emerson, 1819, and Description of the Building for a Literary, Scientific and Military Academy, 1819. University Archives and Special Collections, Kreitzberg Library, Norwich University, Northfield, Vt.

86. Ibid.

87. Thompson, *A Gazetteer of the State of Vermont*, p. 37 and engraving; Ellis and Dodge, *Norwich University, 1819–1911*, vol. 1, p. 68; *Catalogue of the Officers and Cadets of the American Literary, Scientific and Military Academy for 1827*, p. 42; Turner, *Campus*, pp. 36–37.

88. Ellis and Dodge, *Norwich University, 1819–1911*, vol. 1, p. 4.

89. Thompson, *A Gazetteer of the State of Vermont*, p. 37.

90. Ellis and Dodge, *Norwich University, 1819–1911*, vol. 1, p. 122; Dewey, *The Life and Letters of Admiral Dewey*, p. 89.

91. White and Johnson, *Early Houses of Norwich, Vermont*, p. 42; Ellis and Dodge, *Norwich University, 1819–1911*, vol. 1, pp. 139–40.

92. *"Know Your Town,"* p. 54.

93. White and Johnson, *Early Houses of Norwich, Vermont*, p. 42.

94. Ibid.; Goddard and Partridge, *A History of Norwich, Vermont*, p. 110; Dewey, *The Life and Letters of Admiral Dewey*, p. 89.

95. Goddard and Partridge, *A History of Norwich, Vermont*, p. 107.

96. Goddard and Partridge, *A History of Norwich, Vermont*,

p. 269; *Some Pages of Norwich History*, p. 53; White and Johnson, *Early Houses of Norwich, Vermont*, p. 43.

Chapter 5: The Continuing Massachusetts Legacy

1. Turner, *Campus*, p. 44; Tolles, "College Architecture in New England in Printed and Sketched Views," *Magazine Antiques* 103, no. 3 (March 1973): 505–6.

2. Fuess, *Amherst*, p. 24; Richardson and Clark, *The College Book*, pp. 255–56; Gay, *Gazetteer of Hampshire County, Massachusetts, 1654–1887*, pp. 132–33.

3. Fuess, *Amherst*, pp. 39, 41, 50–51, 287, 344; Norton, *Amherst*, p. 83; *A Guide to Amherst Architecture* (1921), p. 15; Hitchcock, *The Handbook of Amherst, Massachusetts* (1891), p. 135; Tyler, *History of Amherst College*, pp. 63–65, 73; Carpenter and Morehouse, *History of the Town of Amherst, Massachusetts*, pp. 159–61, 165; Richardson and Clark, *The College Book*, pp. 256–57; King, *"The Consecrated Eminence,"* pp. 9–10.

4. Fuess, *Amherst*, pp. 56, 83–84, 287; Norton, *Amherst*, p. 81; *A Guide to Amherst College* (1921), p. 15; Hitchcock, *The Handbook of Amherst, Massachusetts* (1891), p. 136; King, *"The Consecrated Eminence,"* pp. 13–14, 112; Tyler, *History of Amherst College*, pp. 74–75. Both North and South colleges received new library rooms in 1933, the gift of Stanley King, the president from 1932 to 1946, and designed by architect Frederick J. Woodbridge. Both buildings were remodeled on their interiors in 1953 according to plans prepared by the New York architectural firm of McKim, Mead and White ("North and South Colleges to Be Rebuilt," *Amherst Alumni News*, March 1953).

5. Tyler, *History of Amherst College*, pp. 176–77, 409; Norton, *Amherst*, p. 82; Fuess, *Amherst*, pp. 84, 86, 164, 287, 330, 343; "The College Chapel," *Amherst Student*, 19 March 1892; Sinnott and Mentor, *Meetinghouse and Church in Early New England*, pp. 107–10, 127; Withey, *Biographical Dictionary of American Architects (Deceased)*, p. 160; James Kellum Smith, "The Architecture of the Johnson Chapel," from *Amherst College—Dedication of the Johnson Chapel* (1934), pp. 11–14; Emerson, "High Upon Her Living Throne," *Amherst Graduate's Quarterly* (May 1948): 198–200; Records of the Prudential Committee, Meetings of 20 September and 4 November 1825, Amherst College Archives; *Annals of Amherst College* (1860), pp. 66–67; Merrill, "Isaac Damon and the Architecture of the Federal Period in New England," Ph.D. diss. (Yale University, 1965), pp. 184–206, 391–98; Hitchcock, *The Handbook of Amherst, Massachusetts* (1891), pp. 135–36; *A Guide to Amherst College* (1921), pp. 15–16; Hitchcock, *The Visitor's Guide to the Public Rooms and Cabinets of Amherst College* (1862), p. 14; King, *"The Consecrated Eminence,"* pp. 19–23, 74, 126, 213–19, 310–11. John Leland was appointed by the Prudential Committee

to serve as coordinating agent for the construction of the Johnson Chapel.

6. Fuess, *Amherst*, pp. 90–91, 156–57; Norton, *Amherst*, p. 80; Tyler, *History of Amherst College*, pp. 177–79; Richardson and Clark, *The College Book*, p. 259; King, "*The Consecrated Eminence*," pp. 23–24, 56–57, 310–11. In 1834, as student enrollments continued to grow, the college trustees considered erecting a fourth, predominantly residence hall, to be placed on the south end of the original row and to relate to the three central buildings in the same manner as North College (Hall). The site, later to be occupied by the Appleton Cabinet, was actually prepared for construction, but the project was cancelled as a result of the Panic of 1837.

7. King, "*The Consecrated Eminence*," pp. 26, 67–68, 119, 314–15; Fuess, *Amherst*, pp. 26, 67–68, 91–92, 287, 290, 330; Norton, *Amherst*, p. 74; "College Hall," *Amherst Student*, 21 May 1892; "College Hall," *Amherst Student*, 27 June 1905, pp. 260a, 260b; Beardslee and Plimpton, *Popular Guide to the Public Buildings and Museum of Amherst College* (1875), p. 81; Hitchcock, *The Handbook of Amherst, Massachusetts* (1891), p. 113; *A Guide to Amherst College* (1921), p. 22.

8. King, "*The Consecrated Eminence*," pp. 35–43, 310–13; Fuess, *Amherst*, pp. 90, 96, 130–31, 134, 291; Tyler, *History of Amherst College*, pp. 316–17; Norton, *Amherst*, p. 79; "The Octagon," *Amherst Student*, 26 March 1892; Donnelly, "Astronomical Observatories in New England," *Old-Time New England* 50, no. 3 (Winter 1960): 74–75; Allen, "The Octagon: A Building with a Rich History," *Amherst Student*, 20 October 1986, p. 9; Hitchcock, *The Visitor's Guide to the Public Rooms and Cabinets of Amherst College* (1862), pp. 21–35; *Annals of Amherst College* (1860), pp. 68–69; Beardslee and Plimpton, *Popular Guide to the Public Buildings and Museum of Amherst College* (1875), pp. 25–34; Hitchcock, *The Handbook of Amherst, Massachusetts* (1891), pp. 136–41. The Octagon occupies the site of the old First Congregational Society church, which stood there from 1782 to 1828.

9. Norton, *Amherst*, p. 74; Fuess, *Amherst*, p. 136; Tyler, *History of Amherst College*, p. 327; "The Morgan Library," *Amherst Student*, 23 January 1892; King, "*The Consecrated Eminence*," pp. 43–48, 90–91, 312–13; "Amherst's Library," *Amherst Student*, 17 February 1894; "Plan of the New Library," *Catalogue of Amherst College* (1852–53), lithograph; Hitchcock, *The Handbook of Amherst, Massachusetts* (1891), pp. 114–17; *Guide to Amherst College* (1921), pp. 15–16; *Annals of Amherst College* (1860), p. 70; Hitchcock, *The Visitor's Guide to the Public Rooms and Cabinets of Amherst College* (1862), p. 15; Beardslee and Plimpton, *Popular Guide to the Public Buildings and Museum of Amherst College* (1875), pp. 81–82.

10. King, "*The Consecrated Eminence*," pp. 28–29, 47–48, 312–13; Norton, *Amherst*, p. 84; "Appleton Cabinet," *Amherst Student*, 6 February 1892; Tyler, *History of Amherst College*, pp. 397–98; *Annals of Amherst College* (1860), pp. 65–66; Beardslee and Plimpton, *Popular Guide to the Public Buildings and Museum of Amherst College* (1875), p. 14; Hitchcock, *The Handbook of Amherst, Massachusetts* (1891), pp. 131–32; *A Guide to Amherst College* (1921), pp. 20–21.

11. King, "*The Consecrated Eminence*," pp. 58–60, 62, 312–13; Fuess, *Amherst*, pp. 157, 164; "East College," *Amherst Student*, 23 April 1892; Tyler, *History of Amherst College*, p. 400.

12. King, "*The Consecrated Eminence*," pp. 58–62, 284–85, 312–15; Tyler, *History of Amherst College*, p. 400; Fuess, *Amherst*, pp. 99, 157–58; "Williston Hall," *Amherst Student*, 12 December 1891; Norton, *Amherst*, p. 80; "The Art Gallery," *Amherst Record*, 8 July 1874; *Annals of Amherst College* (1860), p. 68; Beardslee and Plimpton, *Popular Guide to the Public Buildings and Museum of Amherst College* (1875), p. 35; Hitchcock, *The Visitor's Guide to the Public Rooms and Cabinets of Amherst College* (1862), pp. 15–16; Hitchcock, *The Handbook of Amherst, Massachusetts* (1891), pp. 118, 123; *A Guide to Amherst College* (1921), p. 19.

13. King, "*The Consecrated Eminence*," pp. 63–66, 314–15; Fuess, *Amherst*, pp. 197, 282, 290; Norton, *Amherst*, p. 93; "The Barrett Gymnasium," *Amherst Student*, 7 May 1892; "Barrett Gymnasium," *Amherst Student*, 28 January 1909; Phillips, "The Truth About Barrett Gymnasium," *Amherst Graduate's Quarterly* 21 (1931–33): 34–41; Tyler, *History of Amherst College*, p. 401; Hitchcock, *The Visitor's Guide to the Public Rooms and Cabinets of Amherst College* (1862), p. 16; Beardslee and Plimpton, *Popular Guide to the Public Buildings and Museum of Amherst College* (1875), p. 78; Hitchcock, *The Handbook of Amherst, Massachusetts* (1891), pp. 123–24; *A Guide to Amherst College* (1921), p. 20. Barrett Hall (Gymnasium) is claimed to be the only extant college gym in the United States predating the Civil War. Dr. Barrett not only contributed to its construction but throughout his life also contributed almost every year for building repairs, improvements, and exterior landscaping. On his death, he left a bequest to perpetuate these areas of support.

14. Turner, *Campus*, pp. 101, 313.

15. Nutt, *History of Worcester and Its People*, vol. 2, p. 745; Kuzniewski, *Thy Honored Name*, pp. xiii, 1, 30; Kuzniewski, "This Holy Cross," p. 56. In 1876, the original two-story seminary (academy) building (central house with side wings), reduced in size in around 1898, was moved up the hill to the northeast and was used for campus farm workers' housing, and then student housing after 1936. Today, expanded as Campion House, it accommodates the offices of the college chaplains.

16. Kuzniewski, *Thy Honored Name*, pp. 30, 42; Lapomarda, "A Study of Fenwick Hall Relative to Nomination to the National Register of Historic Places" (1979), p. 1; Meagher and Grattan, *Spires of Fenwick*, pp. 37–41; *Historical Sketch of the College of the*

Holy Cross, pp. 5–12; Nutt, *History of Worcester and Its People*, vol. 2, p. 745; Devitt, "History of the Maryland–New York Province, XV: College of the Holy Cross," *Worcester Letters* 64 (1935), photocopy, Archives and Special Collections, Dinand Library, College of the Holy Cross.

17. Kuzniewski, *Thy Honored Name*, p. 49; Lapomarda, "A Study of Fenwick Hall," p. 1; Meagher and Grattan, *Spires of Fenwick*, pp. 46, 92, 96; Devitt, "History of the Maryland–New York Province, XV: College of the Holy Cross," *Woodstock Letters* 64 (1935), photocopy, Archives and Special Collections, Dinand Library, College of the Holy Cross.

18. Kuzniewski, *Thy Honored Name*, pp. 76, 80, 81, 92, 96; Lapomarda, "A Study of Fenwick Hall," p. 2; Meagher and Grattan, *Spires of Fenwick*, pp. 85–93; *Historical Sketch of the College of the Holy Cross*, pp. 19–22.

19. Kuzniewski, *Thy Honored Name*, pp. 31, 124–25; Meagher and Grattan, *Spires of Fenwick*, pp. 108–9; Devitt, "History of the Maryland–New York Province, XV: College of the Holy Cross," *Woodstock Letters* 64 (1935), photocopy, Archives and Special Collections, Dinand Library, College of the Holy Cross; Lapomarda, "A Study of Fenwick Hall," pp. 2–3; Nutt, *History of Worcester and Its People*, vol. 2, p. 746; Withey, *Biographical Dictionary of American Architects (Deceased)*, p. 70; *Historical Sketch of the College of the Holy Cross*, pp. 24–26, 28. The new west wing contained the college library, debating society meeting rooms, and rooms for senior students and the Jesuits. Improved steam heating was introduced in the full complex, including all student rooms. These two expansion phases of Fenwick Hall resulted in utilities being introduced there and campuswide—city water in 1871, and gas lighting in 1875 (temporarily replacing electricity, which had initially been unsuccessful).

20. Lapomarda, "A Study of Fenwick Hall," p. 3; Kuzniewski, *Thy Honored Name*, pp. 138, 148–49, 152, 154; Nutt, *History of Worcester and Its People*, vol. 2, p. 747; Kuzniewski, "*This Holy Cross*," p. 62; Meagher and Grattan, *Spires of Fenwick*, pp. 112, 114; Lapomarda, "A Study of O'Kane Hall Relative to Nomination to the National Register of Historic Places" (1979), pp. 1–2; *Worcester Telegram*, 7 March 1980.

21. Turner, *Campus*, pp. 76–87, 106.

22. This portion of the section of the book devoted to Tufts is a revised version of my illustrated article, "Gridley J. F. Bryant and the First Building at Tufts College," *Old-Time New England* 63, no. 4 (April–June 1973): 89–99.

23. The building remained unnamed officially until 1892, when it was christened "Ballou Hall" by the Tufts College Board of Trustees following recommendations made by the students and the Executive Committee. See the Records and Minutes of the Board of Trustees of Tufts College, Meeting of 15 July 1892, Digital Collections and Archives, Tufts University.

24. Tufts College was founded under a Commonwealth of Massachusetts charter, granted on 21 April 1852. The movement resulting in its establishment was initiated in 1847 by Reverend Thomas J. Sawyer of New York, Reverend Hosea Ballou, 2nd of Medford, and Reverend Thomas Whittemore of Cambridge. See Start, *History of Tufts College*, p. 20.

25. Edward C. Rollins, Ballou Hall References, "Tufts Buildings," vol. 1, Digital Collections and Archives, Tufts University.

26. Records and Minutes of the Board of Trustees of Tufts College, Meetings of 21 July and 21 September 1852.

27. "Tufts (Universalist) College, Somerville, Massachusetts," *Ballou's Pictorial* 11, no. 15 (11 October 1856): 225; Records and Minutes of the Board of Trustees of Tufts College, 3 May 1853.

28. Miller, *Light on the Hill*, p. 51; *Trumpet and Universalist Magazine* 25 (13 November 1852): 2, and 26 (11 June 1853): 2; Records of the Board of Trustees of Tufts College, Meeting of May 1853.

29. *Trumpet and Universalist Magazine* 26 (23 July 1853): 26. A large black-and-white lithograph portraying the cornerstone festivities and showing the magnificent tent is at the Digital Collections and Archives, Tufts University.

30. Start, *History of Tufts College*, p. 24.

31. Miller, *Light on the Hill*, p. 61.

32. "The Tufts College," *Trumpet and Universalist Magazine* 26 (11 June 1853), p. 2.

33. Miller, *Light on the Hill—Volume II*, p. 39; "Ballou Hall Restoration," *Tufts Alumni Review* 2 (February 1956): 18a–18d; Tufts College Public Relations News Release (1955), Digital Collections and Archives, Tufts University.

34. Rollins, Ballou Hall References, "Tufts Buildings," vol. 1, pp. 9–10; *Tufts Weekly* 43 (2 November 1939): 1, 3. The porch was presented to the college by alumnus Eugene B. Bowen and was formally dedicated on 28 October 1939 by then-president Leonard Carmichael. The new Bowen Porch added coherence and monumentality to the north facade. Its four Greek Ionic columns were taken from an old academy building (Maplewood Institute, Pittsfield, Mass.) and were transported to the Tufts campus. The porch was built somewhat wider than the south porch to permit automobiles to pass underneath it. During the 1955–56 renovation of Ballou Hall, the north doorway became the main entrance to the structure, facing the grassed, tree-shaded central mall (The Green).

35. For enlightening discussions of the Italian Renaissance Revival style, consult Henry-Russell Hitchcock, *Architecture: Nineteenth and Twentieth Centuries*, chap. 5, and Clay Lancaster, "Italianism in American Architecture Before 1860," *American Quarterly* 4 (1952): 127–48.

36. Rollins, Ballou Hall References, "Tufts Buildings," vol. 1, "Remodeling of Ballou Hall," pp. 8–10; "Ballou Hall," *Tufts Alumni Review* n.s. 1 (October 1955): 4; "Ballou Hall Restoration," *Tufts*

Alumni Review 2 (February 1956): 18a–18d; "Ballou Hall Restoration Will Centralize Admin.," *Tufts Weekly* 59 (13 May 1955): 1; "Ballou Hall Atop Tufts Hill Will Undergo Renovation," *Medford (Mass.) Daily Mercury*, 12 August 1955. The contractor for the project was the Arnold S. Grant Construction Company of Somerville, Mass.

37. Rollins, Ballou Hall References, "Tufts Buildings," vol. 1, p. 10.

38. In the 1955–56 interior renovations, the Large Chapel was reconstructed, albeit not too faithfully. Now known as the Coolidge Room, today it serves as an attractive lounge and as a spacious meeting room for faculty, trustees, and students. Present here are replicas of the original ornamental wall cornices of the former chapel, as well as the original cast-iron support columns in the center of the room.

39. Rollins, Ballou Hall References, "Tufts Buildings," vol. 1, pp. 1–6; "The Tufts College," *Trumpet and Universalist Magazine* 26 (11 June 1853): 2.

40. Treasurer's Cash Book entry, 15 January 1855, p. 3, and Ledger Book, entries of 17 January 1856, pp. 2 and 38, Digital Collections and Archives, Tufts University. An installment of $250 was paid to Bryant on the first occasion, and $700 was added a year later on completion of the building interior. Curiously, at no place in the Records and Minutes of the Trustees of Tufts College is Bryant's name mentioned. See also Award of Arbitors in the Case of Coburn and Richards (Suffolk County Court), 19 July 1854, Digital Collections and Archives, Tufts University.

41. "The Tufts College," *Trumpet and Universalist Magazine* 26 (11 June 1853): 2. See also Brooks, *History of the Town of Medford*, p. 298.

42. Kilham, *Boston After Bulfinch: An Account of Its Architecture, 1800–1890*, p. 67.

43. "A Complete Catalogue of Plans, Specifications, Architectural Drawings, Photographs, etc., of Gridley J. F. Bryant (In Custody of Henry T. Bailey, North Scituate, Mass., 1890)," University of Oregon Library, Eugene [1890].

44. Ibid., p. 11; *Catalogue of the Officers and Students of the Maine State Seminary* (Lewiston, Maine: Journal Office, 1857), p. 22; *Maine State Seminary Advocate* 6, no. 1 (April 1861): 2.

45. Short, *History of Tufts College*, pp. 21, 35; Miller, *Light on the Hill*, pp. 62, 72; Records and Minutes of the Board of Trustees of Tufts College, Meetings of 29 May 1855 and 27 May 1856; Rollins, Packard Hall, "Tufts Buildings," vol. 1, pp. 11–12. At the rear of the dormitory was the wooden college barn, erected about the same time and razed in 1876.

46. Miller, *Light on the Hill*, pp. 63, 72, 201, 456, 537–38, 552; Miller, *Light on the Hill—Volume II*, pp. 417, 427; Buildings and Grounds Committee, "Packard Hall Renovation," 13 September 1979, Digital Collections and Archives, Tisch Library; *Tufts Weekly* 7, no. 12 (17 December 1901); Rollins, Packard Hall, "Tufts Buildings," vol. 1, pp. 1–3; "Packard Hall, 1856," Concise Encyclopedia of Tufts History (2000–2004), Digital Collections and Archives, Tufts University; telephone interview with Ned Baxter of the architectural firm of William Rawn Associates, Boston, 3 March 2009. When Ballou Hall was totally remodeled in 1955–56, Packard Hall served as the temporary headquarters of the college's administrative offices.

47. Rollins, Packard Hall, "Tufts Buildings," vol. 1, pp. 1–3.

48. The third academic structure to be erected on College Hill was a small, two-story, vernacular wooden dormitory (1857) known as Building B. Intended to relieve crowded student living conditions on the campus, it was originally situated on the north side of the mall (The Green) where West Hall (1871–72) is located today. Used as a twelve-student dormitory for just three years, it became a faculty dwelling and in 1870 was relocated to Professors Row. In 1910, with the new name Richardson House, it was renovated and became a women's dormitory for Jackson College. In 1923, it was renovated again and doubled in size, the original building serving as the western half of the still-intact structure. See Miller, *Light on the Hill*, pp. 63–64, 96, 203, 549–50; Rollins, Building B, The Wooden Dormitory, "Tufts Buildings," vol. 1, p. 15; "Richardson House, 1857," Concise Encyclopedia of Tufts History (2000–2004), Digital Collections and Archives, Tufts University; Sauer, *Tufts University*, p. 84.

49. Miller, *Light on the Hill*, pp. 63, 97–99; Records and Minutes of the Board of Trustees of Tufts College, Meetings of 13 January and 26 May 1857, 24 May 1859, 29 May 1860, 28 May 1861; Withey, *Biographical Dictionary of American Architects (Deceased)*, p. 554; Building Committee Contract of 3 March 1860 with Griswold S. Adams of Boston.

50. Miller, *Light on the Hill*, pp. 63–64; Rollins, East Hall, "Tufts Buildings," vol. 1, pp. 18–19; *Tufts Alumni Bulletin* 15 (October 1941): 18.

51. Rollins, East Hall, "Tufts Buildings," vol. 1, pp. 19–21; Miller, *Light on the Hill*, pp. 64, 286; Doane, ed., *Here and There at Tufts*, p. 38; *Tuftonian* 8 (October 1881): 2; *Tufts Weekly* 41 (21 October 1937): 8; *Tufts Weekly* 49 (12 April 1945): 1; *Tufts Weekly* 71 (11 March 1966): 1; Miller, *Light on the Hill—Volume II*, p. 51; Rollins, "College Pictures." At an undetermined date in the late nineteenth century, the central stairway was replaced by interior stairways at each end of the building. East Hall was wired for electrical lights soon after 1900. Twice, in World War I and World War II, the building served as a temporary U.S. Army barracks.

Chapter 6: Trinity and Wesleyan in Connecticut

1. Trinity (Washington) College was preceded by two institutions in Connecticut established under the auspices of the Episco-

pal Church. The first of these, known as Seabury College and then The Episcopal Academy of Connecticut, was located in Cheshire, and despite efforts to convert it to a college, it remained a secondary school and never had the authority to grant degrees. The second, the General Theological Seminary of the Protestant Episcopal Church, was moved to New Haven from New York in 1820, but remained there for just two years; it returned to New York in 1822. See Steiner, *The History of Education in Connecticut*, pp. 237–39.

2. Steiner, *The History of Education in Connecticut*, pp. 239–40; Weaver, *Hartford*, pp. 70–72; Weaver, *The History of Trinity College*, vol. 1, pp. 26–27; Brocklesby, "Trinity College, Hartford," *Scribner's Monthly* 11 (March 1876): 602–3; Records of the Board of Trustees, Washington College, 10 August 1824; Richardson and Clark, *The College Book*, pp. 263–64.

3. Trumbull, *The Memorial History of Hartford County, Connecticut, 1633–1884*, vol. 1, p. 436; Burpee, *History of Hartford County, Connecticut, 1633–1928*, vol. 1, p. 305; Brocklesby, "Trinity College, Hartford," p. 603.

4. Weaver, *The History of Trinity College*, vol. 1, pp. 27, 36, 60, 186; Barber, *Connecticut Historical Collections*, p. 6; Perry, *The History of the American Episcopal Church, 1587–1883*, vol. 2, p. 541; Steiner, *The History of Higher Education in Connecticut*, p. 241; Hollister, *The History of Connecticut*, pp. 623–24. The chief contractor for Seabury Hall is identified as William Hayden of Hartford in bills and receipts present in the collections of the Trinity College Archives. Hayden served in the same role for the concurrent building of Jarvis Hall.

5. Weaver, *The History of Trinity College*, vol. 1, pp. 27, 36, 48, 186; Barber, *Connecticut Historical Collections*, p. 6.

6. Perry, *The History of the American Episcopal Church, 1587–1883*, vol. 2, p. 541; Brocklesby, "Trinity College, Hartford," p. 603; *Dictionary of American Biography*, vol. 20, pp. 241–42; Withey, *Biographical Dictionary of American Architects (Deceased)*, p. 659; Placzek, *Macmillan Encyclopedia of Architects*, vol. 4, pp. 400–401; Kilham, *Boston After Bulfinch*, pp. 28–30.

7. Brocklesby, "Trinity College, Hartford," p. 604; Adams, "The Founding of Trinity College [Washington College, 1823–45]," *Historical Magazine of the Episcopal Church* 14 (March 1945): 53; Steiner, *The History of Education in Connecticut*, p. 246; Richardson and Clark, *The College Book*, p. 267.

8. Weaver, *The History of Trinity College*, vol. 1, p. 82; Calendar of Trinity College, Hartford, 1847; Brocklesby, "Trinity College, Hartford," p. 603. The inscribed cornerstone of Brownell Hall was saved after the building's demolition and preserved for 130 years in the basement of the second Seabury Hall on the current Rocky Ridge campus. In 2007, it was recovered during the Long Walk's renovation, and in August 2008 it was installed, along with a plaque, in the Downes Memorial Archway, a central point of passage on the campus. This interesting historical relic is a tangi-

ble link with the former Washington College campus, at the present site of the State Capitol in downtown Hartford.

9. Weaver, *The History of Trinity College*, vol. 1, pp. 176–77; *Catalogue of Trinity College, 1876–77*, appendix; Steiner, *The History of Education in Connecticut*, p. 250; Davis, ed., *The New England States*, vol. 2, p. 727; Burpee, *The Story of Connecticut*, vol. 2, p. 648; Trumbull, *The Memorial History of Hartford County, Connecticut, 1633–1884*, vol. 1, pp. 443–44; Withey, *Biographical Dictionary of American Architects (Deceased)*, pp. 343–44.

10. Potts, *Wesleyan University, 1831–1910*, pp. 3, 6, 8, 9–14, 17; Osborn, *The History of Connecticut*, vol. 5, pp. 252–53; Clark, *The History of Connecticut*, p. 242; *History of Middlesex County, Connecticut*, pp. 119–20; Richardson and Clark, *The College Book*, pp. 303–6; Crofut, *A Guide to the History and Historic Sites of Connecticut*, pp. 496–97; Steiner, *The History of Education in Connecticut*, pp. 258–60; Davis, *The New England States*, vol. 2, pp. 729–30.

11. Connecticut Historical Commission, Historical Resources Inventory Form (1978) for South College (Lyceum), Wesleyan University, Middletown; Potts, *Wesleyan University, 1831–1910*, pp. 78–79, 196; Dutcher, "Wesleyan's Buildings and Grounds in the Earliest Years," typescript, pp. 1155–56; Ellis and Dodge, *Norwich University, 1819–1911*, vol. 1, p. 3; Price, *Wesleyan's First Century*, pp. 20, 21, 27, 39, 156, 187. When Wesleyan acquired the property from the A.L.S.&M. Academy in 1831, there were two small, 10-by-12-foot guard houses on either side of the High Street entrance to the fenced, informally landscaped campus, but these were immediately removed by the new ownership.

Even as late as the mid-1850s, there was hope in certain circles that an edifice matching North College could be constructed, thereby completing the symmetrical three-building row (Joint Board, Meeting of 31 July 1855) along the lines of the original Yale row.

12. Connecticut Historical Commission, Historical Resources Inventory Form (1978) for North College (The Dormitory), Wesleyan University, Middletown; Potts, *Wesleyan University, 1831–1910*, pp. 78–79, 195–96; Dutcher, "Wesleyan's Buildings and Grounds in the Earliest Years," typescript, pp. 1156–57; Ellis and Dodge, *Norwich University, 1819–1911*, vol. 1, p. 63; Price, *Wesleyan's First Century*, pp. 21, 156–57. The reconstructed North College was renovated in 1955 to house the offices of the Dean of Admissions, and again in 1962 to accommodate the offices of the Provost and other administrators. When residential use was terminated in 1965, only the upper two floors were being used for this purpose. There have been other interior modifications since.

13. Potts, *Wesleyan University, 1831–1910*, p. 79; Ellis and Dodge, *Norwich University, 1819–1911*, vol. 1, pp. 64–68; Dutcher, "Wesleyan's Buildings and Grounds in the Earliest Years," typescript, p. 1159; Price, *Wesleyan's First Century*, pp. 21, 39, 79; Minutes of the Board of Trustees, Meetings of 7 August 1839 and 3 August 1847.

14. Potts, *Wesleyan University, 1831–1910*, p. 79; Price, *Wesleyan's First Century*, p. 22; Building File, Special Collections, Wesleyan University Library; Record of the Proceedings of the Prudential Committee of Wesleyan University, Meetings of 1 May 1833, 23 May 1833, 30 June 1835, 12 April 1836; Crawford, "As We Were: A Building with a History," *Wesleyan Literary Monthly* 13 (1904–5): 341–43; "Electricity at Wesleyan," *Electrical Engineer* 16, no. 277 (23 August 1893): 172–73.

15. Potts, *Wesleyan University, 1831–1910*, pp. 70, 79–81; Price, *Wesleyan's First Century*, pp. 39, 40, 42, 63, 65, 104, 110, 187, 211; Dutcher, "Wesleyan's Buildings and Grounds in the Earliest Years," pp. 1160–62; Richardson and Clark, *The College Book*, p. 311; Donnelly, "Astronomical Observatories in New England," *Old-Time New England* 50, no. 3 (Winter 1960): 75; Milham, "Early American Observatories," *Popular Astronomy* 45, no. 9 (November 1937): 24; Minutes of the Board of Trustees, Meetings of 6 November 1835, 29 January 1836, 23 March 1836, 31 July 1838, 7 August 1839; Trustees and Visitors Minutes, Meetings of 22 August 1837, 31 July 1838; Minutes of the Prudential Committee, 21 December 1838, 9 January 1839, 5 May 1839, 3 October 1839, 22 January 1840, 5 November 1840. The first wooden observatory was twice moved from its original site and ultimately served as a henhouse at an off-campus location!

Chapter 7: Colby and Bates in Maine

1. Colby College was chartered in 1813 as the Maine Literary and Theological Seminary for the education of Baptist ministers. From 1821 to 1867 it operated under the name Waterville College. In 1867 it was retitled Colby University in recognition of a $50,000 gift by Gardner Colby, a wealthy Baptist philanthropist from Boston. On Dr. Nathaniel Butler's assumption of the presidency in 1899, the institution received its present name. This section of the book is an edited version of my illustrated article, "'The Bricks' at Colby (Waterville) College: The Origins of a Lost Campus," *Maine History* (Maine Historical Society) 39, no. 4 (Winter 2000–2001): 241–55.

2. In September 1952, the first Waterville campus was formally abandoned. The presence of a large, noisy, pollution-generating paper pulp mill across the river was another factor influencing the decision to shift sites. For a full, recent account of the relocation of the college, see Smith, *Mayflower Hill*, chap. 1.

3. Tolles, "College Architecture in New England Before 1860 in Printed and Sketched Views," *Magazine Antiques* 103, no. 3 (March 1973): 507–8. The artist Esteria (Butler) Farnam (1814–99) was a miniaturist and landscape painter from Winthrop, Maine. Her works were known for their precise detail and balanced composition. Thomas Moore of Boston published her view of Bowdoin College at about the same time as the Colby scene.

4. White, "Linking the Old and the New Colby," *Colby College Alumnus* 31 (1941), p. 5. For references to other New England college row plans, see Turner, *Campus*, chaps. 1 and 2.

5. The president's house, the first building at Colby (Waterville) College, was a modest-sized wooden structure completed in 1819 and intended as a home for theological students and for Professor of Divinity Jeremiah Champlin and his family. It was ultimately removed from the campus, and the site was occupied by Memorial Hall (1869). See Marriner, *The History of Colby College*, p. 37; Records of the Trustees of Waterville College, Meeting of 19 May 1819, Colby College Special Collections, Waterville, Maine.

6. The final cost was $2,700. See Whittemore, *History of Colby College, 1820–1925*, p. 32.

7. Waterville College, *Origin, Progress and Present State of the College*, p. 1.

8. Marriner, *The History of Colby College*, p. 49.

9. Whittemore, *The Centennial History of Waterville*, p. 299; Hall, *History of Higher Education in Maine*, p. 106.

10. Albert W. Paine to Warren Foss, 1895, Colby College Special Collections, Waterville, Maine.

11. *A Brief Description of Colby College and Its Equipment*, p. 22.

12. Records of the Trustees of Waterville College, Meeting of 1 May 1822, Colby College Special Collections, Waterville, Maine.

13. Whittemore, *History of Colby College*, p. 36.

14. *Waterville Morning Sentinel*, 13 March 1911; Marriner, *The History of Colby College*, p. 298.

15. Whittemore, *History of Colby College*, p. 188.

16. Marriner, *The History of Colby College*, p. 85; Champlin, *An Historical Discourse Delivered at the Fiftieth Anniversary of Colby University, August 2nd, 1870*, p. 11.

17. Records of the Trustees of Waterville College, Minutes of the Annual Meeting, 1835.

18. Hall, *History of Higher Education in Maine*, p. 106.

19. Marriner, *The History of Colby College*, p. 85.

20. Ibid.; Hall, *History of Higher Education in Maine*, p. 111.

21. Whittemore, *The Centennial History of Waterville*, p. 300; Rush, *History of Maine College Libraries*, p. 28.

22. Hall, *History of Higher Education in Maine*, p. 111. See William S. Rusk, "Thomas U. Walter and His Works," *Americana* 33 (1938): 151–79; Robert E. Ennis, "Thomas U. Walter," in Placzek, ed., *Macmillan Encyclopedia of Architects*, vol. 4, pp. 365–70; Ennis, "Walter, Thomas U(stick)," in Turner, ed., *The Dictionary of Art*, vol. 32, pp. 827–28. The attribution was subsequently repeated in other printed works pertaining to Colby College and Maine history.

23. See "The Girard College Architectural Competition," *Journal of the Society of Architectural Historians* 16, no. 2 (1957): 20–27; and George L. Hersey, "Thomas U. Walter and the University of Lewisburg," *Journal of the Society of Architectural Historians* 16, no. 1 (1957): 20–24.

24. Thomas U. Walter journal (1834–36), 9 January 1836, The Athenaeum of Philadelphia, Penn.; conversations with Roger W. Moss, Jr., Director, The Athenaeum of Philadelphia, and Marilyn C. Solvay (former Walter project assistant), Curator, William A. Farnsworth Library and Art Museum, Rockland, Maine, 30 September 1987. The entry is noted in Moss and Tatman, *Biographical Dictionary of Philadelphia Architects, 1700–1930*, p. 824.

25. Hall, *History of Higher Education in Maine*, p. 116; Marriner, *The History of Colby College*, p. 174.

26. Hall, *History of Higher Education in Maine*, p. 111.

27. See Tolles, "Gridley J. F. Bryant and the First Building at Tufts College," *Old-Time New England* 63, no. 4 (1973): 88–99.

28. *A Brief Description of Colby College and Its Equipment*, p. 21.

29. Four other plain, functional wooden structures supplemented the row buildings on Colby (Waterville) College's first campus. Between 1827 and 1833, the one- and two-story mechanics workshops were erected. These were used until 1842 and were removed soon thereafter. In 1832 college administrators authorized the construction of a boardinghouse at the north end of the campus on the spot later occupied by Coburn Hall (1871–72). This building was used as a student commons facility until the early 1870s, when the trustees, disenchanted with mass dining, voted to sell it. Despite this action, it was retained by the college and used for other purposes. See Whittemore, *History of Colby College*, pp. 70, 178; and Whittemore, *The Centennial History of Waterville*, p. 300.

30. The Bates College portion of the chapter is a revision of my illustrated article, "Maine State Seminary: Gridley J. F. Bryant and Antebellum Architectural Master Planning," *Old-Time New England* 70, no. 268 (Spring/Summer 2000): 41–53.

31. For an enlightening explanation of the creation of Bates College from the Maine State Seminary, see Charles E. Clark's *Bates Through the Years*, pp. 19–23. See also Anthony, *Bates College and Its Background*, pp. 87, 133–36, 180–81, 208–9; James A. Howe, "Bates College," in Merrill, *History of Androscoggin County, Maine . . .*, pp. 183–86; and *Lewiston Journal Magazine Section*, 3 August 1957, p. 3A.

32. *Seminary Advocate*, April 1861, p. 2. Bryant's fee is documented in Construction Bills, 21 November 1856, Maine State Seminary Plans, Muskie Archives, Bates College, Lewiston, Maine. For general biographical information on Bryant, see Henry T. Bailey, "An Architect of the Old School," *New England Magazine* 25 (1901): 326–49; Withey, *Biographical Dictionary of American Architects (Deceased)*, p. 87; Robert B. MacKay, "Gridley J. F. Bryant," in Placzek, ed., *Macmillan Encyclopedia of Architects*, vol. 1, pp. 315–16; MacKay, "Bryant, Gridley J(ames) F(ox)," in Turner, ed., *The Dictionary of Art*, vol. 5, pp. 63–64; and a relatively recent work (2007), Roger Reed, *Building Victorian Boston*.

33. *Seminary Advocate* (Maine State Seminary), January–December 1856, p. 1; "A Complete Catalogue of Plans, Specifications, Architectural Drawings, Photographs, etc . . . [of] Gridley J. F. Bryant" (in custody of Henry T. Bailey, North Scituate, Mass., 1890), University of Oregon Library, Eugene.

34. Tolles, "College Architecture in New England Before 1860 in Printed and Sketched Views," *Magazine Antiques* 103, no. 3 (March 1973): 508–9; Merrill, ed., *History of Androscoggin County, Maine*, p. 186; *Atlas and History of Androscoggin County, Maine*, p. 89; *Catalogue of the Officers and Students of the Maine State Seminary, Lewiston . . .*, frontispiece.

35. *College Crescent* (Bates College), April 1864: 1. Bryant later designed a major connected educational complex for the Boston City Hospital, erected from 1861 to 1865. See Roger G. Reed, "'To Exist for Centuries': Gridley Bryant and the Boston City Hospital," *Old-Time New England* 77, no. 266 (Spring/Summer 1999): 65–89.

36. Records of the Board of Trustees of the Maine State Seminary, Meetings of 28 June and 8 October 1855, Bates College.

37. *Seminary Advocate*, March 1856, p. i.

38. Howe, "Bates College," in Merrill, ed., *History of Androscoggin County, Maine*, p. 186; *Seminary Advocate*, May 1856, p. 3; Anthony, *Bates College and Its Background*, p. 141.

39. Gridley J. F. Bryant to [W. R. Frye], 11 July 1856, and Bryant to Frye, 12 November 1856, Bates College; Ebenezer Knowlton to Rev. Oren B. Cheney, 30 October 1856, from *Seminary Advocate*, October 1856, p. 1.

40. *Seminary Advocate*, December 1856, p. 3.

41. *Seminary Advocate*, May 1857, p. 2; Anthony, *Bates College and Its Background*, pp. 140–41.

42. "Venerable Hathorn Hall Claims Picturesque Past," *Bates Student*, 16 December 1931, p. 3.

43. Rush, *History of Maine College Libraries*, p. 35.

44. "Venerable Hathorn Claims Picturesque Past," p. 3.

45. *Catalogue of the Officers and Students of the Maine State Seminary for 1857–58* (Lewiston, Maine: Journal Office, 1857), p. 22.

46. Merrill, ed., *History of Androscoggin County, Maine*, p. 188; *Catalogue of the Officers and Students of the Maine State Seminary for 1860–61*, p. 31; Records of the Board of Trustees of the Maine State Seminary, Meeting of 12 July 1859.

47. Gridley J. F. Bryant, "Original Drawings for Parker Hall, Maine State Seminary, Lewiston, Maine (Front, Rear and End Elevations; Vertical Transverse and Longitudinal Sections; Basement Principal, Second, Third and Revised Basement Floor Plans; First, Second, Third Floor Framing). Completed in Boston from September 1 to November 11, 1856," Muskie Archives, Bates College, Lewiston, Maine.

48. *Catalogue of the Officers and Students of the Maine State Seminary for 1857–58*, p. 20.

49. "Old Parker 'Reverts' to Women," *Bates College Bulletin* 44 (1947): 81.

50. W. H. Littlefield, "Meeting of the Building Committee," *Seminary Advocate*, September 1856, p. 1.

51. *Catalogue of the Officers and Students of Bates College for 1864–65* (Lewiston, Maine: Daily Journal Office, 1864).

52. *Bulletin of Bates College*, 15 May 1906, p. 9.

53. Littlefield, "Meeting of the Building Committee," p. 1; Bryant, "Original Design Drawings for Parker Hall" (Basement).

54. Ada Louise Huxtable, "Commercial Buildings—c. 1850–1870, Boston, Mass.—Gridley James Fox Bryant, arch.," *Progressive Architecture* 39 (1958): 108.

55. *Bates Student* 56 (c. 1928), p. 99.

Bibliography

The bibliography for this book is arranged by general categories and lists both published and manuscript materials that have been utilized both in the research and writing stages. Published items include selected book, booklet, brochure, magazine, journal, newsletter, and newspaper titles. Not included in this bibliography, but cited in the preceding chapter notes, are seldom used printed and manuscript materials, visual images, contemporary letters concerning the project, e-mails, Web sites, oral history interviews, and certain ephemera items.

I. General Works

Addison, Agnes. *Romanticism and the Gothic Revival*. New York: R. R. Smith, 1938.

Andrews, Wayne. "Alexander Jackson Davis." *Architectural Review* 109, no. 643 (May 1951): 307–12.

———. *Architecture, Ambition and Americans*. New York: Harper and Brothers, 1955.

"Astronomical Observatories in the United States." *Harper's Weekly* 8, no. 73 (June 1856): 25–52.

Avery Obituary Index of Architects (Columbia University). 2nd ed. Boston: G. K. Hall and Company, 1970.

Bailey, Henry Turner. "An Architect of the Old School." *New England Magazine* n.s. 25, no. 3 (November 1901): 326–49. Gridley J. F. Bryant.

Barber, John Warner. *The History and Antiquities of New England, New York, New Jersey and Pennsylvania*. Hartford, Conn.: H. S. Parsons and Company, 1842.

Blumenson, John J.-G. *Identifying American Architecture: A Pictorial Guide to Styles and Terms, 1600–1945*. Nashville, Tenn.: American Association for State and Local History, 1977.

Boone, Richard G. *Education in the United States: Its History from the Earliest Settlements*. New York: D. Appleton and Company, 1889.

Brubacher, John S., and Willis Rudy. *Higher Education in Transition: An American History, 1636–1956*. New York: Harper and Brothers, 1958.

Burchard, John, and Albert Bush-Brown. *The Architecture of America: A Social and Cultural History*. Boston: Little, Brown, 1961.

Bush-Brown, Albert. "College Architecture: An Expression of Educational Philosophy." *Architectural Record* 112, no. 2 (August 1957): 154–57.

Condit, Carl W. *American Building: Materials and Techniques from the First Colonial Settlements to the Present*. Chicago: University of Chicago Press, 1968.

———. *American Building Art: The Nineteenth Century*. New York: Oxford University Press, 1960.

Coolidge, A. J., and J. B. Mansfield. *A History and Description of New England, General and Local*. 2 vols. Boston: Austin J. Coolidge, 1860.

Cremin, Lawrence A. *American Education: The Colonial Experience, 1607–1783*. New York: Harper and Row, 1970.

———. *American Education: The National Experience, 1783–1876*. New York: Harper and Row, 1982.

Davis, William T. *The New England States: Their Constitutional, Judicial, Educational, Commercial, Professional, and Industrial History*. 4 vols. Boston: D. H. Hurd and Company, 1897.

Dean, Eldon. "Early College and Educational Buildings in New England." *Pencil Points* 20 (December 1934): 597–603.

Dober, Richard P. *Campus Planning*. New York: Reinhold, 1963.

Donnelly, Marian Card. "Astronomical Observatories in New England." *Old-Time New England* 50, no. 3 (Winter 1960): 72–80.

Dwight, Timothy. *Travels in New England and New York*. 4 vols. New Haven: By the author, 1821–22.

Early, James. *Romanticism and American Architecture*. New York: A. S. Barnes, 1965.

Fein, Albert. *Frederick Law Olmsted and the American Environmental Tradition*. New York: George Braziller, 1972.

Fitch, James M. *American Building: The Forces That Shape It*. 2nd ed. Boston: Houghton, Mifflin, 1966.

Francis, Dennis S. *Architects in Practice, New York City, 1840–1900*. New York: Committee for the Preservation of Architectural Records, 1979.

Gelernter, Mark. *A History of American Architecture: Buildings in Their Cultural and Technological Context*. Hanover, N.H.: University Press of New England, 1999.

Gowans, Alan. *Images of American Living: Four Centuries of Architecture and Furniture as Cultural Expression*. New York: Harper and Row, 1976.

Hamlin, Talbot F. *Greek Revival Architecture in America: Being an Account of Important Trends in American Architecture and American Life prior to the War between the States.* New York: Oxford University Press, 1944.

Hammett, Ralph W. *Architecture in the United States: A Survey of Architectural Styles since 1776.* New York: John Wiley and Sons, 1976.

Handlin, David P. *American Architecture.* London: Thames and Hudson, 1985.

Harris, Cyril M. *American Architecture: An Illustrated Encyclopedia.* New York: W. W. Norton, 1998.

———, comp. and ed. *Dictionary of Architecture and Construction.* New York: McGraw-Hill, 2000.

Hayward, John. *The New England Gazetteer.* 14th ed., rev. Boston: John Hayward, 1841.

Hislop, Codman, and Harold A. Larrabee. "Joseph Jacques Ramee and the Building of North and South Colleges." *Union Alumni Monthly* 27, no. 4 (February 1938): 1–16.

Hitchcock, Henry-Russell. *Architecture: Nineteenth and Twentieth Centuries.* Baltimore, Md.: Penguin, 1958.

Howard, Rodney H., and Henry E. Crocker. *A History of New England.* 2 vols. Boston: Crocker and Company, 1880.

Kilham, Walter H. *Boston after Bulfinch: An Account of Its Architecture, 1800–1890.* Cambridge: Harvard University Press, 1946.

Kirker, Harold. *The Architecture of Charles Bulfinch.* Cambridge: Harvard University Press, 1969.

Klauder, Charles Z., and Herbert C. Wise. *College Architecture in America and Its Part in the Development of the Campus.* New York: Charles Scribner's Sons, 1929.

Kornwolf, James D. *"So Good a Design"; The Colonial Campus of the College of William and Mary: Its History, Background, and Legacy.* Williamsburg, Va.: Joseph and Margaret Muscarelle Museum of Art, The College of William and Mary, 1989.

Lancaster, Clay. "Italianism in American Architecture before 1860." *American Quarterly* 4 (Summer 1952): 127–48.

Larson, J. F., and Archie M. Palmer. *Architectural Planning of the American College.* New York: McGraw-Hill, 1933.

Llewellyn, Robert, and Douglas Day. *The Academical Village: Thomas Jefferson's University.* Charlottesville, Va.: Thomasson-Grant, 1982.

Loomis, Elias. "Astronomical Observatories in the United States." *Harper's New Monthly Magazine* 13 (1856): 44–45.

Loth, Calder, and Julius T. Sadler, Jr. *The Only Proper Style: Gothic Architecture in America.* New York: New York Graphic Society, 1975.

Maddox, Diane. *Master Builders: A Guide to Famous American Architects.* Washington, D.C.: Preservation Press of the National Trust for Historic Preservation, 1985.

Meeks, Carroll L. V. "Henry Austin and the Italian Villa." *Art Bulletin* 30 (June 1948): 145–49.

———. "Romanesque before Richardson in the United States." *Art Bulletin* 35 (1953): 17–33.

Milham, Willis I. "Early American Observatories." *Popular Astronomy* 45, no. 9 (November 1937), and no. 10 (December 1937).

———. *Early American Observatories: Which Was the First Astronomical Observatory in America?* Williamstown, Mass.: Williams College, 1938.

Millar, John Fitzhugh, and Suzanne Carlson. *The Architects of the American Colonies or Vitruvius Americanus.* Barre, Mass.: Barre Publishers, 1968.

Morrison, Hugh S. *Early American Architecture: From the First Colonial Settlements to the National Period.* New York: Oxford University Press, 1952.

Morse, Jedediah, and Elijah Parish. *A Compendious-History of New England.* Charlestown, Mass.: S. Ethnege, 1804.

Moss, Roger W., Jr., and Sandra L. Tatman. *Biographical Dictionary of Philadelphia Architects, 1700–1830.* Boston: G. K. Hall, 1985.

O'Gorman, James F. *Henry Austin: In Every Variety of Architectural Style.* Middletown, Conn.: Wesleyan University Press, 2008.

"Our Colleges." *Emerson's Magazine and Putnam's Monthly* 5, no. 6 (December 1857): 688–91. Williams, Bowdoin, and Union Colleges.

Pease, John, and John Niles. *Gazetteer of the States of Connecticut and Rhode Island.* Hartford, Conn.: William Marsh, 1819.

Pevsner, Nikolaus, John Fleming, and Hugh Honour. *A Dictionary of Architecture.* Rev. and enl. ed. Woodstock, N.Y.: Overlook Press, 1976.

Pierson, William H., Jr. *American Buildings and Their Architects: The Colonial and Neoclassical Styles.* Garden City, N.Y.: Doubleday and Company, 1970.

———. *American Buildings and Their Architects: Technology and the Picturesque, the Corporate and Early Gothic Styles.* Vol. 1. Garden City, N.Y.: Doubleday and Company, 1978. Vol. 2, 1986.

Place, Charles A. *Charles Bulfinch, Architect and Citizen.* Boston: Houghton Mifflin, 1925.

Placzek, Adolf K., ed. *Macmillan Encyclopedia of Architects.* 4 vols. New York: Free Press, Macmillan, 1982.

Poppeliers, John C., S. Allan Chambers, Jr., and Nancy B. Schwartz. *What Style Is It?: A Guide to American Architecture.* Washington, D.C.: Preservation Press for the Historic American Buildings Survey and the National Trust for Historic Preservation, 1983.

Reed, Roger. *Building Victorian Boston: The Architecture of Gridley J. F. Bryant.* Amherst: University of Massachusetts Press, 2007.

Richards, J. M., ed. *Who's Who in Architecture from 1400 to the Present.* New York: Holt, Rinehart and Winston, 1977.

Richardson, Charles F., and Henry A. Clark, eds. *The College Book.* Boston: Houghton, Osgood, 1878.

Rifkind, Carole. *A Field Guide to American Architecture.* New York: New American Library, 1980.

Roper, Laura Wood. *FLO: A Biography of Frederick Law Olmsted.* Baltimore: Johns Hopkins University Press, 1973.

Roth, Leland M. *The Architecture of McKim, Mead and White.* New York: Garland, 1978.

———. *A Concise History of American Architecture.* New York: Harper and Row, 1980.

Rudolph, Frederick. *The American College and University: A History.* New York: Alfred P. Knopf, 1962.

Schrock, Nancy C., ed. *Dictionary of Boston Architects, 1846–1970.* Cambridge: Committee for the Preservation of Architectural Records, 1984.

Schuyler, Montgomery. "The Architecture of American Colleges: VI—Dartmouth, Williams and Amherst." *Architectural Record* 28 (1910): 423–42.

———. "The Architecture of American Colleges: VII—Brown, Bowdoin, Trinity, Wesleyan." *Architectural Record* 29 (January–June 1911): 145–66.

Scully, Vincent J., Jr. *American Architecture and Urbanism.* New York: Frederick A. Praeger, 1969.

———. *The Shingle Style and the Stick Style: Architectural Theory and Design from Downing to the Origins of Wright.* Rev. ed. New Haven: Yale University Press, 1971.

Sinnott, Edmund W., and Jerould A. Manter. *Meetinghouse and Church in Early New England.* New York: McGraw-Hill, 1963.

Tatman, Sandra L., and Roger W. Moss. *Biographical Dictionary of Philadelphia Architects: 1730–1930.* Boston: G. K. Hall, 1985.

Tewkesbury, Donald G. *The Founding of American Colleges and Universities before the Civil War.* New York: Teachers' College, Columbia University, 1932. Repub., 1965.

Thorndike, Joseph J., Jr. *Three Centuries of Notable American Architects.* New York: American Heritage, 1981.

Thwing, Charles. *A History of Higher Education in America.* New York: D. Appleton and Company, 1906.

Tishler, William H. *American Landscape Architecture: Designers and Places.* Washington, D.C.: Preservation Press of the National Trust for Historic Preservation, and the American Society for Landscape Architects, 1988.

Tolles, Bryant F., Jr. "College Architecture in New England Before 1860 in Printed and Sketched Views." *Magazine Antiques* 103, no. 3 (March 1973): 502–9.

———. "College Architecture in Northern New England Before 1860: A Social and Cultural History." Ph.D. diss., Boston University, 1970.

———. "Colleges and Campuses," in *The Encyclopedia of New England: The Culture and History of an American Region,* ed. Burt Feintuch and David H. Watters, pp. 93–96. New Haven: Yale University Press, 2005.

———. "Early Medical School Architecture in Northern New England." *Vermont History* 42, no. 4 (Fall 1974): 257–77.

Turner, Jane, ed. *The Dictionary of Art.* 34 vols. New York: Grove; London: Macmillan, 1996.

Turner, Paul Venable. *Campus: An American Planning Tradition.* Cambridge: MIT Press, 1984.

Upjohn, Everard M. *Richard Upjohn: Architect and Churchman (1802–1878).* New York: Columbia University Press, 1939.

Upton, Dell. *Architecture in the United States.* New York: Oxford University Press, 1998.

Vose, George L. *A Sketch of the Life and Works of Loammi Baldwin, Civil Engineer.* Boston: George H. Ellis, 1885.

Walter, Thomas U. "Richard Upjohn, F.A.I.A.—1802–1878." *Journal of the Society of Architectural Historians* 8, no. 6 (December 1947): 272–76.

Wertenbaker, Thomas J. *Princeton, 1746–1896.* Princeton, N.J.: Princeton University Press, 1946. Includes Nassau Hall.

Wheelwright, John Brooks. "Richard Upjohn, Churchman and Architect." *New England Quarterly* 12, no. 3 (September 1939): 500–509.

Whiffen, Marcus, and Frederick Koeper. *American Architecture, 1607–1976.* Cambridge: MIT Press, 1981.

Williard, Ashton R. "The Development of College Architecture in America." *New England Magazine* n.s. 16, no. 5 (July 1897): 513–34.

Withey, Henry F., and Elsie R. Withey. *Biographical Dictionary of American Architects (Deceased).* Los Angeles: New Age, 1956.

II. New England State and County Histories, and Atlases

A. Connecticut

Barber, John Warner. *Connecticut Historical Collections. . . .* New Haven, Conn.: John W. Barber, 1836.

Brigham, Harold J. *History of Connecticut.* 4 vols. New York: Lewis Historical Publishing, 1962.

Burpee, Charles W. *History of Hartford County, Connecticut, 1633–1928.* 3 vols. Chicago: S. J. Clarke Publishing, 1928.

———. *The Story of Connecticut.* 4 vols. New York: American Historical Company, 1939.

Clark, George L. *History of Connecticut, Its People and Its Institutions.* 2nd ed. New York: G. P. Putnam's Sons, 1914.

Crofut, Florence S. M. *A Guide to the History and Historic Sites of Connecticut.* 2 vols. New Haven, Conn.: Yale University Press, 1937.

Dwight, Theodore. *History of Connecticut, from the First Settlement to the Present Time.* New York: Harper and Brothers, 1841.

Harwood, Phiny L. *History of Eastern Connecticut.* 4 vols. Chicago: Pioneer Publishing, 1931–32.

History of Middlesex County, Connecticut. New York: J. B. Beers and Company, 1884.

Mitchell, Mary H. *History of New Haven County.* 3 vols. Chicago: Pioneer Historical Publishing, 1930.

Morgan, Forrest, ed. *Connecticut as a Colony and as a State.* 4 vols. Hartford: Publishing Society of Connecticut, 1904.

Osborn, Norris Galpin, ed. *The History of Connecticut in Monographic Form.* 5 vols. New York: States History Company, 1925.

Pease, John C., and John M. Niles. *A Gazetteer of the States of Connecticut and Rhode Island. . . .* Hartford: William S. Marsh, 1819.

Rockey, J. L., ed. *History of New Haven County, Connecticut.* 2 vols. New York: W. W. Preston, 1892.

Sanford, Elias B. *A History of Connecticut.* Rev. ed. Hartford: S. S. Scranton and Company, 1922.

Steiner, Bernard C. *The History of Education in Connecticut.* Washington, D.C.: Government Printing Office, 1893.

Trumbull, James Hammond, ed. *The Memorial History of Hartford County, Connecticut, 1633–1884.* Vol. 1. Boston: Edward L. Osgood, 1886.

Van Dusen, Albert E. *Connecticut.* New York: Random House, 1961.

Works Progress Administration (Federal Writers' Project). *Connecticut: A Guide to Its Roads, Lore, and People.* American Guide Series. Boston: Houghton Mifflin, 1938.

B. Rhode Island

Arnold, Samuel Greene. *History of the State of Rhode Island and Providence Plantations.* 2 vols. New York: D. Appleton and Company, 1859–60. 4th ed., Providence: Preston and Rounds, 1899.

Bayles, Richard M., ed. *History of Providence County, Rhode Island.* 2 vols. New York: W. W. Preston and Company, 1891.

Bicknell, Thomas W. *The History of the State of Rhode Island and Providence Plantations.* 5 vols. New York: American Historical Society, 1920.

Carroll, Charles. *Rhode Island, Three Centuries of Democracy.* 4 vols. New York: Lewis Historical Publishing, 1932.

Field, Edmond, ed. *State of Rhode Island and Providence Plantations at the End of the Century: A History.* 2 vols. Boston: Mason Publishing, 1902.

Jordy, William H. *Buildings of Rhode Island.* New York: Oxford University Press, 2004.

Richman, I. B. *Rhode Island, Its Making and Meaning.* 2 vols. New York: Putnam's, 1902. 2nd ed., 1908.

Talman, William H. *History of Higher Education in Rhode Island.* Washington, D.C.: U.S. Bureau of Education, 1894.

Works Progress Administration (Federal Writers' Project). *Rhode Island: A Guide to the Smallest State.* American Guide Series. Boston: Houghton Mifflin, 1937.

C. Massachusetts

Aldrich, Peleg E. *History of Worcester County, Massachusetts. . . .* Boston: C. F. Jewett, 1879.

Barber, John Warner. *Historical Collections, . . . Relating to the History and Antiquities of Every Town in Massachusetts. . . .* Worcester, Mass.: Dorr, Howland and Company, 1839.

Bush, George G. *History of Higher Education in Massachusetts.* Washington, D.C.: U.S. Government Printing Office, 1891.

Child, Hamilton. *Gazetteer of Berkshire County, Mass., 1725–1885.* Syracuse, N.Y.: Journal Office, 1885.

Clark, Will L. *Western Massachusetts, A History, 1636–1925.* 4 vols. New York: Lewis Historical Publishing, 1926.

Conklin, Edwin P. *Middlesex County and Its People.* 5 vols. New York: Lewis Historical Publishing, 1927.

Drake, Samuel Adams. *History of Middlesex County, Massachusetts.* 2 vols. Boston: Estes and Lauriat, 1880.

Field, David Dudley, ed. *A History of the County of Berkshire, Massachusetts.* Pittsfield, Mass.: Samuel W. Bush, 1829.

Gay, William B. *Gazetteer of Hampshire County, Massachusetts, 1654–1887.* Syracuse, N.Y.: W. B. Gay and Company, [1887].

Hart, Albert Bushnell. *Commonwealth History of Massachusetts.* 5 vols. New York: States History Company, 1927–30.

History of the Connecticut Valley in Massachusetts. . . . 2 vols. Philadelphia: Louis H. Everts, 1879.

Holland, Josiah Gilbert. *History of Western Massachusetts. . . .* 2 vols. Springfield, Mass.: Samuel Bowles and Company, 1855.

Hurd, D. Hamilton, ed. *History of Middlesex County, Massachusetts. . . .* 3 vols. Philadelphia: J. W. Lewis and Company, 1890.

———, ed. *History of Worcester County, Massachusetts. . . .* Philadelphia: J. W. Lewis and Company, 1889.

Lockwood, John H.. et al. *Western Massachusetts, A History, 1636–1925.* 4 vols. New York: Lewis Historical Publishing, 1926.

Marsh, Daniel L., and William H. Clark. *The Story of Massachusetts.* 4 vols. New York: American Historical Society, 1938.

Nelson, John. *Worcester County; A Narrative History.* 3 vols. New York: American Historical Society, 1934.

Smith, J. E. A., and Thomas Cushing, eds. *History of Berkshire County, Massachusetts, with Biographical Sketches of Its Prominent Men.* 2 vols. New York: J. B. Beers, 1885.

Wikander, Lawrence E., Helen Terry, and Mark Kiley. *The Hampshire History, Celebrating 300 Years of Hampshire County, Massachusetts.* Northampton, Mass.: Hampshire County Commissioners, 1964.

Works Progress Administration (Federal Writers' Project). *Massa-

chusetts: A Guide to Its Places and People. American Guide Series. Boston: Houghton Mifflin, 1937.

Wright, Harry Andrew. *The Story of Western Massachusetts.* 4 vols. New York: Lewis Historical Publishing, 1949.

D. Maine

Atlas and History of Androscoggin County, Maine. Philadelphia: Sanford, Everts and Company, 1873.

Blanding, William F., and Philip W. McIntyre, eds. *Men of Progress: Biographical Sketches and Portraits of Leaders in Business and Professional Life in and of the State of Maine.* Boston: New England Magazine, 1897.

Clayton, W. W. *History of Cumberland Co., Maine.* Philadelphia: Everts and Peck, 1880.

Halfpenny, H. E. *Atlas of Kennebec County, Maine.* Philadelphia: Caldwell and Halfpenny, 1879.

Hall, Edward W. *History of Higher Education in Maine.* Washington, D.C.: U.S. Government Printing Office, 1903.

Kingsbury, Henry D., and Simeon L. Deyo, eds. *Illustrated History of Kennebec County.* 2 vols. New York: H. W. Blake and Company, 1892.

Merrill, Georgia Drew, ed. *History of Androscoggin County, Maine.* Boston: W. A. Fergusson and Company, 1891.

Rush, N. Orwin. *History of Maine College Libraries.* Worcester, Mass.: Clark University Library, 1946.

Works Progress Administration (Federal Writers' Project). *Maine: A Guide "Down East."* Boston: Houghton Mifflin, 1938.

E. New Hampshire

Belknap, Jeremy. *History of New Hampshire.* 3 vols. Dover, N.H.: J. Mann and J. K. Remick, 1812.

Bush, George G. *History of Education in New Hampshire.* Washington, D.C.: U.S. Government Printing Office, 1898.

Charlton, Edwin A. *New Hampshire as It Is.* 3rd ed., rev. Claremont, N.H.: A. Kenney and Company, 1857.

Farmer, John, and Jacob B. Moore. *A Gazetteer of the State of New Hampshire.* Concord, N.H.: Jacob B. Moore, 1823.

Fogg, Alonzo F. *The Statistics and Gazetteer of New Hampshire.* Concord, N.H.: D. L. Guernsey, 1874.

Hayward, John. *Gazetteer of New Hampshire.* Boston: John P. Jewatt, 1849.

McClintock, John N. *History of New Hampshire.* Boston: B. B. Russell, 1889.

Merrill, Eliphalet, and Phineas Merrill. *Gazetteer of the State of New Hampshire.* Exeter, N.H.: Norris and Company, 1817.

Pillsbury, Hobart. *New Hampshire: Resources, Attractions and Its People.* 8 vols. New York: Lewis Historical Publishing, 1927–28.

Sanborn, Edwin D. *History of New Hampshire from Its First Discovery to the Year 1830.* Manchester, N.H.: John B. Clarke, 1875.

Stackpole, Everett S. *History of New Hampshire.* 4 vols. New York: American Historical Society, 1917.

Tolles, Bryant F., Jr., with Carolyn K. Tolles. *New Hampshire Architecture: An Illustrated Guide.* 1979; reprint, Hanover: University Press of New England, 2004.

Whiton, John M. *Sketches of the History of New Hampshire, from 1623 to 1833.* Concord, N.H.: Marsh, Capen and Lyon, 1834.

Works Progress Administration (Federal Writers' Project). *Hands That Built New Hampshire.* Brattleboro, Vt.: Stephen Daye Press, 1940.

———. *New Hampshire: A Guide to the Granite State.* American Guide Series. Boston: Houghton Mifflin, 1938.

F. Vermont

Aldrich, Lewis Cass, and Frank R. Holmes, eds. *History of Windsor County, Vermont.* Syracuse, N.Y.: D. M. Mason and Company, 1891.

Allen, Ira. *The Natural and Political History of the State of Vermont.* London: J. W. Meyers, 1798. Reprinted in the *Vermont Historical Society Collections* 1 (1870).

Bearse, Ray, ed. *Vermont: A Guide to the Green Mountain State.* Rev. ed. Boston: Houghton Mifflin, 1966. An expanded new edition of the Federal Writers' Project (W.P.A.) American Guide Series volume for Vermont, published in 1936.

Beckley, Hosea. *The History of Vermont, with Descriptions, Physical and Topographical.* Brattleboro, Vt.: George H. Salisbury, 1846.

Bush, George G. *History of Education in Vermont.* Washington, D.C.: U.S. Government Printing Office, 1900.

Child, Hamilton, ed. *Gazetteer and Business Directory of Addison County, Vermont for 1881–82.* Syracuse, N.Y.: Journal Office, 1882.

———, ed. *Gazetteer and Business Directory of Chittenden County, Vermont for 1882–83.* Syracuse, N.Y.: Journal Office, 1883.

Crockett, Walter H. *History of Vermont.* 5 vols. New York: Century History Company, 1921.

Hemenway, Abby Maria, ed. *The Vermont State Historical Gazetteer: A Local History of All the Towns in the State. . . .* 5 vols. Burlington, Vt.: Published by the author, 1867–92.

Hoskins, Nathan. *A History of the State of Vermont from Its Discovery and Settlement to the Year 1830.* Vergennes, Vt.: J. Shedd, 1831.

Mussey, Barrows. *Vermont Heritage: A Picture Story.* New York: A. A. Wyn, 1947.

Newton, Earle W. *The Vermont Story: A History of the People of the Green Mountain State, 1749–1949.* Montpelier: Vermont Historical Society, 1949.

Rann, W. S., ed. *History of Chittenden County, Vermont.* Syracuse, N.Y.: D. Mason and Company, 1886.

Smith, H. Perry. *History of Addison County, Vermont.* Syracuse, N.Y.: D. Mason and Company, 1886.

Stone, Arthur F. *The Vermont of Today: With Its Historic Background, Attractions and People.* 4 vols. New York: Lewis Historical Publishing Company, 1929.

Stone, Mason S. *History of Education, State of Vermont.* Montpelier, Vt.: Published by the author, 1934.

Thompson, Zadock. *A Gazetteer of the State of Vermont.* Montpelier, Vt.: E. P. Walton and the Author, 1824.

———. *History of Vermont, Natural, Civil and Statistical.* Burlington, Vt.: Chauncey Goodrich, 1842.

Works Progress Administration (Federal Writers' Project). *Vermont: A Guide to the Green Mountain State.* American Guide Series. Boston: Houghton Mifflin, 1937.

III. Institutional Source Materials

A. Harvard University (College), Cambridge, Massachusetts

Andrews, William Loring, ed. *A Prospect of the Colledges in Cambridge in New England . . . Engraved by Wm. Burgis in 1726.* New York: Dodd Mead and Company, 1897.

Bail, Hamilton Vaughan. *Views of Harvard: A Pictorial Record to 1860.* Cambridge: Harvard University Press, 1949.

Bailyn, Bernard, and Donald Fleming, et al. *Glimpses of the Harvard Past.* Cambridge: Harvard University Press, 1982.

Baker, Daniel Weld. *History of the Harvard College Observatory during the Period 1840–1890.* Cambridge: n.p.,1890.

Batchelder, Samuel F. *Bits of Harvard History.* Cambridge: Harvard University Press, 1924.

———. "The Singular Story of Holden Chapel." *Harvard Alumni Bulletin* 23, no. 18 (3 February 1921): 405–16.

Bentinck-Smith, William. *The Harvard Book.* Cambridge: Harvard University Press, 1982.

Bolton, Charles Knowles. "The Harvard University Library." *New England Magazine* (Second Series) 9, no. 4 (December 1893): 433–49.

Bond, William C. "Description of the Observatory at Cambridge, Massachusetts." *Memoirs of the Academy of Arts and Sciences* n.s. 9 (1849): 177–88, plus plates.

———. "History and Description of the Astronomical Observatory of Harvard College." *Annals of the Observatory of Harvard College* 1 (1856).

Bradford, Alden. "Historical Sketch of Harvard University." *American Quarterly Register* 9, no. 4 (May 1837): 321–66.

Brown, John P. "Notes on Bulfinch Church at Lancaster, Mass." *Old-Time New England* 17, no. 4 (April 1937): 148–51. Design details of University Hall, Harvard.

Brown, Walter. *Harvard Yard in the Golden Age.* New York: A. A. Wyn, 1948.

Brown, William G. *Official Guide to Harvard University.* Cambridge: [Harvard] University Press, 1899. Edited for the Harvard Memorial Society.

Building Harvard: Architecture of Three Centuries. Cambridge: Information Center, Harvard University, 1964. Also 1968, 1973, 1975, etc.

Bunting, Bainbridge, and Margaret Henderson Floyd. *Harvard: An Architectural History.* Cambridge: Belknap Press of Harvard University Press, 1985.

Cambridge Historical Commission. *Survey of Architectural History in Cambridge. Report Two: Mid-Cambridge.* Cambridge: MIT Press, 1967. By Antoinette F. Downing, Elizabeth MacDougall, and Eleanor Pearson.

———. *Survey of Architectural History in Cambridge. Report Four: Old Cambridge.* Cambridge: MIT Press, 1973. By Bainbridge Bunting and Robert H. Nylander.

Cambridge, Massachusetts. Harvard University Archives, Pusey Library. College Buildings (volume of papers concerning the erection of Holworthy and University Halls).

———. Harvard University Archives, Pusey Library. College Buildings card file (sources and notes).

———. Harvard University Archives, Pusey Library. Indexes to Buildings and Locations in the Harvard Area (computerized lists by Chris Hail, 1982).

Chamberlain, Samuel, and Donald Moffat. *Fair Harvard.* New York: Hastings House, 1948.

Davis, Andrew McFarland. "The Early College Buildings at Cambridge." *American Antiquarian Society Proceedings* n.s. 6 (1889–90): 323–49.

———. "The Indian College at Cambridge." *Magazine of American History* 24 (1890): 33–39.

———. "A Search for a Lost Building." *Atlantic* 66 (1890): 211–19. Harvard's first building in Cambridge.

———. *The Site of the First College Building at Cambridge.* Worcester, Mass.: Press of Charles Hamilton, 1889. Published initially in the *American Antiquarian Society Proceedings* n.s. 5 (1887–88): 469–84.

"Description of the Colleges at Cambridge." *Massachusetts Magazine* 2 (June 1790): 323–26.

"The Eastern Front of University Hall." *Harvard Alumni Bulletin* 19, no. 36 (14 June 1917): 713.

Education, Bricks and Mortar: Harvard Buildings and Their Contribution to the Advancement of Learning. Cambridge: Harvard University, 1949.

Eliot, Samuel A. *A History of Cambridge, Massachusetts.* Cambridge: Cambridge Tribune, 1913.

Eustis, Henry L. "The Lawrence Scientific School." *Harvard Register* 3 (1881): 375–78.

"The Faculty Room in University Hall." *Harvard Alumni Bulletin* 15, no. 20 (12 February 1913): 324–28.

Foster, F. Apthorp. "The Burning of Harvard Hall, 1764, and Its Consequences." *Publications of the Colonial Society of Massachusetts* 14 (1913): 2–43.

"Founding Fathers." *Journal of the Bostonian Society of Civil Engineers* 23 (July 1936): 173. Biographical sketch of Loammi Baldwin, the designer of Holworthy Hall.

Gardiner, John H. *Harvard.* New York: Oxford University Press, 1914.

Gore Hall: The Library of Harvard College, 1838–1913. Cambridge: Harvard University Press, 1917.

Green, Samuel Abbott. "The Earliest Print of Harvard College." *Harvard Graduates' Magazine* 5, no. 19 (March 1897): 325–26.

Harris, Seymour. *The Economics of Harvard.* New York: McGraw-Hill, 1972.

"Harvard College." *Columbian Magazine* 2 (December 1788): 669.

Hatch, Mary R. P. "Harvard University: Some Account of Its Makers, Its Library, and Other Buildings and Its Club Life." *New England Magazine* n.s. 33, no. 3 (November 1905): 307–22.

"Hollis Hall, 1763–1913." *Harvard Alumni Bulletin* 15, no. 24 (12 March 1913): 395–98.

"Holworthy Hall." *Harvard Alumni Bulletin* 14, no. 30 (1 May 1912): 482–85.

Hudnut, Joseph. "The Architecture of the Yard." *Harvard Alumni Bulletin* 48, no. 12 (30 March 1946): 481–84.

King, Moses. *Harvard and Its Surroundings.* 4th ed. Cambridge: Moses King, 1882.

Kirker, Harold. "The Architect of Stoughton Hall." *Harvard Alumni Bulletin* 68, no. 2 (9 October 1965): 64–65, 67.

Lane, William C. "The Building of Holworthy Hall, 1812." *Harvard Graduates' Magazine* 12, no. 47 (1903–04): 349–58.

———. "The Building of Massachusetts Hall, 1717–1720." *Publications of the Colonial Society of Massachusetts* 24 (1923): 81–110.

———. "Early Views of Harvard College." *Harvard Graduates' Magazine* 12, no. 47 (1903–4): 349–58.

———. "Paul Revere Engraving of Harvard." *Harvard Graduates' Magazine* 12, no. 46 (1903–4): 338–39.

———. "Two Landmarks: Foundations of the First College Buildings." *Harvard Graduates' Magazine* 18, no. 71 (March 1910): 451–52.

"Massachusetts Hall." *Harvard Alumni Bulletin* 10, no. 20 (19 February 1908): 1–2.

Moe, Alfred K. *A History of Harvard.* Cambridge: Harvard University, 1896.

Morison, Samuel Eliot. "A Conjectural Restoration of the 'Old College' at Harvard." *Old-Time New England* 23, no. 4 (April 1933): 130–58.

———, ed. *The Development of Harvard University since the In-auguration of President Eliot, 1869–1929.* Cambridge: Harvard University Press, 1930.

———. *The Founding of Harvard College.* Cambridge: Harvard University Press, 1935.

———. *Harvard College in the Seventeenth Century.* 2 vols. Cambridge: Harvard University Press, 1936.

———. *Three Centuries of Harvard University, 1636–1936.* Cambridge: Harvard University Press, 1936.

———. "Needlework Picture Representing a Colonial College Building." *Old-Time New England* 24, no. 2 (October 1935): 67–72.

———. *Three Centuries of Harvard.* Cambridge: Harvard University Press, 1936.

Paige, Lucius R. *History of Cambridge, Massachusetts, 1630–1877, with a Genealogical Register.* Boston: H. O. Houghton and Company, 1877.

Palfrey, Cazneau. "Holden Chapel." *Harvard Register* 3 (1881): 83.

———. "Massachusetts Hall." *Harvard Register* 3 (1881): 222–25.

———. "A Study of Holden Chapel." *Harvard Register* 1–2 (1880): 238–39.

"The Passing of Gore Hall." *Harvard Alumni Bulletin* 15, no. 16 (15 January 1913): 260–64.

"Passing of Gore Hall." *Boston Christian Science Monitor,* 18 January 1913.

Peabody, Andrew. *Harvard Reminiscences.* Boston: Ticknor and Company, 1888.

Peabody, Reverend Francis G. "The Spiritual History of Divinity Hall." *Harvard Graduates' Magazine* 24, no. 95 (March 1916): 462–71.

Peirce, Benjamin. *A History of Harvard University.* 2 vols. Cambridge: Brown, Shattuck and Company, 1833.

Quincy, Josiah. *History of Harvard University.* 2 vols. Cambridge: John Owen, 1840; Boston: Crosby, Nichols, Lee and Company, 1860.

Rettig, Robert Bell. *Guide to Cambridge Architecture: Ten Walking Tours.* Cambridge: MIT Press, 1969.

Schuyler, Montgomery. "The Architecture of American Colleges: I—Harvard." *Architectural Record* 26 (1909): 243–69.

Shand-Tucci, Douglass. *The Campus Guide: Harvard University.* New York: Princeton Architectural Press, 2001.

Specifications and floor plan for Holworthy Hall, Harvard University. William L. Clements Library, University of Michigan, Ann Arbor. 11 sheets.

Thayer, William Roscoe. "John Harvard and the Early College." *New England Magazine* n.s. 25, no. 2 (October 1901): 131–46.

Thayer, William Roscoe, and Charles E. L. Wingate. *Harvard University: Its History, Influence, Equipment, and Characteristics. . . .* Boston: R. Herndon, 1900.

Thompson, Grace Agnes. "The Harvard College Observatory and

Its Photographic Work." *New England Magazine* n.s. 33, no. 2 (October 1905): 194–203.

Vaille, F. O., and H. A. Clark, eds. *The Harvard Book: A Series of Historical, Biographical and Descriptive Sketches.* 2 vols. Cambridge: Welch, Bigelow and Company, 1875; Boston: Houghton, Osgood and Company, 1878. Essays on individual buildings, etc.

Walton, Clarence E. "An Historical Prospect of Harvard College, 1636–1936." *Old-Time New England* 28, nos. 2–3 (October 1936 and January 1937): 39–66 (no. 2), and 99–109 (no. 3).

Ware, Henry. "The Harvard College Library." *Harvard Register* 1–2 (1880): 184, 201–4.

———. "Stoughton Hall." *Harvard Register* 3 (1881): 72–74.

Waters, Henry F. "The College Fire in 1764—A Contemporary Account." *Harvard Register* 3 (1881): 294–97.

Wiley, Franklin Baldwin. *The Harvard Guide-Book.* 2nd ed. Cambridge: Charles W. Sever, 1895.

Winsor, Justin, ed. *The Memorial History of Boston.* 4 vols. Boston: J. R. Osgood, 1880–81.

B. Yale University (College), New Haven, Connecticut

Allen, Walter. "New Haven." *New England Magazine* n.s. 20, no. 4 (June 1899): 481–501.

Atwater, Edward E. *History of the City of New Haven to the Present Time.* New York: W. W. Munsell and Company, 1887.

Austin, Henry. "Ground Plan for the Yale Library," New Haven, 1842. Beinecke Rare Book Library, Yale University, New Haven.

Baldwin, Ebenezer. *Annals of Yale College from Its Foundation to the Year 1831.* New Haven: B. and W. Noyes, 1838.

Baldwin, Simeon Eben. "The Three Earliest Architects in New Haven." *New Haven Colony Historical Society Proceedings* 10 (1951): 226–39.

Barber, John Warner. *History and Antiquities of New Haven, from Its Earliest Settlement to the Present Time.* New Haven: J. W. Barber, 1831. Also, 1856 ed., with Lemuel S. Punderson.

Bartlett, Ellen S. *Historical Sketches of New Haven.* New Haven: Tuttle, Morehouse and Taylor, 1897.

[Belden, Ezekial P.]. *Sketches of Yale College.* . . . New York: Saxton and Miles, 1843.

Blake, Henry T. *Chronicles of New Haven Green from 1638 to 1862.* New Haven: Tuttle, Morehouse and Taylor, 1898.

Bolton, Dorothea. "A Senior Notebook, 1803." *Yale Library Gazette* 10 (1936): 59–62.

Brockway, Jean L. "John Trumbull as Architect at Yale." *Magazine Antiques* 28 (September 1935): 114–15.

Brown, Elizabeth Mills. *New Haven: A Guide to Architecture and Urban Design.* New Haven: Yale University Press, 1976.

Carmalt, L. J. *Guide Book of New Haven and Yale University.* New Haven: Van Dyke and Company, 1933.

Carroll, Richard, ed. *Buildings and Grounds of Yale University.* New Haven: Yale University Printing Service, 1979.

Clap, Thomas. *The Annals or History of Yale College (1700–1766).* New Haven: Printed for John Hotchkiss and B. Mecom, 1766.

"College Edifices and Their Relation to Education." *American Literary Magazine* 1 (November 1847). Description of the Yale Library.

Cooper, Helen A. "John Trumbull at Yale." *Magazine Antiques* 123 (January 1983): 202–13.

Cuningham, Charles E. *Timothy Dwight, 1752–1817.* New York: Macmillan, 1942.

Dana, Arnold C. "Yale Old and New." Personal scrapbook, 1933–43. 78 vols. Manuscripts and Archives, Yale University Library, New Haven.

Decrow, William E. *Yale University.* New Haven: Tuttle, Morehouse and Taylor, 1893.

———. *Yale and "The City of Elms."* 2nd ed. Boston: W. E. Decrow, 1885.

Deming, Clarence. *Yale Yesterdays.* New Haven: Yale University Press, 1952.

Dexter, Franklin B. *Biographical Sketches of Yale College with Annals of the College History, 1701–1792.* 6 vols. New York: H. Holt and Company, 1885–1904.

———, ed. *Documentary History of Yale University . . . 1701–1745.* New Haven: Yale University Press, [c. 1916]; repub., New York: Arno Press and New York Times, 1969.

———, ed. *The Literary Diary of Ezra Stiles.* 3 vols. New York: Charles Scribner's, 1901.

———. "New Haven in 1784." *Papers of the New Haven Colony Historical Society* 4: 122–38.

———. *Sketch of the History of Yale University.* New York: H. H. Holt and Company, 1887.

Donnell, Edna. "A. J. Davis and the Gothic Revival." *Metropolitan Museum Studies* 5 (September 1936): 183.

Eggleston, Percy Coe. "Yale and Her President, 1777–1795." *New England Magazine* n.s. 34, no. 2 (April 1909): 137–47.

Fisher, George P. *Life of Benjamin Silliman.* . . . New York: Charles Scribner and Company, 1866.

Fulton, John F., and Elizabeth H. Thomson. *Benjamin Silliman, 1779–1864, Pathfinder in American Science.* New York: H. Schuman, [1947].

A Graphic View of New Haven. New Haven: New Haven Colony Historical Society, 1976. Views of Yale included.

Guilbert, Juliette. "Something That Loves a Wall: The Yale University Campus, 1850–1920." *New England Quarterly* 68, no. 2 (June 1995): 257–77.

Heinz, Bernard. "Old Yale: Doubling the College—Connecticut Hall Was a Big Undertaking." *Yale Alumni Magazine* 50, no. 2 (November 1986): 40–42.

Holden, Reuben A. *Yale: A Pictorial History*. New Haven: Yale University Press, 1967.

Isham, Norman M. "The Original College House at Yale." *Yale Alumni Weekly* 26, no. 5 (20 October 1916): 115–20.

Keith, Elmer D., and William L. Warren. "Peter Banner, a Builder for Yale College." *Old-Time New England* 45, no. 4 (Spring 1955): 93–102; 47, no. 2 (Fall 1956): 49–53; 49, no. 4 (Spring 1959): 104–10. Three articles treating the President's House, Berkeley Hall, and The Lyceum.

———. "Peter Banner, Architect, Moves from New Haven to Boston." *Old-Time New England* 58, no. 3 (Winter 1967): 57–76.

———. "Peter Banner, His Building Speculations in New Haven." *Old-Time New England* 53, no. 4 (Spring 1963): 102–9.

Kelley, Brooks Mather. *Yale: A History*. New Haven: Yale University Press, 1974.

Kingsley, James L. *A Sketch of the History of Yale College in Connecticut*. Boston: Perkins, Marvin and Company, 1835.

———. *Yale College: A Sketch of Its History*. 2 vols. New York: Henry Holt and Company, 1879. Large folios.

Lambert, Edward R. *History of the Colony of New Haven, Before and After the Union with Connecticut. . . .* New Haven: Hitchcock and Stafford, 1838.

Morgan, Edmund S. *The Gentle Puritan: A Life of Ezra Stiles, 1727–1795*. New Haven: Yale University Press, 1962.

"A Needlework Picture of Connecticut Hall, Built 1752." *Bulletin of the Association in Fine Arts* (Yale University) 12 (June 1943): 2–4.

Office of the Secretary, Yale University. *The Buildings of Yale University*. New Haven: Yale University, 1965.

"The Old Chapel in the Sixties; Undergraduate Memories of an Historic Yale Structure." *Yale Alumni Weekly* 18 (7 May 1909): 799–800.

"The Old College Campus: Its Physical Life and Aspects Fifty Years Ago." *Yale Alumni Weekly* 19 (18 February 1910): 535–36.

Osterweis, Rollin G. *Three Centuries of New Haven, 1638–1938*. New Haven: Yale University Press, 1953.

Oviatt, Edwin. *The Beginnings of Yale (1701–1726)*. New Haven: Yale University Press, 1916.

———. "The Making of Yale." *New England Magazine* n.s. 25, no. 4 (December 1901): 426–42.

Peters, Absalom. "American Colleges: Yale College, New Haven, Conn." *American Journal of Education and College Review* 1 (May 1856): 463–79.

Pierson, George Wilson. *Yale: A Short History*. 1976; reprint, New Haven: Office of the Secretary, Yale University, 1991.

———. *Yale: College and University, 1871–1937*. 2 vols. New Haven: Yale University Press, 1952–55.

Pinnell, Patrick. *The Campus Guide: Yale University*. New York: Princeton Architectural Press, 1999.

———. "Old Campus Building History." Unpublished ms., 1996. Manuscripts and Archives, Yale University Library, New Haven.

Pratt, Anne S. "John Trumbull and the Brick Row." *Yale University Library Gazette* 9, no. 1 (July 1934): 11–20.

Schuyler, Montgomery. "The Architecture of American Colleges: II — Yale." *Architectural Record* 24 (1909): 393–416.

Scully, Vincent, Catherine Lynn, Erik Vogt, and Paul Goldberger. *Yale in New Haven: Architecture and Urbanism*. New Haven: Yale University Press, 2004.

Seymour, George Dudley. "Henry Caner, 1680–1731, Master Carpenter, Builder of the First Yale College Building, 1718, and of the Rector's House, 1722." *Old-Time New England* 15, no. 3 (January 1925): 98–124.

———. *New Haven*. New Haven: Printed for the author, 1942.

———. *Researches of an Antiquary*. New Haven: Yale University Press, 1928. Five essays.

Shumway, Floyd M., and Richard Hegel, eds. *New Haven: An Illustrated History*. New Haven: New Haven Colony Historical Society, 1981.

Sizer, Theodore, ed. *The Autobiography of Col. John Trumbull: Patriot—Artist, 1746-1843*. New York: Kennedy Graphics/Da Capo Press, 1970.

———. "John Trumbull, Amateur Artist." *Journal of the Society of Architectural Historians* 8, nos. 3–4 (July–December 1949): 1–6.

———. *John Trumbull, Museum Architect*. N.p.: n.p., [c. 1941]. Pamphlet.

———. "The Trumbull Gallery, 1832–1932: The Centenary of America's Earliest College Art Museum." *Yale Alumni Weekly* 42 (28 October 1932): 143–46.

———. *The Works of John Trumbull, Artist of the American Revolution*. New Haven: Yale University Press, 1967.

Tolles, Bryant F., Jr. "Henry Austin (1804–91)—Architect: The Eclectic Revival." Unpublished paper, 1961, author's collection.

Tucker, Louis Leonard. *Puritan Protagonist: President Thomas Clap of Yale College*. Chapel Hill: University of North Carolina Press, 1962.

"The Twilight of Alumni Hall: Life Story of a Familiar Yale Structure." *Yale Alumni Weekly* 19 (11 March 1910): 607–9.

"A Visit to Old Yale." *Appleton's Journal* 3, no. 42 (15 January 1870): 57–60.

Warch, Richard. *School of Prophets: Yale College, 1701–1740*. New Haven: Yale University Press, 1873.

Welch, Lewis S., and Walter Camp. *Yale: Her Campus, Class-Rooms, and Athletics*. Boston: L. C. Page and Company, 1899.

Whitlock, Reverdy. "Who Killed the Old Brick Row." *Yale Alumni Magazine* 38, no. 4 (January 1975): 25–29.

Woodward, Sarah Day. *Early New Haven*. New Haven: Edward P. Judd, 1929.

C. Brown University (Rhode Island College), Providence

Barry, Joy, and Martha Mitchell. *A Tale of Two Centuries: A Warm and Richly Illustrated History of Brown University, 1764–1985.* Providence: Brown Alumni Monthly, 1985.

Batt, Reverend William J. "University Hall in the Fifties." *Brown Alumni Monthly* 28, no. 6 (January 1928): 144–45.

Bingham, Clarence S. "Old University Hall: An Attempt to Identify Its Rooms and Occupants." *Brown Alumni Monthly* 8, no. 6 (January 1908): 113–19.

"Brief History of Brown University, 1764–1961." Typescript prepared by the Office of the Secretary, 28 pp., 1961. Brown University Archives, John Hay Library, Providence.

Bronson, Walter C. *History of Brown University, 1764–1914.* Providence: Brown University, 1914.

Brown, Robert P., et al. *Memories of Brown: Traditions and Recollections Gathered from Many Sources.* Providence: Brown Alumni Magazine Company, 1909.

Brown Family Papers (1767–80; 1819–24; 1831–36; 1841). Brown University, John Carter Brown Library, Providence.

Cady, John Hutchins. *The Civic and Architectural Development of Providence, 1636–1950.* Providence: Book Shop, 1957.

———. "Manning Hall, Centenarian." *Brown Alumni Monthly* 34, no. 9 (April 1934): 209–11.

"Campus Revisions." *Brown Alumni Monthly* 40, no. 3 (October 1939): 60.

Catalogue of the Officers and Students of Brown University (1821–71). Title variations.

Clancey, Gregory K. *Exterior Paint Survey: Manning Hall, Brown University, Providence, R.I.* Boston: Society for the Preservation of New England Antiquities, 1990.

Downing, Antoinette F., Principal Architectural Historian. *College Hill Demonstration Grant Study.* Providence, R.I., 1958–.

"Exercises Celebrating the Reopening of University Hall, Middle Campus, Brown University, Providence, Rhode Island, May 4, 1940, 11 a.m." Typescript. [Springfield, Mass.: Massachusetts Sterotype Reporters, 1940.] Brown University Archives, John Hay Library, Providence.

Exercises Commemorating the Restoration of University Hall, Brown University, October the Twentieth-Fourth A. D. MDCCCCV.... Providence: [Standard Printing Company], 1905.

Extracts from "Corporation Records—Buildings and Grounds, 1769–1914." Typescript. Brown University Archives, John Hay Library, Providence.

"For the Reconstruction of Hope College." *Brown Alumni Monthly* 41, no. 8 (April 1941): 221.

"For University Hall, a $100,000 Gift." *Brown Alumni Monthly* 39, no. 7 (February 1938): 189.

Frieberg, Malcolm. "Brown University's First 'College Edifice.'" *Old-Time New England* 50, no. 4 (April–June 1960): 85–93.

Gerold, William. *College Hill: A Photographic Study of Brown University in Its Two Hundredth Year.* Providence: Brown University Press, 1965. Foreword by Carl Bridenbaugh.

Guild, Frederick Taft. "The Old College Edifice of Rhode Island College." *Daughters of the American Revolution Magazine* 71 (1937): 202–3. University Hall.

Guild, Reuben. "History of the University," 1897. Typescript in binders. Brown University Archives, John Hay Library, Providence.

Guild, Reuben A. "Brown University." *New England Magazine* o.s. 4, no. 1 (January 1886): 1–12.

———. *Early History of Brown University, Including the Life, Times, and Correspondence of President Manning, 1756–1791.* Providence: Snow and Farnham, 1897.

———. *Historical Sketch of Brown University.* Providence: Snow and Greene, 1858.

———. *History of Brown University, with Illustrative Documents.* Providence: [Providence Press Company], 1867.

———. *Life, Times, and Correspondence of James Manning, and the Early History of Brown University.* Boston: Gould and Lincoln, 1864.

Historical Catalogue of Brown University, 1764–1914. Providence: Published by the University, 1905. Contains "History of the University," pp. 1–9.

Hitchcock, Henry-Russell. *Rhode Island Architecture.* Providence: Museum Press, 1939. Reprint ed., New York: Da Capo Press, 1968.

"Hope College." *Brown Alumni Monthly* 57, no. 5 (February 1957): 4–7, 13.

"Hope College: A Venerable Dorm Is Ready for an Interesting Experiment." *Brown Alumni Monthly* 59, no. 9 (July 1959): 28–29, 54.

Hope College: For the Promotion of Virtue, Science and Literature. Providence: n.p., 1959. Reconstruction of Hope College.

"Hope College—'Go Ahead.'" *Brown Alumni Monthly* 58, no. 5 (February 1958): 18.

"In Homage to University Hall." *Brown Alumni Monthly* 41, no. 1 (June 1940): 7–8.

Iselin, Diane C. *Ivied Halls: Two Centuries of Housing at Brown University.* Providence: Brown University, 1981.

Keen, William W. *The Early Years of Brown University (1764–1770).* Boston: n.p., 1914. Pamphlet.

Kenny, Robert W. "How the College Edifice Was Built on a Spot Made for the Muses on the Inaccessible Mountain." *Brown Alumni Monthly* 72, no. 1 (October 1971): 26–31.

King, Moses, ed. *King's Pocket-Book of Providence, R.I.* Cambridge: Moses King, 1882.

Locke, Edwin Allen. *Brown University: An Illustrated Historical Souvenir.* Providence: Preston and Rounds, c. 1897.

"Manning Hall Centennial Celebration, February 22, 1934." Typescript address, articles, and newspaper clippings. Brown University Archives, John Hay Library, Providence.

Manuscripts Pertaining to the Building of University Hall, three boxes (1769–1775). Brown University, John Carter Brown Library, Providence.

Mitchell, Martha. *Encyclopedia Brunoniana*. Providence: Brown University Library, 1993.

Munro, Walter Lee. "The Old Back Campus: Memories of the Area Known Since 1880 as the Middle Campus." *Brown Alumni Monthly* 28, no. 3 (October 1927): 67–68.

———. "The Old Back Campus II: Concerning Hope College and the Hope College Gas Light Association." *Brown Alumni Monthly* 28, no. 5 (December 1927): 119–20.

———. "The Old Back Campus III: Concerning the Hope College Attic and Prohibition of Bonfires." *Brown Alumni Monthly* 28, no. 7 (February 1928): 166–67.

———. "The Old Back Campus IV: Concerning Manning Hall." *Brown Alumni Monthly* 28, no. 8 (March 1928): 192–94.

———. "The Old Back Campus V: Concerning University Hall." *Brown Alumni Monthly* 28, no. 10 (May 1928): 245–46.

———. "The Old Back Campus VI: Concerning Rhode Island Hall." *Brown Alumni Monthly* 29, no. 1 (June 1928): 3–5.

"National Historic Landmark." *Brown Alumni Monthly* 50, no. 9 (July 1963): 17. University Hall.

"Natural History." *The Brunonian* 5, no. 5 (May 1872): 246–48. Rhode Island Hall.

"The New U.H." *Brown Alumni Monthly* 40, no. 5 (December 1939/ January 1940): 115. University Hall.

Old Providence: A Collection of Facts and Traditions Relating to Various Buildings and Sites of Historic Interest in Providence. Providence: Merchants National Bank of Providence, 1918. University Hall and Hope College.

Palmer, Henry Robinson. "Brown University." *New England Magazine* n.s. 20, no. 3 (May 1899): 293–314.

Presidential papers, c. 1770–1872. Brown University Archives, John Hay Library, Providence.

"Rededicating the 'College Edifice'" and "The Restoration." *Brown Alumni Monthly* 40, no. 8 (April 1940): 199–201.

"The Restoration of Hope College: 'Of National Importance.'" *Brown Alumni Monthly* 58, no. 6 (March 1958): 19.

"Restoration of University Hall." *Brown Alumni Monthly* 5, no. 7 (February 1905): 133–35.

"The Restoration of University Hall." *Brown Alumni Magazine* 6, no. 3 (October 1905): 49–53.

"The Restoration of University Hall." *Brown Alumni Monthly* 39, no. 8 (March 1939): 220.

The Sesquicentennial of Brown University, 1764–1914. Providence: Published by the University, 1915. Contains "The Early Years of Brown University, 1764–1770," an essay by William W. Keen.

"To Make a Brown Centennial." *Brown Alumni Monthly* 39, no. 7 (February 1939): 195.

"University Hall." *Brunonian* 13, no. 5 (6 December 1879): 48–49.

University Hall, Built in 1770, Reconstructed in 1940. Providence: Brown University, 1940.

Wayland, Francis. *The Dependence of Science upon Religion: A Discourse Delivered at the Dedication of Manning Hall, the Chapel and the Library of Brown University, February 4, 1835*. Providence: Marshall, Brown and Company, 1835. Building descriptions.

"Where a Man May Worship: Manning Hall, 60 Years Brown's Chapel, Will So Serve Once More." *Brown Alumni Monthly* 58, no. 6 (March 1958): 3–5.

Woodward, William McKenzie, and Edward F. Sanderson. *Providence: A Citywide Survey of Historical Resources*. Providence: Rhode Island State Historical Preservation Commission, 1986.

[Wriston, Henry H.]. "And the Years Look Down: President Wriston's Biography of University Hall, Written for the Rededication, May 4, 1940." *Brown Alumni Magazine* 41, no. 1 (June 1940): 9–10, 16.

Wriston, Henry M. "Our Architecture on College Hill." *Brown Alumni Monthly* 47, no. 3 (November–December 1946): 69–71.

Wroth, Laurence C. "The Construction of the College Edifice, 1770–1772 . . . A Study of the History of Brown University and Providence, Rhode Island." Typescript, 1962. Brown University Archives, John Hay Library, Providence.

D. Dartmouth College, Hanover, New Hampshire

Accepted and Rejected Plans for Wentworth and Thornton Halls and for Renovation of Dartmouth Hall by Ammi Burnham Young, 1828–29. Rauner Special Collections, Dartmouth College Library, Hanover.

Account of Expense of Erecting the College Edifice, Commenced, Feb. 7th, 1839 (Notebook of Reed Hall and Observatory Building Materials and Labor Expenditures). Rauner Special Collections, Dartmouth College Library, Hanover.

"Ammi Burnham Young, Architect of the Boston Custom House." *American Architect and Building News* 38 (19 November 1892): 124.

Barrett, Frank J., Jr. *Hanover, New Hampshire*. "Images of America." Dover, N.H.: Arcadia, 1997.

Bartlett, Edwin Julius. "Pen and Camera Sketches of Hanover and the College Before the Centennial, IV—The Old Chapel," *Dartmouth Alumni Magazine* 13 (May 1921): 442–50. Dartmouth Hall.

Bartlett, Samuel C. "Dartmouth College Sixty Years Ago." *Dartmouth Literary Monthly* 8, no. 5 (March 1894): 215–20.

———. "Eleazar Wheelock and Dartmouth College." *Granite Monthly* 11, nos. 8–10 (August–October 1888): 277–81.

Benezet, Roger P. "The History of Reed Hall." Student thesis, 1932. College Archives, Dartmouth College Library

Bisbee, Marvin Davis. "History of Dartmouth College from Its Beginning Until 1869." Unpublished ms., n.d. College Archives, Dartmouth College Library.

Bramen, Harold F. "The Fated Morning." *Dartmouth College Alumni Magazine* 56, no. 5 (1964): 28–30. Dartmouth Hall fire, 1904.

Bridenbaugh, Carl. "Peter Harrison Addendum." *Journal of the Society of Architectural Historians* 18 (December 1959): 158–59. Updates his 1949 book (below).

———. *Peter Harrison: First American Architect.* Chapel Hill: University of North Carolina Press, 1949.

"A Brief Account of Dartmouth-College in New-England." *American Museum* 2, no. 4 (October 1787): 343–44. Dartmouth Hall description.

"Brief Description of Dartmouth College with a View." *Massachusetts Magazine* 5 (February 1793): 67–68.

Centennial Celebration at Dartmouth College, July 21, 1869. Hanover: J. B. Parker, 1870.

Chase, Francis L., ed. *Hanover, New Hampshire: A Bicentennial Book.* Hanover: Town of Hanover, 1961.

Chase, Frederick. *A History of Dartmouth College and the Town of Hanover, New Hampshire*, ed. John K. Lord. Cambridge: J. Wilson and Son, 1891. First of a two-volume history of the college (to 1815), the second written by the editor, John K. Lord (below).

Childs, Francis Lane. "Dartmouth Hall—Old and New." *Dartmouth Alumni Magazine* 28 (January 1936): 7–17.

Currier, Amos N. "Dartmouth College." *Dartmouth Bi-Monthly* 1, no. 5 (July 1906): 244–55. Physical plant.

"Dartmouth College." *Gleason's Pictorial and Drawing-Room Companion* 5, no. 18 (29 October 1853): 280.

Dartmouth College Board of Trustees Records, 5 vols. plus index, 1770–1909. Rauner Special Collections, Dartmouth College Library, Hanover.

Dartmouth Hall Subscription Form, 1784. Rauner Special Collections, Dartmouth College Library, Hanover.

Eleazar Wheelock Papers. Rauner Special Collections, Dartmouth College Library, Hanover.

General Catalogue of Dartmouth College and the Associated Schools, 1769–1900, Including a Historical Sketch of the College Prepared by Marvin Davis Bisbee. Hanover: Printed for the college, 1900.

Gerould, James Thayer, and Marvin D. Bisbee. *Bibliography of Dartmouth College and Hanover, N.H.* Concord, N.H.: Edward N. Pearson, 1894.

Hapgood, Herbert. J., ed. *Echoes from Dartmouth: A Collection of Poems, Stories, and Historical Sketches by Graduate and Undergraduate Writers of Dartmouth College.* Hanover: C. M. Stone and Company, 1895.

Hill, Ralph Nading, ed. *The College on the Hill: A Dartmouth Chronicle.* Hanover: Dartmouth Publications, 1964.

Hoefnagel, Dick, with Virginia Close. *Eleazar Wheelock and the Adventurous Founding of Dartmouth College.* Hanover: Durand Press for the Hanover Historical Society, 2002.

Hopkins, Ernest H., ed. *Exercises and Addresses Attending the Laying of the Cornerstone of the New Dartmouth Hall . . ., October 25 and 26, 1904.* Hanover: Printed for the College, 1905.

[Kelly, Eric P.]. "The Burning of Dartmouth Hall." *Dartmouth Alumni Magazine* 21, no. 5 (March 1929): 287, 289–90.

Kenney, R. L. "The History of Wentworth and Thornton Halls." Student thesis (1935), College Archives, Dartmouth College Library.

Lenning, Henry F. "A History of Dartmouth Hall." Unpublished ms. (c. 1937), College Archives, Dartmouth College Library.

Lord, John King. *A History of Dartmouth College (1815–1909).* Concord, N.H.: Rumford Press, 1913. Sequel to 1891 history by Frederick Chase (above).

———. "The Building of Dartmouth Hall." *Dartmouth Alumni Magazine* 14, no. 5 (March 1922): 346–47.

McCallum, James Dow. *Eleazar Wheelock, Founder of Dartmouth College.* Hanover: Dartmouth College Publications, 1939.

Meacham, Scott. *The Campus Guide: Dartmouth College.* New York: Princeton Architectural Press, 2008.

Moran, Geoffrey P. "The Post Office and Custom House at Portsmouth, New Hampshire, and Its Architect, Ammi Burnham Young." *Old-Time New England* 58, no. 4 (April–June 1967): 85–102.

Morgan, William. "A Case for the Permanent Preservation of the Dartmouth College Observatory." Student thesis, 1966, College Archives, Dartmouth College Library.

Morris, Edwin B. "Ammi B. Young." *Journal of the American Institute of Architects* 1 (February 1944): 69–71.

Orsenigo, Eugene J. "The Medical School at Dartmouth College, Hanover, New Hampshire." Typescript, 1934, College Archives, Dartmouth College Library.

Overby, Osmund R. "Ammi B. Young: An Architectural Sketch." *Magazine Antiques* 81 (May 1962): 530–33.

———. "Ammi B. Young in the Connecticut Valley." *Journal of the Society of Architectural Historians* 29, no. 3 (October 1960): 119–20.

Patrick, Vanessa E. "The Dartmouth College Green: Union of New England Town and American Campus." Master's thesis, University of Virginia, 1978. College Archives, Dartmouth College Library.

Plan Sheets for the [Shattuck] Astronomical Observatory by Ammi Burnham Young (c. 1854). Rauner Special Collections, Dartmouth College Library, Hanover.

Quint, Wilder D. *The Story of Dartmouth*. Boston: Little, Brown, 1914.

Rejected Plan Sheet for Dartmouth Hall by William Gamble (c. 1773). Rauner Special Collections, Dartmouth College Library, Hanover.

"Reminiscences of Hanover" [Made at Dartmouth College, Hanover, New Hampshire, in 1842 at the request of President Nathan Lord] by William W. Dewey. Edited and published by the Hanover Historical Society, 1964. Frederick Chase Collection, Rauner Special Collections, Dartmouth College Library, Hanover.

Reports of the Presidents of Dartmouth College (1828–60). Rauner Special Collections, Dartmouth College Library, Hanover.

Renovation Drawings for Dartmouth, Wentworth, Thornton and Reed Halls. Department of Grounds and Buildings, Dartmouth College Library, Hanover.

Richardson, Charles F. "Dartmouth Architecture." *Dartmouth Magazine* 15, no. 1 (November 1900): 1–19.

Richardson, Leon B. *History of Dartmouth College*. Hanover: Dartmouth College Publications, 1932.

———. "Brief Biographies of Buildings: I—Wentworth and Thornton Halls." *Dartmouth Alumni Magazine* 35, no. 1 (October 1942): 11–12.

———. "Brief Biographies of Buildings: II—Reed Hall." *Dartmouth Alumni Magazine* 35, no. 2 (November 1942): 21.

Rugg, Harold G. *Dartmouth College Engravings*. Hanover: Dartmouth College Press, 1925.

Smith, Perry Baxter. *The History of Dartmouth College*. Boston: Houghton Osgood and Company, 1878.

Tolles, Bryant F., Jr. "Ammi Burnham Young and the Gilmanton Theological Seminary." *Old-Time New England* 61, no. 2 (October–December 1970): 47–54, 56.

———. "The Evolution of a Campus: Dartmouth College Architecture Before 1860." *Historical New Hampshire* 42, no. 4 (Winter 1987): 329–82.

Vallentine, B. B. "Dartmouth College." *Manhattan Magazine* 3, no. 3 (March 1884): 195–205. Contains building illustrations.

Wheelock, John. *Sketches of the History of Dartmouth College and Moor's Charity School, with a particular account of some late remarkable proceedings of the Board of Trustees, from the year 1779 to the year 1815*. Newburyport, Mass.: n.p., 1815.

Williams, Wendell H. "The Architectural History of the Observatory." Student thesis, 1934. College Archives, Dartmouth College Library.

Wodehouse, Lawrence. "Ammi Burnham Young, 1798–1874." *Journal of the Society of Architectural Historians* 25, no. 4 (December 1966): 268–80.

———. "Ammi Young's Architecture in Northern New England." *Vermont History* 36, no. 2 (Spring 1968): 54–58.

Younger, Charlotte K. "Dartmouth Hall (1784–1984): A Bicentennial Tribute." *Dartmouth Alumni Magazine* 77, no. 4 (December 1984): 44–47.

E. Williams College, Williamstown, Massachusetts

"The Architecture of a Lamented Genius, Thomas Alexander Tefft." M.A. thesis, Brown University, 1971. Brown University Archives, Providence.

Ballinger, Richard A. "Williams College." *New England Magazine* n.s. 42, no. 2 (April 1910): 143–53.

Bidwell, O. C. "Early Williams." *Williams Literary Monthly* 1, no. 3 (July 1885): 122–28.

Brooks, Robert R. R., ed. *Williamstown: The First Two Hundred Years, 1753–1953*. Williamstown: McClelland Press, 1953. 2nd ed., Williamstown Historical Commission, 1954.

Cash Book, 1825–30. Williams College Archives and Special Collections, Williamstown.

Catalogue of the Corporation, Officers, and Students of Williams College. Williamstown: Williams College, 1822–92.

Creese, Walter. "Fowler and the Domestic Octagon." *Art Bulletin* 28, no. 2 (January 1946): 89–102. Hopkins Observatory.

Collections of the Berkshire Historical and Scientific Society. 3 vols. Pittsfield, Mass.: Sun Printing, 1892–99.

The Crank. "Concerning the Hermitage." *Williams Athenaeum* 10, no. 3 (26 May 1883): 36–37. Magnetic Observatory.

Davis, Horace. "Williams College in 1845." *University of California Chronicle* 14, no. 1 (c. 1911).

Denison, John H. *Mark Hopkins: A Biography*. New York: Charles Scribner's Sons, 1935.

"Description of College Buildings in Existence, c. 1840." Typescript excerpts from printed sources. Williams College Archives and Special Collections, Williamstown.

Durfee, Reverend Calvin. *A History of Williams College*. Boston: A. Williams and Company, 1860.

Egleston, Nathaniel H. *Williamstown and Williams College*. Washington, D.C.: Judd and Detweiler, 1884.

"Griffin Hall." *Williams Quarterly* 9, no. 1 (August 1861): 65.

Hopkins, Albert. *An Address Delivered at the Opening of the Observatory at Williams College, June 12, 1838*. Pittsfield, Mass.: Phineas and Allen and Sons, 1838.

Hopkins, Mark. *Religious Teaching and Worship; A Sermon Preached at the Dedication of the New Chapel Connected with Williams College, September 22, 1859*. Boston: T. R. Marvin, 1859.

"Jackson Hall, 1855–1908." Typescript by John Adams Lowe, n.d. Williams College Archives and Special Collections, Williamstown.

"Lawrence Hall—A New Design." B.A. honors thesis, Lawrence Ward Chapman, 1953. Williams College Archives and Special Collections, Williamstown.

Lewis, R. Cragin, ed. *Williams, 1793–1993: A Pictorial History.* Williamstown: Williams College Bicentennial Commission, 1993.

Lowe, John Adams. "The Story of a College Building." *Williams Literary Monthly* 17, no. 9 (April 1902): 437–42. Griffin Hall.

———. "Williams in 1830." *Williams Literary Monthly* 21, no. 3 (October 1905): 138–40.

———. "Williams of Yesteryear—VI. Kellogg Hall, 1847." *Williams Literary Monthly* 21, no. 8 (March 1906): 402–3.

———. *Williamsiana: A Bibliography of Pamphlets and Books Relating to the History of Williams College, 1793–1911.* Williamstown: Trustees of Williams College, 1911.

"Magnetic Observatory." *Williams Quarterly* 10, no. 2 (November 1862): 144.

Malmstrom, R. E. *Lawrence Hall at Williams College.* Williamstown: Williams College Museum of Art, [1979].

Mehlin, Theodore Grefe. "Williams College Renovates Hopkins Observatory." *Sky and Telescope* 23, no. 2 (February 1962): 1–4.

Milham, Willis I. *The History of Astronomy in Williams College and the Founding of Hopkins Observatory.* Williamstown: Williams College, 1937.

"Nathan Jackson, Benefactor." *Williams Alumni Review* 29, no. 8 (June 1927): 354–57. Jackson Hall.

Niles, Grace G. "Albert Hopkins and Williamstown." *New England Magazine* n.s. 31, no. 6 (February 1905): 665–80.

"Old Williams" photograph album, n.d. Williams College Archives and Special Collections, Williamstown.

"Old Williamstown Memories: Its Main Streets and College Buildings a Half Century Ago." *Berkshire Hills* n.s. 1 (1904–5): 25–28.

"Our Campus Architecture." *Williams Graphic* 1, no. 2 (1921): 10–11.

Perry, Arthur Latham. *Williamstown and Williams College.* Williamstown: Privately printed, 1899. 3rd ed., Norwood, Mass.: Norwood Press, 1904.

Records of the Trustees of Williams College (microfilm). Williams College Archives and Special Collections, Williamstown.

"Records of Various Donations and Legacies, 1793–1885." Unpublished ms. Williams College Archives and Special Collections, Williamstown.

Rice, Richard A., and Leverett W. Spring. *Williams College, Williamstown, Mass.: Historical Sketch and Views.* Boston: Geo. H. Ellis Company, 1904.

Rudolph, Frederick. *Mark Hopkins and the Log: Williams College, 1836–1872.* New Haven: Yale University Press, 1956.

Safford, Truman H. *A Discourse Read June 25, 1888, to Commemorate the Fiftieth Anniversary of the Dedication of the Hopkins Observatory at Williams College.* Williamstown: Williams College, 1888.

Salisbury, Elon G. *In the Days of Mark Hopkins: Story of Williams College.* Phelps, N.Y.: Salisbury Press, 1927.

Spring, Leverett W. *A History of Williams College.* Boston: Houghton Mifflin, 1917.

———. "Williams College." *New England Magazine* n.s. 9, no. 2 (October 1893): 161–79.

Statement of Costs Relating to the Moving of Griffin Hall, unpublished ms., n.d. Williams College Archives and Special Collections, Williamstown.

Stoddard, Whitney S. *Reflections on the Architecture of Williams College.* Williamstown: Williams College, 2001.

"The Story of a College Building." *Williams Literary Monthly* 17, no. 9 (April 1902): 438–42. Griffin Hall.

"Three Chapels." *Argo* 2, no. 1 (29 April 1882): 4–5; and no. 2 (20 May 1882): 20–21. West College, Griffin Hall, and College Chapel.

Warren, Philip H., Jr. *What's in a Name: The Buildings of Williams College: A Collection of Essays.* Williamstown: Williams College, 1999.

Wells, David Ames, and Samuel H. Davis. *Sketches of Williams College, Williamstown.* Springfield, Mass.: H. S. Taylor, 1847.

"Williams College." *American Advocate* 2, no. 75 (10 September 1828): 90–91.

Williams College: Indelible Photographs. New York: Albertype Company, 1890.

Williams College. 1886. West Gardner, Mass.: Adams and Aldrich, c. 1886. Phototypes.

"Williams College Architecture, 1790–1860." 2 vols. B.A. honors thesis, Bruce Burr McElvein, 1979. Williams College Archives and Special Collections, Williamstown.

"Williams College Architecture and Physical Plant Projects," Department of Buildings and Grounds. Williams College Archives and Special Collections, Williamstown.

"Williams College Library." *Norton's Literary Gazette and Publisher's Circular* 3, no. 3 (18 March 1853).

Williams College Records of the Faculty, 1821–71. Williams College Archives and Special Collections, Williamstown.

Williamstown Free School file. Williams College Archives and Special Collections, Williamstown.

Wriston, Barbara. "The Architecture of Thomas Tefft." *Bulletin of the Rhode Island School of Design* 28, no. 2 (November 1940): 37–45.

F. Bowdoin College, Brunswick, Maine

Anderson, Patricia McGraw. *The Architecture of Bowdoin College.* Brunswick: Bowdoin College Museum of Art, 1988. Photographs by Richard Cheek.

Bowdoin College, 1794–1949: An Historical Sketch. . . . Portland, Maine: Anthoensen Press, 1950.

"Bowdoin College." *American Magazine of Useful and Entertaining Knowledge* 3, no. 6 (March 1837): 215–17.

Boyer, Kenneth J. "Library Facilities at Bowdoin College, 1802–1960." *Bowdoin Alumnus* 34 (December 1959): 2–7.

Brault, Gerald Joseph. "A Checklist of Portraits of the Campus of Bowdoin College Before the Civil War." Typescript, Bowdoin College, 1960. Special Collections and Archives, Bowdoin College Library.

———. "The Earliest Painting of the Bowdoin College Campus." *Old-Time New England* 51, no. 4 (Spring 1961): 101–3.

———. "Notes on Samuel Melcher, III and Bowdoin College." Typescript, 1961. Special Collections and Archives, Bowdoin College Library.

Building Agreement . . . Samuel Melcher and Sons . . . and the President and Trustees of Bowdoin College (1843). Special Collections and Archives, Bowdoin College Library.

Building Files, miscellaneous mss. (12 boxes). Special Collections and Archives, Bowdoin College Library.

Building Files, miscellaneous printed and photocopied materials (3 boxes). Special Collections and Archives, Bowdoin College Library.

Calhoun, Charles C. *A Small College in Maine: Two Hundred Years of Bowdoin.* Brunswick: Bowdoin College, 1993.

Campus views (4 boxes of prints, photographs). Special Collections and Archives, Bowdoin College Library.

Cleaveland, Nehemiah, and Alpheus Packard. *History of Bowdoin College with Biographical Sketches of Its Graduates from 1806 to 1879, Inclusive.* Boston: James Ripley Osgood and Company, 1882.

College Records, boxes (1796–1846). Special Collections and Archives, Bowdoin College Library.

Daggett, Athern P. "The Chapel." *Bowdoin Alumnus* 20 (November 1945): 3–4.

"Domestic Correspondence from Bowdoin College." *World* (New York), 9 August 1860. Physical description of Bowdoin College.

Durall, Frank J. "Bowdoin College." *High School Rostrum* (Guilford High School, Guilford, Maine) 3, no. 1 (October 1896): 2–7. Architecture and campus plan.

Hatch, Louis C. *The History of Bowdoin College.* Portland, Maine: Loring, Short and Harmon, 1927.

Hawthorne, Manning. "Nathanial Hawthorne at Bowdoin." *New England Quarterly* 13, no. 2 (June 1940): 246–79.

"Historical Sketch of Bowdoin College." *American Quarterly Register* 8, no. 2 (November 1835): 105–17.

Howell, Roger, Jr. "Evidences of the Massachusetts Hall Cupola." *Bowdoin Alumnus* 33 (February 1959): 13.

Leonard Woods–Robert Gardiner Letters (1839–66). Special Collections and Archives, Bowdoin College Library.

Letter Copy Book of Joseph McKeen, College Treasurer (1837–63). Special Collections and Archives, Bowdoin College Library.

Little, George T. "Historical Sketch of the Institution During the First Century." *General Catalogue of Bowdoin College and the Medical School of Maine, 1794–1894.* Brunswick: Bowdoin College, 1894.

The Medical School of Maine and Seth Adams Hall. Brunswick: Bowdoin College, 1965.

Minutes of the Visiting Committee of the Boards of Trustees and Overseers of Bowdoin College (1826–64). Special Collections and Archives, Bowdoin College Library.

"The Old Chapel." *Bowdoin Orient* 13, no. 15 (5 March 1884): 212–14.

"The Old Chapel and the New." *Bowdoin Orient* 2, no. 12 (3 February 1873): 180–81.

"Old Massachusetts." *Bowdoin Orient* 13, no. 11 (19 December 1883): 156–58.

Packard, George T. "Bowdoin College." *Scribner's Monthly* 12, no. 1 (May 1876): 47–60.

Paul A. Chadbourne Letters. Special Collections and Archives, Bowdoin College Library.

Putnam, Henry. *"A Description of Brunswick, (Maine); in Letters by a Gentleman from South Carolina, to a Friend in That State."* Brunswick: Joseph Griffin, 1820. A letter passage describes the early Bowdoin open quadrangle campus.

Records of the Boards of Trustees and Overseers of Bowdoin College (1793–1863). Special Collections and Archives, Bowdoin College Library.

"Richard, Richard M., Hobart Upjohn, Architects, 1833–1933." *Architectural Record* 73, no. 5 (May 1933): 322.

"Richard Upjohn." *American Architect and Building News* 4, no. 139 (24 August 1878): 60. Obituary notice.

"Richard Upjohn." *American Architect and Building News* 4, no. 141 (7 September 1878): 82–84.

Samuel Melcher, III Ledger (Day) Books (1803–57). Pejepscot Historical Society, Brunswick. Special Collections and Archives, Bowdoin College Library.

Shipman, William D. *The Early Architecture of Bowdoin College and Brunswick, Maine.* Brunswick: Brunswick Publishing, 1973.

———. "Samuel Melcher II, 1775–1862." *A Biographical Dictionary of Architects in Maine* 5, no. 13. Augusta: Maine Historic Preservation Commission, 1988.

Slattery, Charles Lewis. "Brunswick and Bowdoin College." *New England Magazine* n.s. 5, no. 4 (December 1891): 448–69.

Time Book for the Construction of the Bowdoin College Chapel (May 1851–December 1854), Samuel Melcher, III, et al. Special Collections and Archives, Bowdoin College Library.

Treasurer's Account Books (1803–21). Special Collections and Archives, Bowdoin College Library.

Wheeler, George Augustus, and Henry Warren Wheeler. *History of Brunswick, Topsham and Hartswell, Maine*. Boston: Alfred Mudge and Son, 1878.

Woods, Leonard. *Address on the Opening of the New Hall of the Medical School of Maine*. Brunswick: Telegraph Office, A. G. Tenney, 1862.

G. University of Vermont, Burlington

Allen, Charles E. *About Burlington, Vermont*. Burlington: Hobart J. Shanley and Company, 1905.

———. "Early History of the University of Vermont and the First Graduating Class." *Burlington Free Press*, 2 July 1904.

Auld, Joseph. *Picturesque Burlington: A Handbook*. 2nd ed. Burlington: Free Press Association, 1894.

Benedict, G. G. "Burlington, Vermont." *New England Magazine* n.s. 11, no. 5 (January 1895): 547–63.

Benedict, George Wyllys. "History of the University of Vermont." *American Quarterly Register* 13 (May 1841): 391–402.

[Benedict, George W.]. "The University Buildings in the Past." *Burlington Free Press*, 15 August 1882.

Buckham, Matthew H. "One Hundred Years of the University of Vermont." *The Areil*, 1905, 18, pp. 209–12. Yearbook of the University of Vermont.

Catalogue of the Officers and Students of the University of Vermont for 1825. Burlington: University of Vermont, 1825.

Chapin, William A. R. *History: University of Vermont College of Medicine*. Hanover, N.H.: Dartmouth Printing, 1951.

Clark, Prof. N. G. "University of Vermont." In Abby Maria Hemenway, *The Vermont State Historical Gazetteer*, vol. 1. Burlington: Published by the author, 1867–92. Pp. 521–30.

Crockett, Walter Hill. "The Beginnings of the University of Vermont." *Vermont Alumnus* 5 (11 November, 2 and 16 December 1925; 24 February 1926): 83–84, 131, 137–38, 166, 169–70, 282. Covers the period 1777–1806.

Daniels, Robert V., ed. *The University of Vermont: The First Hundred Years*. Hanover: University Press of New England, 1991.

"Early Architecture in Vermont." *Burlington Free Press*, 12 July 1922.

Gayer, Diane Elliott. "UVM's 'Old Mill' Enters 21st Century." *AIA Vermont Report*, June 1997, p. 1.

Goodrich, John E. "One Hundred Years Ago: The Beginnings of the University of Vermont." *The Areil, 1905*, 18, pp. 213–18.

———. "Sketch of the University of Vermont." *The University Cynic* 19, no. 8 (9 November 1901): 143–48; no. 9 (23 November 1901): 159–63; no. 10 (7 December 1901): 175–77; no. 11 (21 December 1901): 192–97; no. 12 (11 January 1902): 209–14.

———. "The University of Vermont." *Vermonter* 2, no. 10 (May 1897): 157–65.

Graffagnino, Kevin. "John Johnson." *Vermonter* magazine section, *Burlington Free Press*, 6 July 1980, pp. 3–4.

Hill, Ralph Nading. "The Clock Maker of Old Burlington (Lemuel Curtis)." *Vermont Life* 21, no. 1 (Autumn 1966): 42–46. Banjo clock painting of the "College Edifice," University of Vermont.

Jennings, James. "The University of Vermont: A State University Reassesses Its Past and Lays Plans for the Future." *Vermont Life* 3, no. 3 (Spring 1949): 54–57.

John Johnson Papers. Special Collections, University of Vermont Libraries.

Letters of Professor George W. Benedict. Special Collections, University of Vermont Libraries.

Lewis, Robert E. "The University of Vermont." *New England Magazine* n.s. 15, no. 1 (September 1896): 64–79.

Lindsay, Julian Ira. *Tradition Looks Forward: The University of Vermont: A History, 1791–1904*. Burlington: University of Vermont and State Agricultural College, 1954.

———. "University of Vermont Also Is Celebrating Sesquicentennial." *Burlington Daily News* 74, no. 53 (4 March 1941): 4–6.

Minutes of the Board of Trustees of the University of Vermont (1791–1860). Special Collections, University of Vermont Libraries.

Mudgett, Katherine. "Medical Building at Century Mark." *Vermont Alumni Weekly* 9, no. 1 (2 October 1929): 7.

Poole, George Howard. "Vt. Campus Tradition Centers About Venerable 'Old Mill.'" *Vermont Alumnus* 7 (8 February 1928): 231, 235.

President Daniel Clarke Sanders Papers. Special Collections, University of Vermont Libraries.

Records of the Trustee Meetings at the University of Vermont (1827–60). Special Collections, University of Vermont Libraries.

Thomas, John D. *University of Vermont*. "The Campus History Series." Charleston, S.C.: Arcadia, 2005.

Tolles, Bryant F., Jr. "The 'College Edifice' (1801–1807) at the University of Vermont." *Vermont History* 40, no. 1 (Winter 1972): 1–9.

———. "The 'Old Mill' (1825–29) at the University of Vermont." *Vermont History* 57, no. 1 (Winter 1989): 22–34.

Torrey, Joseph. "The 'Old Brick Mill.'" *The Ariel, 1913*, pp. 7, 191–93.

"University of Vermont at Burlington." *Vermont Sentinal* (Burlington), 24 July 1805, p. 2.

"The University of Vermont and State Agricultural College." *Vermonter, the State Magazine* 16, no. 1 (January 1911): 53–59.

"UVM History," typescript by Joseph L. Hills. Accounts of buildings. Special Collections, University of Vermont Libraries.

Wheeler, John F. *A Historical Discourse . . . Semi-Centennial Anniversary of the University of Vermont*. Burlington: Free Press Print, 1854.

Wilbur, James Benjamin. *Ira Allen: Founder of Vermont, 1751–1814*. 2 vols. Boston: Houghton Mifflin, 1928.

H. Middlebury College, Middlebury, Vermont

Addresses and Proceedings at the Semi-Centennial Celebration of Middlebury College held at Middlebury, Vermont, August 20, 21 and 22, 1850. Middlebury: Justus Cobb, Register Office, 1850.

Andres, Glenn M. *A Walking History of Middlebury, Vermont*. Middlebury: Middlebury Bicentennial Commission, 1975.

Bain, David H. *The College on the Hill: A Browser's History for the Bicentennial—1800 Middlebury College 2000*. Middlebury: Middlebury College Press, 1999.

Blake, Clarence E. "Middlebury College." *New England Magazine* n.s. 11, no. 2 (October 1894): 129–46.

Cady, Frank W. "History of Middlebury College, 1800–1920." Unpublished typescript, n.d. College Archives, Special Collections, Middlebury College.

Catalogue of Middlebury College, Middlebury, Vermont . . ., 1902–03. Middlebury: Middlebury College, 1902. Historical section, pp. 3–9.

Celebration of the Sixtieth Anniversary of Middlebury College: Addresses and a Poem on Laying the Cornerstone of a New Edifice. Middlebury: Register Book and Job Office, 1860. Starr Hall, the last of the "Old Stone Row" buildings.

Connell, Edward A. "Middlebury—the Beauty of Variety." *American Landscape Architect* 11, no. 2 (February 1932): 21–25.

Fowler, William C. "Historical Sketch of Middlebury College." *American Quarterly Register* 9 (February 1837): 220–29.

Gamaliel Painter's Day Book for "Stone College" (1811–16). College Archives, Special Collections, Middlebury College.

Hendrie, Edwin J. "History of Middlebury College." Unpublished typescript, 1931. College Archives, Special Collections, Middlebury College.

Labaree, Reverend Benjamin, President of the College. "Outline History of His Several Endeavors to Obtain Funds for Middlebury College from 1840 to 1868 together with some peculiar facts connected with that History." Unpublished handscript booklet, [c. 1868]. College Archives, Special Collections, Middlebury College. Construction and reconstruction of Starr Hall.

Lee, W. Storrs. *Father Went to College: The Story of Middlebury*. New York: Wilson-Erickson, 1936.

———. *Town Father: A Biography of Gamiel Painter*. New York: Hastings House, 1952. Chapter on the founding of Middlebury College.

Merrill, Thomas A. *Semicentennial Sermon Containing a History of Middlebury, Vermont*. Middlebury: E. Maxhorn, 1841.

Middlebury College: A Souvenir Published by Class of '98. Rutland, Vt.: Tuttle Company, 1898. Commentary about academic and residential facilities.

"Middlebury College." *Addison County Newspaper List*, Pictorial Supplement, 3 May 1923. Contains campus views.

"Middlebury College—Centennial Anniversary." *Vermonter* 6, no. 1 (August 1900): 3–8.

Middlebury College Bulletin, Catalogue Number, 1969–70. Middlebury: Middlebury College, June 1969. Information section contains building data.

Prentiss, Charles E. "Middlebury College." *University Magazine* 1, no. 2 (August 1904): 9–29.

President and Fellows Minutes of the Annual Meetings, November 4, 1800–June 28, 1899. College Archives, Special Collections, Middlebury College.

Renovation Plans for Painter Hall, Old Chapel and Starr Hall. Maintenance Department, Middlebury College.

Robinson, Duane. "Sesquicentennial at Middlebury." *Vermont Life* 4, no. 4 (Summer 1950): 22–29. Campus illustrations.

Smith, Albee. "The Burning of Starr Hall." *The Undergraduate* (Middlebury College) (April 1899): 48–49.

Stameshkin, David M. *The Town's College: Middlebury College, 1800–1915*. Middlebury: Middlebury College Press, 1985.

———. *The Strength of the Hills: Middlebury College, 1915–1990*. Middlebury: Middlebury College Press, 1996.

Subscription Books (1812–60). Maintenance Department, Middlebury College.

Swift, Samuel. *History of the Town of Middlebury in the County of Addison, Vermont*. Middlebury: A. H. Copeland, 1859.

Treasurer's Accounts Books (1801–62). Maintenance Department, Middlebury College.

Wiley, Edgar J. *Catalogue of the Officers and Students of Middlebury College . . ., 1800–1927*. Middlebury: Middlebury College, 1928. Historical essay, pp. xi–xviii.

Wright, Charles B. "Sketch of Middlebury College." *Education* 19, no. 10 (June 1899): 594–603.

I. Norwich University (American Literary, Scientific and Military Academy), Northfield, Vermont

"American Literary, Scientific and Military Academy at Norwich, Vermont." *American Journal of Education* 13 (n.s. 3), no. 1 (March 1863): 65–72.

"American Literary, Scientific, and Military Academy at Norwich, Vermont." In *Military Schools and Courses of Instruction in the Science and Art of War*, ed. Henry Barnard (New York: E. Steiger, 1872), pp. 857–88.

Articles of Agreement . . . between Pierce Bouton, Alden Partridge, and Thomas Emerson, 1819. Norwich University Archives and Special Collections, Kreitzberg Library.

Captain Alden T. Partridge Letters (1807–35). Norwich University Archives and Special Collections, Kreitzberg Library.

Catalogue of the Officers and Cadets of the American Literary, Scientific and Military Academy for 1827. Middletown, Conn.: A.L.S.&M. Academy, 1827.

Description of a Building for a Literary, Scientific and Military Academy, 1819. Norwich University Archives and Special Collections, Kreitzberg Library.

Dewey, Adelbert M. *The Life and Letters of Admiral Dewey.* New York: Wadfall Company, 1899. Norwich University, pp. 79–100.

Dodge, Major General Grenville M., and William A. Ellis. *Norwich University, 1819–1911: Her History, Her Graduates, Her Roll of Honor.* 3 vols. Montpelier, Vt.: Capital City Press, 1911.

Ellis, William A. *Norwich University: Her History, Her Graduates, Her Roll of Honor.* Concord, N.H.: Rumford Press, 1898. Superseded by 1911 Dodge and Ellis history (above).

Goddard, M. E., and Henry V. Partridge. *A History of Norwich, Vermont.* Hanover, N.H.: Dartmouth Press, 1905.

"Know Your Town"—The 1940 Survey of Norwich, Vermont. Norwich: Norwich Woman's Club, 1942.

"Norwich University." *University Quarterly* (April 1861): 415–20.

"Norwich University." *University Reveille* 1 (December 1860): 5–6.

Shelden, N. L. "Norwich University." *New England Magazine* n.s. 20, no. 1 (March 1899): 65–88.

Some Pages of Norwich History: A Bicentennial Publication. Norwich, Vt.: Bicentennial Committee, 1961. Brief history of Norwich University by Professor Allen Foley, pp. 43–56.

White, Reverend Homer. *History of Norwich University, Northfield, Vermont.* Northfield: C. N. Whitmarsh, 1891.

White, Philip Aylwin, and Dana Doane Johnson. *Early Houses of Norwich, Vermont,* ed. Hugh S. Morrison. Hanover, N.H.: Dartmouth College, 1938. 2nd ed., Norwich: Norwich Historical Society, 1973. Sections devoted to Norwich University buildings.

J. Amherst College, Amherst, Massachusetts

Account Book of John Leland, Jr., Treasurer of Amherst College. Archives and Special Collections, Amherst College Library.

Allen, Rebecca. "The Octagon: A Building with a Rich History." *Amherst Student* (20 October 1986): 9.

Amherst College—Dedication of Johnson Chapel. Amherst: Amherst College, 1934.

"Amherst College Buildings and Grounds: Historical Information." Looseleaf notebook, 2007 ed. revised, by Ralph C. McGoun and M. B. Taft. Archives and Special Collections, Amherst College Library.

Amherst College Trustees—Prudential Committee Votes Concerning Buildings and Grounds, 24 November 1824–4 August 1835. Archives and Special Collections, Amherst College Library.

Amherst Student (Amherst College) (1891–94 series on Amherst College buildings).

"Amherst's Library." *Amherst Student,* 17 February 1894.

Amherst, the Village Beautiful. Amherst: Press of Carpenter and Morehouse, 1892.

Annals of Amherst College . . . together with a Popular Guide to the College Buildings and Various Cabinets. Northampton, Mass.: Trumbull and Gore, and Amherst: J. S. and C. Adams, 1860.

Beardslee, Clark S., and G. A. Plimpton. *Popular Guide to the Public Buildings and Museum of Amherst College.* Amherst: By the College, 1875.

"The Art Gallery." *Amherst Record,* 8 July 1874.

"Barrett Gymnasium." *Amherst Student,* 28 January 1909.

Buildings and Grounds Files, 1820s+. Archives and Special Collections, Amherst College Library.

Carpenter, Edward W., and Charles F. Morehouse. *History of the Town of Amherst, Massachusetts.* Amherst: Carpenter and Morehouse, 1896.

Emerson, Margaret R. "High upon Her Living Throne." *Amherst Graduate's Quarterly* (May 1948): 198–200.

Field, Thomas P. *A Brief History of Amherst College, 1821–1900.* Washington, D.C.: Government Printing Office, 1889.

Fuess, Claude Moore. *Amherst: The Story of a New England College.* Boston: Little, Brown, 1935.

A Guide to Amherst College. Amherst: Exhibits Committee for the Centennial Celebration, 1921.

Guide to Amherst College. Amherst: Alumni Council, 1934.

Guide to Amherst College Buildings for Campus Guides. Typescript, c. 1965. Archives and Special Collections, Amherst College Library.

Hitchcock, Charles H. *The Visitor's Guide to the Public Rooms and Cabinets of Amherst College. . . .* Amherst: Published by the College, 1862.

Hitchcock, Edward. *A Popular Description of the New Cabinet and Astronomical Observatory of Amherst College for the Use of Visitors.* Amherst: J. S. and C. Adams, 1848.

———. *Reminiscences of Amherst College. . . .* Northampton, Mass.: Bridgeman and Childs, 1863.

Hitchcock, Frederick H. *The Handbook of Amherst, Massachusetts.* Amherst: n.p., 1891. Rev. ed., Amherst: F. H. Hitchcock, 1894.

Humphrey, Heman. *Sketches of the Early History of Amherst College.* N.p.: F. W. Stearns, [1905]. Pamphlet.

Kirkwood, Robert. "Johnson Chapel at Amherst College." Student paper, 1975. Archives and Special Collections, Amherst College Library.

King, Stanley. *"The Consecrated Eminence": The Story of the Campus and Buildings of Amherst College.* Amherst: By the College, 1951.

Le Duc, Thomas H. A. *Piety and Intellect at Amherst College, 1865–1912.* New York: Columbia University Press, 1946. Reprint, New York: Arno Press and the New York Times, 1969.

McCarthy, Colleen. "Classicism, Chemistry and the Campus Center: Amherst's Architecture Defines a Small College." *Amherst Student* (8 November 1996): 8–9.

Merrill, David O. "Isaac Damon and the Architecture of the Federal Period in New England [with] Illustrations." Ph.D. diss., Yale University, 1965.

———. "Isaac Damon and the Southwick Column Papers." *Old-Time New England* 54, no. 2 (Fall 1963): 48–58.

Morsman, Whitney H. "The Foundations of Amherst College: A Landmark of Education." Student paper, 1996. Archives and Special Collections, Amherst College Library.

Norton, Paul F. *Amherst: A Guide to Its Architecture.* Amherst: Amherst Historical Society, 1975. College buildings, pp. 73–99.

Phillips, Paul C. "The Truth About Barrett Gymnasium." *Amherst Graduates Quarterly* 21 (1931–32): 37–41.

Rand, Frank Prentice. *The Village of Amherst: A Landmark of Light.* Amherst: Amherst Historical Society, 1958.

Riley, H. E. *An Amherst Book: A Collection of Stories, Poems, Songs, Sketches and Historical Articles by Alumni and Undergraduates of Amherst College.* Amherst: n.p., 1896.

Todd, David. "Early History of Astronomy at Amherst College." *Popular Astronomy* 106 (January 1903).

Tyler, Reverend William Seymour. *A History of Amherst College During Its First Half Century, 1821–1871.* Springfield, Mass.: Clark W. Bryan and Company, 1873.

———. *History of Amherst College . . . from 1821–1891.* New York: Frederick H. Hitchcock, 1895.

Waff, Craig B. "Providence will send us a fitting telescope . . . just at the right time [Amherst College's Lawrence Observatory]." *Griffith Observer* 71, no. 9 (August 2007): 2–13.

Webb, Matthew Scott. "Buildings for Investigative Learning: Changing Architecture on the Amherst College Campus of the 1840s and 1850s." Student paper, 1996. Archives and Special Collections, Amherst College Library.

Wilson, Douglas, ed. and contributor. *Passages of Time: Narratives in the History of Amherst College.* Amherst: Amherst College Press, 2007.

Young, Malcolm Oakman. *Amherstiana: A Bibliography of Amherst College.* Amherst: Amherst College, 1921.

K. *The College of the Holy Cross, Worcester, Massachusetts*

"Architecture—Description of Buildings at Holy Cross College." Looseleaf notebook by Linda Nelson, 1974. Archives and Special Collections, Dinand Library, College of the Holy Cross.

Catalogue of the Officers and Students of College of Holy Cross, Worcester, Mass., for the Academic Year, 1856–57. Worcester: Printed by Henry J. Howland, [1856]. Also, catalogues under varying titles for 1858–59 to 1890–91.

Cassidy, Francis Patrick. *Catholic College Foundations and Development in the United States (1677–1850).* Washington, D.C.: Catholic University of America Press, 1924.

Devitt, Father Edward I. "History of the Maryland–New York Province, XV: College of the Holy Cross, Worcester, Mass., 1843–1914." *Woodstock Letters* 64 (1935): 204–37.

Diary of Father Thomas Mulledy, S.J. (first president of Holy Cross), 21 June 1843–29 July 1845. Archives and Special Collections, Dinand Library, College of the Holy Cross.

Fitton, Reverend James. *Sketches of the Establishment of the Church in New England.* Boston: Patrick Donahoe, 1872. College of the Holy Cross section, pp. 289–310.

Historical Sketch of the College of the Holy Cross, Worcester, Massachusetts, 1843–1883. Worcester: Press of Charles Hamilton, 1883.

"Histories of Holy Cross," ms. and printed historical materials. Archives and Special Collections, Dinand Library, College of the Holy Cross.

Kuzniewski, Anthony J., S.J. *Thy Honored Name: A History of the College of the Holy Cross, 1843–1994.* Washington, D.C.: Catholic University of America Press, 1999.

———. *"This Holy Cross."* Worcester: College of the Holy Cross, 2002.

Lapomarda, Vincent A. *The Jesuit Heritage in New England.* Worcester: Jesuits of Holy Cross College, 1977.

———. "A Study of Fenwick Hall Relative to Nomination to the National Register of Historic Places." Typescript, plus copied illustrations, 1979. Archives and Special Collections, Dinand Library, College of the Holy Cross.

———. "A Study of O'Kane Hall Relative to Nomination to the National Register of Historic Places." Typescript, plus copied illustrations, 1979. Archives and Special Collections, Dinand Library, College of the Holy Cross.

Lincoln, William. *History of Worcester.* 2 vols. Worcester: C. Hersey, 1862. Second volume by Charles Hersey.

Lord, Robert H., John E. Sexton, and Edward T. Harrington. *History of the Archdiocese of Boston.* 3 vols. New York: Sheed and Ward, 1944.

Meagher, Walter J., and William Grattan, Jr. *Spires of Fenwick: A History of the College of Holy Cross, 1843–1963.* New York: Vantage Books, 1966.

Mooney, Richard H. "College of the Holy Cross." *Worcester Magazine* 2 (1901): 139–56.

Nutt, Charles. *History of Worcester and Its People.* 4 vols. New York: Lewis Historical Publishing, 1919.

"125 Years." *Purple Patcher.* Worcester: College of the Holy Cross, 1969. Special issue of the College of the Holy Cross yearbook.

Roe, Alfred S. "The City of Worcester." *New England Magazine* n.s. 23, no. 5 (January 1901): 543–67.

Power, Edward J. *A History of Catholic Higher Education in the United States.* Milwaukee, Wis.: Bruce Publishing, 1958.

Sears, Edward I. "College of the Holy Cross." *National Quarterly Review* 9 (June 1864): 93–111; and 13 (September 1866): 344.

L. Tufts University (College), Medford, Massachusetts

Award of Arbitrators in the case of Coburn and Richards (Suffolk County Court), 19 July 1854. Digital Collections and Archives, Tisch Library, Tufts University.

"Ballou Hall." *Tufts Alumni Review* n.s. 1 (October 1955): 4.

"Ballou Hall Restoration." *Tufts Alumni Review* 2 (February 1956): 18a–18d.

"Ballou Hall Restoration Will Centralize Administration." *Tufts Weekly* 59 (13 May 1955): 1.

Ballou, Hosea Starr. *Hosea Ballou, 2nd, D.D., First President of Tufts College: His Origin, Life and Letters.* Boston: E. P. Guild and Company, 1896.

Brooks, Charles. *History of the Town of Medford, Middlesex County, Massachusetts, from Its First Settlement, in 1630, to the Present Time, 1855.* Boston: James M. Usher, 1855. Edited and extended to 1885 by James M. Usher, Boston: Rand, Avery and Franklin, 1886.

Bryant, Gridley J. F. *Specifications of Public Buildings for Which Plans and Instructions Were Supplied.* Pamphlets, 2 vols. Massachusetts State Library, Statehouse, Boston.

Capen, E. H. "Tufts College." *New England Magazine* o.s. 4, no. 2 (1886): 99–112.

Carmichael, Leonard. *Tufts College.* Princeton, N.J.: Newcomen Society of North America, 1952.

A Catalogue of the Officers and Students of Tufts College (1854–91). Boston: Bazin and Chandler; J. S. Spooner, John Wilson, and Son, etc., [c. 1891].

A Centennial View: Yesterday and Today at Tufts College. Medford: Tufts College, 1952.

Coggan, Linus Child. "A History of Tufts College." *Tuftonian* 30 (May 1905): 267–79.

"College Pictures," looseleaf notebook, compiled by Edwin C. Rollins, n.d. Digital Collections and Archives, Tisch Library, Tufts University.

Coolidge, Richard B. "Walnut Tree Hill." *Medford Historical Register* 39 (June 1936): 21–37.

"Dedication of Bowen Porch." *Tufts Alumni Bulletin* 13 (December 1939): 11. Ballou Hall.

Doane, Lewis, ed. *Here and There at Tufts—Published by the Class of Nineteen Hundred and Nine.* Medford: Tufts College, 1907.

"E. B. Bowen, Carmichael Speak at New Bowen Porch Dedication." *Tufts Weekly* 43 (2 November 1939): 3. Ballou Hall.

Extract of payments from contract between the Trustees of Tufts College, and Richards and Coburn, 1854. Digital Collections and Archives, Tisch Library, Tufts University.

Facilities Management, Buildings and Grounds Collection. Digital Collections and Archives, Tisch Library, Tufts University.

Gittleman, Sol. *An Entrepreneurial University: The Transformation of Tufts, 1976–2002.* Hanover: University Press of New England for Tufts University Press, 2004.

"Historic East Hall Undergoing Complete Interior Remodeling." *Tufts Weekly* 49 (12 April 1945): 1.

Ledger Book (1853–76) from basement vault, Ballou Hall. Digital Collections and Archives, Tisch Library, Tufts University.

Medford Past and Present: 275 Anniversary of Medford, Massachusetts, June, 1905. Medford: Medford Mercury, 1905. "Tufts College" by Samuel Elder, pp. 51–64.

Miller, Russell E. *Light on the Hill: A History of Tufts College, 1852–1952.* Boston: Beacon Press, 1966.

———. *Light on the Hill: Volume II—A History of Tufts University Since 1952.* Cambridge: Mass Market Books, 1986.

"New East." *Tufts Alumni Bulletin* 15 (October 1941): 18.

"Original Tufts Structure Undergoes Many Changes." *Tufts Weekly* 29 (23 September 1925): 1. Ballou Hall.

Papers of Reverend Hosea Ballou, 2nd. Digital Collections and Archives, Tisch Library, Tufts University.

Records and Minutes of the Board of Trustees of Tufts College (16 September 1851–28 May 1872). Includes Executive and Building Committees, and Treasurer's Annual Reports. Digital Collections and Archives, Tisch Library, Tufts University.

Rollins, Edwin C. "Reminiscences." Looseleaf notebook, n.d. Digital Collections and Archives, Tisch Library, Tufts University.

———, comp. "Tufts Buildings." 3 looseleaf notebooks, n.d. Digital Collections and Archives, Tisch Library, Tufts University.

Sauer, Anne. *Tufts University.* "The College History Series." Charleston, S.C.: Arcadia, 2001.

"Staid Ballou Hall Is Campus Landmark." *Tufts Weekly* 57 (27 February 1953): 7.

Start, Alaric Bertrand, ed. *History of Tufts College Published by the Class of 1897.* Cambridge, Mass.: John Wilson and Son, 1896.

Tolles, Bryant F., Jr. "Gridley J. F. Bryant and the First Building at Tufts College." *Old-Time New England* 113, no. 4 (April–June 1973): 89–99.

Traditions Committee for the Tufts University Alumni Council.

High on the Hill: Tufts Then and Now. Medford: Tufts Alumni Council, 1979.

Treasurer's Cash Book (1853–76) from basement vault, Ballou Hall. Digital Collections and Archives, Tisch Library, Tufts University.

Tufts College—1887. West Gardner, Mass.: Phototypes by Adams and Aldrich, 1887.

"Tufts College, Medford, Massachusetts." *Ballou's Pictorial* 11, no. 5 (11 October 1856): 225. Printed view, Ballou Hall.

Woods, Amy. "Tufts College." *New England Magazine* n.s. 32, no. 4 (June 1905): 415–30.

M. Trinity (Washington) College, Hartford, Connecticut

Accounts of Washington College, 3 July 1824–1 December 1826. Trinity College Archives, Trinity College.

Adams, Arthur. *The Founding of Trinity College [Washington College, 1823–1845].* New Brunswick, N.J.: n.p., [c. 1945]. Reprinted from the *Historical Magazine of the Protestant Episcopal Church* 14 (March 1945): 53–65.

Architectural Drawings and Elevations of Buildings on the Original Campus of Washington (later Trinity) College, Hartford, c. 1824, by Solomon Willard. Trinity College Archives, Trinity College.

Brocklesby, W. C., delineator. "Plans of Trinity College, Showing Arrangement of Rooms, 1871." Jarvis and Brownell Halls. Trinity College Archives, Trinity College.

———. "Trinity College, Hartford." *Scribner's Monthly* 11 (March 1876): 601–15.

Building Agreement (draft) for Jarvis Hall ("The College"), William Hayden, Contractor, and the Building Committee for Washington College, [c. 1824]. Trinity College Archives, Trinity College.

Calendar of Trinity College, Hartford, 1847. Hartford: Wm. Faxon, 1847.

Catalogue of the Library and Members of the Athenaeum, Trinity College. Hartford: Elihu Geer, 1853. Rear cover printed view.

Gaines, Edith. "Collectors' Notes." *Magazine Antiques* 77, no. 4 (April 1960): 390. Connecticut scrimshaw views, including "Eastern View of Washington College."

Geer's Hartford City Directory, for 1852–3. . . . Hartford: Elihu Geer, 1852. Printed view. Also, 1853 edition, printed view.

Hart, Samuel, D. D. "Trinity College, Hartford." *New England Magazine and Bay State Monthly* o.s. 4, no. 5 (May 1886): 393–408.

"Historical Sketch of Trinity College." *Trinity College Bulletin* 2 (February 1905): 47–72.

Old Campus—Papers Related to the Construction: Plans, Specifications, Contracts, Letters, etc., 1820s. Trinity College Archives, Trinity College.

Perry, William Stevens. *The History of the American Episcopal Church, 1587–1883.* 2 vols. Boston: James R. Osgood and Company, 1885. "Trinity College," vol. 2, pp. 538–46.

Plans and Photographs of the Washington and Trinity College Campuses. Looseleaf ring binder compiled by Robert S. Morris, Class of 1916. Trinity College Archives, Trinity College.

Record of the Doings of the Trustees of Washington (later Trinity) College, in the City of Hartford, State of Connecticut, May 1823–May 1887. Trinity College Archives, Trinity College.

Royce, George M. "Trinity College." *The Churchman* 73 (9 May 1896): 635–43.

Specifications Book for the Chapel, [c. 1824]. Trinity College Archives, Trinity College.

Specifications Book for the College, [c. 1824]. Trinity College Archives, Trinity College.

Subscription Book for Washington College, 1 April 1824–1 December 1826. Trinity College Archives, Trinity College.

Thomas C. Brownell Papers (1821–39). Trinity College Archives, Trinity College.

Weaver, Glenn. *Hartford: An Illustrated History of Connecticut's Capital.* Woodland Hills, Calif.: Windsor Publications, Inc., with the Connecticut Historical Society, 1982.

———. *The History of Trinity College,* vol. 1. Hartford: Trinity College Press, 1967.

———. "Trinity College Moves to the New Campus." *Trinity College Alumni Magazine* 5 (January 1964): 1–11.

Wheildon, William W. *Memoir of Solomon Willard, Architect and Superintendent of the Bunker Hill Monument.* Boston: Monument Association, 1865.

N. Wesleyan University, Middletown, Connecticut

Alumni Records of Wesleyan University, Middletown, Conn. Hartford, Conn.: Case, Lockwood and Brainard Company, 1883. Contains historical sketch.

Annual Reports, 1831–38, 1838–63, and 1863–89, photocopies of mss. Special Collections and Archives, Wesleyan University Library.

Appendix A ("Wesleyan Buildings and Grounds in the Earliest Years") from George M. Dutcher, "Wesleyan: The First Years," typescript, n.d. Special Collections and Archives, Wesleyan University Library.

Appendix B. ("The Early Pictorial History of Wesleyan University") from George M. Dutcher, "Wesleyan University: The First Years," typescript, 1948. Special Collections and Archives, Wesleyan University Library.

Catalogue of the Officers and Students of Wesleyan University (1831–32 to 1883–84).

Crawford, Morris B. "As We Were: A Building with a History." *Wesleyan Literary Monthly* 13 (1904–5): 341–43. The gun-house of the A.L.S.&M. Academy.

"Electricity at Wesleyan University." *Electrical Engineer* 16, no. 277 (23 August 1893): 172–73. "Old Laboratory."

Harrington, Karl P. *The Background of Wesleyan: A Study of Local Conditions About the Time the College Was Founded. . . .* Middletown: Wesleyan University, 1942.

Middletown, Connecticut: A Survey of Historical and Architectural Resources. 3 vols. Middletown: Greater Middletown Preservation Trust, 1979.

Minutes of the Board of Trustees, 1830–1870. Special Collections and Archives, Wesleyan University Library.

Minutes of the Joint Board of Trustees and Visitors, 1830–1868. Special Collections and Archives, Wesleyan University Library.

Potts, David B. *Wesleyan University, 1831–1910: Collegiate Enterprise in New England.* Hanover: University Press of New England for Wesleyan University Press, 1992.

Price, Carl Fowler. *Wesleyan's First Century.* Middletown: Wesleyan University, 1932.

Record of the Proceedings of the Prudential Committee of Wesleyan University, 28 June 1831–21 June 1841. Also index volume. Special Collections and Archives, Wesleyan University Library.

Rice, William North. "The History and Work of Wesleyan University." In *1831–1906: Celebration of the Seventy-Fifth Anniversary of the Founding of Wesleyan University.* Middletown: Wesleyan University, 1907.

Spaeth, John W., Jr. "Brown Old Row of College Halls." *Wesleyan Alumnus* 56 (Fall 1971): 22–24.

Trager, Philip. *Wesleyan Photographs.* Middletown: Wesleyan University Press, [c. 1982].

Wesleyan Buildings: Lists and Indexes, n.d. Special Collections and Archives, Wesleyan University Library.

O. Colby (Waterville) College (University), Waterville, Maine

Bixler, Julius Seelye. *Colby College (1813–1853), A Venture in Faith.* New York: Newcomen Society of North America, 1953.

A Brief Description of Colby College and Its Equipment. Waterville: Published by the College, 1907.

Burrage, Henry S. *History of the Baptists in Maine.* Portland, Maine: Marks Printing House, 1904.

———. "The Beginnings of Waterville College, now Colby University, with a Sketch of Its First President, Rev. Jeremiah Champlin." *Collections of the Maine Historical Society,* series 2, vol. 4 (1893): 124–45.

Campioli, Mario E. "Thomas U. Walter, Edward Clark and the United States Capitol." *Journal of the Society of Architectural Historians* 23, no. 4 (December 1964): 210–13.

Champlin, James T. *A Historical Discourse Delivered at the Fiftieth Anniversary of Colby University, August 2nd, 1870.* Waterville: Published by the Trustees, 1870.

Chipman, Charles P. *The Formative Period in Colby's History.* Waterville: Colby College Library, 1912.

Fotiades, Anestes. *Colby College: A Venture of Faith.* Augusta, Maine: Alan Sutton, 1994.

"The Girard College Architectural Competition." *Journal of the Society of Architectural Historians* 16, no. 1 (1957): 20–24. Thomas U. Walter.

Haynes, George H. *Souvenir of Waterville, the University City of Maine.* New York: Andrew H. Kellogg, 1898. Section on Colby University.

Hersey, George L. "Thomas U. Walter and the University of Lewisburg." *Journal of the Society of Architectural Historians* 16, no. 1 (March 1957): 20–24. Bucknell University.

Marriner, Ernest C. *The History of Colby College.* Waterville: Colby College Press, 1963.

———. *Maine Yesterdays.* Waterville: Colby College Press, 1964.

Mason, George C., Jr. "Thomas U. Walter, F.A.I.A.—1804–1887." *Journal of the American Institute of Architects* 8, no. 5 (November 1947): 225–30.

Newcomb, Rexford. "Thomas Ustick Walter." *Architect* 10, no. 5 (August 1928): 585–89.

Records of the Trustees of Waterville College (1819–65). Colby College Special Collections.

Rusk, William S. "Thomas U. Walter and His Works." *Americana* 33, no. 2 (April 1939): 151–79.

Small, Albion W. "Colby University." *New England Magazine* o.s. 6, no. 4 (August 1888): 309–20.

Smith, Earl H. *Mayflower Hill: A History of Colby College.* Hanover: University Press of New England for Colby College, 2006.

"Thomas Ustick Walter" (obituary). *American Architect and Building News* 22, no. 620 (12 November 1887): 225.

Tolles, Bryant F., Jr. "'The Bricks' at Colby (Waterville) College: The Origins of a Lost Campus." *Maine History* 39, no. 4 (Winter 2000–2001): 241–55.

Waterville College. *Origin, Progress and Present State of the College.* Portland, Maine: Argus Office, 1822. References to South College in the row.

White, Clarence H. "Linking the Old and the New." *Colby Alumnus* 31, no. 1 (October 1941): 5–6. Relates the original Waterville row campus to its successor at Mayflower Hill.

Whittemore, Reverend Edwin C., ed. *The Centennial History of Waterville, Kennebec County, Maine.* Waterville: Executive Committee of the Centennial Celebration, 1902.

———. *History of Colby College, 1820–1925: An Account of Its Beginnings, Progress, and Service.* Waterville: Trustees of Colby College, 1927.

P. Bates College (Maine State Seminary), Lewiston, Maine

Anthony, Alfred Williams. *Bates College and Its Background: A Review of Origins and Causes.* Philadelphia: Judson Press, 1936.

Bliss, Muriel. "A Short History of Parker Hall." *Bates Student* 56, no. 25 (16 November 1928): 3.

Buck, Marjorie Louise. "Bates College: A Bibliography of Publications Dealing With Its Foundation and Growth, 1857–1943." Thesis for a degree in Library Science, Simmons College, Boston, 1943.

Catalogue of the Officers and Students of Bates College, Lewiston, Me. Lewiston: Daily Journal Office, and Nelson Dingley, Jr., Company, 1863–1872.

Catalogue of the Officers and Students of the Maine State Seminary. Lewiston: Daily Journal Office, 1857–62.

Chase, Clarence A. "Lewiston and Bates College." *New England Magazine* n.s. 13, no. 4 (December 1895): 513–32.

Cheney, Emeline Burlingame. *The Story of the Life and Work of Oren B. Cheney, Founder and First President of Bates College.* Boston: Morning Star Publishing House for Bates College, 1907.

Clark, Charles E. *Bates Through the Years: An Illustrated History.* Lewiston: Bates College, 2005.

Freewill Baptist Education Society Annual Report: 1st to 41st, 1841–1880. 2 vols. Dover, N.H.: William Burr, 1841–80. Reports on the first buildings for the Maine State Seminary.

"Hathorn Hall." *Bates Student* 53, no. 21 (9 October 1925): 3.

"Lewiston, Maine." *Ballou's Pictorial and Drawing-Room Companion* 12, no. 13 (28 March 1857): 200. Printed view of campus as planned by Gridley J. F. Bryant.

MacKay, Robert B. "Gridley J. F. Bryant, 1816–1899." *A Biographical Dictionary of Architects in Maine* 3, no. 9. Augusta: Maine Historic Preservation Commission, 1986.

Nute, Sylvia. "A Short History of Hathorn with Digressions." *Bates Student* 56, no. 21 (19 October 1928): 3.

"Old Parker 'Reverts' to Women." *Bates College Bulletin* 44, no. 13 (May 1947): 81.

Original design drawings for Parker Hall, Bates College, completed in Boston, 1 September–11 November 1856, by Gridley J. F. Bryant. Edward S. Muskie Archives and Special Collections Library, Bates College.

"Parker Hall." *Bates Student* 53, no. 22 (16 October 1925): 3.

"Present Parker Hall Differs from Civil War Version." *Bates Student* 84, no. 16 (5 March 1958): 4.

Ramsdell, Harriet J. "Hathorn Hall, Now 100 Years Old, Is the Heart of Bates." *Lewiston Journal Magazine Section* (Sunday, 3 August 1957): 3-A, 8-A.

Stanley, Professor Richard C. "Historical Sketch of Bates College," from the 23rd annual *Report of the Superintendent of Schools, State of Maine.* Augusta, Maine: n.p., 1877. Brief summary of Bates College history, pp. 108–18.

Tolles, Bryant F., Jr. "Maine State Seminary: Gridley J. F. Bryant and Antebellum Architectural Master Planning." *Old-Time New England* 78, no. 268 (Spring/Summer 2000): 41–55.

"Venerable Hathorn Hall Claims Picturesque Past." *Bates Student* 59, no. 19 (16 December 1931): 3.

Index